WALL
STREET
JOURNAL
BOOKS

TEARING DOWN THE WALLS

HOW SANDY WEILL
FOUGHT HIS WAY TO THE TOP
OF THE FINANCIAL WORLD...
AND THEN NEARLY LOST IT ALL

MONICA LANGLEY

A WALL STREET JOURNAL BOOK
PUBLISHED BY SIMON & SCHUSTER
NEW YORK LONDON TORONTO SYDNEY SINGAPORE

WALL
STREET
JOURNAL
BOOKS

A Wall Street Journal Book
Published by Simon & Schuster Inc.
Rockefeller Center
1230 Avenue of the Americas
New York, NY 10020

For information regarding special discounts for bulk purchases, please contact Simon & Schuster
Special Sales at 1-800-456-6798 or business@simonandschuster.com

Manufactured in the United States of America

1   3   5   7   9   10   8   6   4   2

Library of Congress Cataloging-in-Publication Data
Langley, Monica.
Tearing down the walls : how Sandy Weill fought his way to the top of the financial
world—and then nearly lost it all / Monica Langley.
p. cm.
Includes bibliographical references and index.
1. Weill, Sandy. 2. Bankers—United States—Biography. 3. Stockbrokers—United States—
Biography. 4. Capitalists and financiers—United States—Biography. 5. Financial services
industry—United States. 6. Consolidation and merger of corporations—United States—History.
7. Wall Street. 8. Shearson Lehman Brothers. 9. Citigroup (Firm). I. Title: Sandy Weill fought
his way to the top of the financial world—and then nearly lost it all. II. Title.

HG2463.W45L36 2003
332.1'092—dc21
[B] 2003041091

ISBN 0-7432-1613-X

To Roger and Langley Grace

CONTENTS

CAST OF CHARACTERS

Arron, Judith Carnegie Hall's executive director from 1986 until her death in 1998, she introduced Sandy to classical music and sat on the boards of Travelers and Citigroup.

Berlind, Roger One of Sandy's first partners on Wall Street, he left the business after losing his wife and three of his four children in a plane crash. He became an award-winning producer in his first passion, the theater.

Bialkin, Kenneth A leading securities lawyer, he began representing Sandy in a Wall Street shake-up in 1968 and became his close friend and a longtime corporate director of companies Sandy headed.

Bibliowicz, Jessica Sandy's daughter, with her mother's good looks and her father's ambition, followed her dad into the securities business and caused friction between Sandy and Jamie Dimon, his heir apparent.

Budd, Ed The chairman and CEO of Travelers, as a last resort, sought Sandy's help with the troubled insurance giant but found himself out of a job when Sandy bought the entire company.

Buffett, Warren The billionaire investor from Omaha, who stood ready to help Sandy during his final days at American Express, later sold Berkshire Hathaway's big stake in Salomon Brothers to Sandy.

Calvano, James Recruited by Sandy to leave Avis for American Express, he later joined Sandy in building his second empire but wisely refused to stay in the same hotel with his boss.

Campbell, William The Philip Morris U.S.A. chairman behind the "Marlboro Man" campaign, he became John Reed's retail and marketing guru at Citibank and pitched banking as a consumer product.

Carpenter, Michael Given a second chance by Sandy after his ouster from Kidder, Peabody, he ran Citigroup's investment-banking and securities business until scandal rocked the firm in 2002.

Carter, Arthur The neighbor with whom Sandy dreamed about starting their own Wall Street firm dominated the fledgling brokerage until Sandy and the other partners rebelled. He later became a millionaire publisher and sculptor.

Cogan, Marshall An early partner on Wall Street whose intense focus on deals helped usher in Wall Street's go-go years in the late 1960s and led to a power struggle with Sandy.

Cohen, Peter The brash financial wizard and operations expert worked tirelessly at Sandy's side in building the first securities empire until he decided to escape Sandy's shadow.

Collins, Paul Citicorp's vice chairman, he was the liaison between Sandy and John Reed in negotiating the blockbuster merger of Travelers and Citicorp.

Dimon, Jamie The "golden boy" protégé, he began working with Sandy straight out of Harvard Business School and was like a son to Sandy until he tangled with Sandy's daughter and paid dearly.

Dimon, Theodore "Ted" Jamie's father, he was a hugely successful stockbroker whose family became close friends with the Weills after Sandy took over Shearson in 1974.

Druskin, Robert One of Sandy's trusted aides, he held many operations and financial posts in both of Sandy's empires.

Falls, Alison Sandy's executive assistant, she followed him into exile from American Express and provided key support until he regained his footing with the purchase of Commercial Credit.

Fishman, Jay A zealous cost cutter, he helped turn around Travelers' insurance operation but ultimately grew impatient waiting for Sandy to formulate a succession plan.

Ford, Gerald The former president of the United States became a "trophy" director in Sandy's companies, a position that gave him wealth beyond the dreams of many career politicians.

Gerstner, Louis Sandy's rival at American Express, he worried that the brazen Shearson crew would tarnish the carefully cultivated image of his green and gold cards. He later became CEO of RJR Nabisco and then IBM.

Glucksman, Lew The tough-talking trader, onetime Lehman Brothers CEO, plotted with Sandy over martinis how to shake up the sleepy and comfortable Smith Barney.

Golub, Harvey Granted his wish by Sandy to run an American Express division, he rose to become the CEO of the credit-card giant. He returned the favor by selling Shearson back to Sandy.

Greenhill, Robert With much fanfare, the star investment banker brought his Morgan Stanley cronies and their fat paychecks to Smith Barney but failed to deliver the M&A business Sandy expected.

Grubman, Jack Sandy's controversial $20-million-a-year telecommunications analyst was the darling of the soaring 1990s but was quickly dubbed the villain—and posed a threat to Sandy—when it all came crashing down.

Harris, J. Ira A longtime friend of Sandy's, the seasoned deal maker shrewdly steered the delicate negotiations of the Primerica acquisition that nearly broke down over jets and golden parachutes.

Jackson, Jesse The civil rights leader developed a mutually beneficial bond with Sandy, forged by their respective encounters with racism and anti-Semitism.

Levitt, Arthur An early partner, he saved Sandy in a firm shake-up but grew frustrated at Sandy's claiming exclusive credit for Shearson's huge success. He ultimately became chairman of the Securities and Exchange Commission.

Lipp, Robert The Chemical Bank president joined Sandy in his high-risk comeback and did much of the heavy lifting in the construction of Sandy's second financial-services empire.

Loeb, John Snubbing Sandy as an upstart on Wall Street, the proud financier and leader of the Jewish "Old Crowd" ultimately succumbed to the modern forces taking hold of the financial district and sold his distinguished firm to Sandy.

Magner, Marge Determined to make it in the man's world of finance, she toiled in the bowels of consumer lending and rose to become Citigroup's highest-ranking female executive.

Mannes, Barry The head of Sandy's least favorite department, the human-resources professional implemented many of his boss's harshest measures to resuscitate bloated and troubled financial companies.

Mark, Reuben The CEO of Colgate-Palmolive, originally on John Reed's board, became the behind-the-scenes advocate for better corporate practices in the Citigroup boardroom.

Maughan, Deryck A dapper Brit who fraternized with Sandy on the Carnegie Hall board, he headed Salomon Brothers until he sold it to Sandy. He then endured the "he's in, he's out" machinations that were part of Sandy's control of Citigroup.

McDermott, Mary From the lowly position of "gal Friday" in Sandy's first firm, she became a public-relations maven for Sandy's subsequent empires.

Miller, Heidi Initially an aide to Jamie Dimon at Smith Barney, she rose to become the CFO of Travelers and then Citigroup, bearing the brunt of the conflicting styles of Sandy and John Reed.

Pearson, Andrall The ex-president of PepsiCo and former professor at Harvard Business School, he became a pivotal director in Sandy's second empire and a critical voice in the crisis of leadership at Citigroup.

Pike, Bill The young investor-relations manager helped Sandy boost his visibility on Wall Street and learned much about life with a financial mogul.

Prince, Charles "Chuck" Commercial Credit's general counsel, the smart workaholic was one of the "treasures" of Sandy's acquisition binge. A Sandy loyalist, he assumed more important and sensitive roles at Citigroup.

Reed, John The cerebral visionary, whose push for ATMs and credit cards ushered in the modern banking era, astonishingly agreed to merge his prestigious Citicorp with Sandy's Travelers. The banker faced the final power struggle of his long career against Sandy.

Robinson, James D. III Scion of an Atlanta banking dynasty, the patrician chairman of American Express brought Sandy into the WASP nest, where he became a president without portfolio. Years later, he helped Sandy break into the exclusive old-boys' club, Augusta National.

Rubin, Robert The highly regarded Treasury secretary was the most sought-after financier in the world when Sandy wooed him to Citigroup. He soon became a kingmaker in the boardroom drama over leadership.

Sheinberg, George After Sandy put clients in his company's stock, the Bulova CFO became a close friend and then executive for Sandy—until he challenged his boss in a high-stakes meeting at American Express.

Simmons, Hardwick When his family's old-line securities firm became Sandy's first acquisition, the well-bred Bostonian became the "token WASP" as Sandy pushed for bigger targets with better names than his own.

Spitzer, Eliot The New York attorney general, dubbed "the Enforcer," launched a crusade to reform Wall Street's conflicts of interest and set his sights on Citigroup, as well as his own political future.

Stern, Isaac The virtuoso violinist and passionate president of Carnegie Hall offered Sandy the platform from which he could strengthen a New York institution and smooth his own entrée into Manhattan society.

Thomas, Franklin The ex-head of the Ford Foundation, appointed to the Citicorp board by Reed, became the acting chairman in the boardroom showdown and a key director on the succession and governance dilemmas.

Tsai, Gerald Jr. A mutual-funds gunslinger in the 1960s, the conglomerateur rapidly transformed American Can into a hodgepodge of financial companies called Primerica before bailing out with millions of dollars.

Warner, Sandy The CEO of the elite but staid J.P. Morgan rebuffed Sandy's merger offer, and then found himself scrambling to compete with the man and the company he had rejected.

Weill, Etta Sandy's quiet and reserved mother passed down to her son her knack for numbers.

Weill, Joan Marrying Sandy against her parents' wishes, the ultimate corporate wife became her husband's closest confidante. His marriage to Joan was Sandy's most important merger.

Weill, Marc As Sandy's son, he rose to high-level posts in companies run by his father, until his lifestyle forced him out.

Weill, Max Sandy's father hurt his son so deeply that Sandy spent his life trying to be the opposite of him.

Williams, Arthur L. An insurance industry renegade who staged revival-style stadium events to promote term-life policies, he sold his company to Sandy and repeatedly taunted his new boss until the association ended in a tearful confrontation.

Willumstad, Robert The unassuming, masterful manager from Chemical Bank rose steadily through Sandy's consumer-finance and banking operations. Quietly heading Citigroup's most profitable units, he became the "stealth" candidate to succeed Sandy when he was unexpectedly named president.

Woolard, Edgar The former DuPont chairman, he served as Reed's staunchest advocate in the battle between the co-CEOs.

Wright, Joe The ex–Reagan administration official and W.R. Grace executive saw his friendship with Sandy wane, then ultimately end, as Sandy's prominence rose.

Zankel, Arthur A longtime friend to whom Sandy confided on a beach vacation in 1961 that he wanted to build a great financial company one day, he gave Sandy unvarnished, shrewd advice as a director on all of Sandy's companies.

Zarb, Frank Brought into Sandy's first securities firm to set up a "back office," he helped set the stage for Sandy's unlikely growth through acquisitions in the 1970s.

TEARING
DOWN THE
WALLS

———

PROLOGUE

Sanford I. Weill had been rehearsing his speech all day long, hoping he would be more comfortable when he addressed an exclusive gathering of the nation's best-known chief executives that evening. But, as usual, it was only making him increasingly nervous.

There was, of course, no reason to be nervous. As the chairman and chief executive officer of Citigroup, Sandy Weill was one of the world's most powerful executives and his company was the most profitable of all. He met frequently with other distinguished men and women, including presidents, and in those one-on-one sessions he was charming, smart, and funny. But tonight's gathering held special significance for Sandy. It would take place in the vast confines of the New York Stock Exchange, epicenter of world finance and the place that inspired him years earlier to seek a career in finance. That career had been a remarkable test of will and spirit. In the 1950s, as the son of Polish immigrant Jews, Sandy had struggled to get even the lowliest job on Wall Street. But using his remarkable analytical abilities, coupled with an appetite for money and respect, he had pulled off one coup after another, taking over bigger and bigger companies and melding them into what was now the world's largest financial empire.

Still, Sandy remained insecure. His rise to power had come at a price. His corporate victories often reflected class warfare: Jew against WASP, immigrant against *Mayflower* descendant, poor against rich, entrepreneur against establishment. In certain lofty and influential circles, Sandy Weill was disparaged as a street fighter, a brash and ruthless predator who picked off vulnerable prey, companies with big names and bigger troubles. But tonight could change all that.

His chauffeur-driven Cadillac sedan pulled up to the guarded VIP entrance of the New York Stock Exchange, and as Sandy pulled himself out of the backseat, he was awash in glaring camera lights and flashing strobes. A publicity hound, Sandy relished the media attention. Straightening up in his tailor-made Savile Row tuxedo, Sandy, a connoisseur of rich food and fine wine, still looked rumpled with his expansive girth on his five-foot-nine-inch frame. He grinned broadly as he walked through the Big Board's trading floor, which only a few hours earlier had been packed with screaming traders and clerks frantically tracking the fluctuations of thousands of stock prices. Now some two hundred high-ranking executives and their guests mingled amid the sound of clinking cocktail glasses and easy banter.

And here, pushing his way through the crowd to welcome the guest of honor, came computer wunderkind Michael Dell. At this same event last year, the founder of Dell Computer had been honored as CEO of the Year by *Chief Executive* magazine, at thirty-six years old the youngest ever selected. Tonight, Sandy Weill would be crowned 2002's CEO of the Year, at sixty-nine the oldest honoree. As camera crews suddenly veered toward the high-profile and handsome Dell to question him about the emerging crisis of confidence in corporate America, Dell demurred: "This is Sandy's night."

The portly financier was strangely childlike in his excitement at the star treatment. When the magazine had informed him of the honor, Sandy actually began shivering. "It's something I've always wanted, and I was running out of time," he had said. For tonight's gala Sandy had even had flown in from California his ninety-one-year-old mother-in-law, who had strongly opposed her daughter's marriage to Sandy when he was an unemployed loser without a college degree. Tonight the Citigroup CEO would show her—and countless others who had underestimated and never fully accepted him—just what he had accomplished.

The lustrous night seemed to be going perfectly. Surrounded by well-wishers and camera crews, Sandy beamed, his wife, Joan, by his side. Some of the nation's most important chief executives lined up to pay their respects to the man many would have voted "Least Likely to Succeed" when he had started on Wall Street and, for that matter, when he had been ousted from American Express years later. Forced into corporate exile but driven to make a comeback, Sandy had built piece by piece, from out-of-favor, down-on-their-luck corporate dregs, the globe-girdling financial supermarket of the twenty-first century.

Sandy had secured his lifelong climb to the top just two years earlier, when he pushed out his last rival, John Reed, to become sole heir to the

Citigroup crown. After boldly convincing the world's best-known banker to merge Citicorp's credit-card and consumer-bank behemoth into Travelers' insurance and securities concern, Sandy had agreed to share power with the unlikely partner. But after a tumultuous collaboration, the brazen and instinctual Sandy outmaneuvered the reserved and cerebral Reed.

Even as he basked in the congratulations of his fellow executives, Sandy was growing increasingly anxious. He fidgeted, glancing often at his watch. While he enjoyed the adulation, he seemed ready to get upstairs to dinner so he could get his acceptance speech behind him. This night's message couldn't be the easy "thank you and good night" he was accustomed to delivering. In an economic environment of impoverished investors and company scandals, he had prepared a rallying cry for corporate chiefs. Now that the long bull market had come crashing down, investors, politicians, and regulators were out for blood. No longer an underdog, Sandy Weill and Citigroup—and American business in general—were under attack as symbols of the soaring 1990s' corporate greed and excess. Sandy's own empire was feeling the heat: His bankers had done deals with World-Com and Enron, both now bankrupt and mired in scandal, and the media was full of stories about the unseemly favoritism of giving hot stock issues to corporate fat cats at the expense of small investors. The pressure on Sandy could only have been intensified by the joking comment made by Andrall Pearson, a longtime director of first Travelers, then Citigroup, when Pearson learned that Sandy had been tapped as CEO of the Year. "Get your parachute ready," Pearson had warned. "I've never seen anyone get that big an honor who doesn't come tumbling down the mountain. When you're at the peak of your recognition, the seeds of your disaster have already been sown."

Tonight, Sandy hoped to put much of the mounting criticism behind him. The tension was telling: The bags under his eyes were dark and puffy, and he was beginning to break out in a sweat.

But before he could begin, giant television screens prominently positioned throughout the Stock Exchange floor flashed a picture that caught his attention—and that of nearly everyone else. There on the screen was Jack Grubman, the controversial $20-million-a-year Wall Street analyst who worked for Sandy. The footage was of Grubman's appearance that very afternoon before a congressional panel probing his close ties with the bankrupt and fraud-plagued WorldCom.

A congressman unexpectedly asked the star telecommunications analyst of Salomon Smith Barney, Citigroup's securities unit, if he ever doled out scarce shares in hot stock issues to WorldCom executives, a practice known as "spinning."

On every TV above the trading floor, the dark and intense Grubman looked stunned.

"I can't recall. I don't—I'm not saying no. I'm not saying yes," Grubman fumbled.

Sandy gamely tried to ignore the television but couldn't help glancing nervously over his shoulder at the screen above his head. The guests in black tie and evening gowns mingling on the Stock Exchange floor had several opportunities to watch the damaging Grubman video. CNBC repeatedly ran the hearing footage as the day's top business story.

Citigroup executives there to honor their boss instantly knew Grubman's remarks meant big trouble. Chuck Prince, longtime general counsel and now chief operating officer, disgustedly thought Grubman was coming off almost like John Dean during the Watergate hearings. *And of all days for this to happen,* Prince worried. He knew Sandy regarded tonight's ceremony as the equivalent of a sports figure being inducted into the Hall of Fame. Sandy had eagerly confided to Prince how much he looked forward to having his head "cast" for the bronze bust of his likeness, which would join those of corporate luminaries Bill Gates and Jack Welch.

Bob Willumstad, Citigroup's president, worried about Grubman's ominous image depriving Sandy of his glorious night. *Miserable timing,* he thought as he moved with the other guests from the trading floor to the Stock Exchange's wood-paneled and chandelier-filled boardroom. Willumstad took his seat at the head table next to Sandy's mother-in-law.

As they suspected, the video took its toll on Sandy. Already nervous about his speech, the Citigroup chairman was now visibly distraught. He ate his ketchup-doused filet mignon quickly and guzzled his red wine. His celebration was looking more and more like punishment. Rather than enjoying the festivities, he looked around uneasily. Several times, he complained that the occasion was behind schedule. At 9:30, he finally asked the event's host, "It's getting late, isn't it?"

By the time Michael Dell introduced him as this year's CEO of the Year, Sandy looked pasty and sweaty. He raised the crystal trophy above his head in a victory salute and joked about the age difference between the baby-faced billionaire and himself, a much older billionaire. Then he began to read his speech.

"Tonight is a time to be serious," he began, noting the year's extraordinary business challenges, including the global recession, terrorism, the meltdown in Argentina, and the largest bankruptcy in American history.

"These corporate scandals have shaken our faith in America's financial system," Sandy said, as beads of perspiration spread across his forehead. "They have also called into question the integrity of our corporate executives."

Within minutes, sweat was rolling down Sandy's cheeks. The script he nervously clutched was originally designed to show his leadership in addressing the public's concern about corporate abuses. But the words he spoke tonight would mean little. It would be his actions in the coming days and weeks and months that would make—or break—his reputation.

"We must begin asking what we, as CEOs, have to do, however challenging and uncomfortable it may be," Sandy said, adding what would have been heresy to him even a few weeks earlier: "We must be conscious of a broader purpose than simply delivering profits."

As soon as the speech was over, a champagne toast was offered to Sandy. Visibly relieved to be finished, Sandy yelled out—far louder than decorum allowed—"I want some gin!"

Joan Weill rushed to her husband's side. Sandy wiped his drenched face with a handkerchief. Then Joan took his hand to lead him off the small stage. She gasped, "Sandy, your hand is like ice!"

1

CRASHING THE GATES

At age twenty-two, when most young men are eagerly laying plans for their careers, Sandy Weill was facing failure. In one shattering night the future that he had thought would be his had utterly evaporated. His dreams of joining the family business were in ruins, his beloved mother was suddenly facing life alone, his classmates would soon be graduating without him, and the woman he desperately wanted to marry was being told to dump him. All because his father, Max Weill, went out for cigarettes one night and didn't come back.

For Sandy, the pain of failure was all the worse for how hard and long he had struggled to achieve even a smattering of success. As a child growing up in the Bensonhurst section of Brooklyn, short and chubby Sandy was an easy target for the bullies who often sent him scurrying to his mother's protective skirts. Shy and reclusive, he made no close friends at school and stood in fear and awe of his handsome, ebullient father, Max, who often scolded Sandy for not being more rough and tumble and not standing up for himself. His only real friend was his little sister, Helen, who worshiped her brother. During summers at their grandparents' farm, Sandy would dig worms so that he and Helen could fish in the pond and then dutifully bait her hook and remove any wriggling fish she caught. But even with her, Sandy kept his feelings to himself. The two could sit together for hours listening to New York Yankees games on the radio without exchanging a word.

All that began to change when fourteen-year-old Sandy was enrolled at the Peekskill Military Academy, a boarding school near his grandparents' farm. The school emphasized both sports and scholarship and kept students' days full of activities. At five feet nine inches Sandy was too small for the football team, but much to his own surprise, he honed his tennis skills, acquired during earlier summer camps, to win many school tournaments. He became captain of Peekskill's tennis team and even played in the Junior Davis Cup. The physical regimen of calisthenics every morning and sports every afternoon melted away some of the baby fat. At the same time Sandy realized he liked learning and was good at it. He would bang out his homework assignments in an hour or two and then nag his roommate, Stuart Fendler, to finish his assignments so the two could head for the school canteen for ice cream. Yet while excelling at both sports and academics, Sandy never became a leader on campus or even a very popular student. At graduation, when seniors predicted what would become of their classmates, no one predicted Sandy would do anything exceptional. He told classmates he planned to join his father's steel-importing business. In a school skit, Sandy even cast himself as the owner of Super Deluxe Steel Plating Co., with five plants across the country.

Max Weill's inaptly named American Steel Co.—it dealt almost exclusively in imported steel—was his second business venture. Like many young Jewish men whose parents had emigrated from Eastern Europe, Max first went into the rag trade, where his good looks, flirtatious ways, and free spending won him a strong clientele as a dressmaker. Etta Kalika, whom Max married in 1932, couldn't have been more different. Plain, conservative, and thrifty, Etta refused to wear the fancy clothes Max brought her and preferred to spend her time visiting her parents, who lived downstairs from Max and Etta in a three-family home the parents owned, and caring for her two children, Sandy and Helen. While the dressmaking business was successful, Max Weill, who treated himself to a weekly haircut and manicure, was always on the lookout for the next big opportunity. One opportunity he found—to violate wartime price-gouging regulations— earned him a $10,000 fine and a suspended prison sentence and prompted him to leave dressmaking for good. After an abortive move to Miami during the war, Max and Etta were back in Brooklyn by 1945, this time in the Flatbush neighborhood, and Max had set up American Steel.

Sandy's outstanding academic record at Peekskill opened the doors of prestigious Cornell University where, true to his intentions to join his father's business, he declared a major in metallurgical engineering. But as so many college freshmen discover, college is about a lot more than classes. With thirteen Jewish fraternities eager to sign up new pledges, Sandy found himself a hot property. AEPi was particularly interested in recruiting him, and Sandy wanted to make a good impression. The composure and confidence—or at least the appearance of it—developed in military school, as well as the free-flowing alcohol, helped him overcome his innate shyness. Though never comfortable in social settings, he found he could be sociable and even charming. His tennis skills, applied to the game of table tennis, impressed the fraternity brothers.

Once AEPi accepted him, Sandy fell into a common pattern: alcohol and parties at night, missed classes in the morning, and weekends full of dates. By Thanksgiving of his freshman year Sandy was on probation and realized that the rigors of metallurgical engineering were not conducive to his new lifestyle. A switch to Cornell's liberal-arts program enabled him to resuscitate his grade-point average without making a serious dent in his heavy schedule of dating, eating, and drinking. Indeed, it was during his freshman year that Sandy began to indulge what would become a lifelong passion: food. Sandy and his frequent Ping-Pong partner Lenny Zucker, who shared Sandy's obsession with eating, would plan weekends around where they were going to eat. It helped that Sandy had a car, a new yellow Pontiac convertible, and a credit card, both supplied by his father. Yet he wasn't extravagant. On the way to pick up their dates for a dinner at a famous Finger Lakes restaurant, Sandy warned Zucker to let the girls order first. "They'll order the liver, the cheapest thing on the menu, and then we can have steaks," a prediction that turned out to be dead on.

Despite his shortish stature and less-than-suave manners, Sandy had more than his fair share of dates at Cornell. He was especially adept at spotting and romancing the Cornell coeds who came from moneyed families. But when he was twenty-one and visiting home during his junior year, his aunt Mabel, a self-professed matchmaker, told her nephew about Joan Mosher, a student at Brooklyn College who lived with her parents in Aunt Mabel's neighborhood of Woodmere, Long Island. Overcoming an initial bout of shyness, Sandy telephoned Joan and came away from the call convinced he really wanted to meet this woman. Their first date, April Fool's Day, 1954, ended in the wee hours of the next morning as the two found one thing after another to talk about. Smitten, Sandy vowed to friends that he was going to marry Joan Mosher and, true to that pledge, he never dated anyone else. Joan's gracious poise, empathetic manner, and tall, slender figure were an irresistible package to the Brooklyn boy who was just about the opposite—awkward, short, and stocky with a cockiness that tended to hide his shyness. To be closer to her, Sandy would spend weekends with his aunt Mabel, sleeping on her sofa during the few hours he wasn't with

Joan. Joan's family lived in a new upscale development in Woodmere, in an upper-middle-class home with a large yard. Her father, Paul, was in public relations, and the family lived in a country-club milieu that Sandy had never experienced. While the Moshers didn't directly object to Sandy, it wasn't hard for Sandy to recognize that they weren't thoroughly pleased that Joan was getting serious with someone who didn't seem to be as ambitious or as polished as they might have liked.

While his brief foray into metallurgical engineering ended in near disaster, Sandy still intended to join his father's business. With that certain opportunity ahead, he thought little about career planning, unlike friends who were aiming for law school or joining professionally oriented groups on campus. He continued to coast through school, posting reasonable grades in easy courses while spending as much time with Joan as he could. By spring of 1955 the young couple began planning an elaborate wedding to be held shortly after Sandy graduated.

Then Max Weill sprang his stunning surprise. Leaving the house on the pretext of going for a pack of cigarettes, Max phoned his unsuspecting wife to tell her he had long been having an affair with a younger woman and now he intended to divorce Etta and marry his lover. Reeling, all Etta could think to do was call her son. The news floored Sandy. He had known his parents were very different from each other, but he had never even considered the possibility that they might divorce. As soon as he recovered his wits, Sandy jumped into his convertible, sped off to pick up his sister at Smith College in western Massachusetts, and then drove through the night to confront Max, who was living with his mistress. It was only then, as he and Helen tried desperately to convince Max to come home, that his father struck a second shocking blow: He had secretly sold American Steel months earlier. There was no steel business and no job for Sandy.

Defeated and despondent, Sandy returned to Cornell. His family was disintegrating before his eyes, and his long-held dream of setting up as a prosperous steel importer had evaporated, literally overnight. Yet more was in store. While he and Helen were comforting their mother in Brooklyn, Sandy missed a crucial exam in his accounting class. The professor wouldn't listen to explanations or excuses, and suddenly the shaken senior didn't have enough credits to graduate with his class. Joan's parents seized on the crisis as ammunition to foil the pending wedding. Their daughter's suitor wouldn't have a college degree. Worse, his parents were divorcing in a scandalous affair. "The apple doesn't fall far from the tree," Paul Mosher warned his daughter before offering her a trip to Europe if she wouldn't marry Sandy.

But Joan and Sandy had forged a bond that neither scandal nor parents could break. In a last-ditch effort to remove at least one of the Moshers' objections to him, Sandy convinced the Cornell administration to let him take a make-up exam for his accounting course. He took the exam on the Monday before the planned wedding and was notified he had passed on Thursday. Cornell wouldn't be issuing diplomas again until the next fall, but at least Sandy had graduated. The wedding went ahead as planned, despite the obvious tension between Sandy and Joan's parents and without the presence of Max Weill, whom Sandy had forbidden to attend lest his presence upset Etta. The elegant ceremony took place at the Essex House in Manhattan, across from Central Park. Sandy was ecstatic to be marrying the beautiful and graceful woman who had become his closest friend. And while Sandy was neither a debonair nor an elegant groom, Joan Weill recognized a diamond in the rough. She loved him for his loyalty, drive, and sense of humor—and for putting her on a pedestal. The honeymoon took the couple to Florida for the entire summer, courtesy of Max Weill, who now lived there with his new wife. Sandy and Joan toured the state, putting their hotels and meals on his father's credit card. The expenses-paid honeymoon was more than Max Weill's wedding gift—it was his effort at reconciliation with his still-angry son.

LEARNING THE BACK OFFICE

Usually Sandy got no further than the receptionists' desks. By the fall of 1955, Wall Street had gotten a reputation as a good place to make some money, and Sandy spent weeks trudging through Lower Manhattan making cold calls on the firms lining the narrow streets. Often he passed directly in front of the City National Bank, its facade decorated with a frieze called "The Titans of Finance." But with his heavy Brooklyn accent, cheap suits, and perennially sweat-soaked shirts, about all Sandy could persuade the receptionists to do was take his resumé. He knew it wasn't much of a resumé. A liberal-arts degree, even from a prestigious school like Cornell, didn't do much to prepare a guy for a job in what was then called "high finance." And his work experience consisted of two weeks selling the Greater New York Industrial Directory to local businesses, a job from which he was fired after making only one sale in those two weeks. What it took Sandy longer to realize was that the banks and securities firms crowded into the financial enclave considered themselves a culture operating in a world apart from other industries. Only the well-bred, the well-dressed, the well-off, and the well-connected need apply. For decades the Street had been dominated by firms like J.P. Morgan and Morgan Stanley, whose managing directors and brokers enjoyed memberships in the prestigious clubs along Hanover Square that openly or informally prohibited blacks, Jews, and women. Moreover, many of those men had attended the same prep schools and colleges and could trace their Protestant roots to the *Mayflower.* Certain brokerage houses and investment banks, such as Goldman Sachs, welcomed and promoted Jews, but only those descendants of German Jewish emigrés; they carried a distinct bias against the sons and grandsons of Eastern European Jews, like Sandy.

Pervasive as they seemed, Wall Street's prejudices were focused mostly among the brokers and managing directors, the "front office" that solicited and cared for clients, mostly wealthy individuals. The "back office," where the accounting, record keeping, and other mundane tasks of high finance were carried out, was a different story. And that's where Sandy finally got a break. More of a crack, really. Bear Stearns, very much a second-tier firm among Wall Street's powerful brokerage houses, needed another runner to deliver securities certificates to other firms. "Runner" wasn't really an apt description of the job. The brokerage firms preferred reliability over speed, and most of the runner jobs went to old men looking to augment their Social Security checks or to escape the boredom of retirement. But business was good for Wall Street, and the twenty-two-year-old Weill seemed reliable enough. The job paid only $35 a week, but it literally opened doors for Sandy. Delivering stock certificates around Wall Street, anchored by the New York Stock Exchange with its colossal Corinthian columns and marble-walled, gilt-ceilinged trading room, gave Sandy a chance to watch brokers in action. Each lunch hour was devoted to close observation as brokers slammed down phones, raced to fill out trading slips, and shouted to one another about the latest blip disclosed by the chattering Dow Jones News Service machines. The adrenaline rush he got from simply watching the action was addictive. Sandy *had* to be part of that club.

One day it dawned on Sandy that a detour might take him where he wanted to go. At Cornell he had been a member of the Reserve Officers' Training Corps—ROTC—an organization designed to prepare college students for a stint in the military as officers. Sandy's ROTC unit was affiliated with the U.S. Air Force. It wasn't a big leap, then, to calculate that serving four years as an Air Force pilot would give a guy—even a guy of Eastern European Jewish descent—a credential that could gain him admission to the broker training programs that had once rejected him. The plan might have worked. Pilots had to have fast reactions and good decision-making skills—excellent prerequisites for a broker's job—and military service carried some clout on Wall Street. But he never got the chance to find out. With the Korean War long since ended, the military was winding down and setting tough new standards for new recruits. An Air Force dentist examining potential recruits found a spot of decay on one of Sandy's teeth. Application denied.

Now desperate—he and Joan were expecting their first child—Sandy pleaded with his bosses at Bear Stearns to at least let him have a crack at taking the mandatory brokerage licensing examination. He would study on his own while continuing to do his daily chores in the back office. They consented: If he could pass the examination, he would get a shot at being a broker. In the meantime, whether to encourage or discourage him, they began giving Sandy more responsibilities in the back office. First they made him a quote boy, a post in which he worked directly for a boisterous trader named Cy Lewis, who would later become a legend among Wall Street traders. Lewis would yell for a price quote on some stock, and Sandy would punch the necessary symbol into the quote machine to get it for him. Next he became a margin clerk, keeping track of the loans Bear Stearns made to customers to allow them to buy more stock, which was in turn used as collateral against the loan. If a stock's price fell—that is, the collateral securing the loan declined in value—it was Sandy's job to let a broker know that his client needed to either put up more cash as collateral or sell the stock to repay the loan. Few brokers had any concept of how important these and dozens of other menial back-office jobs were to the smooth functioning of their firm. Fewer still had any idea about how to do those jobs. But Sandy was fascinated by the intricacies of the back office, even while studying for the exams that might let him move to the front office. Less than a year after his desperate plea, Sandy Weill passed his exams and became an officially licensed broker at Bear Stearns.

THE COINCIDENTAL PARTNER

It wasn't much as apartments go, a one-bedroom next to the railroad tracks in East Rockaway. But the monthly rent of $120 was affordable and the commute to the city was easy. More important, it let the young couple get away from Joan's parents and Sandy's mother, with whom they had been alternately living since returning from their Florida honeymoon. But the best thing about the new apartment was that they lived across the hall from Arthur and Linda Carter, another young Jewish couple. The two couples formed an instant bond. Linda, who had just given birth to the Carters' first child, offered comfort and advice as Joan neared the end of her pregnancy. Arthur had majored in French at Brown University and had considered a career as a concert pianist before joining the U.S. Coast Guard during the Korean War. As the war wound down, Arthur began looking for a job on Wall Street. Dressed in his Coast Guard uniform, he managed to secure an interview with Bobbie Lehman, the head of Lehman Brothers and grandson of one of the founders. A former army man, Lehman, who ran the firm as his own personal fiefdom, liked the urbane and handsome young man and hired him as a rookie investment banker in the department that advised industrial concerns. But Carter had no upper-class pedigree, no Wall Street connections, no family money, and he soon discovered he wasn't being paid as much as his colleagues. When the Weills moved in across the hall, Arthur Carter suddenly found himself with a neighbor who shared the brunt of Wall Street's prejudices. The two families often cooked dinner together, Arthur and Sandy rode the train together each day, and they frequently met for lunch, since neither was invited to join the private clubs to which other brokers belonged. The conversation always concerned business and the Street, and how they would run the place if they were in charge.

Sandy's brokerage career began in a decidedly different way from most others. Rather than making phone calls or personal visits to solicit clients, Sandy found he was far more comfortable sitting at his desk, poring through companies' financial statements to see how fast they were growing or examining the disclosures they made to the Securities and Exchange Commission about their business. He often found little nuggets of information that persuaded him a company's stock was a good buy or to be avoided at all costs. For weeks his only client was his mother, Etta. Joan, who knew very well Sandy's tendency to avoid public contact, managed to double his clientele one weekend when they ran across one of her old boyfriends, Michael Weinberg, at the beach and Joan persuaded him to let Sandy sign him up for a brokerage account. She began calling Sandy at the office each day, sometimes several times a day, to warn him to "get off your duff and make some calls." Her nudges helped Sandy overcome his shyness, and he began building a client base centered around his Brooklyn roots. The area merchants and professionals Sandy convinced to open accounts also became a source of new business as word spread about the successful stock picks he had put in their portfolios.

But there were limits to working at Bear Stearns. Bigger brokerage firms had a wider array of financial products, from mutual funds to hog bellies, to offer their clients. If a broker could sell two or three commission-generating products to each client rather than just one, each sales call would be far more profitable. With his track record on stocks and a solid, if small, client base, Sandy moved in 1956 to Burnham & Co., a Jewish firm run by I. W. "Tubby" Burnham. Each night as Burnham headed out the door, he could see young Sandy hunched over his desk, searching for tidbits of information in company reports or making cold calls to pitch new clients. With new products to sell to his old clients and the wide array of product offerings to attract new clients, Sandy grossed $25,000 in sales in his first year at Burnham and took home a third of it, or about $8,000.

While Sandy was building his brokerage business, Arthur Carter decided that he could further his career at Lehman Brothers if he had a business degree. Although Sandy argued against it—Carter already had a job at one of the most powerful Wall Street firms—Carter applied to and was accepted by Dartmouth's Amos Tuck School of Business Administration, his tuition to be paid by the government under legislation for veterans of the Korean War. When Carter left for school he gave Sandy $5,000 to put into a brokerage account for him. He called Sandy daily from Hanover, New Hampshire, to compare notes about stocks that might be good buys and to share some of the insights he was gaining from his classes and classmates. By graduation, Carter's investment, managed by Sandy, had grown to $60,000. Carter was right about what additional education might do for him: When he returned to Wall Street with his business degree, he joined an old-line investment banking firm, Lee Higginson & Co., that offered him 50 percent more money.

Despite their success, Sandy and Carter never stopped talking about how they would run a business. As 1960 dawned, the two men could do more than talk. They were experienced, they were earning good salaries, they had moved their families into bigger suburban homes in affluent neighborhoods (although Sandy and Joan rented rather than owned their home) where Jews were welcomed, and they had some money in the bank. The idea of starting their own firm was immensely appealing. If they owned the firm, they could keep all the fees and commissions they generated. But it was also frightening. Sandy's brokerage business would generate immediate commissions if, as he presumed, his clients followed him to the new firm. It was much less likely that the companies Carter advised at his investment-banking firms would follow him to a small new outfit. There was no way to know how long it might take for Carter to begin generating fees. One solution, Carter suggested, would be to bring in another broker who, like Sandy, could begin generating commissions immediately. And he had just the person in mind, an old friend named Roger Berlind, a Princeton English major working at Eastman Dillon. Like Sandy, Roger Berlind was Jewish and had endured the same humiliation trying to break into Wall Street—thirty consecutive rejections before Eastman Dillon hired him—and it wasn't hard to persuade him to join them. While his first impression of Sandy was of someone gruff and unsure of himself, Berlind recognized that Sandy knew the brokerage business thoroughly and was very smart. Berlind also suggested that they attempt to recruit his friend Peter Potoma, another broker at Eastman Dillon. Not only was Potoma married to money, he was an Italian, and so more welcome on the New York Stock Exchange floor than a Jew.

Before the quartet made their final move, Sandy went to Tubby Burnham, who had started Burnham from scratch twenty-five years earlier. Would he support Sandy's effort to start a new firm by agreeing to handle the fledgling firm's back-office business? With Burnham's blessing, the four young partners each contributed $60,000 for a total of $240,000—enough to buy a seat on the New York Stock Exchange for $160,000, rent a tiny office, and hire one secretary. To fund his share Sandy went to Etta. She lent him $30,000—more than half of what she had—and Sandy used all but $1,000 of his and Joan's savings, money they had set aside to buy a new house, to make up the rest. In May 1960 the new firm of Carter, Berlind, Potoma & Weill opened in a cramped two-room office at 37 Wall Street. The four partners shared one room; a secretary and reception area occupied the other. At the end of their first day in business, the firm, minus the secretary, took itself to a celebratory dinner at a fine French restaurant on Third Avenue. But without their wives—the four didn't think they could afford to bring them—the dinner wasn't much fun. Sandy felt the fear of failure gnawing at his gut. He was risking nearly everything he and Joan had.

DIGGING FOR DETAILS

New firms, even on Wall Street, don't just start minting money. True, Carter, Berlind, Potoma & Weill began with the customer base that the three brokers brought with them. But they knew that to survive, much less thrive, they would need something that brought them to the attention of the professional money managers and wealthy individuals who typically gravitated toward the well-known names of Wall Street. In 1960 Wall Street was still basking in the lucrative "fixed-commission" system, in effect a government-backed price-fixing scheme that forbade brokers from undercutting one another's prices to attract business. So like any other small firm trying to break into the near monopoly that the big Wall Street firms enjoyed, Carter, Berlind needed a gimmick. That gimmick turned out to be Sandy's brain.

Brokers at the big Wall Street firms may have come from good schools and respected families, but they weren't known for towering intellects. Life was easier if they wined and dined their clients, took them to baseball games or Broadway shows, and then recommended mostly big blue-chip stocks, instantly recognizable companies whose names appeared almost daily in *The Wall Street Journal*. After all, these big companies had a well-known history and provided familiar products or services. And if clients didn't want the big blue-chip companies, the brokers could offer them hot new technology stocks from companies in electronics, atomic energy, or space exploration. It wasn't necessary for a broker to build a detailed case for why an investor should buy any of those stocks. More to the point, the brokers' commissions were fixed: They would make the same amount of money regardless of whether they put in hours of tedious research.

But socializing repelled Sandy. He wasn't articulate or polished, and he hated making small talk. Let his partners take care of that. He much preferred sitting at his desk, a Te-Amo cigar clenched in his teeth, mining documents for information. Sandy's desk was always overflowing with sheafs of pink paper. The "pink sheets," as they were aptly called, were printed by the National Quotation Bureau, the forerunner of the NASDAQ market and a listing agent for companies that weren't big enough, profitable enough, or respected enough to be listed on the exclusive New York Stock Exchange. The pink sheets listed that day's "bid" and "ask" for individual companies whose stocks could be bought "over the counter," another way of saying that the stocks were handled not through a central exchange like the NYSE, but by individual brokerage firms that "made a market" in a particular stock. Sandy would spend hours poring over the pink sheets, looking for unknown companies with the right combination of growth rates, debt levels, profit margins, and other financial details that signaled a good investment. After he had identified a possible target, he would start checking other sources, including documents filed with the Securities and Exchange Commission and anything else that might give him some insight into the company's growth potential and its stock's value. One of the first little gems he discovered was a small company called Associated Transport Inc., a freight hauling company whose stock traded between $7 and $13 a share in 1960. Based on his research into the obscure company, Sandy concluded it had good growth potential both as a company and as a stock, and he began recommending that clients buy it. By 1964 the stock was selling as high as $43. Investors who followed Sandy's advice would have quadrupled their money in four short years.

But most wealthy investors didn't appreciate the benefits of research and didn't want to risk their money on the stocks of unfamiliar companies. They were content to accept whatever returns they could get from their big blue-chip stocks. Thus a firm like Carter, Berlind held little interest for them. And Carter, Berlind's one measly, unattractive office—as opposed to a firm like Merrill Lynch with its vast network of branches—wasn't exactly inviting to well-heeled individual investors. Fortunately, however, some fundamental changes taking place in the nature of investing in 1960 ensured that Carter, Berlind would prosper nevertheless. One of those changes was the growth of mutual funds, investment vehicles that pool the financial resources of thousands of individual investors to buy stocks and bonds in bulk cheaper, with more knowledge, and with less fuss than the individuals could do by themselves. Mutual funds had been around for years, but only in the 1950s did they become an important part of the investment scene. Incomes were rising fast enough to allow more families to save part of their paychecks, and the stock market's spectacular rise in the 1950s, when the Dow Jones Industrial Average tripled in value, lured increasing numbers of small investors who were not welcome customers at the big brokerage houses. Then, as now, mutual-fund companies competed against one another based on how much they could increase their customers' money. Consequently, fund managers began to look for undiscovered companies with quick growth potential.

One day in 1960 a Bostonian named Edward C. "Ned" Johnson III called the firm to discuss one of its highly detailed research reports. Ned Johnson was a research analyst at Fidelity Management & Research Co., which his father had founded years earlier to advise the Fidelity Fund, one of the earliest mutual funds. Soon the young Ned Johnson was picking the brains of Carter, Berlind in weekly phone calls and executing profitable trades following their research. With Fidelity as their first institutional client, the founders realized their research prowess could be a powerful tool to attract other institutional clients such as pension funds, for which they would execute much larger trades—generating bigger fees—without having to support a capital-intensive branch network. The firm, along with another upstart called Donaldson, Lufkin & Jenrette, quickly developed a niche as a "research boutique."

Sandy didn't confine his research to the office. One weekend in 1963 an acquaintance complained about all the overtime he was putting in at the Bulova Corporation factory where he worked. Bulova had just introduced a new watch called the Accutron, the first wristwatch to use electronics rather than springs and levers to keep time, and they were flying out of the stores as fast as they could be made. After grilling the man for more details about the new watch, what it cost to make, and what Bulova charged jewelers for the watch, Sandy came to the office the next Monday and told his colleagues to start buying Bulova stock for the firm's account and recommending it to clients as a "buy." Carter, Berlind's buying was so persistent that it soon attracted the attention of Bulova's assistant treasurer George Sheinberg, who began inquiring about Carter, Berlind. None of his fellow executives at Bulova had ever heard of the firm. Likewise, Sheinberg's contacts on Wall Street knew nothing about it. Finally Sheinberg called Sandy directly to find out why the firm was so eager to own Bulova stock. The two met over a chicken Kiev dinner and began a friendship.

The next year Bulova needed more working capital to expand its production of Accutron watches. To raise the money, the company hired Goldman Sachs, a prestigious and powerful firm whose senior partner, John Weinberg, sat on Bulova's board. Goldman would be in charge of putting together a syndicate, a group of Wall Street firms that would buy bonds from Bulova, then resell them to investors. Typically the syndicates were composed of a dozen or so well-regarded Wall Street firms. Sheinberg, however, suggested that Carter, Berlind be included in the syndicate. Weinberg checked with his colleagues at Goldman Sachs, who told him that Carter, Berlind was a firm of "nobodies" and shouldn't be part of the syndicate. But Sheinberg was adamant; without Carter, Berlind's heavy purchases of Bulova stock and research reports recommending that their clients buy it, too, Bulova's stock would not be nearly so high and raising money would be much more difficult. Goldman relented and let Carter, Berlind into the syndicate, but only for a minuscule 1.9 percent of the deal. Still, it was the first time the firm had been admitted into a syndicate run by one of Wall Street's old-guard firms. Goldman made sure, however, that the upstarts at Carter, Berlind knew who was in charge: The name of the tiny firm was left out of the standard "tombstone" ad announcing the deal in *The Wall Street Journal.*

In their first year in business the three brokers each brought in about $75,000 in commissions, reinvesting all but their meager—at least by Wall Street standards—$12,000 salaries. Each of the three had a different approach to the business. Sandy let his thinking do his selling. It was his ideas and roll-up-the-sleeves analysis that attracted clients who made money on his smart though often obscure stock picks. Because of his unease in social settings, he preferred letting the other partners do the client hand-holding. His colleagues happily obliged because they feared Sandy's disheveled working-class appearance and his habit of endlessly smoking or chewing cheap cigars would drive away clients. At their urging, he bought a hat like one he had seen President John F. Kennedy wear. But it looked absurd on the chunky twenty-seven-year-old, and he wore it only once.

Roger Berlind, a tall, thoughtful, soft-spoken man with horn-rimmed glasses, was almost the antithesis of a fast-talking stockbroker. His blood didn't pulse with the market gyrations as did the others'; he simply went into the business after his first love of writing show tunes didn't pay the bills. He was the most pleasant of the four to be around, the most presentable, and therefore the most likely to meet with the institutional clients such as Ned Johnson. His sweeter disposition made him an easy target for his hard-charging colleagues, who deemed him "barely Jewish" because of his tony Princeton degree and his Gentile wife and friends.

Peter Potoma was the wild card among the four founders. A savvy stockbroker, he could sell stocks better than either Sandy or Berlind. But Potoma frequently disappeared for days at a time. The partners let him get away with it for longer than they should have, primarily because his rich father-in-law sent Carter, Berlind a significant chunk of business.

While the three brokers worked the phones, Arthur Carter, the aspiring investment banker, was quietly assuming control of the firm, even though the partners never elected him or anyone else to be the head. Precisely at 5:00 P.M. each day, Carter brought out the firm's ledger book, in which he had meticulously recorded the number of shares traded by each of the three brokers and compared their commissions against the day's cost of operating, creating a daily profit-and-loss statement. If one of the brokers had an especially good day, he would leave the office after the daily ledger review feeling like the king of the mountain. A bad day, however, made whoever experienced it feel like the world's worst loser. Carter's domineering and dry personality reflected his worries about the down-and-dirty nature of the firm that bore his name. Fancying himself a graphic designer of sorts, he fashioned the stationery and business cards for Carter, Berlind, Potoma & Weill. The design was elegant, crisp, and traditional, an effort to make the hole-in-the-wall firm that no one had heard of look like one of the mainstays of the Wall Street Club.

But the outlander firm was faced with a crisis in credibility early on. In the winter of 1962 the New York Stock Exchange notified Carter, Berlind that it was bringing disciplinary proceedings against Potoma for violating the exchange's rules. The troubled broker had engaged in a pattern of "free-riding" in his and his wife's accounts by buying stock on its way up without paying for it and then selling later to cover the original purchase price. Having a partner disciplined by the New York Stock Exchange could destroy the firm, especially among the institutional clients it was so ardently courting. Moving quickly to save themselves, the other three partners took over Potoma's New York Stock Exchange seat, forced his resignation, and dropped his name from the firm. When news of Potoma's suspension moved over the Dow Jones news ticker that July, there was no mention of the new firm of Carter, Berlind & Weill.

BUILDING A TALENT BANK

The mid-1960s were a golden time on Wall Street. Known as the "go-go" years, it was a time when the public experienced one of its periodic love affairs with stocks. Wall Street firms large and small scrambled to open new offices and hire new brokers and researchers to meet the booming demand. The trend was evident in Lower Manhattan, where opportunistic builders began throwing up nondescript modern office buildings among the area's imposing monuments to capitalism. The new buildings were quickly occupied by firms short on history but long on greed and guts. Among them was Carter, Berlind & Weill, which used some of the capital its partners had plowed back into the firm to rent a full floor at 55 Broad Street, one of the primary narrow streets that make up the southern tip of Manhattan. The three founding partners continued sharing an office, although the one they now shared was fully forty feet long. The rest of the office space was decorated with gray carpet, chrome and red upholstered chairs, and fake wood desks. Maps and tip sheets covered the walls, and a pervasive fog of cigarette and cigar smoke hung over it all.

The firm also began to use its growing capital to hire more brokers and research analysts, typically young opportunists like themselves who were rejected by the establishment firms. Among their first hires was a well-spoken young man with piercing blue eyes named Arthur Levitt Jr. Levitt had worked as a newspaper writer and had dabbled at the fringes of Wall Street, acting as a salesman for cattle that were used as tax shelters for rich individuals. He had been rejected by all the old-line brokerage houses despite the fact that his father had long served as New York State's comptroller. His family background, polished style, and persuasive presentation all impressed Sandy. But Levitt wasn't at all sure he wanted to go to work for a "peanut firm" like Carter, Berlind & Weill. First, he quickly noticed that these men didn't treat their work as a job. Rather, it was their life. Second, he was stunned that the partners didn't associate with—indeed, didn't even know—Wall Street's richest and most powerful figures, people like Billy Salomon, from the founding family of Salomon Brothers, and John Loeb, a founder of Loeb Rhoades, whom he had met in his tax-shelter dealings. But Carter, Berlind & Weill, he saw, was counting on performance, not connections, to be successful. Finally, there was the matter of salary: $25,000 annually, a lot less than people he knew were getting when they started at the bigger firms. But it was the only offer he had, so he took it.

Levitt regretted his decision almost immediately. He was the odd man out among the office staff. The three partners would sit in their big office speaking their own shorthand and using obscure hand signals to carry on conversations amid the ringing phones and clattering quote machines, leaving Levitt to guess at what they meant. Walking in on big laughs that ceased in his presence, he got the impression he was the object of their jokes and jeers. After a few months of such tension, Levitt was at a crossroads. He would have to leave unless he could get their attention and respect. One morning he puffed himself up, strode into the partners' office, and announced, "I'm the syndicate manager." Startled, Sandy, Berlind, and Carter looked at Levitt, then at one another. They didn't have any such position. With a few exceptions like the Bulova deal, Carter, Berlind & Weill wasn't invited to join any syndicates. But if Levitt wanted to be the syndicate manager, then he could be the syndicate manager. The three immediately resumed their staccato repartee. Levitt, neither challenged nor endorsed, went back to his desk at least mildly satisfied. He had upped the ante for himself at Carter, Berlind & Weill. Indeed, his bid for status left the partners impressed with their new colleague. He has chutzpah, Sandy concluded. And it wasn't such a bad idea. Levitt's superior contacts and his confident, diplomatic demeanor might actually get the firm into a few syndicates.

Something of a renegade, Carter, Berlind & Weill wasn't reluctant to break some of Wall Street's unwritten "rules," one of which was that blacks had no place on the Street. In the early '60s, there were almost no African Americans employed in the downtown brokerages. Only one black-owned brokerage house operated in that decade. Special Markets Inc., however, couldn't get office space on Wall Street because landlords refused to rent to the fledgling firm "run by and for Negroes." As the 1960s progressed, the number of African Americans working for the New York Stock Exchange grew quietly, with an estimated forty black men serving as floor carriers by 1969. The job, taking used punch cards from traders and sticking them into mechanized reading devices to register trades on the ticker, was hardly emblematic of any positive recruitment effort; more middle-class white kids simply preferred to go to college rather than serve as clerks. The first black to actually trade securities on the Exchange floor was thirty-one-year-old Joseph Louis Searles III, who purchased a seat in 1970. He was completely ignored, even having a remote seat designated for him in the Big Board's lunchroom. Searles braved the hostile treatment with tremendous ambition to succeed, but he lost his seat a couple of years later when the market downturn wiped out his firm.

Clarence Jones received his law degree from Boston University in 1959 and soon became counsel to the man he most admired in the world, the Reverend Martin Luther King Jr. Jones acted both as an advisor to King on legal matters—he helped negotiate a settlement with the City of Birmingham, Alabama, over civil rights demonstrations aimed at desegregating department stores and public accommodations—and as a draft speechwriter, brainstorming with King the night before the civil rights leader's "I Have a

Dream" speech and securing its copyright afterward. But Jones also had a taste for business and sensed that huge opportunities lay in America's black population, then largely ignored by most big businesses. With another lawyer and an insurance manager, Jones set up an insurance company to focus on the black middle class. When the up-and-coming company needed more funds, a friend suggested that Carter, Berlind & Weill might be more hospitable to Jones than the old-line investment banks. Sandy and his partners didn't just find a source of funds, it found a company—Colonial Penn Group of Life Insurance Companies—that wanted to buy Jones's company outright. Of course, that meant Jones lost the helm of his concern, but Carter, Berlind & Weill promptly offered him a job. The partners had been so impressed with Jones's business plan, his Rolodex of contacts, and his charismatic personality that they gave him a phone and a desk, and told him to put his skills to work. Soon Jones brought in big union accounts, including the National Maritime Union and various locals of the International Brotherhood of Teamsters. Even Muhammad Ali stopped by Carter, Berlind & Weill for business meetings with Jones. Jones felt a tremendous kinship with Sandy and the other Jewish partners. He got the feeling that Sandy wondered, "Imagine if I were a Negro."

Women didn't find Wall Street nearly so inhospitable. In the 1960s more women were going to work, either to supplement their families' incomes or because they were waiting longer to marry. But while Wall Street was receptive to women, it invariably steered them toward such menial jobs as secretary, receptionist, and switchboard operator. One catchall job in many Wall Street firms was "gal Friday," a job that involved doing whatever the bosses wanted done, from bringing back lunch for deskbound traders to making restaurant reservations for the bosses and their wives. Mary McDermott was a twenty-one-year-old graduate of Catholic girls' schools when she applied for a gal Friday position at Carter, Berlind & Weill. Her father, an accountant, had checked with his friends in the financial district and warned her that "no one has heard of this dinky outfit. You're going to work for a bucket shop." But McDermott figured it might be more fun than the alternative, teaching high school English, and she took the job to see what she could learn. For a young woman in her first job, surrounded by swirling cigar smoke, verbal epithets, and lots of male posturing, McDermott proved remarkably observant. When new recruits joined the firm, she gave them this summation of the major players: "Arthur Carter runs the place and has at least one secretary in tears every day. Roger Berlind wants to write Broadway songs; he's miscast in this business, but he's the stabilizing influence. Arthur Levitt is smooth and well connected. Sandy Weill is quiet, stays in his little corner, and looks at the tape all day. You can stand on this desk and take off your clothes, and he won't even notice."

It didn't take McDermott long to realize that there was a bigger role for her in the firm. Hearing the men discuss investment ideas, she realized that while the ideas were good, they weren't being very well articulated. With her language and writing skills McDermott could translate those abstruse ideas into plain English, making it easier for investors to understand. The partners saw the value in easier-to-understand reports, and so McDermott became the firm's first "research editor." That often meant following the analysts around, jotting down notes, then retreating to an office to figure out the best way to explain the idea in simple terms, but it was a major step up for a woman working on Wall Street.

The most important early hire, however, was a brassy, pudgy Harvard Business School graduate named Marshall Cogan. A born salesman, Cogan had put himself through business school selling cars for a Boston-area dealership. After rejections from Goldman Sachs and Lehman Brothers, Cogan came to Carter, Berlind & Weill through an employment agency. His arrogant spiel during interviews with the partners would surely have offended the old-line Wall Street executives, but it didn't bother anyone at Carter, Berlind & Weill.

"If he can do half as much as he says he can, he'll be terrific," Carter told his colleagues.

With his experience selling cars, Cogan was a natural to become the firm's first auto analyst, and his real-world expertise quickly paid off. His research indicated that among the Big Three automakers Chrysler was undervalued as a stock. Sure enough, delighted clients soon found Chrysler's stock moving higher. But Cogan was brimming with too much energy to spend his days doing stock research. His nervous tics bothered his colleagues, and they were a little afraid of him, not the least because he would literally bite pencils in two when he got excited about an idea. And one of the ideas that most excited him was the business of mergers and acquisitions.

Mergers had been around for a long time. Indeed, some of America's biggest companies—U.S. Steel and General Motors, for example—had grown through the early 1900s largely by buying and absorbing other steel companies or automakers. But the merger business in the late 1950s and early 1960s was shaping up to be something different: Big companies weren't buying smaller companies in the same business; they were buying *big* companies in *different* businesses. The idea behind these "conglomerates"—conglomerations of different businesses—was very simple: Just as individual investors were urged to own several stocks in different industries to diversify their portfolios and protect against any single stock plunging in value, the conglomerates wanted to own a diversified portfolio of businesses to protect against a downturn in any single business. An additional motive was that the stocks of some companies could be bought very cheaply, especially if the companies were having a hard time, with the conglomerates' high-priced shares. A conglomerate typically would buy an ailing company, oust the management, and replace it with managers loyal to the new parent company. Often such routine functions as accounting or personnel would be taken over by the parent company's staff, making it easier for the newly acquired company to make a profit. All this was made possible by the public's captivation with stocks, which made it easy for brash entrepreneurs to raise the money to assemble conglomerates. The men who assembled these vast but disparate empires became the celebrities of the 1960s financial world. Charles "Tex" Thornton put together Litton Industries, which held electronics companies, a shipyard, and various other assorted businesses. Harold Geneen, who in his teens was a Wall Street clerk, launched a massive expansion of International Telephone & Telegraph (ITT) beyond its basic business of making telephones to acquire such diverse brands as Avis Rent a Car, Hartford Insurance, and Sheraton hotels.

Carter, Berlind & Weill got its share of the conglomerate business, attracting as major clients a couple of the most aggressive players, including Charles Bluhdorn, who masterminded the growth of Gulf + Western Industries. Bluhdorn aggressively sought big names, such as Paramount Pictures, or cash-rich companies selling cheaply that he could milk for funds. Marshall Cogan got the firm most involved with James Ling, who parlayed a business of supplying electrical components into an aerospace concern called Ling-Temco-Vought, later renamed LTV Corp. The two men fed each other's ambitions as they sought bigger deals, eventually taking LTV into the meatpacking and steel businesses as well. Cogan made sure that one of his assistants was in almost daily contact with the flamboyant Jimmy Ling, even sending someone weekly to LTV headquarters.

A CHANGE AT THE TOP

The value of good research was rapidly becoming clear to everyone at Carter, Berlind & Weill. Clients who bought or sold stocks based on the firm's recommendations made money. And entrepreneurs like Bluhdorn and Ling used Carter, Berlind & Weill's research to find companies they could target for eventual acquisition. In both cases, the firm profited from commissions and fees. But no one at Carter, Berlind & Weill had any inkling that a single research report would be the genesis of the company's biggest triumph and its ultimate undoing.

The report was the product of Edward Netter, Sandy's friend who had worked as an actuary for Metropolitan Life. He had joined Carter, Berlind & Weill as an insurance analyst and spent a year studying the property and casualty industry. Stocks of companies in that business were trading at less than the apparent value of their assets. That wasn't surprising, because technology and other exciting sectors were much more interesting than insurance stocks. But Netter discovered a little secret about the industry: "surplus surplus." His lengthy report, turned into English prose by Mary McDermott, revealed that many of these fundamentally boring companies were hoarding huge cash reserves. The cash poured into the companies as policyholders paid their regular premiums, then the companies put the cash aside to cover future payouts on claims. Actually there wasn't much of a secret about it. The facts were there for anyone willing to dig into the companies' financial statements. But the implications of surplus surplus were stunning: Anyone who purchased one of the companies at or near the price of its stock could largely recoup the purchase price by simply raiding the acquired company's trove of cash. Basically, someone could buy one of these companies for nothing! Netter drew up a chart of the ten largest property and casualty companies listing their low returns on equity, trading prices below book value, and overcapitalization—their surplus surplus. Then to confirm his analysis, Netter befriended the chairman of one of these companies, Continental Insurance, and visited its headquarters to fine-tune his untried idea that companies could be acquired for less than the sum of their rich assets.

Carter and Cogan, the firm's aspiring investment bankers, instantly realized that Netter's discovery could be a windfall for one of the acquisitive conglomerateurs building their empires of miscellaneous businesses. They also knew that a successful deal would be a windfall for Carter, Berlind & Weill, too. They had just the acquirer in mind to do the deal: Saul Steinberg, the head of a computer leasing company called Leasco Data Processing Equipment Corp. The twenty-nine-year-old Steinberg—young, brash, Jewish, and from Brooklyn—was a Young Turk like them. Steinberg's lawyer Kenneth Bialkin, a rising securities attorney, had gotten to know Arthur Levitt through his work for the Jewish Guild for the Blind. Both young and ambitious, Bialkin and Levitt had an instant rapport, chatting about Wall Street and deal makers. They sensed that although Steinberg liked to brag about being a self-made man—his perennial claim was that his business "wasn't started by my grandfather"—like the partners of Carter, Berlind & Weill, he yearned for acceptance by the financial establishment.

The next step was picking the right target. Reviewing Netter's list of prospects, the partners chose an old Philadelphia company, Reliance Insurance Co.—stodgy, unsuspecting, ripe for the picking—and code-named the project "Raquel," after the actress Raquel Welch: highly desirable and very well endowed. Carter, Berlind & Weill quietly began buying up Reliance shares as they pitched the stock to institutional investors. In May 1968, rumors began circulating that Leasco was trying to secure a position in Reliance; Leasco's stock shot up more than $16 a share to close at a new high of $167 on the day of the speculation. Reliance's chairman and CEO told Dan Dorfman, writing *The Wall Street Journal*'s "Heard on the Street" column about the trading activity in Reliance stock, that he had an idea who was buying a stake and promised that Reliance wouldn't just roll over and play dead in the face of an unwanted suitor.

Soon after, SEC disclosures showed that Steinberg's Leasco paid $4.6 million for 3 percent of Reliance's outstanding shares. Steinberg told *The Wall Street Journal* that he had been "studying companies in the fire and casualty insurance field in which Reliance is engaged"—basically Carter, Berlind & Weill's groundbreaking report. Yet when Leasco launched its formal and hostile tender offer for all the remaining shares of Reliance, it used established investment bankers—Lehman Brothers and White Weld & Co.—not the upstart firm that gave Steinberg the bold idea. Carter, Berlind & Weill appealed to Steinberg and his lawyer Kenneth Bialkin that it should get at least a place in the tombstone ad, which White Weld was fighting tooth and nail. The outsiders can get a fee, but not get into our lofty realm, the elite bankers argued. But Carter, Berlind & Weill wanted prestige as much as profit.

Ultimately, the scrappy firm's involvement got Wall Street's attention.

To combat Steinberg, Reliance sought a white knight, Data Processing Financial & General Corp., to make a competing offer. But Data Processing didn't match Leasco's 3 percent stake. More decisive, however, came the revelation that Carter, Berlind & Weill, identified as Steinberg's investment advisor, controlled more than 30 percent of Reliance. By August 1968, Leasco sweetened its tender offer for the insurer and offered its management five-year contracts if Reliance would abandon its opposition.

After Steinberg's conquest, the insurance industry report by Carter, Berlind & Weill became a hot commodity, essentially a playbook for other deal makers. Thereafter, eight of the ten insurers in the report were taken over, including Loews Corp.'s purchase of Continental Insurance and American Express's buyout of Fund American Cos. The trend provoked an outrage about raiding the nation's insurers, sparking congressional and SEC hearings as well as New York and American Stock Exchange inquiries. Carter, Berlind & Weill was called before each panel. The famous surplus surplus strategy was stopped, but its purveyors achieved a new-found notoriety. Emboldened and flush with cash, Steinberg quickly shook the financial establishment again with an audacious but unsuccessful attempt to take over Chemical Bank, the nation's sixth-largest commercial bank.

Steinberg's raid on Reliance was a stunning victory for Carter, Berlind & Weill. The deal reaped the firm $750,000 as a finder's fee and $47,000 in commissions from its initial purchases of Reliance stock. Moreover, it forced even the biggest investment firms to sit up and take note of the brash young firm that had identified the opportunity and set the deal in motion. But it also set up a deep conflict within the once close partnership that ran the firm. Arthur Carter's skills as an investment banker were finally beginning to come to the fore, and he wanted the firm to get out of the hurly-burly of brokerage and focus exclusively on the more urbane—and potentially more lucrative—business of finding and doing deals like Reliance. If he couldn't transform Carter, Berlind & Weill, Carter decided he would leave and start his own investment banking firm. Carter had other changes going on in his life, as well. He had divorced his wife and married an aspiring singer and actress, a Southerner named Dixie Carter. He also had been elected to the boards of four companies, including the automaker Studebaker.

But Reliance had a huge impact on Sandy Weill as well. As a broker, Sandy had to always be on the lookout for the next trade, the next deal, the next client. His firm had been instrumental in doing the Reliance deal, but here was twenty-nine-year-old Saul Steinberg at the head of a huge company, while Sandy was still working the phones and digging into research reports to keep his stable of clients happy. Maybe, he thought, it would be better to work on building a company than simply being just the outside deal person who found companies for others. The revelation gave him a focus he had lacked before. Suddenly he was intent on building a real Wall Street firm, not just working on the fringes of the Street.

For eight years the three partners, who together had collected some one hundred rejections from Wall Street firms, had been united in proving that their brains and chutzpah could beat the pedigree and connections of the clubby financial establishment. Now, however, the camaraderie was wearing thin. Arguments broke out frequently over who was making the most money for the firm. Carter would warn his two colleagues that they weren't "scratching the pad enough," stock trader lingo for taking buy or sell orders from clients. Worse still from the viewpoint of Sandy and Berlind, Carter was clearly favoring the strong personalities and financial contributions of Arthur Levitt and Marshall Cogan, both of whom had joined the three founders on the executive committee. Levitt's connections had brought the firm its first acquisition, a small investment-management firm called Bernstein-Macaulay in 1967, and Cogan was clearly becoming a star deal maker with his high-profile transactions. Neither Sandy nor Roger Berlind confronted Carter, but they were becoming deeply resentful of his imperious attitude toward them. After all, if it hadn't been for their early successes in attracting clients to buy and sell stocks discovered by Sandy's research, there wouldn't even be a Carter, Berlind & Weill.

Arthur Carter was questioning whether he wanted to stay in the brokerage business or take the firm in another direction. He had discussions with both Cogan and Levitt, suggesting that the three of them use their majority votes on the executive committee to slash his cofounders' shares of the firm to a mere 1 percent, a level that would surely force them to leave. Neither Cogan nor Levitt committed themselves to the coup, but neither did they outright reject it.

When Carter called an executive committee meeting on September 10, 1968, the five men gathered in a conference room. Carter began to set the stage, telling Sandy and Berlind "you aren't pulling your weight." But before he could make his motion to weaken the two men's hold on the firm, Arthur Levitt stepped in with a motion to adjourn for a brief recess. Levitt drew Sandy and Berlind aside and told them what was about to happen, that Carter was setting them up for the firing squad.

"You've heard it with your own ears," Levitt warned the two men. "If Arthur will do this to you, it's just a matter of time before he pulls the same stunt on me." He told the stunned pair that he had hurriedly consulted with Bialkin, who reviewed the firm's charter and bylaws and concluded that the partners could override Carter. "I propose we kick Carter out and do it today," Levitt said. Sandy resisted, his long friendship with Carter balanced against the man's duplicity. Perhaps they should warn him to start looking for another job, Sandy suggested. But Levitt pressed his point: "I'm telling you, if you keep Arthur in the firm, he'll be like a wounded animal who'll come back to kill us all."

When the meeting reconvened minutes later, Levitt took the role of executioner. "You're out," he told Carter. "You're either out at three-thirty today or we issue a press release that you're fired."

Carter stared for a minute at the colleagues he had so long dominated. "Okay, fine," he said and left.

The next morning's *Wall Street Journal* reported on page sixteen that Carter had made "an amicable parting." Arthur Levitt was quoted as saying "This wasn't a shake-up." And the thirty-six-year-old Carter, characterizing his departure as "friendly," explained that he had resigned "because basically I wanted to do something else. And that something else was to become involved in the operations of a publicly owned concern." Indeed, within a month Carter had founded his own investment banking firm and soon took it public.

The remaining partners summoned their more than fifty employees, and Berlind and Levitt explained briefly that Arthur Carter had left the firm. No further details were forthcoming. Sandy, traumatized by the sudden turn of events, stood quietly in a corner during the meeting. He realized that this was an opportunity to fill the leadership void, but he couldn't muster the courage. *I'm afraid to be out front,* he thought, *where people can see my mistakes.*

The break between Carter and Sandy Weill, the original founders who plotted over dinners with their wives and little boys, was especially hard on Sandy. After the shocking disappointment he had experienced years earlier at the hands of his father, Sandy valued loyalty deeply. And Carter would come to realize that his cold demeanor meant the end of his good friendship with Sandy.

Although the restructuring of the firm went swiftly, Sandy was scared. None of the partners had any experience managing what had become a decent-sized firm. Sandy, Berlind, and Levitt knew they needed Cogan, who had become the firm's biggest revenue generator. To prevent him from leaving—Carter tried to entice him away to join his new venture—they offered him top billing in the new firm. He agreed and Cogan, Berlind, Weill & Levitt was born. Soon afterward the Weills and Levitts went out to dinner together, the wives trying to relieve their husbands' worries by bantering about ways they could save money, including buying just one set of Bar Mitzvah clothes that their sons could share. But Sandy couldn't make light of the firm's suddenly perilous future. He had been shaken to the core. Practically his only comment that evening, made over and over: "God, can we survive?"

2

CORNED BEEF WITH LETTUCE

T he new firm of Cogan, Berlind, Weill & Levitt may have been a trau-
matic victory for the participants, but it didn't inspire any respect on
Wall Street. Mocking the Jewish partners' initials, the Street's merciless
jokesters quickly branded the firm "Corned Beef With Lettuce." Thus it
wasn't very difficult for Sandy Weill and Roger Berlind, the two remaining
cofounders, to take an important step in their firm's growth: abandon Wall
Street. What was the benefit of remaining in the financial district where the
establishment held court every day and excluded them? Wall Street can
run its club; we'll run a business, Sandy vowed. The firm would take its expertise to its prospective clients, the big companies and wealthy individuals in midtown Manhattan. The result: a suite of offices on the thirty-fourth
floor of the gleaming new General Motors Building, a prestige address on
Fifth Avenue, across the street from the elegant Plaza Hotel and command-
ing spectacular views of Central Park.

If the intention was to generate more business, the move worked well.
CBWL boomed through the rest of 1968 and well into 1969. In fact, business grew so quickly—the company was generating fees and commissions
at an annual pace of $18 million in 1969 compared to just $4 million
two years earlier—that Burnham & Co., the firm's original clearinghouse,
couldn't keep up with the mounting flow of transactions. Moreover, Tubby
Burnham was wary of the securities that CBWL's Marshall Cogan was promoting on behalf of his high-flying merger-and-acquisition clients. Sandy's
old boss told the young firm to take its clearing business elsewhere.

The logical place to turn was the esteemed firm of Loeb Rhoades, which
handled clearing operations for many smaller firms of CBWL's size. Because John Langeloth Loeb, one of the patriarchs of German Jews on Wall
Street, insisted that his firm would clear trades only for firms of the highest

quality and prestige, hooking up with Loeb Rhoades would be a sign to the rest of the financial community that CBWL was no joking matter. Yet when Sandy asked John Loeb if he would take on their clearing business, the patrician Mr. Loeb told him in no uncertain terms that his firm already was operating at capacity and would not handle their clearing. Sandy knew Loeb Rhoades could easily deal with the volume of CBWL's business if it wanted to. It was a snub he wouldn't forget. And one that John Loeb would come to regret.

Stung by Loeb's insult, Sandy began to think about setting up a back-office facility at CBWL to clear its own trades. Such a move wouldn't have been possible in the earliest days, when the partners were struggling to pay office rent. But the firm had incorporated a few years earlier and the owners had been plowing nearly all their profits back into the business rather than distributing the proceeds to the partners as did many of the old-line firms. There was enough cash to set up a back-office operation, and the decade's bull market had given the CBWL executives the confidence that their fees and commissions would cover the significant fixed costs until they could grow enough to use all that clearing capacity.

Who would set up and run the back-office operation? Arthur Levitt, capitalizing on his many contacts in the financial community, came up with the name of Frank Zarb, who had developed and was running a training program for another firm's back office. Zarb, thirty-five, was the Brooklyn-born son of an immigrant refrigerator mechanic. He had never seen a stock certificate until he got his first job in the back office of Goodbody & Co. Zarb, an "operations expert," liked to joke that the front office of a brokerage firm was for "rich Yalies" and the back office for "poor kids like me." Not surprisingly, he took an instant liking to the four men he met in the General Motors Building. To his delight, they were a lot like him—blunt, brash, roll-up-your-sleeves managers. Much of his "interview" consisted of the four CBWL executives talking simultaneously to him and to one another, raising their voices or cursing to try to get the others' attention.

But it was Sandy who bowled over Zarb. Once the two began focusing on the nuts and bolts of becoming a "self-clearing" operation, Zarb quickly realized that Sandy knew more about the subject than anyone he had ever met. *Brokers think of the securities business as a telephone and a customer,* Zarb thought, *but Sandy is intimately familiar with every aspect of the business.* Sandy ticked off a list of problems, inefficiencies, and ineptness that marked most clearing operations, pausing to be sure Zarb agreed that none of those problems would plague a CBWL back office. Already the antiquated clearing systems in use were being overwhelmed by the massive paperwork that a long bull market created. The paralyzing "paper crunch" forced the New York Stock Exchange to begin closing on Wednesdays simply to allow brokerage houses some breathing room to catch up on the transfer of money and securities.

Now Sandy demanded the attention of his colleagues. To avoid the mess other brokerage firms were experiencing and to provide room for the future growth of their clearing business, Sandy and Zarb concluded that they would have to start from scratch with the most advanced automated-processing technology, and they would have to build a system that could handle triple their current volume.

"This pipeline will be our platform for growth," Sandy told his fellow executives. Cogan, Berlind, and Levitt didn't seem to know or care what that meant. They were tired of hashing out details of back-office plans. It was mundane, menial, and money losing. They knew that the front office is where a firm makes its money. Still Sandy persisted in his lecture, recalling a lesson from his military boarding school days. He quoted Sir Halford John Mackinder, the father of "geopolitics," who said, "he who rules the heartland . . . commands the world." Then he concluded, "our back-office operation is our heartland."

Sandy's fervor shocked his partners. They didn't realize he was so well read, articulate, or thoughtful. Even more surprising, Sandy, usually the guy at the back of the room who played the role of kibitzer and second-guesser, was taking the lead. Yet no one felt threatened by Sandy's display of leadership—after all, this was the back office he was talking about. He was welcome to be the leader of that! Eager to flee the meeting, they quickly agreed to hire Zarb and to give him a $1-million budget to set up a state-of-the-art clearing operation.

The looming expansion brought new vigor to the seemingly endless debate of who should lead the firm. No one had stepped forward to take over Arthur Carter's role after his departure, and the arguments about who should run the firm were usually held as the four CBWL executives dined on steak in the back room of the Christ Cella restaurant. It wasn't so much that one man thought he should be in charge; it was that none of them was willing to cede authority to anyone else. But the arguments would soon have to end. The firm's lawyer, Ken Bialkin, told the foursome that a chief executive was necessary to sign the leases on the new back-office space and to purchase the equipment.

The issue came to a head one night at Christ Cella when the four executives invited Bialkin to join them for dinner. What he witnessed was four grown men full of testosterone, ambition, and alcohol yelling, cursing, and trading insults. "You're a jerk," said one to another. "You're stupid" was the reply. "You can't be trusted," said a third. After a brief but futile effort by Sandy to persuade Bialkin himself to take the role of CEO, the attorney pressured his clients to take a vote. Sandy, who was too scared and shy to take full responsibility for the firm, nevertheless wanted to be able to influence the firm's direction. Still hurt by the final clash with Arthur Carter, he voted for Roger Berlind as "the least likely to go and do something on his own." Levitt supported Berlind as the nicest and most trustworthy of the group. And Cogan, who badly wanted to run things but knew he could never get the backing of Sandy and Levitt, cast his vote for Berlind on the assumption he could push Berlind around more easily than either of the other two. Berlind had no delusions. He accepted the job and told his colleagues that he knew why he had been given the CEO post: "I got the job because I'm the least threatening."

Meantime Frank Zarb had CBWL's back office up and operating on two leased floors at 100 Wall Street. The clearing operation was staffed by a bunch of Italians who described themselves as "goodfellas from Brooklyn." As the firm's new CEO, Roger Berlind invited them to a welcoming get-together at the General Motors Building. Trying to impress their boss, the new hires launched into a technical discussion of "fail-to-receive" securities and "out-of-balance" accounts, liberally interspersed with references to competitors as "dem guys" and "dose guys." Berlind's eyes glazed over in boredom. But then he came up with a solution: "Come on, I want to buy you guys a drink." He led them to a posh piano bar near the GM Building, the new staffers beside themselves at the prospect of free booze in such elegant surroundings. But they were even more astonished when Berlind sat down at the piano and began playing Broadway standards. This guy, the goodfellas agreed, was a far cry from the tough and aggressive bosses they knew from previous experience at other firms.

THE MOUSE THAT ATE THE ELEPHANT

As the good times continued to roll in early 1969, the executives at CBWL began to indulge themselves in the kinds of excesses that have long been part of Wall Street, yet with their own twist. A decorator was hired to spiff up the offices. But rather than the Oriental carpets and dark wood paneling that were the hallmarks of old Wall Street, CBWL wound up with gleaming modern modular furniture sitting on a boldly geometric wall-to-wall carpet. No still lifes, portraits, or hunt scenes adorned the walls. It was nude drawings by Aristide Maillol and signed prints by contemporary artists. Sandy, much more passionate about food than art, hired a chef for the office to whip up gourmet lunches in the thirty-fourth-floor kitchen each day.

Yet all good things come to an end, and the long bull market of the 1960s began to fade away in 1969 before plunging in 1970. As the pace of trading slowed and commissions began to evaporate, the partners at CBWL worried about how to cover the much larger overhead costs they had incurred in setting up their own clearing operation. Berlind, Cogan, and Levitt debated various plans to attract new business. But when the market plummeted and the outlook grew really grim, Sandy argued for a much different, more immediate response. "You can't control income. It varies based on conditions outside of our control," he told his partners. "But you can control expenses." The logic was unassailable, but none of the others was willing to take on the challenge of cost control. They deferred to Sandy, who seemed to have an instinctive knowledge of how to go about paring costs out of the firm. They hadn't minded when he assumed the leadership role of the back office. Indeed, they were delighted he was willing to take on that onerous task. Now Sandy was taking on another unwanted job, but this time he was making big decisions on expenses that affected everyone. All managers were told they would have to take 25 percent pay cuts; all other employees a 10 percent pay cut. Sandy's ax spared nothing; he even fired his beloved chef.

On March 13, 1970, McDonnell & Co., a sixty-five-year-old elite securities firm with longtime ties to the Ford family and other wealthy investors, announced it would close its doors, the victim of a back-office breakdown and bad management. Wall Street was stunned. The New York Stock Exchange began a desperate search for potential acquirers who might buy some or all of McDonnell's twenty-six branch offices around the country. In the past the Big Board would have looked almost exclusively at a potential acquirer's capital base to ensure that it was adequate. But the Exchange, keenly aware that the growing numbers of lost or wrongly recorded customer accounts was threatening investor confidence in the stock market, began looking at acquirers' clearing operations, too. The largely unknown firm of Cogan, Berlind, Weill & Levitt, still profitable— albeit barely—and boasting a brand-new back office, passed both tests and was allowed to snap up McDonnell's Beverly Hills office for mere pennies on the dollar. In one swoop CBWL expanded its retail brokerage business, successfully carried out an acquisition, and established its first turf outside of New York City.

McDonnell was just the beginning of Wall Street's woes. Up and down the Street, firms began faltering or failing. The New York Stock Exchange named Felix Rohatyn, a respected financier and expert troubleshooter, to head a Crisis Committee that would try to save or sell what firms it could. CBWL felt the pain as well: Its earnings plunged from $2.6 million in 1969 to just $500,000 in 1970. The back office processed a mere forty trades a day, far from the numbers necessary to justify the investment. There were months when CBWL had to wait for one more trade just to pay the rent.

As summer arrived, serious cracks began to show in some of the most prestigious firms. Hayden Stone & Co.—the firm where Joseph Kennedy began to build much of his fortune—had already been struggling to bolster its financial structure because its elderly partners were withdrawing their stakes as they retired. To stay afloat, Hayden Stone borrowed $17.5 million from a consortium of Oklahoma businessmen who were investment-banking clients. But as conditions worsened on Wall Street, Hayden Stone was coming near the edge of failure. The Oklahomans, fearful of losing their entire investment, hired a crafty, down-home Oklahoma lawyer, Larry Hartzog, to investigate the situation. He found Hayden Stone's pencil-and-eyeshade accounting system in complete disarray. The firm literally didn't know who owned what. Securities were being held in "suspense" accounts until the firm could figure out who owned them. Worse, the firm had $7 million of securities on its books that somehow weren't in the vault. He also learned that the New York Stock Exchange, deeply concerned about the market impact of such a large and prestigious firm's failure, was already searching for another brokerage house to rescue Hayden Stone. Hartzog knew that to save his clients' investment in Hayden Stone, a rescuer would have to be able to untangle the firm's back-office mess. Thus he urged the Big Board to find out which firm on Wall Street had the best back office. With their recent experience in auctioning off the pieces of McDonnell, exchange officials recalled a little-known firm—the name had something to do with corned beef—that had an impressively modern and efficient clearing operation.

Hartzog was floored when he found that CBWL was a tiny firm with offices only in New York and Beverly Hills; in contrast, Hayden Stone boasted a nationwide system of sixty-two branches. Could a mouse swallow an elephant? More important, would a bunch of blue bloods work for these scrappy Brooklyn Jews? The only way to find out was to send Hardwick Simmons, the Hayden Stone executive who was the great-grandson of the firm's founder, Gaylen Stone, over to meet the CBWL guys. "Never heard of them, or 'Corned Beef and Mustard' or whatever it is," the aristocratic Simmons told Hartzog. "They're not even on our radar screen." The Hayden Stone heir, who harbored dreams of one day running his family's esteemed firm, was incredulous. But the firm was broke and headed for disaster, so he had no choice but to make the trek from Wall Street to midtown.

What this child of privilege from one of Wall Street's founding families discovered in the General Motors Building sent his head spinning. He stood in a garish lobby surrounded by chrome and brass furniture and blobs of paint that passed for art. Could this possibly be Corned Beef With Lettuce? He was horrified to find that the initials on the firm's sign matched the nickname. A man who had inhabited a particularly charmed world since birth, Hardwick Simmons thought he had arrived on another planet.

Then suddenly he was shaking hands with one of the Corned Beef principals, Sandy Weill. With a half-chewed cigar stuck in his mouth and his shirttail bloused out over his paunch, Sandy welcomed the tall and trim Simmons. "Let's grab a hot dog on the street," Sandy blurted. Stunned, Simmons followed him out of the building and across the street to a hot-dog vendor's cart. Sandy ordered his hot dog, paid for it, and wolfed it down before Simmons could decide whether he wanted his with mustard or ketchup. As the hot July sun beat down on them, Sandy, sweat running down his face and soaking his shirt under his arms, fired one question after another about Hayden Stone's business at the uncomfortable Simmons, who remained in his dark suit jacket despite the relentless heat. Back at the office, Simmons met the other principals. Berlind and Levitt seemed nice enough and were certainly more presentable than Sandy, Simmons thought. But Marshall Cogan, with his nervous tics and bore-a-hole-in-you intensity, actually shocked him.

When Simmons was out the door, Sandy and his partners looked at one another in disbelief. They had just ushered out the ultimate WASP who had asked them—the Jews from Brooklyn—to bail out his stricken white-shoe firm. If they could pull this off, CBWL would gain not only a huge retail presence, but also a distinguished name and reputation—instantly. "We need the legitimacy of history," Cogan said over and over. Levitt opposed the deal, fearful that the team couldn't manage a firm ten times larger than theirs. There wasn't much talk about culture clashes. Rather, the partners were salivating at the prospect of finally gaining access to "the club" through Hayden Stone.

Sandy began applying his sharp analyst's pencil to the Hayden Stone numbers, but he continued to fret that CBWL would be exposed to Hayden Stone's liabilities and further losses. He reviewed the details with his partners and Bialkin. The attorney noticed for the first time that Sandy seemed to have a special financial genius. *He may not be the best talker, but the numbers sure seem to speak to Sandy,* Bialkin thought. Equally impressed by Sandy's reasoning and knowledge, his partners reluctantly gave him the authority to negotiate on their behalf.

Sandy had to deal with several players interested in saving the once-proud brokerage house. Simmons, of course, represented the firm and his family. Hartzog was dealing on behalf of the Oklahoma creditors. And the New York Stock Exchange's Crisis Committee had to be consulted. All would have preferred that Hayden Stone be rescued by a firm that wasn't known on the Street as Corned Beef With Lettuce. But other potential acquirers were either in trouble themselves or not as hungry as Sandy and his firm. With the September 10, 1970, deadline—when regulators would suspend Hayden Stone from the securities business because of insolvency—looming, the talks proceeded rapidly. Hungry but not stupid, Sandy extracted major concessions from the participants. The New York Stock Exchange would provide a $7.6-million cash infusion and assume Hayden Stone's liabilities, estimated at nearly $10 million. Sandy would be able to "cherry pick" the branches, buying only those that were the most profitable. And his firm would assume the prestigious Hayden Stone name, jettisoning once and for all the hated Corned Beef With Lettuce moniker.

As the parties blessed the deal, one of the Oklahoma lenders, Jack Golsen, balked. Angry at losing much of his investment, he wanted an example made of Hayden Stone, for "justice to be done." On September 10, while Sandy and the operations crew labored into the night to prepare their system to handle 57,000 new accounts from Hayden Stone on top of the measly 5,800 already in the system, Cogan, Berlind, and Hartzog were flying through blinding storms on a chartered Learjet to Oklahoma City. Early the next morning they confronted Golsen, who was also getting phone calls from the New York Stock Exchange, his fellow Oklahoma investors, and even the White House. All were urging him to relent in the stock market's best interests. Then Marshall Cogan asked for a few minutes alone with the holdout. "You're a Jew. I'm a Jew," Cogan told Golsen. "If this deal falls through, and if there's a disaster, the story will be 'a tough Jew brought down Wall Street.'"

Minutes later Cogan burst out of Golsen's office and called the Big Board. Berlind called Sandy: "We've got him." With the market set to open for trading in just minutes, an announcement was made from the Exchange balcony: "From now on, tickets will be marked 'CBWL–Hayden Stone.'" A cheer rang across the massive trading room.

Hayden Stone's takeover by a band of Brooklyn Jews didn't go over well inside the older firm. Brokers and employees, mostly Protestant and many anti-Semitic, gathered around news tickers in Hayden Stone's many branches with the same gloom that had greeted the news that John F. Kennedy had been assassinated. Thirty top Hayden Stone branch managers were invited to the General Motors Building to meet the new principals. Roger Berlind offered polite but bland welcoming remarks. When Sandy, sitting to the side of the conference table, was introduced, he murmured only "hi."

How was it, the Hayden Stone managers wondered, that these meek upstarts could best people as popular and sophisticated as Wick Simmons? Then Marshall Cogan jumped up onto the conference table with a shocking thud. He began to stride up and down the table, ranting about the possibilities of the combination, his spit showering down in the faces of managers sitting below. When Cogan finished, there was dead silence. What on earth could be next? Then CBWL's head of research recovered his wits, stood up, and said, "Now I know what it's like to follow a wild animal." The resulting laughter was as much in relief as in genuine appreciation of the humor, but it was enough to restore some equilibrium. As the Hayden Stone managers began asking questions of their new leaders, the power in the room moved swiftly to Sandy. On nearly every technical issue, from deal points to trade execution, Berlind said, "Let's hear what Sandy has to say." Though reluctant to speak extemporaneously, Sandy became a different person in a question-and-answer format—smart, confident, and even funny. The Hayden Stone managers returned to their branches with lots of stories to tell.

A MILLIONAIRE'S DEBUT

Fresh from their Hayden Stone triumph and no longer the subject of overt ridicule on Wall Street, Sandy and his colleagues were eager to capitalize on their success by selling shares of the new CBWL–Hayden Stone to investors. Ironically, public ownership of securities firms—the very firms that both arrange for other companies to sell stock and then buy and sell those shares for investors—hadn't been allowed until just a year earlier, when Donaldson, Lufkin & Jenrette persuaded the New York Stock Exchange to change its rules over the strenuous objections of many more established Wall Street partnerships. In June 1971, with the stock market enjoying a summer rally, CBWL–Hayden Stone filed with the Securities and Exchange Commission to sell 1 million shares of stock, 600,000 of which would be new shares with the remaining 400,000 owned by the four partners and some of their employees. The four partners indicated in the filing that they intended to sell 56,733 shares each. The cash they raised from the sale would be used in part to help finance their increasingly lavish lifestyles. In the early 1970s the $140,000 annual salaries the partners paid themselves were substantial, but far from real wealth. Sandy and Joan, for instance, had their eye on a fancy cooperative apartment in Manhattan. Another reason the partners wanted to sell some stock was to pay back loans they had taken from the firm. Sandy owed the firm $44,000, the least among the four partners. The flamboyant Marshall Cogan, always one to push the edges of the financial envelope, had taken a $590,000 loan from the company.

Shortly after their filing, Sandy and his cohorts were stunned when the SEC declared its opposition to allowing insiders to cash in their own shares when a company went public. Arthur Levitt and Sandy tracked down SEC Chairman William Casey, who was meeting with New York Stock Exchange officials in New York. Levitt, who had come to know Casey when Levitt was selling tax shelters, caught him as he was leaving the Exchange to go to a meeting in Bethpage, Long Island. Sandy and Levitt jumped into the cab with Casey, and as they sped through the streets of Manhattan and then out of the city, they argued the unfairness of changing the rules in midstream. After Casey got out of the cab for his meeting, Sandy demanded of the taxi driver, "How do you think we did?" The driver thought their arguments were persuasive, but he added, "You guys are some kind of crazy." The $43 cab fare was worth it: The SEC ruled that the partners could sell their shares in the public offering.

The initial public offering went without a hitch, selling out at $12.50 a share, netting each partner more than $700,000 in cash. Coupled with the value of the shares they still held, CBWL had made each partner worth more than $3.5 million on paper. A few weeks later Sandy and Joan threw their first big function for the firm in what amounted to a "coming-out" party for the couple, aglow with their much improved social and financial stature. More than one hundred CBWL–Hayden Stone executives and staffers gathered for drinks and dinner in the posh fourteen-room cooperative apartment that the Weills had recently purchased in a building on the corner of Sixty-seventh Street and Fifth Avenue. Sandy's colleagues marveled at their upscale surroundings and at Sandy's increasing ease at socializing, especially with the gracious and effervescent Joan at his side. The party was a milestone for the brokerage house and the Weills. Sandy's expertise in all facets of the securities business was what had made CBWL–Hayden Stone the success it was, and he was assuming his rightful role of father figure. At the same time, Joan was shouldering both the burden and the glory of becoming the ultimate corporate wife. Together, the Weills had arrived.

Intentionally or not, Sandy and his partners had picked precisely the right moment to sell stock in their company. Shortly after the initial public offering, or IPO, the stock market turned down and stayed down for the next few years. At the firm's first annual meeting, Roger Berlind told the assembled shareholders that "volume levels are pitifully low, and at today's level of activity, our company is essentially a break-even activity." The shares that had sold for $12.50 eventually hit a low of $1.63.

Although the slower pace of business was very worrisome, it also gave Sandy time to walk around CBWL–Hayden Stone's headquarters and to stop and chat and, ultimately, to build relationships with a variety of his colleagues and employees. Edwin Gill and Peter Cohen, two young analysts who earlier had considered Sandy some kind of recluse glued to his desk, now found the gruff executive had a probing mind and a dry wit. Sandy especially liked to stroll down the stairs to the thirty-third floor, where the firm's trading desk was situated, each day at 5:30 P.M. to see who was still working.

Sandy also used the slowdown as an excuse to batten down the hatches in the firm's operations, which represented a big part of CBWL–Hayden Stone's fixed costs. Managers of the firm's back-office departments, including treasury, data processing, and clearing services, were summoned weekly for a thorough review. Each Tuesday morning Sandy pored over the prior week's revenue, errors, margin calls, fail ratios, and expenditures. Chomping on his cigar, the once shy stockbroker pulled no punches with his managers. "That's crappy," he would say about a line item he didn't like. "You stupid son of a bitch," he would bark at someone who had screwed up. The operations staff had never worked for someone like this. Sandy's persistent questioning, the degree of detail he sought, the rigor of his reviews, his uncanny ability to sniff out a problem, and his hair-trigger temper were like nothing they had ever seen before in a senior brokerage executive. If a manager tried to explain away a number, Sandy would cut him off: "You better check your facts." He could make fast decisions. If he didn't like a proposal, he would shove it back at the author. "No fucking way. Get outta here."

The back-office crew soon learned that they could interpret Sandy's mood and mind-set by watching his cigar. If he was putting the cigar in and out of his mouth and saying "right, right, right," he was listening to the latest explanation and thinking about it. If he was rolling the cigar back and forth between his lips and muttering "'kay, 'kay, 'kay," they knew it was time to shut up or end the meeting. Behind his back the operations managers called Sandy "The Cigar" and did imitations of him. The nickname was a term of endearment tempered with a healthy dose of fear. The weekly meetings engendered among them a tremendous respect and loyalty for their boss. They even invited him to play on the company softball team and had T-shirts made that proclaimed them THE WEILL ONES. As far as they were concerned, "The Cigar" was the only brokerage bigwig who believed that operations—and by extension its staff—wasn't a second-rate part of the company but a crucial component in building the business.

SHOWDOWN

In early 1973 the New York Stock Exchange once again turned to CBWL–Hayden Stone for a rescue operation. This time H. Hentz & Co. was in trouble. Like Hayden Stone, Hentz had a prestigious name, a chain of branch offices, and big financial problems. It also had a very desirable commodities business and an international presence. Once again Sandy led the negotiations for CBWL–Hayden Stone. The Hentz executives arrived at CBWL–Hayden Stone's offices dressed in sober pin-striped suits and suspenders, with pocket watches on chains and boutonnieres. Sandy, sloppily dressed as usual, skipped the formalities of greetings and launched right into hard-nosed negotiations. Scribbling numbers on a blackboard, he overwhelmed the Hentz executives with his knowledge, diagramming Hentz's troubled divisions and how little they were worth. "This is your fail-to-deliver," he barked, referring to the money still owed the firm by other securities firms. "That's coming off the price." Clueless about their own fail-to-deliver accounting—it was one of those disdainful back-room functions—the Hentz officers could do nothing to challenge Sandy. Only Sandy himself knew that good management could collect much of the amount.

The night before the deal closed, the CBWL–Hayden Stone operations crew warned their boss that their Hentz counterparts intended to get drunk. "Stock certificates might start disappearing," Charles Bachi, the firm's data processing manager, told Sandy. As soon as darkness fell, Sandy and a few of his operations staffers went to the Hentz back office. With his cigar smoke filling the vault, Sandy and his crew counted every stock certificate to be sure nothing was missing. Then his men carted off the securities to CBWL–Hayden Stone's office. The next morning Arthur Levitt, on a visit to the firm they were about to acquire, spied the open vault, its floor littered with empty baskets. He phoned Sandy in a panic: "Something's wrong here. Everything's been stolen." Sandy replied, "Relax. The stock certificates are already in our vault."

Sandy's intimate knowledge of the brokerage business and his willingness to take on more and more responsibility began to lead to increasing clashes with the strong-willed Marshall Cogan. Their difficult personalities were part of the problem. But the direction the firm was taking led to the biggest conflict. As the head of investment banking, Cogan had gone along with the acquisitions of the retail brokers Hayden Stone and Hentz because their branch offices would provide a distribution outlet to sell the stocks of companies that Cogan was helping bring public. But now, to Cogan's displeasure, the retail side of the house was dominating the firm as Sandy pursued his "failing firms" strategy to increase CBWL–Hayden Stone's size exponentially and cheaply. Furthermore, with its state-of-the-art back office and all those branches, there was a huge need to bring in even more retail clients. Sandy had built a giant salami slicer; now the firm had to bring in more salami.

Peter Cohen, a young Columbia Business School graduate hired as an analyst a few years earlier and who had since become Cogan's assistant, felt the tension and saw the suspicion growing between Cogan and Sandy. "Where's Marshall sending you?" Sandy would ask Cohen if they met in the hall or elevator. "What's he planning?" Cohen would then go back to Cogan and tell his boss, "By the way, I told Sandy what I'm doing. I don't want to get caught between you two guys."

In August 1973 the simmering confrontation boiled over. The four partners, who together owned nearly half the firm's stock, gathered in a conference room to choose either Sandy or Cogan as the new CEO. As he had in the earlier power struggle with Arthur Carter, Arthur Levitt once again played kingmaker. Noting that Cogan was more one-dimensional, Levitt argued that Sandy had more of the skills necessary to run the business. Roger Berlind indicated his support for Sandy as well. But then Sandy, nervous and thrilled at the prospect of being the CEO of a company at the age of forty, made his single demand: Cogan had to go. "If people really want me to run this place, then I must have the ability to do that." With Levitt and Berlind backing Sandy, Marshall Cogan had little choice. He left not only the firm but also Wall Street, joining one of his big clients, Jimmy Ling, who had started a new conglomerate, Omega-Alpha Inc., after being forced out of LTV.

The next day Sandy invited Peter Cohen, Cogan's bright twenty-six-year-old assistant, to join him for lunch at the Harmonie Club. The Harmonie Club had been founded in 1852 by German Jewish immigrants who were denied admittance to the city's oldest and most select enclave, the Metropolitan Club. Until World War II, membership in the club was restricted to New York's German Jewish banking dynasties that made up what was known as "Our Crowd"—the Lehmans, Goldmans, Sachses, Warburgs, and Schiffs. But after the war, membership was opened to "the other kind." Cohen, a Jew, was eager just to dine at the Harmonie, dubbed "Jewish heaven" and famous for its blintzes slathered with lingonberries, chopped chicken liver, and challah dipped in egg batter. Yet Cohen also expected lunch to be quick—he assumed he was about to be fired for his close relationship with Cogan.

"I know you don't really know much about running a business like this, and I really don't either. I have to learn," Sandy said between sips of his martini. "I know you're willing to work very hard to get to the bottom of things. You can be a great help to me."

"How?" Cohen asked, relieved he wasn't being fired.

"Would you like to be my assistant? Together we can figure this thing out," Sandy said.

Too shocked to say much, Cohen replied, "I want to think about it," and the pair returned to their offices. Thirty minutes later Cohen strode into Sandy's office and said, "I'm in."

Soon Sandy and his young assistant seemed almost inseparable. Cohen's quick mind easily grasped intricate financial and procedural details that even Sandy missed. Their workday extended late into the night, with Cohen often accompanying Sandy back to the Weills' apartment, where the two reviewed the day's events and numbers. They even worked in the apartment on Sundays and did it so often that Joan Weill took pity on Cohen's young wife, Karen, and began inviting her to bring the Cohens' baby daughter and join them.

NEW FRIENDS

As the new CEO it didn't take Sandy long to formally change the firm's name to simply Hayden Stone, eliminating any vestige of the hated "Corned Beef With Lettuce." Yet the new name didn't last long. Free to pursue his strategy of growth by acquisition, and backed by a handpicked staff of senior executives, Sandy found his next target: Shearson Hammill & Co., a seventy-four-year-old private retail brokerage house that was even bigger than Hayden Stone. Better yet, it had a more prestigious name associated with Wall Street's past. But there was risk involved, too. Shearson was in serious financial trouble and needed to be bailed out, but Hayden Stone was losing money, too. The entire securities industry was suffering, and a third of the brokers who worked on the Street had been forced to take up other jobs, some as menial as driving taxis or waiting tables, to supplement their meager commissions.

Alger "Duke" Chapman, Shearson's CEO, dreaded his meeting with Sandy. But his search for a brokerage house more like his own had yielded nothing. Fearful that being seen with Sandy might start rumors, Chapman suggested they meet over lunch at an out-of-the-way restaurant in Manhattan's Little Italy. In the dark dining room, he and Sandy ate traditional red-sauce dishes, smoked a pack of cigarettes, finished a bottle of red wine, and talked about deal possibilities. To Chapman's surprise, he and Sandy liked each other. When they emerged into the afternoon sun, they had agreed to explore a purchase by Hayden Stone.

The negotiations took place in a dozen sessions in Sandy's apartment. Peter Cohen, who toiled at the dining room table with spreadsheets and a calculator, backed Sandy. Each piece of Shearson Hammill's business was taken apart and examined minutely before a value was placed on it. Chapman was accompanied by his deputy, Fred Joseph, who, with his feet propped on a glass coffee table in the living room, tried to play tough and questioned Sandy's valuations. It didn't take long for Sandy to decide that Joseph wouldn't be asked to stay after the merger. "Get your feet off my table," he snarled at Joseph. Chapman was more amenable. A pleasant man, he earned the loyalty of his brokers by knowing the names of their children and even their pets. He swallowed hard when Sandy told him that to make the deal work, Shearson would have to fire half of its 2,400 employees. Never before had such wide-scale layoffs been seen on Wall Street. When news of the layoffs broke not long after the deal was concluded, Sandy instantly gained a reputation as a ruthless predator.

Shortly after the deal creating Wall Street's fifth-largest firm was announced—Sandy proclaimed the new firm would be named Shearson Hayden Stone—Sandy received a call from the Justice Department's Antitrust Division. "Sir, would you mind if I record the conversation?" Sandy asked. "My mother would never believe that I'd do something so important that the antitrust division of this country would call." He never heard back from the Justice Department, and the sale closed in September 1974.

Buying another company was one thing. Actually merging the operations of two disparate companies was quite another. When Arthur Levitt arrived in San Francisco shortly after the deal closed to meet the branch staff, the last broker was walking out the door. The word had gone out throughout Shearson that "you don't want to work for people like that." George Murray, who had been at Hayden Stone before becoming one of

Sandy's deputies after CBWL bought Hayden Stone, told his boss that the phrase "people like that" was WASP code for "New York Jews."

But Sandy knew exactly how to counter that problem: trot out the house WASP, Hardwick Simmons, whose lineage could be traced back to the *Mayflower.* Suddenly Simmons was accompanying Sandy to visit the Shearson branches. Sandy didn't have to tell Simmons to show how well the Jew and the Gentile could work together; Simmons knew his presence would serve a powerful purpose in setting the tone for what was now his company, too. He, who had grave doubts about working for CBWL when it was acquiring his family's firm, had come to appreciate Sandy's emergence as a great brokerage chief. Part of Sandy's management strength was his ability to use the right person in the right place at the right time. Wick Simmons didn't mind playing the part of the WASP; hell, he was having the time of his life.

Once the brokerage ranks had settled down, Shearson Hayden Stone sent them new employment contracts requiring them to concede a few percentage points of their sales commissions. One of Shearson's top brokers, Theodore "Ted" Dimon, didn't like that at all, and he promptly fired off a detailed memo to Sandy, who then invited him to lunch at the Harmonie Club. The forty-three-year-old Dimon had joined Shearson after college to work with his Greek immigrant father. Together they had built a huge clientele among Greek Americans, and now Dimon was living on Park Avenue and putting three sons through private schools.

"Did you read my memo?" he asked Sandy as they settled in to lunch.

"I threw it out," Sandy responded, still puffing his cigar at the table.

That didn't deter Dimon, who laid out what he expected in order to stay at Shearson. Sandy answered on the spot. Some were yes, others no, but Dimon came away from the lunch respecting Sandy's decisiveness and candor.

The two men became friends after the lunch. Later, when their wives ran into each other in a psychology class they were taking at the New School in Manhattan, the two families became close. That summer the Dimons invited Sandy and Joan to lunch in the tony Hamptons, where the three teenaged Dimon boys—Peter and twins Ted and Jamie—hung out with the Weill teens, Marc and Jessica. Soon the two families were sharing outings every few months, including the Weills' Passover seders, where Ted would play his violin. The young Jamie Dimon, who worked in his dad's brokerage office during the summers, became interested in hanging around his father and Sandy to listen in on their lively conversations about the securities business. With a knack for numbers and a keen interest in business, the bright, blue-eyed young man thought he might one day want to get into the business. Indeed, in one of his college economics courses Jamie used the Shearson takeover by CBWL–Hayden Stone as the topic of a term paper. His mother gave a copy to Sandy when the Dimons and Weills next got together. Sandy liked the paper enough that he sent Jamie a note: "Terrific paper. Can I show it to people here?"

"Absolutely," Jamie responded. "Can I have a summer job?"

The young Dimon worked that summer at Shearson as a gofer in the budget department.

ABANDONED AT THE ALTAR

Even as the firm under his command grew by leaps and bounds, Sandy Weill remained a hands-on manager, fanatical about operations, who led by example. If he couldn't control the stock market's every movement or the brokers' every sales call, he would control the back office so it never caused Shearson Hayden Stone to miss a minute of business. He would be on the scene the moment anything went wrong. When the computers stalled, Sandy, who wasn't allowed to smoke in the computer room, darted nervously back and forth from the computers to a nearby stairwell, where he had a quick puff or two until the problem was solved. Returning from lunch one day, he discovered his brokers and traders standing in the street; the GM Building was being evacuated because of a bomb threat. "I'm going back in," he yelled to them. "Who has the guts to follow me?"

He expected his employees to put the firm first in everything. When a fire broke out in the building housing Shearson's back-office operations, Sandy and Peter Cohen rushed to the scene to find people milling around outside the building as fire trucks pulled up and began deploying their hoses. They made a beeline for Anthony Fedele, who oversaw the vault.

"Is everything locked in the cage?" Cohen asked him.

"No," Fedele replied. He and his colleagues had just escaped from a room rapidly filling with smoke and had carried a wheelchair-bound colleague down a stairwell.

"You mean there are stock certificates, bearer bonds, and checks laying around with firemen in the building?" Sandy screamed. "You go right now and put that stuff away."

"Sandy, the fucking building is on fire," Fedele retorted.

"Not on your floor, it's not," Sandy said. "Go!"

Within minutes Cohen and a contingent of Shearson processors, clad in street clothes, joined the gear-laden firemen rushing into the building.

Sandy's obsession with cost control had always given his firm a competitive advantage over the rest of Wall Street. With commissions fixed by law, Shearson's relatively low costs enabled it to post fatter profits than its competitors in the good times and smaller losses in the bad. But the old cartel-like ways of Wall Street changed on May 1, 1975, when the fixed-commission system was abolished. Suddenly brokers could charge whatever they wished to execute a trade for a client. True competition had come to the Street, and there was no fiercer competitor than Sandy Weill. With its low cost structure Shearson could offer big investors cheaper trades and still make money. Indeed, the establishment of a free market on Wall Street propelled Shearson Hayden Stone to record earnings that year.

But there was little time to savor the triumph of true competition. On the night of June 24, Roger Berlind's wife and three of his four children were killed when the Eastern Airlines jet on which they were passengers crashed during its approach to Kennedy Airport in a severe storm. Berlind was waiting in the baggage claim area when told of the crash. He was overcome by the loss and by the fact that he was now the only parent of his two-year-old son, William. A week later, he resigned from the firm. "The whole idea of earning a living makes no sense," he told Sandy. "I have no motivation and no desire and no interest in business. There is no reason for me to be here."

Sandy looked at the last cofounder of their original firm and told him, "You do whatever you wish."

Berlind had always been a calming influence on the firm. Without that influence Sandy was free to mold Shearson in his own image, and he set out on a buying binge. He snapped up Lamson Brothers, a Chicago-based commodities broker, in 1976, then bought Faulkner, Dawkins & Sullivan, a big institutional brokerage house, in 1977. Shearson's stock was listed on the prestigious New York Stock Exchange as earnings continued to set records. Gaining confidence with each deal completed and each quarter of higher earnings, Sandy exerted more and more control. He expected subordinates to follow his way or the highway. When he visited the Faulkner Dawkins brokers in their downtown office, they sought new deals giving them higher commission splits to stay with Shearson.

Sandy refused. "We have other brokers, and we won't give you a better split."

"Then we'll leave Shearson," threatened one broker.

"Well, good-bye," Sandy said curtly. All but one broker—the only woman at Faulkner Dawkins—left. But it didn't worry Sandy. He was on a roll and had a much bigger target in his sights—the elite investment bank of Kuhn Loeb, a legendary name on Wall Street with powerful corporate finance clients.

Sandy began negotiating in the fall of 1977 with Kuhn Loeb. The talks eventually resulted in an agreement on the broad terms of a purchase of Kuhn Loeb by Shearson. On a Friday afternoon, Kuhn officials asked Sandy to draw up a final agreement and a press release announcing the deal for them to review the following Monday at the offices of Shearson's attorney, Ken Bialkin. On Monday Sandy could hardly contain himself while waiting for the Kuhn officials to review the documents. When they hadn't shown up an hour after the appointed time, Sandy tried to call Kuhn executives, but they couldn't be located. Then someone rushed Sandy an item that had just crossed the news wires: Kuhn Loeb had just announced it would merge with Lehman Brothers. The Kuhn officials all along had been negotiating on parallel tracks with Lehman and had dumped Shearson. The reason? In essence, the wealthy Schiff family, which controlled the old-line Kuhn Loeb, as well as some Kuhn officials, didn't want to combine with the upstart Sandy Weill and his firm. Sandy was simultaneously furious, embarrassed, and deeply hurt. Peter Cohen, who was standing beside Sandy when he got the news, realized that this wasn't just business; it was personal.

Sandy wore the devastating personal affront on his sleeve. His already erratic mood swings became wider, his temper worse. If Sandy felt that anyone was standing between him and his overwhelming desire to succeed, he exploded. Always prone to manage by roaming around asking questions, Sandy started interrupting and criticizing more. When he spied the head of the compliance department reading a newspaper, he growled, "You fucking guys have nothing to do?!" and was gone before the manager could explain that he was reading about a compliance scam.

One day Sandy stopped by the general services department and began reviewing fixed expenses. Anthony DeMeo, the young man recently promoted to head the unit, was hoping Sandy would praise him for his cost control.

"Why are these mailing expenses for research so high?" Sandy asked.

DeMeo explained that Faulkner Dawkins, the firm Shearson had recently bought, did several mailings, including A and B lists.

"Show me," Sandy demanded.

DeMeo fetched the lists for Sandy, who reviewed them quickly, then slammed them on the table.

"You fucking idiot! You're sending the same research to the same people," Sandy screamed. His face reddened as he leaned over the table, inches from DeMeo's frightened face. "You fucking idiot. How many people are on the same lists?"

When DeMeo couldn't answer, his sympathetic colleagues volunteered to help him figure it out that day. But Sandy's tirade continued. "Fucking A-B-C-D lists! How much is this costing us?" Leonard Haynes, an operations executive, leaned forward in his seat, prepared to physically restrain Sandy, who seemed on the verge of attacking DeMeo. Dejected and shaking, the young manager left the room with the mailing lists. "This is a guy who would kill for you, and you just shot him," Haynes told Sandy.

Now more disappointments piled up. Arthur Levitt, who had served as president of the firm under Sandy and knew his own ambitions would be stymied as long as Sandy was on top, left to become president of the American Stock Exchange. Levitt's resignation opened the position of president, and Sandy offered it to Frank Zarb, the man who had built the firm's sophisticated and efficient back office from scratch. But Zarb decided to move to the investment banking firm of Lazard Frères instead.

With Zarb's departure, Peter Cohen felt that the way was clear for Sandy to offer him the presidency. Instead, Sandy called his old friend George Sheinberg, the chief financial officer of Bulova, whom he had gotten to know a decade earlier after buying up enough Bulova stock to attract Sheinberg's attention. Over dinner in the Plaza Hotel's fancy Edwardian Room, Sandy offered Sheinberg a position in Shearson. Without even negotiating a salary or title, Sheinberg agreed based solely on their long friendship. Sandy said, "There's only one person I want you to meet—Peter Cohen."

When Sheinberg met Cohen, he asked him, "What kind of problems do you have at Shearson?"

"There's only one problem," Cohen replied. "Sandy."

Cohen was exhausted from being around Sandy all the time. Now with a young son in addition to his daughter, Cohen resented having to do personal tasks for Sandy's family—he had to set up their stereo system and buy Marc Weill a college wardrobe—when he should have been with his own. As the person at Shearson closest to Sandy, Cohen bore much of the brunt of Sandy's temper tantrums. Sandy's decision not to offer him the presidency was the final blow. Cohen resigned shortly after his meeting with Sheinberg to go to work for Edmond Safra, the rich owner of Republic National Bank. Severing his ties to Shearson, Cohen sold his stock, infuriating Sandy. At Cohen's farewell party, when Sandy lashed out at his deputy, accusing him of being a "traitor," the festivities came to an abrupt halt.

When George Sheinberg showed up for work in March 1978, he found Sandy champing on his cigar and looking surprised that his friend was there to go to work. "Go downtown and learn the accounting," Sandy ordered. "And by the way, Peter is leaving." Sheinberg soon found that he was expected to assume many of Cohen's duties. On a trip to a regional sales meeting, Sandy started screaming at Sheinberg as soon as they checked into the hotel. In a rage about the cost of the hotel room and the airplane tickets, Sandy blamed Sheinberg, who until that moment had no idea the travel department reported to him. Then the former Bulova executive, accustomed to hotel suites in Geneva, found he was sharing a room with another Shearson executive. *Here,* Sheinberg thought, i*s one of the secrets of Sandy's stunning success: It's not about nickels and dimes; it's about pennies.* However uncomfortable he might be sharing the bathroom with another man, Sheinberg nevertheless concluded that it was the proper approach.

Over the years, Sandy had saved enough of his own pennies to buy an idyllic eight-acre estate in Greenwich, Connecticut. Sandy and Joan spent their weekends there, surrounded by lush gardens, an apple orchard, and a tennis court. Sandy often invited other securities-industry executives to play tennis, including Tommy Kempner, the nephew of high-and-mighty John Loeb. Kempner, a Yale graduate, ran the family's Loeb Rhoades investment banking and brokerage house. He and his wife, Nan, partied in the high-society circles that still excluded Sandy and Joan. During their games Sandy would badger Kempner about selling his firm to Shearson. Kempner just laughed off the entreaties, until the fall of 1978, when he stopped laughing.

In the years since the patrician John Loeb had insulted Sandy by flatly refusing to handle his growing firm's back-office business, Loeb Rhoades had acquired the large brokerage firm of Hornblower, Weeks, Noyes & Trask. The merger had turned out to be an operational and financial disaster. Now the proud seventy-six-year-old John Loeb, faced with the task of saving his firm and his family's capital, called Sandy to ask him to stop by his office. Both men knew they were talking about Shearson taking over Loeb Rhoades, but John Loeb kept referring to a possible "combination." It was a humbling experience for Loeb, whose marriage years before to Frances Lehman had elevated him to the highest levels of German Jewish society. As a managing director of Loeb Rhoades he had been a stubborn opponent of change on Wall Street, railing often and loudly against "unrestrained and unrestricted competition," the very forces that had helped Sandy achieve his many successes.

A few weeks later, Sandy and Sheinberg ran into Loeb at a black-tie event. The old man uncharacteristically praised the Shearson CEO in front of others. When Loeb walked away, Sheinberg turned to Sandy. "Shit, Sandy, this is going to happen."

Sandy caught his breath. "Do you really think so?"

Then Sheinberg added, "If we're going to do this, we need Peter back." That fall the Weills invited the Cohens and others to break the Yom Kippur fast, an annual event at their home, with a dinner of homemade chopped liver, coleslaw, potato salad, rugelach, and a noodle pudding from Joan's grandmother's recipe.

In front of the guests, Sandy told Cohen, "You made a mistake."

"No, you made a mistake," Cohen shot back.

"If you tell me you want to come back, I want you to come back," Sandy said.

In December the estranged mentor and his protégé met for drinks in the Plaza Hotel's Oak Bar. Sitting on dark leather chairs the pair discussed Cohen's return to Shearson. Sandy drank gin and Cohen drank vodka, and the night turned to early morning. At one point Sandy laid down the cards he was holding: "If you come back, I think we can take over Loeb Rhoades." By the time they stumbled out of the bar, Cohen had agreed to return to Shearson as chief administrative officer and a director. The pair didn't really like or trust each other anymore. But the prospect of taking over Loeb Rhoades, one of Wall Street's biggest prizes, had pulled them back together. Neither Sandy nor Cohen would admit it, but they needed each other.

ATOP THE WORLD AND RUNNING SCARED

The return of Peter Cohen, whose mastery of intricate financial and procedural details had been sorely missed, spurred Sandy to begin serious talks for Loeb Rhoades, Hornblower & Co. As with his earlier acquisitions, this one was bigger than its acquirer: Loeb Rhoades had 150 offices and 1,800 brokers while Shearson fielded 1,700 brokers in 130 offices. Loeb Rhoades also would give Shearson a lot more clout in the investment-banking business, which had languished after Marshall Cogan's ouster. Perhaps more important, Sandy's takeover of the last great German Jewish securities firm would go a long way to assuage both the Kuhn Loeb put-down and John Loeb's snub.

Word of the negotiations leaked to the press on Friday, May 11, 1979, forcing the two firms to try to work out an agreement over the weekend. On Saturday morning, they convened at Sandy's Greenwich estate, inside the Weills' Normandy-style house with its pool, sauna, and wine cellar. They gathered in the spacious living and dining rooms, but as negotiations got thornier, each contingent staked out an upstairs bedroom to use as a private conference room. Sandy, padding through his mansion in pants and a golf shirt, offered the negotiators plates of Joan's homemade chicken salad, leaving Cohen and Sheinberg to handle the nitty-gritty deal points. John Loeb stayed in touch by telephone from his estate in nearby Westchester County, New York.

The Shearson and Loeb Rhoades teams didn't get to the financial structure of the proposed new firm until Sunday, again meeting at the Weills' country home. As Joan welcomed the executives that morning, Mother's Day, she reminded them to call their mothers. After the twenty-eight-hour marathon, the negotiators, surviving on more batches of chicken salad, had a deal. Shearson would issue $90 million of its debt and equity securities to partners of the privately held Loeb Rhoades. The aristocratic John Loeb would become the largest single shareholder and convert his troubled investment into liquid form: Shearson shares that were listed on the New York Stock Exchange. Sandy would own about 5 percent of the company, but he would be running it as chairman and chief executive officer.

The merger of the two firms' computer and processing systems was so massive that the deal was set up to be done, in effect, as three mini-mergers. After the second transfer of accounts and branches, the system went haywire, resulting in a steady stream of mistakes in processing customer orders and recording transactions. Sandy's famed back office finally had more salami than it could slice. Customers screamed at their stockbrokers about the foul-ups; the brokers in turn screamed at the firm management and back office. The mayhem and the resulting hostility in the firm, not just between the two merging firms but among his own people, was more than Sandy could tolerate. Even two of his top executives, Peter Cohen and Wick Simmons, were at each other's throats.

His leadership needed as never before, Sandy realized his exhausted team needed to share some downtime to rekindle the bonds that united them when the firm was small and scrappy. The cockiness of recent years, stoked by the takeovers of one prestigious firm after another, was turning into fear that they had finally taken on a challenge that was too great. George Sheinberg confided to Sandy that he was scared. Like the other Shearson executives, his net worth was tied up in the firm. "This isn't just a huge business," he told Sandy. "This is still us, this is still our money."

Sandy summoned his senior managers to a retreat at the posh Greenbrier Resort in White Sulphur Springs, West Virginia. For two days, the dozen executives ate, drank, roomed, and golfed together. When the finger-pointing and blame game subsided, Sandy weighed in. "We're all in this together," the CEO told his closest advisors. "We can refuse to go through with the third phase of the merger, if that's what it takes to save this firm."

The Shearson executives knew that Sandy, who had sold his beautiful Fifth Avenue co-op apartment during the bear market when the firm needed more cash, would do anything to keep his firm alive. On their last night together in the cabin, the hostilities faded along with their sobriety. Before the night was over, these men who had followed Sandy Weill to the top of the brokerage heap made a pact to stick together. In their drunken enthusiasm, some of them even used a kitchen knife to draw blood to seal their oath.

The third mini-merger went forward, consolidating the two firms' operations in customer sales, bonds, marketing, block trading, and research. With Shearson's acquisition of Loeb Rhoades complete, the first board meeting on a cold, overcast day in December 1979 signaled the unofficial passing of the old guard. Emerging from his chauffeur-driven Cadillac limousine, walking past the polished marble columns of the Harmonie Club, John Loeb headed for the private reception for the new board of directors. The cigar-chomping, loud-talking New Crowd from Shearson was relishing its victory while the impeccably tailored, stiff Old Crowd barely moved.

As soon as Sandy saw the tall, erect Loeb enter the banquet room, the excited and genial CEO rushed to greet him. "John, this is going to be one helluva company," Sandy enthused. The elder banker looked down on him politely but stiffly. "The combination of Loeb Rhoades and Shearson makes a lot of sense, Sandy," said the patrician who had just lost his firm to the street-smart kid from Brooklyn. Loeb's sense of loss and remorse was too great for him to make more than an obligatory appearance. Though Sandy had named him the honorary chairman, Loeb departed before the new Shearson Loeb Rhoades's first board meeting began.

After the glowing press reports of Sandy's rise to superbroker stardom, including prominent articles in *The Wall Street Journal* and *The New York Times,* the Shearson CEO had to redouble his efforts to stay on top of his huge and fast-growing firm. His strategy of building through acquisition meant that some important business functions were left to the people he trusted, like Anthony Fedele, who ran the vault. One day a high-ranking colleague reported to Sandy that internal auditors had discovered that Fedele had been running things loosely and in violation of New York Stock Exchange rules. Someone who worked directly for Fedele had been buying securities and paying with checks that didn't have sufficient funds. Fedele would look the other way, simply putting the checks in the vault until the securities were sold and sufficient profits banked to cover the checks.

"You can make a mistake and lose a million dollars for the company, and if you weren't negligent, you can probably keep your job," Sandy told the informant. "But if you steal ten cents, you're gone, you're out of here."

What to do with Fedele, he was asked. Fedele was one of Sandy's hardest-working managers and a fellow Brooklyn native to boot.

"Fire him," Sandy replied, tears welling up in his eyes. "I loved that guy," he said softly.

Another internal crisis required Sandy to take a firm stand. A Shearson commodities client, Bunker Hunt of the ultrarich Hunt family of Dallas, Texas, was buying up all the silver he could get his hands on. When the price of silver went up, Hunt would borrow against his increased account balance, then take the cash to other Wall Street firms to buy more silver on credit, driving the price of silver up still higher. The Shearson CEO, who watched as the Hunt account represented an increasing percentage of his firm's business, became very nervous about the wealthy Texan's position. Sandy asked for his net-worth statement. Hunt replied that he was a billionaire and he didn't give out net-worth statements. Sniffing a problem,

Sandy resorted to raising Hunt's margin on silver even though silver was going up. Required to put up more and more collateral, Hunt and his Shearson broker left in anger. Shearson brokers were incensed that Sandy would run off such a rich and big-name client like that, but Sandy told them that the Hunt account posed a tremendous threat to their firm. He turned out to be dead right. When the silver market crashed in early 1980, so did Bunker Hunt and the securities firm that had happily taken his business, Bache Stuart Halsey Shields.

The start of the 1980s was a heady time for Sandy, a savvy bargain shopper who had exploited Wall Street's misery in the 1970s to build a major securities franchise. Now he was ready to take advantage of his and his company's stature. The first step was getting former president Gerald Ford to join Shearson Loeb Rhoades's board of directors, a major coup that gave the board cachet and credibility. The second step was launching the firm's first television advertising campaign. With commercials airing during the U.S. Open tennis championships, Shearson Loeb Rhoades enjoyed hard-to-get celebrity box seats at the Flushing Meadows stadium, where Sandy held court in the box next to real-estate tycoon Donald Trump. A third step was buying a corporate jet, partly to help Sandy get over his fear of flying, but also to serve as an all-important status symbol. On the business front, Shearson scored the highest profit margins of any publicly traded securities firm and the third highest return on equity of any company in the United States.

Another upward move—literally and figuratively—was the firm's relocation to the top six floors of the south tower of the World Trade Center. Scared of heights and of flying, Sandy hesitated initially about moving Shearson's headquarters into the clouds. But the World Trade Center owners told him that the Twin Towers were built to withstand the crash of a 747 jet plane. What about a fire? Peter Cohen asked. They assured the Shearson executives that helicopters would land on the roof to shuttle them to safety, so they wouldn't have to worry about descending 106 floors in an emergency.

Touring the empty floor before signing the lease, Sheinberg pointed to the nearby fifty-three-story building housing the headquarters of Merrill Lynch & Co., now the only securities firm bigger than Shearson Loeb Rhoades. "We'll look down on Merrill Lynch," he said, laughing. That prospect was appealing enough to Sandy to overcome his fear of heights. When the Trade Center owners agreed to build at their own considerable expense the world's highest working fireplace for Sandy's office—a feature he thought would bring good luck—the ambitious CEO was sold. He quickly staked out a large corner office on the one hundred sixth floor overlooking the Hudson River and Lower Manhattan. Feeling he had arrived, Sandy gave away his old desk to his favorite operations manager and replaced it with an antique semicircular "hunt" desk surrounded by pine-paneled walls bordering the numerous windows. The penthouse headquarters held opulent meeting and reception rooms, a massive kitchen, and a lavish dining room with a mural depicting Wall Street symbols and milestones. The painting showed scenes of Shearson's rise to become the nation's second-largest securities firm, including a depiction of Sandy shaking hands with Gerald Ford. More than decoration, the mural became a symbol of the risky and rocky climb of its forty-six-year-old founder, Sandy Weill.

But the Wall Street striver, who was still viewed as a parvenu in many quarters, was restless. Smoking eight cigars on some days and two packs of cigarettes on others, Sandy constantly punched out stock-market data from two desktop terminals. After leading the consolidation wave in the securities industry since the market's collapse at the start of the 1970s, the aggressive Shearson chief now had to run the fastest-growing financial-services behemoth. It was a challenge he faced publicly with bravado and privately with more than a little fear.

3

INTO THE WASP NEST

S andy gasped, nearly choking on his cigar.

"What is it?" Joan asked. She knew instantly that her husband was upset by whatever he saw flashing across the ticker of the Dow Jones News Service, which he paused to read at their visit to Shearson's Hong Kong office. Sandy and Joan, along with the firm's new trophy director, former president Gerald Ford, had been touring Shearson's Asian branches, savoring the firm's rising position and prominence in the global securities industry. But the newfound empowerment ended at that moment.

The news on this morning of March 20, 1981: Prudential Insurance Corporation of America, a financial titan, was going to buy Bache Halsey Stuart Shields, the well-known securities firm that had been a pillar of Wall Street for a century. The deal suddenly changed everything. Until this moment the consolidation of Wall Street had been *horizontal* as securities firms bought their competitors in a frantic effort to become bigger and more powerful. Right from the start Sandy had been the smartest and over time had become the most powerful player of that game, acquiring one securities firm after another to build his Shearson empire. But Prudential acquiring Bache: This was *vertical!* No longer were securities firms going to be independent players competing against one another. Now one of the richest and most powerful insurance companies in the world—the Rock— would own a strong franchise in what Sandy had presumed was his turf. As a stand-alone brokerage Bache had been no real threat to Shearson Loeb Rhoades, especially after the disastrous collapse of the silver market and its impact on the Hunt brothers and their account at Bache. But backed by Prudential's huge asset base and its thousands of insurance agents with their millions of customers, Bache could find renewed power. Just imagine all those agents selling not just insurance policies but stocks and bonds as well! As large and powerful as Shearson had become, it still was no match for a juggernaut the size of the combined Prudential and Bache. And Sandy knew that the fallout would result in more complementary mergers as other securities firms, realizing the danger posed by this deal, scrambled to find wealthy partners in other parts of the financial-services industry. In a flash, Sandy—and his company—seemed as small and exposed as in their Corned Beef With Lettuce days.

Sandy knew he couldn't afford to be left out, isolated as he was when he first entered the business. He immediately called his deputy, Peter Cohen. "Everything has changed," he urgently told Cohen. "We have to move fast."

Back in New York, a similar panic was spreading at the headquarters of American Express Co. Its chairman and chief executive officer, James D. Robinson III, a courtly patrician, couldn't concentrate during a scheduled management meeting this morning. He darted in and out of the room to make and take calls on what could be the beginnings of a new era of financial conglomerates. The forty-five-year-old Robinson had been pursuing an aggressive, albeit genteel, expansion strategy for his company. While American Express wasn't part of Wall Street, it nevertheless had retained some of the vestiges of the Street's earlier days. It hired only the best, and the best typically were defined by American Express as white, Anglo-Saxon, and Protestant. Yet Robinson's plans for American Express—notwithstanding his own lustrous lineage and his company's blue-chip status—called for the company to become much more than the upscale purveyor of credit cards, trips, and traveler's checks. He wanted his company to have a broader presence in the American economy, to make a bigger mark.

Thus, on opposite sides of the globe, two men as different as they could be, for very different reasons, reached the identical conclusion: pick a partner and do it now!

For Sandy, who had built his empire by merging up, only a company with a better name than his firm's would do. Citicorp, the huge bank with a well-known global presence, would be the ideal match, but current laws prohibited any such merger between a bank and a securities firm. Outside of banking, the most trusted name in financial services was American Express. Its brand and its blue box logo merited the kind of international recognition that only the biggest consumer franchises, such as McDonald's and Coca-Cola, enjoyed. Still hungry to be accepted by the establishment, Sandy relished the thought of running American Express, the ultimate WASP nest, and gaining its imprimatur of respectability.

The scion of a wealthy Southern family, Jim Robinson III—or "little Jimmy Threesticks," as he was called back home—wanted to escape his past as well. Rather than follow in the footsteps of his great-grandfather, grandfather, and father in Atlanta banking, Robinson, with a Harvard MBA in hand, struck out for the world's financial capital, eager to be accepted for his accomplishments rather than his pedigree. He performed with distinction at such blue-blooded firms as Morgan Guaranty Trust Co. and White Weld & Co., two of the most traditional firms on Wall Street, before being recruited to American Express in 1970 by its chairman Howard Longstreth Clark. Robinson knew that with its financial power and the prestige it enjoyed around the world, American Express could probably have its pick of the securities firms that were desperate to merge. If he were guided by prestige, Robinson would think about securities firms like EF Hutton and Merrill Lynch, logical choices consistent with the image and brand of American Express. But given his own success in the hubbub of New York, Robinson was drawn to the entrepreneurial spirit and cockiness of Sandy Weill and Shearson.

A mutual acquaintance had brought Sandy and Jim Robinson together for the first time just a few months before Prudential stunned the financial world with its announcement. Just like the companies they ran, the two were a study in contrasts. Robinson, with his youthful cherubic face and unfurrowed countenance, displayed a courteous, controlled manner and an athletic physique, the result of daily aerobic workouts with a personal trainer. Sandy, pudgy from his daily regimen of heavy meals and ample alcoholic beverages, had a dark complexion and Mediterranean look, with an expression that could change quickly from warmly inviting to cruelly harsh, reflections of his volatile mood swings. While each had used far different means to achieve his success, Robinson and Weill unknowingly shared the same intense, internal drive that results from growing up under the reign of hypercritical fathers. At that meeting they had chatted mostly about ways in which American Express and Shearson might cooperate on various projects that could benefit them both. The topic of an outright merger of two such different companies had been barely mentioned. American Express was driven by marketing, product positioning, and image, while Shearson lived and died on client relationships and market conditions. But they shared a common interest in meeting the challenge posed by Merrill Lynch's very successful new product called a Cash Management Account. The CMA simply wrapped together in one account what would otherwise be a customer's separate checking, brokerage, and money-market accounts. Customers liked the convenience of "one-stop" financial shopping and were willing to pay fat fees to get it. At the same time, the CMA permitted Merrill Lynch to corral much or all of a customer's money under its own roof. Shearson was on the verge of introducing a similar product called a Financial Management Account. Reluctant to give up the free use of customers' balances—Merrill's CMA automatically "swept" a customer's cash into the money-market portion of the CMA each day—Sandy had been slow to offer money-market funds. But Shearson brokers, struggling to counter the popularity of Merrill Lynch's new product, finally prevailed on their boss to give them a similar competitive weapon. To make Shearson's offering more attractive, Sandy had suggested to Robinson at that first meeting that American Express credit cards could be part of the package for Shearson's account holders. Robinson, who discovered that Shearson's clients had a higher net worth than Merrill Lynch's clients, was eager to gain access to that customer base.

Talks had stalled, however, as each company's marketing staff eyed the other with suspicion. Shearson officials felt they were treated worse than second-class citizens. American Express's managers fretted over what such an alliance would do to the prestige of their beloved green cards. The American Express managers disdained their Shearson counterparts as crude and hell-bent on getting their hands on American Express's prized cardholder lists.

Now the unexpected news of the Prudential-Bache merger triggered a second informal meeting between Sandy and Robinson after the Weills returned from Asia. Sandy and Joan invited Jim Robinson and his wife, Bettye, for Sunday brunch at their Greenwich home. Sandy was proud of his lush estate in this prestigious Protestant town, and it gave him a sense of comfort and security to host the Robinsons on his own turf. Sandy had his housekeeper prepare bagels and lox for the Weills and bacon, eggs, and grits for the Robinsons. After brunch, Joan showed Bettye Robinson the gardens and cut her a bouquet of forsythia while the two men retreated to Sandy's dark-paneled study.

Sandy knew from the moment he and Robinson agreed to have this discussion that Shearson could not hope to craft even a so-called merger of equals, much less actually take over American Express. With $20 billion in assets compared to Shearson's $2.5 billion, American Express was simply too large. So as the two settled in to discuss the possibilities, Sandy shed his pose as the gracious host and took on his other persona: the insecure street fighter. If the two companies merged, what would be his role at American Express? What power base would he have? What corporate responsibilities would he have, on top of continuing to head Shearson? Accustomed to being the acquirer rather than the acquired, Sandy wanted to make clear his interest in a top spot at the parent company. His goal if he sold Shearson to American Express: become its president.

Robinson, typically at ease in social settings, was taken aback at Sandy's hard-nosed edge. Evasive while still exuding Southern charm, Robinson assured Sandy he would have an important role at American Express, one that would be worked out with the board of directors. Of course, he told Sandy, "you'll have to prove yourself" over time. Remarkably, Sandy held his volatile temper at that condescending remark. The pair agreed to start negotiations.

By Good Friday 1981, Sandy and Robinson had worked out the parameters of the deal: American Express would buy Shearson for almost $1 billion. At a final negotiating session that day, the CEOs privately hashed out the most sensitive issues that remained open: the number of board seats for Shearson and Sandy's title. Their deputies haggled over the details. Finally, the American Express CEO said he would present their tentative deal on Monday to his board, unofficially led by Howard Clark Sr., who had preceded him as CEO and had recruited nearly every director now on the board.

Robinson quickly dispatched Howard Clark Jr., the former chairman's son who was American Express's investment officer, on the company jet to Hobe Sound, Florida. His mission: persuade his father, as well as several other board members who had retirement places in the rich enclave, to approve the Shearson acquisition. It wouldn't be easy. When he took over as chief executive officer of American Express in 1960, Howard Clark Sr. had gone to great pains to bring onto the company's board the most elite directors he could find, people like Rawleigh Warner Jr., the chairman and chief executive of Mobil Corp.; Richard M. Furlaud, chairman of Squibb Corp.; and Robert V. Roosa, an influential former Treasury Department official who was a partner at the venerable private bank Brown Brothers Harriman & Co. With their backing he had pushed to establish the American Express card as a symbol of prestige as much as a convenient way to pay for things. His efforts were aimed almost exclusively at America's upper crust. It just wouldn't do, for example, to allow Kmart to accept the American Express card.

Thus the junior Clark, known as "H" to distinguish him from his eminent father, knew the board members he would see that weekend would not be happy to associate socially or in the boardroom with the likes of Sandy Weill. Nor would they be happy to associate their very distinguished company with Weill's renegade securities firm. Clark argued that Shearson had the best profit margins in the business, the result of its incredibly efficient operations. He told the men, most of whom were members of the Blind Brook Country Club, one of New York's most exclusive, that if American Express was going to be in the securities business—and it certainly should be—then Sandy's company was in the strongest position to weather that business's cyclical nature.

Excited and nervous, Sandy, Cohen, and Sheinberg left American Express headquarters together and shared a cab to their Upper East Side apartments. They chatted eagerly about getting the Shearson executives together the next day. As Sandy was about to get out of the cab first, he turned to Cohen, who hoped to eventually run Shearson after Sandy moved up to American Express.

"One other thing," Sandy told his right-hand man. "You're not going to be on the board." With that, he slammed the door.

Cohen was stunned. By the time he arrived home he was livid, almost crazed. Sandy had just betrayed him! Figuring the Ivy League bureaucrats at American Express weren't exactly clamoring for more pushy Shearson insiders on their board, he suspected Sandy had sold him out to get the deal. Cohen, the son of a clothing manufacturer, had attended public schools in the middle-class South Shore of Nassau County, Long Island, and graduated from Ohio State University. He knew he wasn't like "them," but neither was Sandy. They should stick together. Sandy's betrayal gnawed at him so that he couldn't sleep that night.

Cohen was a dark-haired, compact man who stood five feet, six inches tall and inch for inch was just as stubborn and scrappy as his boss. The grass was still wet with dew when he arrived at the Weills' Greenwich estate early the next morning. He tore right into Sandy. "I'm mad, because we had an agreement that I would be on the board," Peter said. "It's not right."

"I know you're upset," Sandy responded, keenly aware that he would need Cohen's help in a few hours to convince his management team of the wisdom of selling their company. With his encyclopedic knowledge of the firm and the long hours he worked, Cohen had his own important allies within Shearson. "They're giving us two board seats, not three," Sandy explained. "If you can convince Jim Robinson otherwise, have at it." With only two seats committed and a third seat uncertain, Sandy wanted Shearson's lawyer, Ken Bialkin, or his friend Dan Seymour, former chairman of the J. Walter Thompson advertising agency, on the board. "It's really important we do this deal. Don't screw this up."

Though he was hurt more than he let on, Cohen knew Sandy wanted to propel himself and Shearson into the establishment that had rejected him all his life. "Don't worry. I won't screw it up for you," Cohen said, though he still planned to make a case for himself somehow. He felt oddly as though the bond between Sandy and him had changed forever, that their interests were no longer the same.

When the other executives from Shearson arrived at the Greenwich estate later that morning, Sandy told them he wanted their input and support before going forward with American Express.

"We don't need them," asserted Hardwick Simmons, Shearson's marketing chief. "I'm opposed." As Sandy's token WASP in the 1970s, Simmons didn't share his boss's enthusiasm for breaking into the Gentile crowd. Also, Shearson was booming; that month the Dow Jones Industrial Average had broken above the 1,000 mark. Besides, Simmons and his colleagues expressed doubts about Shearson's compatibility with American Express. They knew it was a stuffy hierarchy filled with memos and committees, all the kinds of things that Shearson's rough-and-ready managers despised.

Sandy countered and cajoled. No longer the shy man on the sidelines, Sandy was powerful and persuasive about the positive reasons for teaming up with American Express. Sherman Lewis, who had become Shearson's president when Shearson took over Loeb Rhoades, sensed that the sale to American Express was as good as done. He realized that Sandy managed by making his executives feel they were part of the decision-making process.

Sheinberg put the whole thing in perspective. "Professionally, we won't be happy running a subsidiary instead of a whole company. Personally, though, we'll all be better off financially. We've been on a roll lately, and now may be the time to take advantage of it." Although he didn't show it,

Sheinberg was deliriously happy at the prospect of becoming really rich if Shearson was sold.

It didn't take long for the Shearson executives to convince themselves that this might work. After buying one ailing firm after another as Wall Street had been falling apart for the past decade, they were the kingpins. They could do it again. We can take those snobs born with silver spoons in their mouths, they crowed. American Express may think it's taking over Shearson, but we can turn the tables. We'll wind up taking over American Express.

With impeccable timing, Sandy was ready to close the deal with his team. "Imagine if you got up tomorrow morning and read that American Express just bought EF Hutton? Would you want that competition?" Sandy said. "Let's pick our partner while we can, rather than let our competitors get the best partners."

The prospect of being left behind in the move toward financial conglomerates dissolved the last remaining opposition. Soon they focused on Sandy's role in the new empire and snickered about how he could run circles around Jim Robinson and assume the helm of American Express. "Do you think I could do it?" Sandy asked with a laugh, suggesting he was joking.

Yet Sandy wasn't entirely kidding. As the meeting broke up, he pulled aside Duke Chapman, who, as the president of Shearson when Hayden Stone took over the firm, was one of the most blue-blooded WASPs Sandy knew. "What are my chances of becoming chairman of American Express?" he whispered.

"None!" Chapman responded. "With this board of directors, a Jew will never be its chairman."

The meeting broke up in time for the Shearson executives, the majority of them Jewish, to get home before sundown, the start of Passover. Sheinberg, recently divorced, stayed at the Weills' to observe the holiday with them. For the traditional Seder, Jessica Weill read the Four Questions, as the family broke matzoh together and drank kosher wine.

The next morning, Easter Sunday, Sheinberg happened to look out his upstairs bedroom window in the Weill home. Coming up the walkway was Louis Gerstner, the highly successful American Express executive in charge of its flagship credit-card and travel business. Gerstner also lived in Greenwich, and as Sheinberg quickly drew the curtain, he guessed from Gerstner's body language that Jim Robinson had ordered him to pay a visit to

Sandy. Brought to American Express in 1977 from McKinsey & Co., the major consulting firm where he handled the American Express account, Gerstner was viewed as the up-and-coming heir apparent to Robinson. At least he had been until the Shearson talks began. The meeting between Sandy and Gerstner lasted only thirty minutes; both men knew that their corporate aspirations could put them on a collision course in coming months.

On Monday, April 20, the board of American Express met to discuss the merger. Robinson had told Sandy he would call him in a couple hours when it was over. But two hours stretched into four and then into the entire day. In the Shearson offices, Sandy was pacing. To Cohen and Sheinberg, he kept barking, "What's going on? What are they doing?" As the meeting dragged on, the Shearson team began to fear there were problems. "It's not the end of the world if we don't do this deal," Cohen remarked, trying to prepare Sandy for the worst. "We're doing all right on our own."

But Sandy was beside himself, chewing his cigars and his fingernails. Finally he called Joan, the one person with whom he could share his insecurity. "You better get down here. I think there's a problem. I don't know what's going on."

When Joan arrived at the World Trade Center offices at six o'clock that evening, she ran into Robinson getting into the elevator. He and Joan were ushered immediately into the private sitting room where Sandy was waiting. The board has approved the merger, Robinson told the Weills, on the financial terms we agreed to, a stock swap valued at $864 million at current stock prices. Sandy was confused; if that's the case, what took so long? What he found out next made him question whether he even wanted to sell his much-loved Shearson to this crowd.

"Sandy, the board doesn't want to name you president, or even chief operating officer, right now," Robinson told him. "You will be chairman of American Express's executive committee, and of course, a director." Sandy and Joan were dumbfounded at such a nebulous, do-nothing corporate position, but Robinson knew he was lucky to get that for Sandy.

Robinson had just spent the entire day being grilled by his directors, who were very uncomfortable with Sandy Weill. Aware of Sandy's no-holds-barred tactics and raw ambition, the directors were terrified that he would take over American Express. Even if they agreed to get into the securities business, they weren't convinced it should be with Shearson and Sandy Weill. Led by the imperious Howard Clark Sr. and Rawleigh Warner, the directors refused to buy Shearson without certain conditions designed to limit Sandy's power. They insisted that Alva Way, a senior executive, be made president, the vacant spot that Sandy badly wanted. To avoid naming a specific person to be Robinson's number two, the directors named Gerstner a vice chairman. Also they rejected Sandy's choice of Bialkin on the grounds that the board didn't want a lawyer as a director. Instead, they chose advertising man Dan Seymour and Sandy's chief deputy, Peter Cohen. Over the weekend, Cohen had presented his case for a director's slot directly to Robinson, noting that without a board seat, he couldn't commit to staying at Shearson beyond the transition.

Of course, Robinson didn't dare confide what lay behind all these machinations to Sandy, who he sensed was about to call off the deal. Instead, he told him that the board had appointed his allies, Seymour and Cohen, and, in his sugarcoated Southern accent, he assured Sandy that he would rise quickly at the blue-chip company as soon as the board got to know him. Without a position of authority from the board, Sandy had to decide whether he could trust Jim Robinson, who was so polished he was difficult to read.

"What's your net worth?" Sandy demanded. Robinson, who was startled at this blunt question, said he was wealthy, but nothing compared to the $30 million Sandy would pocket if he sold Shearson and ended up with 600,000 American Express shares, compared to Robinson's paltry 15,000.

Sandy's confrontational tactic highlighted how different he was from Robinson, who remained calm and diplomatic. Sandy was torn, visibly shaken by his dilemma. While his first instinct was to tell Robinson what to do with his vague promises and WASPy board, he had come close enough to the cachet and clout of American Express to want a role there even more.

Still, Sandy needed a face-saving role, something—anything—to show he would be assuming a top position at American Express. He had an idea: Could he sign the letter to shareholders in the annual report along with Robinson and Way? Sure, conceded Robinson, who knew this gesture was more symbolic than substantive. Increasingly aware that Sandy's role at American Express was more important to him than the price tag of the deal, Robinson promised: "Your time will come."

Sandy looked to Joan, whom he consulted on major decisions. "Should I trust him?" he asked. "Yes," she answered without hesitation.

Sandy turned to Robinson. "Okay, let's do it," he said. When he walked out of the sitting room, he told Cohen with a scowl, "You're on the board."

After final details on an agreement were worked out, the Shearson kitchen staff served steaks and champagne to the exhausted executives at midnight.

At nine o'clock the next morning, Tuesday, April 21, 1981, Sandy got on the nationwide "squawk box" to Shearson's many offices with the news. In a halting voice, he started to explain the rationale behind the merger—American Express's prestige and marketing power. But he stopped suddenly, his chest heaving. Then he finally let his emotions go. With thousands of his employees listening, Sandy sobbed openly.

Fifteen minutes later, the announcement of the groundbreaking merger went out over the news wires. Almost immediately, the media and Wall Street wags, who dubbed the matchup "the Odd Couple," started predicting that the shrewd, calculating Shearson chief would unseat the suave, polite Robinson. Soon Sandy resumed his swagger, confident that he could do at American Express what he had done to a dozen firms in the last decade. "Not bad for a kid from Brooklyn," he confided to a friend. "The Jews are going to take over American Express, and they'll never know what hit them."

Shearson shareholders met to approve the sale on June 29. At the Windows on the World restaurant atop the World Trade Center, Sandy nervously took the ballroom podium. "It's amazing what one has to do to get a crowd," he joked. "Welcome to the wedding," he said to laughter and applause. The Shearson shareholders had always loved Sandy Weill, but never more than now. He had just made them richer than many of them had ever imagined by selling the company at three times book value. "Jimmy, you watch your back. Sandy is smarter than you," one delighted attendee yelled out. Sandy basked in the adoration.

Three of the biggest shareholders in the audience were his early partners: Roger Berlind, Arthur Levitt, and Marshall Cogan. As Sandy reviewed the firm's history from its modest beginnings, they expected to be recognized. "We've survived—and prospered—through too many market cycles to count," Sandy told the friendly audience. "Always charging like bulls, never hibernating with the bears." When Sandy was done, Levitt and Cogan were incensed; they hadn't even been mentioned. Levitt was particularly offended. He firmly believed that Sandy wouldn't be here this day had he, Levitt, not saved Sandy's job in that fateful confrontation with Arthur Carter years ago. But Sandy wasn't sharing the spotlight with anyone.

After getting the approvals of delighted Shearson shareholders and the less excited American Express shareholders, Sandy gleefully noted that

Shearson's stock had risen, making the company worth $988 million on its final day of trading. At 3:30, he left a meeting with Robinson to visit the floor of the New York Stock Exchange. The American Express chief couldn't fathom Sandy's sentimental urge to go to the Big Board. As a man given every advantage in life, Robinson clearly didn't understand the fearsome hurdles that this Brooklyn boy had overcome to get to this day. Sandy fought back tears as he watched Shearson's stock trade for the last time.

A PRESIDENT WITHOUT PORTFOLIO

Sandy Weill certainly did not blend easily into the button-down, hierarchical world of American Express. He wore baggy, rumpled suits on his plump frame rather than the tailored attire of the physically fit American Express upper echelon. When he plopped in his worn, cushy couch and put his feet on the coffee table, which he did a hundred times a day, holes in the soles of his scuffed-up shoes showed. His American Express counterparts, who preferred antique chairs, had their shoes shined daily. Instead of gold cuff links, Sandy wore gold bracelets. When the executives and directors sipped wine at lunch meetings, Sandy would swill a martini. When no one else was smoking, Sandy puffed on his fat Te-Amo cigar. American Express always had a five-year strategy in place. Sandy's long-term planning ran to where he was going to eat dinner that night. While American Express put its charitable dollars to sponsor major art exhibits at the top-tier museums, Sandy had quietly started a very effective charitable foundation that taught poor, mostly minority, high school kids about business and economics. Unhappy with Sandy's poor presence at a podium, the polished and well-spoken Robinson hired Sonya Hamlin, a well-known speaking coach, to tutor him.

The other Shearson executives were equally at odds with their American Express counterparts. At a formal dinner shortly after the merger, Shearson executives sat amidst the American Express officers. They hooted, hollered, cursed, and drank. When one Shearson man stood on a chair to yell at someone across the room, Howard Clark Jr.'s dinner partners were aghast. "Oh my god," whispered the man on his left. "What's going on here? They're animals!" said the man on his right, rolling his eyes.

Even though he didn't dress and behave like his new colleagues, Sandy loved the perks that came with being at American Express. He relished the

Gulfstream jet designated for him and had Sheinberg, an avid photographer, shoot his picture in front of it. The American Express helicopter delivered him to glitzy parties in the Hamptons and onto exclusive golf courses, where the pilot fetched Sandy's clubs. He even appeared on TV in a celebrity-studded golf tournament playing with Jack Nicklaus. He had a car and driver, and attended corporate parties with the likes of Barbara Walters, Karl Malden, and Henry Kissinger. He showed up in the social columns of New York newspapers and even made the cover of *Esquire* magazine. American Express became his passport to more than wealth; it opened the doors to the fame and opulent lifestyle he had always dreamed of.

Accordingly, Sandy was determined to make his mark at his new corporate parent, even though he kept his title as Shearson chairman and CEO. While he initially retained his World Trade Center office with the fireplace, he also took a big corner office on the fortieth floor of the American Express tower. Certain that Cohen could handle the day-to-day operations at the brokerage firm, Sandy rolled up his sleeves to learn as much as he could about the other business units. Sandy's job as chairman of the executive committee gave him responsibility for strategic planning and financial matters. He planned to use these duties to gain enough influence to persuade Robinson to name him chief operating officer, distinguishing him from his rival Gerstner, who was none too eager to share his business strategies for the flourishing green and gold cards with his new colleague. Indeed, Gerstner actively opposed any efforts by Sandy or his Shearson cronies to "cross-market" brokerage products to his cherished cardholders. What if a cardholder lost money on an investment or advice from Shearson? Gerstner argued. He might blame American Express.

Sandy wanted to impress the American Express executives with his knowledge of other businesses, proving he was more than a superbroker. As a director Sandy would be provided monthly financial reports the night before a scheduled board meeting. On those nights he insisted that Sheinberg, who had been named treasurer of American Express, spend the night at his apartment to flesh out questions Sandy could ask. At one early meeting, Sandy turned to a footnote in a report and pointedly asked Gerstner, "Why has the time to answer a customer call gone from thirty-eight seconds to forty-five seconds?"

Another time, Sandy detected weakness in the traveler's-checks unit. Rather than sending a polite memorandum through the proper channels asking for a well-researched report, Sandy called William McCormick, the executive in charge, who was out of town for a weeklong meeting. "Cancel your trip and come back here," Sandy ordered.

McCormick, a vice chairman of the travel-related services division, refused. He told Sandy his staff was studying the situation and that he would be briefed with the other executives at a future meeting. Cursing at such red tape and insubordination, Sandy angrily hung up. When the meeting was held, McCormick started his presentation about traveler's checks. Sandy interrupted him, "We ask the questions and you answer them." Robinson and Gerstner exchanged glances. Sandy's longtime habit of brainstorming and browbeating his managers certainly didn't comport with American Express business etiquette. Yet Sandy was dead right about the trouble. Robinson might not like his new colleague's brusque style, but he was amazed at his alacrity at finding and solving problems, as if they were fires that needed to be put out immediately, lest they spread.

With Peter Cohen preoccupied by his duties at Shearson, Sandy felt the need for someone to work with him as he tried to bone up on the many facets of American Express's business. When young Jamie Dimon, about to receive his MBA from Harvard, called Sandy looking for advice about job offers he was entertaining from Goldman Sachs, Morgan Stanley, and Lehman Brothers, Sandy invited him to his Upper East Side apartment.

"I have a better idea," Sandy told the young man. He offered Dimon the position of his assistant. "I won't pay you as much, but you're going to learn a lot and we're going to have a lot of fun." The handsome and charming Dimon accepted and soon reported to his small office with a window next to Sandy's.

Determined to display his deal-making prowess at American Express, Sandy searched for takeover candidates. He negotiated the purchases of two regional brokerage firms, Foster & Marshall in Seattle and Robinson-Humphrey in Atlanta. Separately, Sandy discovered that the American Express International Bank was attempting to emulate the Geneva-based Trade Development Bank to get into overseas banking for the very rich. That bank, Sandy knew, was run by billionaire Edmond Safra, the international banker Cohen had worked for in his year away from Shearson. Cohen had suggested that American Express explore the acquisition of Safra's bank, and Sandy had given him the go-ahead to make an initial approach. Shuttling between the mysterious banker's Paris apartment and New York, Cohen found Safra was interested and arranged for the Lebanese-born banker to meet Robinson, who was attracted to the Geneva bank's wealthy international client base. Shortly after their amicable meeting, Sandy and Joan flew to Europe so Sandy could have his own powwow with Safra. The pair hit it off, even getting drunk together on New Year's Eve. They called Cohen in New York in the middle of the night and jovially conveyed their intention to strike a deal.

On their way back from Europe, Sandy and Joan gave a lift on the corporate jet to Harvey Golub, a partner at McKinsey & Co. who ran the American Express account. The two had met when Sandy first joined American Express at the behest of Robinson, who wanted Sandy to use McKinsey as the other executives did. Sandy had refused, saying consultants were a waste of money. But Sandy used the ten-hour flight to pick Golub's brain. From his nebulous post as chairman of the American Express executive committee—God, he hated that meaningless title that sounded like corporate purgatory—Sandy had felt the tremors that signaled potential changes in the executive suite.

It didn't take long for Sandy and Golub—both Brooklyn-born cigar smokers—to establish an easy rapport. As he grew to trust Golub during the flight, Sandy peppered him with questions about issues he anticipated arising in the coming weeks: Should he give up the job as chairman and CEO of Shearson to become president of American Express? Should he become the president of American Express if he isn't named chief operating officer at the same time? The two men, wreathed in a thick cloud of cigar smoke, discussed every pro and con.

"Title doesn't matter," Golub told his fellow passenger. "Don't be so hung up on being named chief operating officer." Yet the McKinsey consultant could tell Sandy was bothered by Robinson's consistent refusal to name anyone to the chief operating officer's position.

"It doesn't matter if I give up the CEO title at Shearson, because Peter Cohen will be loyal to me," Sandy offered. Again Golub disagreed. "That loyalty will last about fifteen minutes—at most." Even Joan, who was listening to every word, weighed in on this: Shearson is your power base; don't give up your anchor, she warned.

When the Gulfstream landed in New York, Sandy told Sheinberg, who was on the trip, "I like this guy Golub. He can be an honorary member of Shearson." Golub walked away liking Sandy, but he also saw a man who was used to being in charge struggling to find his way. A minister without portfolio in a foreign culture, Sandy didn't seem all that happy at American Express, Golub thought.

Sandy's premonition about changes in the executive suite proved true. In January 1983, Alva Way, consistently outgunned by Sandy and Gerstner, announced his resignation as president. With the presidency available, Sandy made no secret of his desire for the post. But neither did Gerstner, who thought he deserved the spot as the head of American Express's core travel-related services business, the company's impressive "cash cow." Certainly on paper Gerstner had the upper hand: In 1982 Gerstner's Travel Related Services had contributed $247 million of the company's $581 million of net income, while only $124 million came from investment services.

Robinson, who had gained respect for Cohen's talents after he largely orchestrated the pending acquisition of Safra's Trade Development Bank, asked the young executive for his input. He had come to regard Cohen as quite capable, despite his relative youth; indeed, Robinson had started inviting him to lunch in his private dining room. "Who do you think I should make president?" the American Express CEO asked.

"You have to make Sandy president," replied Cohen, who was still loyal to Sandy despite the strains in their relationship. Besides, if Sandy got more involved at corporate, he would quit meddling at Shearson and give me control, he reasoned.

"Why? Lou is in charge of more revenue-producing divisions for American Express," Robinson countered.

"If you don't make Sandy president, Edmond won't do the deal," Cohen replied. The takeover of Safra's Trade Development Bank was scheduled to close in a few weeks. "Edmond doesn't know Lou Gerstner from a hole in the wall. He knows and trusts you and Sandy."

As Robinson debated his choices in the days that followed, Sandy's nerves got the better of him. He would pace the office floor, pull at his hair, and chew his cigar. He kept hounding Cohen. "Who do you think he's going to pick?" Sandy asked. "Who's going to be president?" When his longtime aide predicted Sandy would get the job, Sandy wanted more information. "How do you know? How can you be sure?" When Cohen said he had recommended Sandy, his boss—unaware of the growing bond between Cohen and Robinson—didn't see how that would carry much weight.

At the start of 1983, Robinson encouraged Sandy to give up the CEO position at Shearson for Cohen. After the American Express chief hinted that Sandy's relinquishing control at Shearson would free him up to do more important work at the parent, Sandy acquiesced. It was the first time Sandy hadn't followed Joan's advice. With mixed emotion, Sandy issued a press release naming Cohen the new president and CEO of Shearson. At age thirty-six, the hardworking and ambitious Peter Cohen became the youngest chief executive of any major securities house.

Within a few days, Robinson called a special board meeting at the Helmsley Palace Hotel to approve the acquisition of Trade Development Bank and select a new president. The directors expressed concerns about the secretive and peculiar Edmond Safra, who refused to come to the United States to meet them, ostensibly for tax reasons. Cohen thought the debate had overtones of anti-Semitism, but Robinson pushed for the lucrative international banking franchise for American Express. After the directors reluctantly approved the $530-million purchase of most of the non-U.S. assets of the Geneva-based bank, Robinson told them, "Peter Cohen is an extraordinary asset." Sandy was floored. Robinson had never showered that kind of praise on him.

Sandy quickly recovered, however, when Robinson recommended him as the next president of American Express. The board approved Sandy only after Gerstner was named chairman of the executive committee. When the new positions were announced on January 16, 1983, Robinson went out of his way to praise both men equally.

Two weeks later, the American Express chairman and CEO handed Sandy a three-page letter detailing—actually limiting—his responsibilities. With the exception of certain financial duties, Sandy couldn't act independently. He had to seek the approval for any major move with the affected operating chiefs of American Express's five divisions or with Robinson. That hit a nerve.

"Jim, I want to be chief operating officer," Sandy declared.

"No," Robinson answered flatly.

Sandy implored Robinson, with assurances that he had the energy and the know-how to do a good job.

Robinson told Sandy that he would lose the "horsepower" of his strong subsidiary heads if he put a COO over them. Jamie Dimon, getting up to speed as Sandy's assistant, couldn't believe his ears. With his Harvard MBA freshly in hand, Dimon was getting a fast lesson in the realities of corporate governance, and he wasn't impressed by what he saw. "Jim Robinson is keeping all the big egos happy and diffusing the power so broadly no one can come close to challenging his authority," Dimon complained to Sandy. "Corporate America is full of children, and it's a waste of fucking time."

While Dimon's observation had some truth to it, neither Dimon nor Sandy knew that Robinson's directors had drawn a line in the sand regarding Sandy's ascent at American Express. The board's controlling clique, centered a little bit north of Palm Beach, would go only so far with Sandy Weill, and he had just reached that limit.

Instead of a cause for celebration, Sandy's so-called promotion felt more like defeat to the hard-charging president. He was at loose ends. Without Shearson, he had no fiefdom to call his own. He would fall into the chair in Sheinberg's office and complain, "I don't have anything to do." When Mary McDermott, who had been with Sandy almost since the beginning, ran into him at a Shearson function, she was astonished at Sandy's appearance. "You look like hell," she told him. "Whatever is making you look this unhappy, it's not worth it."

When his old friend Edwin Gill, who started as an analyst at CBWL, paid Sandy a visit in the American Express tower, he found his old boss in the executive corridor with a martini in his hand at 2:30 in the afternoon. "Edwin, I have nothing to do," Sandy confided. After spending the afternoon having more drinks and reminiscing about the old days when Sandy was the CEO of his own company, Gill left with a heavy heart. *It's as if Sandy has lost his bearings,* Gill thought sadly.

By the summer of 1983, Sandy knew he had to do something to revive his career at American Express—and himself. If he was constrained from managing people, he could at least manage deals. A deal junkie, Sandy thought he had found a good target: Investors Diversified Services. IDS wasn't a sexy or prestigious financial company but a folksy Minneapolis-based firm that sold mutual funds, annuities, and insurance policies through "financial advisors." Selling door to door, the IDS salespeople were the Avon ladies and Fuller Brush men of financial products. After American Express bought Shearson, Sears had snapped up Dean Witter on the theory that Sears could peddle everything from "stocks to socks" to Middle America. IDS would be American Express's chance to go after the middle class too. With a bull market under way, Sandy told Robinson that everyone from teachers to repairmen had a favorite stock or an insurance need. He got the go-ahead to test the waters on an IDS purchase.

Excited and eager, Sandy contacted Fred Kirby II, the chairman of Alleghany Corp., the diversified company that was IDS's parent. Kirby, whose family owned the biggest block of Alleghany stock, was willing to consider a sale on the condition that American Express buy the entire company, including its steelmaking unit. A further condition was that Sandy and his minions couldn't have access to IDS's books to do their due diligence until a purchase price was agreed upon. Such unreasonable provisos normally would have given Sandy pause, but he was so enthusiastic about bringing in a deal that he pushed forward.

The reclusive and obstinate Kirby left to spend the month of June at his remote Adirondack Mountains retreat. But Sandy wouldn't wait for his return. Kirby could be reached only by patching telephone calls through a radio link, but that was good enough for Sandy, who wanted to get this deal rolling. When he reached Kirby, Sandy wasted no time making an offer: "Six hundred million?" Sandy shouted into the phone from his office as he puffed a Marlboro. "How does that sound, Mr. Kirby?" When Sandy couldn't hear a response over the radio's static, he raised his bid to $750 million and then $900 million without apparently getting any response from the other end. Sheinberg and American Express counsel Gary Beller, who were with Sandy, stood by helplessly as Sandy upped the price to a whopping $1 billion in just five minutes.

Sandy wants this deal at any price, Sheinberg thought. *He's negotiating with himself.*

With a $1-billion price tag established, Kirby agreed to let Sandy and his team make an on-site inspection of IDS in Minneapolis. Most of American Express management had been ambivalent about pursuing IDS but were highly skeptical when they got wind of the purchase price. Cohen was particularly outspoken about an atrocious price tag for a Midwestern company with a "farm team" for agents. Hell, this amount was twice what American Express paid Safra for his renowned worldwide bank. Sheinberg and Dimon were about to leave with Sandy for Minneapolis when Cohen said he would join them. Robinson had given the new Shearson CEO his own instructions: "I want a real independent due diligence," Robinson told Cohen privately. "I don't want to be smoked by Sandy."

After the first day of due diligence, Sandy found Cohen and Sheinberg in the hotel bar. "What do you think?" Sandy queried. "Isn't this great? Isn't this really great?"

"I think it's great at the right price, but not at this price," Cohen answered. "Here's why I think we're overpaying."

Before Cohen could explain, Sandy launched into a tirade, screaming, "You don't know what the fuck you're talking about! You better not challenge me on this!"

Remembering Sandy's outburst at his going-away party, Cohen yelled back, "You know what, Sandy? I don't have to take this shit from you. I'm not going to take this shit from you." Looking over at Sheinberg, he added, "George has the same point of view." In an effort to calm Sandy, who was creating a scene at the bar, Cohen asked, "Can we renegotiate the price?"

"Hell no, we're not renegotiating," Sandy fumed. "This is the price, and this is great. You're wrong!"

"Sandy, we're going back to New York. We will not see you tomorrow," Cohen said as he left the bar. Sheinberg paid their tab and walked out behind him. The next morning, Cohen and Sheinberg took the Shearson plane back east to be dropped off in East Hampton, where they planned to spend the weekend at their summer houses.

A senior management meeting was set for the next week, August 15, 1983, to evaluate the IDS purchase. But the meeting would be more than just a consideration of a deal. It would be a vote of confidence in Sandy Weill as well.

As the acquisition's proponent, Sandy made the presentation to the executives seated around the long mahogany table. For the first time in his life, he actually put on a slide show in the American Express tradition. Sheinberg, who had known Sandy for nearly two decades, thought to himself: *This is the reverse of the real Sandy Weill. This is a snow job, a con job. So you're stooping to this, my friend, you're so desperate to get back in the game.*

After the show-and-tell, Robinson went around the room for opinions from the executives, including Gerstner, who had concerns about tarnishing the pristine image of American Express with such a lowbrow operation. When a question arose about taking on a steel subsidiary as part of the deal, one of Sandy's aides jumped in. "Actually, we project a steel-company profit of ten million dollars," he said.

"Where did you get that?" interjected a surprised Sheinberg, who had been assigned the due diligence of the steel unit because of his experience with factories at Bulova. "That's bullshit. This company is lucky if it breaks even. My guess is it will lose money."

Embarrassed and furious that his pitch was being undermined, Sandy exploded. "Why didn't you say anything before this?"

"I just got back from a trip to that site," Sheinberg replied, assuming that the candor that had always marked their relationship at Shearson was what Sandy expected of him. But this time Sandy felt ambushed, stabbed in the back by one of his own men. Sheinberg had committed the cardinal sin of disloyalty. The $1-billion IDS deal died at that meeting.

So did the longtime friendship between Sandy and Sheinberg. Sandy didn't speak to the treasurer for several months, until he left a message for him to meet him for lunch. He coldly informed Sheinberg he was being replaced. (Treasurer was just about the only job over which Sandy had any control.)

"Fine, I'll go back to Shearson," Sheinberg said. "That was our deal when I joined you at corporate."

"I can't have an enemy around, can I?" Sandy responded.

"A deal's a deal," Sheinberg said.

"We'll see," said Sandy.

Sandy succeeded in ousting Sheinberg from the parent company. But Cohen, whose star was rising even as Sandy's was falling at American Express, persuaded Robinson to keep Sheinberg at Shearson. Distraught that his deputies had turned against him and in need of respite, Sandy fled New York for the pampering and luxury of the Hotel du Cap on the French Riviera. There he and Joan vacationed for three weeks among the fragrant pines, splendid gardens, and panoramic views, dining on superb Provençal cuisine and lounging by the seawater pool chiseled into the massive seaside rocks.

When Sandy returned to his office after Labor Day, Cohen asked him to go to lunch "to straighten out the IDS thing."

"You have me all wrong," Cohen told his old mentor.

"You're not loyal, you son of a bitch," Sandy reacted vociferously. "You should show me blood loyalty, cut-your-wrist kind of loyalty. You didn't support me."

"Stop it already," Cohen said. "IDS is a very good idea at the right price. And Kirby has nowhere else to go. So let's structure this transaction so it will fly." Cohen, always a financial wizard, laid out a plan that included a lower purchase price rather than a dilutive pooling of stock, and a tax-efficient scheme of marking up the value of the assets and re-depreciating them.

"That's a great idea," Sandy acknowledged. Beaming, he darted out before finishing his lunch. American Express made another attempt at IDS as a stand-alone, retained Harvey Golub from McKinsey for an impartial due-diligence investigation, and finally agreed with Kirby to pay $773 million in cash and stock.

But the tensions and confrontations in the executive ranks weren't American Express's only troubles by the fall of 1983. While Robinson and his management had been expanding the company's banking and investment activities, the Fireman's Fund, its property-and-casualty insurance unit, was slipping deeper and deeper into debt. The subsidiary had become badly overextended in recent years as premium income declined, competition intensified, and costs rose. Under pressure to deliver earnings to American Express, Fireman's Fund had resorted to accounting gimmickry to paper over its problems. Finally, the bottom fell out in late 1983, forcing American Express to take a massive write-off. On December 12, the company suffered its first earnings decline in thirty-five years because of Fireman's Fund. The news sent American Express shares plunging $3¾ to $28⅜, erasing $750 million of its market capitalization.

Enormous pressure was building on Robinson to show the markets and his board that he was prepared to take all necessary action to stop the decline. Yet only one person in his executive ranks had the reputation as a turnaround artist: Sandy Weill. Under unaccustomed attack after years of kudos, Jim Robinson needed Sandy to rescue his and his company's reputation. At the same time, Sandy, longing for a challenge he could sink his teeth into, needed Fireman's Fund to rescue himself. It didn't take much persuading before he assumed the leadership of the beleaguered insurance unit and departed to its headquarters outside San Francisco. Sandy knew the cross-country assignment removed him from the corporate power base, but he wanted a real job. And as American Express's second-largest shareholder, he wanted to protect his investment.

Diving into his new assignment with his old fervor, Sandy stayed in San Francisco almost full-time at the beginning. At Robinson's behest, he took along Bill McCormick, the traveler's-checks executive with whom he'd had the run-in during his early days at American Express. While McCormick, who had been trained as a nuclear physicist, may have been one of Robinson's favored lieutenants, Sandy nevertheless appreciated his work ethic and methodical dissection of details. Soon, Sandy, McCormick, and Jamie Dimon, who traveled everywhere with Sandy, were spending every waking moment together as they prepared to move quickly and dramatically to turn the company around. At breakfast every morning, Sandy smoked his cigars, until finally McCormick announced, "I can't enjoy my scrambled eggs with that cigar smoke." At the end of eighteen-hour days, the trio often crashed at McCormick's house, purchased so he could stay there full-time while Sandy and Dimon commuted from New York. Plotting the rescue, they smoked cigars and drank gin in the backyard hot tub until midnight.

In early 1984, Sandy launched the turnaround. He fired two thousand employees, sold off the subsidiary's foreign operations, raised premium rates, and slashed expenses. At American Express, McCormick had not been a fan of Sandy's style since their first confrontation over proper procedures. Now, however, McCormick found Sandy an excellent leader, something McCormick had never glimpsed at American Express headquarters. He could count on Sandy to give him straightforward, guileless answers, sprinkled of course with choice expletives, rather than the "glassy-eyed, fishy stare" that McCormick got from most corporate bigwigs.

As Sandy's constant right hand, Jamie Dimon was getting a crash course not only in crisis management but also in eating through four time zones. Wherever they went, Sandy would arrange meetings over meals. With the American Express jet flying them to two cities on some nights, they frequently consumed two complete dinners. After a martini or two, Sandy always ordered whatever he thought was the restaurant's finest dish and an excellent red wine to wash it down. Flying home after that, Sandy wanted a snack available on the plane. The American Express pilots knew to have Domino's pizza—heavy on the jalapeños—sent to whatever airport they were at. Jamie Dimon longed for a simple container of yogurt.

Under Sandy's rule, Fireman's Fund showed a modest improvement in profits in 1984. In March, rejuvenated by his early accomplishments in California, Sandy was looking forward to a dinner at the '21' Club with Robinson and his new fiancée, Linda Gosden, a public-relations maven. A former acupuncturist, Gosden was ambitious and vivacious. She was surfacing not just as Robinson's new love but also his chief advisor. With Joan by his side, Sandy excitedly discussed ideas he was using at Fireman's Fund that could also be implemented at American Express. Yet while Sandy had been away, Gerstner, assuming more responsibility for corporate strategy, recommended that American Express unload the insurance unit.

Sandy saw what was happening. He was still president of American Express, but he was being frozen out. He had never been welcome in the WASP nest, and he had lost the friendships of his closest Shearson colleagues, Cohen and Sheinberg. Still, Cohen, who was forging ahead to expand the securities firm, kept Sandy informed of the unfolding negotiations that spring to buy Lehman Brothers Kuhn Loeb Inc. As one of the last privately held investment banks, Lehman was in turmoil as its co–chief executives, Lewis Glucksman and Peter Peterson, warred over its future. Taking over Lehman would settle a score for Weill and Cohen, who had been snubbed in 1977 when Kuhn Loeb rejected Shearson's offer in favor of merging with the more esteemed Lehman Brothers.

Ending one hundred thirty-four years as a private institution, Lehman agreed to sell to Shearson/American Express in April for $380 million. Cohen, the epitome of the Young Turk reshaping Wall Street, had learned at the feet of a Wall Street master, Sandy Weill. To show his gratitude and a little sympathy for his old boss, who was clearly on the outs, Cohen wanted to tell Sandy himself.

"The day after this deal is closed, you and I are having lunch, just the two of us, right in the middle of their fucking dining room," Cohen told the man who had been humiliated by these old-line firms more than anyone. "It's what you always wanted to do." On May 11, 1984, Sandy and Cohen met for that lunch in the elegant dining room at the Broad Street headquarters of the firm, now renamed Shearson Lehman. As he placed the white cloth napkin in his lap, surrounded by Rembrandts and Renoirs from Bobbie Lehman's collection, Cohen proudly remarked, "Look how far we've come from the day I went to work for you." It was a bittersweet moment for Sandy, who saw this day not as his victory, but as one for his former assistant, who had outmaneuvered him at American Express. Sandy felt betrayed by Cohen. *He's done everything in his power to thwart what I want to do, and driven a wedge between Robinson and me,* Sandy thought.

SWAN SONG

As American Express moved forward with its plan to rid itself of Fireman's Fund, Sandy came up with an idea that could benefit him and American Express as well as provide him with a logical exit. "As long as we're talking about the possible disposition of this thing, would you mind if I see whether I can put together something to buy it?" Sandy asked Robinson.

Robinson wasn't sure; it wouldn't look good to sell to a senior executive.

"Look, Jim, I may not be around the company much longer," Sandy said. "Why not sell to me?" The American Express CEO reluctantly consented that Sandy could explore a buyout—quietly. "It would be a nice gentlemanly way to exit the company."

Sandy swung into full gear. He could have a company of his own to run again! He called his friend Robert Greenhill at Morgan Stanley and other potential investors who might be interested in helping him do a leveraged buyout of the insurance unit, basically borrowing the money to buy Fireman's by pledging its assets as collateral for the loan. Dimon, who loved reading the annual reports of the Berkshire Hathaway Group—which coincidentally had its own insurance holdings—suggested Sandy contact Warren Buffett, the famed investor who served as Berkshire's CEO. A long-time friend of Sandy's, Arthur Zankel, who had made investments with Buffett in the past, arranged a meeting for them when Buffett visited New York the next week. After a productive breakfast at the Plaza Hotel, Sandy and Dimon flew to Omaha, Nebraska, to Buffett's nondescript office in Kiewit Plaza. They drank Cherry Cokes and reviewed Sandy's plan that called for Buffett to put up the funds to buy one fifth of Fireman's Fund.

"I'll take twenty percent and whatever anyone else doesn't want," Buffett said. When Buffett drove Sandy and Dimon back to the airport where the American Express jet was waiting, Sandy invited the financial guru to come aboard and take a look. Buffett, known for his Midwestern penny-pinching values, was impressed. "Mmm, this isn't a bad way of life," he told Sandy before sending them on their way. Dimon was bowled over by what had just happened: "My god, we have an investor!" He and Sandy knew Buffett's reputation for careful investing and utter probity would appeal to American Express.

At the same time that Sandy was preparing a bid for Fireman's Fund, rumors began to crop up about the former Shearson chief's impending departure from American Express. The press picked up on the sales of about half of his American Express stock. Attributing them to "personal financial planning," Sandy denied any plans to leave American Express.

But friends and enemies inside the company knew Sandy was on his way out—one way or another. Robinson and Cohen, who had become close at Sandy's expense, decided to give the man who brought them together a "going-away" party, although it couldn't be called that. Instead, they hatched the idea to throw a lavish gala in honor of the twenty-fifth anniversary of Sandy's start on Wall Street when he and three friends opened Carter, Berlind, Potoma & Weill. Cohen asked Mary McDermott, the firm's first gal Friday and now Shearson's public-relations head, to spare no expense in putting the party together. Asked about a budget, Cohen replied, "Just make it great."

On May 2, 1985, nearly two hundred Shearson employees and friends gathered at the Federal Hall National Memorial on Wall Street from as far away as London, Geneva, and California. Arthur Carter and Roger Berlind attended, despite the difficult circumstances of their exits from the firm. Both men had gone on to very successful careers; Carter made close to $100 million buying and selling companies in the 1970s and had a real-estate and publishing empire, and Berlind, returning to his first love, had produced major Broadway shows including *Amadeus* and *Sophisticated Ladies*. Arthur Levitt still felt some bitterness that his old partner took all the credit when Shearson was sold to American Express. He and Cogan refused to attend despite the fact that they had gone on to their own successes, Levitt as chairman of the American Stock Exchange and Cogan as a co-owner, among other things, of New York's swanky '21' Club.

In the 143-year-old landmark marble building, guests in black tie and evening gowns passed through Corinthian columns for the dinner dance in the massive rotunda. Vases of lilacs and dogwood sat atop tables draped in silver lamé, as oversized white balloons floated overhead. When Mc-Dermott, who had hired a famous party planner for the event, entered the breathtaking room, she burst into tears. Her quiet crying was for more than the room's beauty; she was brokenhearted that this would be Sandy's "swan song."

After dessert, speeches were in order. The Weills' children, Marc and Jessica, spoke about growing up with their father and their Shearson family. Both now worked for the firm: Marc, twenty-nine years old, was a financial consultant in asset management, and Jessica, twenty-five, worked in the marketing department. Cohen took the podium to talk about Shearson's growth to 22,000 employees and to present Sandy with a silver cup inscribed MASTERMIND, MASTER BUILDER AND MASTER CHAIRMAN OF THE BOARD.

Robinson, who had arrived with bodyguards, introduced himself, drawling that he was from "southern Brooklyn." He delivered a parody of the Gettysburg Address: "One score and five years ago, Carter, Berlind and

Weill brought forth in Brooklyn a new firm dedicated to the proposition that all money is created equal . . ." Then the American Express CEO presented Sandy, Carter, and Berlind with 2,300-year-old coins, tetradrachms from the Macedonian Empire. He explained to the crowd, many of them, like Anthony DeMeo and Charles Bachi, from Shearson's back office, that Macedonia, like Shearson, was created in twenty-five years, and gave them all replicas as party favors.

Following the brief remarks of Carter and Berlind, Sandy took the stage, speaking so quietly he could hardly be heard in the vast rotunda. "Arthur Carter lived across the hall from me," he stammered. "We bought a seat on the New York Stock Exchange and . . . here we are." Overcome by emotion, Sandy couldn't continue. The Weills and their friends danced, often in big groups hugging and swaying to the beat, until 1:00 A.M.

A few days later, Sandy offered his plan to take Fireman's Fund private. In a deal worth $1.6 billion, American Express would retain 40 percent of the company, Buffett would get another 40 percent, and Sandy would own the remaining 20 percent. After presenting the plan, Sandy retreated to the fortieth-floor dining room for lunch with Clarence Jones, whom Sandy had made a partner—the first black partner on Wall Street—at CBWL back in the 1960s. While they were eating, one of Sandy's assistants came into the dining room to whisper in his ear. Jones, who didn't hear what she was whispering, watched Sandy simply deflate. The assistant had told Sandy what she had just overheard one American Express executive saying to another in the elevator about Sandy's plan: "What really pisses me off about this deal is that it can make Weill richer." That wasn't a good sign. He was about to be turned down. Having suffered much discrimination in his own life, Jones tried to comfort Sandy, who still seemed like a fish out of water in the WASPy company.

"Sandy, this isn't you," Jones said softly.

"I know," Sandy replied.

With nothing else to do until American Express decided on the proposal, Sandy and Joan, his supporter through good times and bad, returned to the Hotel du Cap to celebrate their thirtieth anniversary. In New York, the American Express board didn't like Sandy's plan. The directors complained that it contained too much debt and asked for too many guarantees. Perhaps more important, they worried that if Sandy did turn around Fireman's Fund, he would make a ton of money and look like a star, while the board could face shareholder lawsuits for selling it to an insider. Instead, the board decided that the parent company would sell it to the public. Robinson called Sandy on June 18 to say that the board had rejected his proposal. The message was clear: American Express didn't mind if Sandy had nothing else to do but resign.

Sandy returned to New York on a Friday afternoon. "I think this is a good time to leave," he told Robinson. "I will go quietly." Then he and the American Express CEO spent most of Saturday at the American Express offices in Lower Manhattan discussing Sandy's departure. On Sunday, Sandy went to the Robinsons' Greenwich home to continue talks on what salary and benefits he would receive as a "consultant" in the future, including an office, pension, stock options, bonus, medical benefits, two secretaries, and car and driver. Sandy met Dimon and his secretary at the office that Sunday night to clean out his office. Sandy also summoned Marty Lipton, his lawyer, to finalize his contract. At 2:00 A.M., Monday, June 25, Sandy left the American Express tower alone, exhausted, and morose. Dimon, knowing Sandy's moods were lifted with a good party, considered orchestrating a last-day event for his boss. "One problem—no one would come," he told their secretary as they finished packing. "They would fear looking like Sandy partisans, a kiss of death at American Express."

Later that Monday morning, American Express announced Sandy's resignation as president and his replacement by Louis Gerstner. In response to a flood of media inquiries, Robinson and Sandy agreed to meet with reporters in the fortieth-floor conference room overlooking New York Harbor. Smoking his Te-Amo cigars, Sandy somehow felt relief, even happiness; as he became more relaxed about his departure, even his humor returned that afternoon. He crowed that he wouldn't be Robinson's "Deputy Dawg" anymore, referring to an old cantankerous but ineffectual cartoon character.

Reporters tried to find out what behind-the-scenes intrigue had led to the unraveling of one of Wall Street's most unusual partnerships. Did Sandy underestimate Robinson's skills as a politician? Was Sandy frustrated by the bureaucracy? The insular board of directors? Didn't Sandy want the number-one job someday?

"Obviously I feel sad about that," Sandy acknowledged. But he couldn't bring himself to criticize Robinson or American Express for his failure to rise to the top. He knew he had made his share of missteps. Much of his undoing was his own. For the first time in his life, Sandy hadn't been true to Sandy. Never again, he vowed to himself.

The big question everyone wanted to know: What will you do now?

Conceding that he had no specific plans, his answer was true to himself: "Maybe I'll build another company. Whatever I do next, I will want to be the top person. I just want to run my own show again."

4

EXILE ON PARK AVENUE

The morning of June 26, 1985, Sandy Weill awakened to face his choices. He could be a CEO in exile, shamed by his defeat at American Express and reluctant to reenter the hurly-burly of corporate life at the highest levels. Or he could be one of the nation's most eligible executives, itching to take the reins of another company and whip it into shape using his legendary managerial and deal-making skills. The long, drawn-out battle with James Robinson and his American Express cronies had sapped Sandy's energy. That morning it occurred to him that he just might indulge one of his longtime fantasies: buy a big boat and take a leisurely cruise with Joan. He shared that thought with his old friend Michael Weinberg, who years ago had become his second client—after his mother—and was now calling to check on Sandy's state of mind. Weinberg sensed the despair in Sandy's tired voice, but he recognized that this wasn't the Sandy Weill he had known for two decades.

"Are you out of your mind?" Weinberg snapped when Sandy began talking about a cruise. "You're the best goddamned CEO I know. You were suffocated by American Express, and now you're free to do whatever the hell you want." With a net worth of more than $50 million, Sandy could put his money and moxie into building another financial empire, Weinberg told him.

It was just the kind of "buck him up" advice that Sandy needed. To hell with cruising into exile. As of this moment Sandy Weill would be Wall Street's most eligible executive. At fifty-two he desperately wanted another shot at the top of the financial industry. American Express simply couldn't be the end of what had been an otherwise brilliant career. He still had a lot to prove, and he intended to prove it as fast as he could.

The first step: find a launching pad, office space that he could use to plot his return to power. Part of Sandy's "exit agreement" with American Express called for the company to provide its ex-president with office space in any of the many properties the huge company had leased or owned around Manhattan. His decision on the location was like many of his judgments—instantaneous, instinctual, and strategic. As he perused the list of available properties, his eyes focused on the Seagram Building. To Sandy that meant only one thing: the Four Seasons restaurant. Other properties might have better views, bigger space, or spiffier décor, but none of that could compete with the Seagram Building's exclusive and exorbitantly expensive eatery. Housed on the building's ground floor on Park Avenue, the Four Seasons had originated the term "power lunch" for its midday gathering of luminaries from finance, fashion, publishing, and entertainment. He might be out of work, but with the Four Seasons as his company cafeteria, Sandy would not be out of circulation. He immediately called American Express to request that his office be set up the very next day, a request that American Express, eager to be rid of the vestiges of its former president, readily obliged.

Sandy wouldn't be plotting his return alone. Jamie Dimon would be right there at his side, offering not only solace and encouragement but also his laserlike mind, capable of analyzing a company's finances faster and more thoroughly than even Sandy. As Sandy's fortunes dimmed at American Express, Dimon had figured that he would be tarred as Sandy's chief accomplice. Yet James Robinson had offered Dimon a continuing post at American Express. And, as something of a financial wunderkind, Dimon would be welcomed by any number of Wall Street firms should he want to leave American Express or Sandy Weill. But as Sandy was negotiating his departure from American Express, he told Dimon, "I would love for you to come with me," and offered to pay him an annual salary of $100,000, not as much as he would make if he stayed at American Express, but a fine salary nevertheless. "It may not work out," Sandy cautioned him. "Do what is right for you."

Dimon accepted on the spot. He pleaded with Sandy to forgo the $100,000 salary, knowing it would come straight out of his boss's pocket. "I wouldn't feel good about it," he said. "I'll go with you. When we get down the road, just give me a little more of any deal." Although the Dimons' first daughter had been born only a few weeks earlier, the family had banked enough that both Jamie and his wife, Judy, who had been a Harvard Business School classmate, were comfortable taking the risk of following Sandy. Nevertheless, Sandy, a multimillionaire, insisted that Jamie would be paid.

The two men would have important support, too, in the form of Alison Falls, who had been Sandy's assistant in the last months of his tenure at American Express. The thirty-one-year-old Falls, a former competitive swimmer with blue eyes, brown hair, and a powerful physique, had worked at American Express and other companies as a paralegal but was eager to break into mainstream business. When word went out around American Express that Sandy Weill was looking for an assistant, Falls bid for the job, despite all the rumors about how Sandy didn't fit into the executive suite and his notorious temper tantrums. During her initial interview with Sandy, she boldly told him, "I hear you're a bear to work for." Impressed by Falls's spirit and self-confidence, Sandy let out a growl. The two laughed and shook hands on the job.

Growing up as part of a large middle-class Irish-Catholic family, Falls soon found Sandy's direct manner, obvious emotion, and lack of pomp or pretense a refreshing change from the emotionless, aloof managers for whom she had worked before. He was no Rhodes scholar, she concluded, but he was someone who would help her grow, help her toughen up. It didn't take her long to figure out how to work with her new boss. Fast and efficient, Falls got things done. But she didn't take any guff. If he yelled, she yelled back. Her respect for Sandy was returned by him. After a tantrum he would often come back to her with a sheepish smile to ask, "Are you mad at me?" Sandy took to calling her "Al," and when his tenure at American Express ended, she had no second thoughts about following him wherever he went.

On the cloudy and unusually cool morning of June 27, 1985, Falls and Dimon were in the Seagram Building waiting when the movers showed up to unload Sandy's semicircular hunt desk and his favorite Chesterfield couch of deep brown leather. Sandy would have the larger office in the suite, and Dimon would take the smaller office with its standard office furniture. Falls set herself up in the reception area, but not before preparing properly for Sandy's imminent arrival. She wanted his first day of unemployment to go as smoothly and routinely as possible and knew the two things he would want the moment he arrived: coffee and stock prices. First, she made sure that Quotron stock quote terminals were installed on his desk and next to the couch. Then she prepared the morning coffee the way she knew he liked it: two scoops of Chock Full o'Nuts coffee supercharged with one scoop of Medaglia D'Oro Italian-style espresso, all brewed up in a Farberware percolator.

While those preparations were under way, Sandy headed to his new office. Crossing the Seagram Building's open plaza, with its reflecting pools and ginkgo trees, he took in the starkness of the building's postwar International style. With dark amber-tinted glass framed by bronze metal, the building looked much like a gigantic brown box. In regulation coat and tie Sandy rode the elevator to his floor. As he entered the new suite he noticed another name on the door: John Loeb. After conquering Loeb and the rest of the Wall Street old guard, Sandy was now a suite mate with a former rival, and both were out of the firms they had built.

"Where do you want the honeymooners?" Falls called out to Sandy as he swept into the office. She was referring to a Mayan pre-Columbian sculpture of an entwined couple. Sandy had long ago laid claim to the sculpture after it was purchased by his old firm, CBWL, when it was decorating its offices in the GM Building. Sandy placed it on a pedestal outside the door to his office. Delighted to see his Quotron terminals winking, he immediately set to checking stock prices, a habit developed in his earliest days as a broker. He was happy, too, to see that Falls had unpacked a dozen or more Lucite boxes encasing miniature copies of the "tombstone" advertisements that had announced each of the triumphant acquisitions that had marked his career before American Express.

A few minutes later Dimon came bounding into Sandy's new office, more animated than usual. "Everybody says you're going to get millions of offers," he reassured his boss. "This is going to be so exciting!"

As Falls began to vacuum up some of the moving debris, the phone rang. Struggling to switch off the vacuum cleaner while grabbing the phone, she heard the familiar sound of former president Gerald Ford's voice. "Just a minute, Mr. President," she chirped, putting him on hold and yelling to Sandy, "It's President Ford! It's President Ford!" The former president's call was the first of many that came in that day. Dozens of Shearson brokers and managers called to tell Sandy how grateful they were for his management skills, skills that had made them millionaires after Sandy had engineered the sale of Shearson to American Express for triple Shearson's book value. Heartened by the many well-wishers, Sandy asked Falls to keep a log of everyone who called so he could remember his friends.

He would also use the log to identify his enemies. Sandy couldn't help but note who didn't call. There was Peter Cohen, for instance, who was now completely out from under Sandy's shadow and running Shearson. And there was his onetime CBWL partner Marshall Cogan. Indeed, Cogan not only didn't call, he predicted to Michael Weinberg, who was friendly with both Sandy and Cogan, that "Sandy is unemployable. Sandy will never get a job anywhere."

Sandy, of course, knew better. He spent that first day in his new quarters discussing the possibilities with Dimon between taking phone calls. The financial-services industry was where Sandy's strengths lay, and he and Dimon discussed dozens of ideas. Dimon programmed Sandy's Quotron machines to display continuous stock quotes of companies the two thought Sandy might one day run, including such globe-girdling powerhouses as Citicorp, J.P. Morgan, and American International Group, Inc. They also put American Express's stock price on display, as well as bellwether stocks like IBM and stocks that Sandy owned, including Ford Motor Co. At one point Dimon suggested that he and Sandy establish a merchant bank, a small firm that would provide financial advice, money management, and loans to other client companies. But Sandy showed no interest in merchant banking or in being a passive investor in someone else's company. He didn't even want to be a turnaround artist, a hired gun brought in to fix someone else's company. All he really wanted was to have his own company to run again, a company that would provide the platform to grow another big business.

Yet he also confided to his young protégé that this "interlude" might not be all bad. As long as it was brief, of course. "You don't realize how hard and how much you've been working until the pressure you feel is finally gone," said the man who for the first time in years didn't have the weight of a huge enterprise pressing down on him. "This morning I didn't wake up gritting my teeth."

Joan Weill took advantage of Sandy's "interlude" to persuade him to travel. Her suggestion: a lengthy sojourn far away, to places such as Australia, New Zealand, or Africa. But the prospects of being away for more than a few weeks from whatever action might arise was more than Sandy could bear. They settled on a two-week trip to two of their favorite cities, Rome and Paris. And unlike the brief vacations they had snatched as part of Sandy's business travel, this time they would take their adult children, including Jessica's new husband (although the kids would fly coach class while Sandy and Joan enjoyed the perquisites of first class). But there was no skimping once they were in Europe. In Rome the family stayed at the venerable Hotel Hassler, perched above the Spanish Steps in the old-fashioned Trinita Dei Monti quarter. Sandy delightedly sipped martinis and wine in the hotel's rooftop garden restaurant, looking out over the dome of St. Peter's Basilica, the Coliseum, and the Pantheon. The Ritz was their home in Paris, and Sandy fully indulged his appetite for spectacular food and wine. He became a little obsessed about sampling the cuisine of Joel Robuchon, whose Paris restaurant Jamin was one of the current infatuations with Parisian gastronomes. From France, Sandy demanded that Falls get the family a reservation on impossibly short notice. He badgered his assistant several times each day: "Am I in? Did you get the reservation?" But even the ever-competent Falls couldn't deal with the time difference between New York and Paris and the restaurant staff's refusal to speak English. She finally told Sandy that if he wanted to eat at Jamin, he would have to get the reservation himself.

But overall the vacation was relaxing and fun. As a less than totally involved father who had been particularly hard on his son, an out-of-work Sandy noticed that he seemed less intimidating to Marc, twenty-nine, and Jessica, twenty-six, both of whom were promising Shearson employees.

If when he returned from Europe Sandy was surprised or disappointed that no employment offers were awaiting him, he didn't show it. Instead of offers, he found himself confronting a mountainous stack of cards and letters. "Best of luck in your new chapter," read one letter. "We hate to see you go," said a missive from a Shearson manager, and another urged Sandy to "take us with you when you land." Sandy's ego demanded such adoration, and he was thrilled at the volume of mail. "Hey, Al," he shouted to his assistant, "let's put all these in a scrapbook."

The next morning Sandy arrived in the office lugging two big white photo albums and put them on Falls's desk. A few hours later he asked her how the scrapbook was coming along. And in the afternoon he asked again. Putting aside her other work, Falls labored over the scrapbooks for much of the day, carefully slipping the letters and cards under the plastic liners. She finally had the books ready for Sandy late that afternoon. As soon as she gave them to him, he turned away from his Quotron and moved to the leather sofa where, with his feet up, he carefully reviewed each letter or note. Mostly he seemed pleased at their sentiments, but occasionally he detected a false note among the well-wishers and would grumble about it to Falls. After he finished with the scrapbooks, he once again wanted to review his phone log. Falls could tell he was still looking for certain names to show up and was hurt that they hadn't.

Still, Sandy wouldn't hold a grudge, as Falls learned the hard way. Kenneth Bialkin had been Sandy's attorney for years, and in 1985 Bialkin was serving as chair of the Anti-Defamation League of B'nai B'rith. Bialkin asked Sandy to chair a fund-raiser, which required him to get donors to buy tables. Once Sandy had recruited several people for the event, he gave Falls the list of well-known businessmen and told her to designate chairs and cochairs. Falls took the task personally. She knew who had called or sent letters after Sandy's ouster and who hadn't. If the individual had been in touch by phone or letter, she named him a chairman. "If not, screw him, just a cochair," she said to herself. She sent her list back to the league.

As soon as he saw it, Bialkin was on the phone to Sandy, noting that some very prominent and generous captains of industry were relegated to cochair status. As soon as Sandy hung up from his conversation with Bialkin, he launched into a screaming rage at Falls.

"What in the world were you thinking?" he yelled. "How can you be this stupid?"

"I did it for you!" Falls cried, her lips quivering and tears streaming down her cheeks. "I didn't like the way these people treated you. Why should we be nice to them?"

Sandy became even more infuriated. "Business is business. Emotion is emotion," he bellowed. "Sometimes you have to get past it or you won't keep moving."

Falls went home that night on the verge of quitting. But then she realized that Sandy had taught her a valuable lesson. He was willing to swallow his pride, his hurt, his shame to do what was right for business.

A MUSICAL INTERLUDE

While he welcomed most phone calls, one day shortly after he moved into his new offices Sandy found a phone message awaiting him that made him a little nervous. The world-renowned violinist Isaac Stern was asking Sandy to call him. A revered musician, Stern was also the president of Carnegie Hall, one of the most cherished classical music venues in the world. Sandy had joined the charitable board of Carnegie Hall in 1983 and valued his membership as a way to see and be seen. In 1984, while still at American

Express, Sandy had agreed to cochair with James Wolfensohn, a senior executive at Salomon Brothers, an ambitious $50-million campaign to restore the deteriorating concert hall. Why was Stern calling now? Now that Sandy no longer had a high-profile job, did Carnegie Hall still want him as a member and fund-raiser? To spare himself the embarrassment of being asked to leave, he decided to offer to resign as soon as Stern came on the line. But when the great musician heard Sandy's offer, he rejected it out of hand. He wasn't calling for any reason but to wish Sandy well. Certainly, he said, Sandy was "very much wanted" at Carnegie Hall, where his energy, brains, and contacts would be invaluable to the effort to resurrect the dilapidated concert hall. Sandy, relieved and happy to be needed, vowed to throw himself into the effort to renew the nearly century-old hall that boasted the world's finest acoustics and that had showcased every important musician, singer, orchestra, and conductor for almost one hundred years.

With his musical experience limited to playing the bass drum in military school, Sandy had not been known as a music lover through most of his adult life. His initial interest in Carnegie Hall's charitable board had almost nothing to do with music and almost everything to do with networking. A pragmatic review of the board of directors—including Wolfensohn, its chairman—convinced Sandy that the board was a place for movers and shakers, and he wanted to be among them. The savvy Stern, a brilliant strategist who had saved Carnegie Hall from the wrecking ball nearly two decades earlier, understood what made corporate moguls like Sandy tick. In his recruitment pitch, Stern told Sandy that Carnegie Hall is "the Fifty-seventh Street version of a golf course"—in other words, another good place to do business outside the office.

Whether they liked classical music or not, board members of Carnegie Hall were expected to attend concerts. Indeed, the administrative staff of the hall kept tabs on which directors attended which concerts. Sandy wasn't a total novice to the world of music—he had, from time to time, been dragged to concerts at Lincoln Center, New York's other great classical music venue—but he was far from a regular subscriber to concert series, and he knew little about music, composers, or musicians. At his first Carnegie Hall concert as a director, Sandy was initially struck by how much warmer and more intimate the hall was compared to the snobbier Lincoln Center. But as he attended more concerts, he also found that he could let the music sweep over him and erase the day's worries and concerns. As his interest in classical music grew, he found himself in a unique position to learn more about it. Besides Stern, Sandy was meeting regularly with other great musicians, including his fellow Carnegie Hall directors Yo-Yo Ma, the famous cellist, and Emanuel Ax, a celebrated pianist. Sandy bombarded the Carnegie Hall staff with questions about coming concerts, artists, and programs. At concerts he often chose to sit with Carnegie Hall's executive director, Judith Arron. Between pieces he would question her closely about the works he particularly liked. At one point she was stunned that he had caught the similarities between two different pieces by Anton Bruckner that were played by two different orchestras at two different concerts. "Sandy, you're really listening," she marveled.

But, of course, as Stern had told him, Carnegie Hall wasn't just about music. Sandy quickly discovered a major business perk: access to the hall's private Club Room, where champagne and hors d'oeuvres were served during intermission by waiters clad in formalwear. There, steps away from the first-tier boxes, the powerful businessmen on Carnegie Hall's board could relax a little, dropping their corporate armor in favor of joking and backslapping. They would whisper in corners and agree to call one another the next day. After two decades of schmoozing with brokers, Sandy was perfectly at home in the intimate confines of the Club Room, a place he called "warm and fuzzy."

Initially Sandy had been reluctant to take on the job of cochairing the fund-raising to restore Carnegie Hall. But then Stern played his trump card. Escorting Sandy onto the stage, Stern had pointed to a spot on the floor. "You know who stood there? Toscanini stood there. And Tchaikovsky conducted from that spot. And over there is where Horowitz sits." Sandy, enthralled, was moved to tears. "Listen, if you're quiet you can hear them," Stern whispered.

With his long workdays at American Express behind him, Sandy could throw himself wholeheartedly into his Carnegie Hall work. He was thrilled that other executives took his calls and agreed to dine with him to discuss the project. "It's going to cost you $100,000 to talk to me about this," he would jokingly warn his target. He confided to Dimon that when he was at American Express he always wondered if people wanted him for himself or because of his position. "It's a turn-on that people listen to me, even though I'm no longer the president of American Express or chairman of Shearson," he said.

Sandy worked out an effective pitch that often began with cocktails at the Weills' apartment, where guests would be shown a video about the hall's history. If a well-known musician was in town, the cocktail hour might include a brief recital. Then it was off to dinner at the Russian Tea Room and on to a concert at the hall. Sandy wanted to get his potential donors into the concert hall not only so they could appreciate the music, but also to provide them with a firsthand look at how their contributions would be used. In addition to pointing out the many cracks in the ceiling, he would encourage his guests to touch the walls in the box seats. "You get a special feeling when you touch the walls," he would say. The feeling was damp—water leaked into the boxes from the restrooms above.

While Sandy genuinely wanted to see Carnegie Hall restored, and he found the business contacts he made working on the board valuable, in the aftermath of American Express his association with the famous hall went beyond all that. If he had learned anything from Jim Robinson and the aloof American Express executives, it was the importance of presentation and persona as much as performance. Despite a lack of social graces or important connections, Sandy had powered his way to the top of Shearson by outperforming everyone around him. Yet he found at the highest reaches of corporate politics, that just being the best executive hadn't been enough. Sandy knew he needed the credentials and clout that would appeal to establishment companies and their boards of directors. Carnegie Hall was becoming the vehicle that would enable Sandy to go beyond the one-note theme of besting everyone in sight and on to orchestrating a place for himself and Joan among the broader cultural and social fabric of New York.

DITHERING

While Carnegie Hall gave Sandy a focal point for some of his energies, it was a far cry from having a company to run. As the summer wore on, Sandy and Dimon fell into a pattern. Both would comb *The New York Times, The Wall Street Journal,* and every major business magazine. On his way home from dinner Sandy would routinely have his driver pull over at a newsstand so he could get an early edition of the next day's *Times.* He scanned it before going to bed, hoping that some tidbit would inspire him to dream about a possible deal he could pursue the next day. Dimon would sit at home in his underwear scanning the *Times* and the *Journal* while sipping his morning coffee. At the office, where Sandy arrived punctually at 8:00 A.M. if he didn't have a power breakfast at the swank Regency Hotel, he would spend much of his time placing phone calls, while Dimon made it his task to accumulate and examine all the financial documents on any companies in which they might conceivably be interested.

Almost any possibility for getting back into business, even some deals that Dimon called "little rinky dinkers," would generate some enthusiasm in Sandy, at least briefly. There was, for instance, a tiny and ailing brokerage firm called Herzfeld & Stern, with only four offices: two in Manhattan, one in Brooklyn, and one in Great Neck, Long Island. Sandy went so far as to ask a top official at Shearson Lehman if his old firm would clear for him, since Herzfeld was far too small to support a back office of its own. But before Sandy could make a decision, Gruntal Financial Corp. came along and gobbled up Herzfeld for $4 million.

Sandy quickly lost interest in such small potatoes and his attention became focused on much bigger prey: EF Hutton Group, one of the few remaining independent brokerages among the leading firms. Earlier that year Hutton, with a national distribution network of more than six thousand brokers, had been rocked by its guilty plea in federal court to two thousand counts of fraud in connection with a check overdrafting scheme. Since then the firm had been labeled a takeover target. A small group of investors approached Sandy about taking the top job at Hutton, along with a major piece of the action if they bought the firm. Even some Hutton board members were talking about Sandy as a possible successor to the firm's chairman and chief executive officer.

In the past Sandy had been obsessive about keeping any pending deals quiet, lest his target or competitors get word that something was up and move to block him. Yet as he was pondering the possibilities in Hutton, he authorized a former aide to talk to some of his old Shearson buddies with an eye to putting together a management team if he decided to pursue Hutton. The associate called several Shearson Lehman officials with a question: "If Sandy took over EF Hutton, would you work for him?" Information is money on Wall Street, and it didn't take long for word of the calls to start leaking out. On September 19, 1985, Hutton stock soared on the rumor that the former American Express president was planning a takeover. Sandy's name still carried weight in the industry he had reshaped, and he liked seeing it move the market. But that gratification was costly. Robert Fomon, Hutton's chairman and chief executive officer, branded the rumors "absolute poppycock" and dug in his heels. With his American Express defeat still looming freshly in his mind, Sandy wasn't up to waging a hostile takeover battle.

Next to come onto his radar screen was Wausau Insurance Companies, a distressed insurer that specialized in property-casualty and workers' compensation policies. The company desperately needed a bailout, but Sandy reached the conclusion that its heavy losses made it too risky to try to save. Soon after, Nationwide Insurance Companies provided Wausau with a $250-million bailout. Even as he was considering Wausau, Sandy was also studying the possibility of buying one of the hundreds of savings and loan associations that littered the financial landscape, another move he eventually concluded was too risky.

Then came an intriguing phone call from Ivan Boesky, the nation's richest and best-known practitioner of what Wall Street called "risk arbitrage." Boesky made his money by betting on whether certain takeovers would happen. If one company made a hostile takeover offer for another company, Wall Street would immediately swing into gear to generate competing hostile or friendly offers for the target company from other companies. If an arbitrageur thought—or, better yet, knew from sources—that a new, higher offer would soon be made, he could make money by buying the stock of the target company at its current price and awaiting the higher offer. On the other hand, if he suspected or knew that the target could successfully fend off erstwhile acquirers, he could sell the stock of the target company "short," that is, borrow shares of the company and sell them at the current price only to buy shares of the target to repay the borrowed shares later, after the potential deal had collapsed and the stock price fallen. Boesky was one of the most controversial players in that arena. His book, *Merger Mania,* had just been published, and his statements on greed were showing up in all the newspapers and magazines that Sandy and Dimon read. Dimon particularly recalled one of Boesky's more outlandish remarks: "Greed is healthy. You can be greedy and still feel good about yourself."

Boesky asked Sandy to come visit him in his office high above Fifth Avenue. When Sandy and Dimon arrived they found the lean, silver-haired arbitrageur standing before a huge bank of high-tech equipment including video terminals, quote machines, news wires, and one hundred sixty telephone lines that connected him with his network of informants, traders, brokers, and staff. Sandy had been set to hear some kind of concrete proposal from Boesky, but the conversation remained on very general terms until Boesky ushered them out.

"I would never do business with that man," Sandy vehemently told Dimon as they rode the elevator down. Dimon shrugged, but he was surprised at Sandy's visceral reaction to Boesky, whom *Fortune* magazine had recently dubbed a "money machine."

As 1985 wore on it was becoming increasingly evident that Sandy wasn't going to get "the call" to go back to work. The office was becoming quieter, the calls from friends further apart, the days more monotonous. Yet it wasn't in Sandy's nature to surrender. Each day he made his way to the office in coat and tie, ready to respond if something happened. Then he would sit staring at the stock prices rolling across his Quotron screen as he smoked one cigar after another. With increasing frequency Falls would quietly phone Joan and whisper, "Call so we can hear the phone ring." Joan would then call, be put through to Sandy, and would propose they do something that afternoon.

"Sandy, let's go to the movies," Joan might say.

"Geez, Joanie, I'm working here," he would reply.

"What do you mean, you're working?" Joan would say. "What do you do?"

"Somebody might call," he would reply.

Increasingly, the best part of Sandy's day became lunch—not just because he loved to eat, but also because he could go downstairs for the daily ritual at the Four Seasons restaurant. The airy monument to modern style had been designed by the eminent architect Philip Johnson. Original art by Picasso and Miró adorned walls that soared twenty feet to the ceiling, and the interior was landscaped with trees that changed with the seasons. The restaurant's Grill Room, with its private club ambiance, was the place to see and be seen at lunch. Regulars included a cross-section of the fabulous and famous in New York: fashion designer Bill Blass, statesman Henry Kissinger, publisher S. I. Newhouse, the mogul brothers Larry and Bob Tisch, financier Ron Perelman, and entertainment executive Barry Diller. Sandy loved the power and energy of the Grill Room, a great rejuvenator for him when things were slow in the office. Coddled by the Four Seasons' impeccably courteous and solicitous managers and waiters, Sandy was among the elite. The moment Sandy was seated, a waiter would place a frosty Gibson—a martini with pickled onions rather than olives—before him. The second Gibson would arrive just as he drained the last of the first one. Although the waiters would invariably recite the entire day's menu, they knew Sandy's favorites: cherrystone clams, "very crisp" duck, veal paillard, raw Belon oysters from France, softshell crabs, or, on the rare occasion he wanted to diet, a simple baked potato with salsa. Always, they knew, he would want a red Bordeaux.

As much as Sandy enjoyed these lunches, they were taking a toll. James Calvano, a vice chairman at American Express, called one day just to check up on Sandy. "How are you doing? What are you doing?" he asked.

"We're looking at a lot of things," Sandy replied. "Very interesting. A lot of opportunities. Don't have one yet. Let's have lunch at the Four Seasons, my company cafeteria."

When Calvano arrived at Sandy's office in the Seagram Building he was reminded of "an elephants' graveyard," with the large lonely offices for Sandy and John Loeb. When he saw Sandy he was startled. Sandy had gone from being just "stocky" to looking bloated. Then, at lunch, he noticed that Sandy had three drinks instead of just two. *Drinking must help him keep his mind off having nothing to do,* Calvano thought.

Often when Sandy returned to his office upstairs there were no phone calls waiting, no meetings scheduled, and no deals to pursue. Full of heavy food and considerable drink, he would take a nap on his leather couch. If a phone call came in that Falls or Dimon knew Sandy would want to take, they would often find him asleep on his sofa with saliva dribbling down the side of his mouth and chin.

One afternoon Skip McElvery, an electrical contractor who had done work on the Weills' Greenwich mansion, came to the office to see Sandy. When he had been working on Sandy's house, McElvery, a tough but affable man, had enjoyed chatting with Sandy. But Sandy owed McElvery money—Sandy mistakenly thought the debt had been paid—and the contractor had gotten tired of waiting for payment. On this day he barged right into Sandy's office, startling the dozing mogul.

"I want my seventy grand," McElvery growled, "or there'll be a lien on your estate tomorrow."

Sandy attempted to apologize for failing to determine if the contractor was entitled to the payment. "I've been so busy I haven't had a chance," Sandy said.

"If you're so goddamned busy, why do you have the imprint of your couch on the side of your head?" the contractor retorted.

Caught with lines on his cheek from the seams of the tufted leather sofa, Sandy asked almost meekly, "Is it that noticeable?"

"Yeah, probably from across the street," McElvery said, now joking with his customer. Sandy told him to sit down and stay awhile, but the contractor found that the former CEO didn't have much to talk about. He could see he was hurting inside. Sandy told Falls to write McElvery a $70,000 check. After the contractor left, a thought hit Sandy. Falls had been complaining that her dating life had suffered along with Sandy's fate. "The guys used to think I was something when I was the assistant to the president of American Express," Falls had told Sandy. "Now you're a nobody, and so am I."

"Listen," he said to Falls, "this might be a match for you. You aren't getting any younger, and he's Irish Catholic, too." Falls, now thirty-two, tried to stop Sandy, but he pressed on. "He's a nice guy, he makes good money. Be nice to him." Soon the two were dating and later planning their wedding. McElvery asked Sandy to be his best man.

As the pace slowed in the office, Falls and Dimon found themselves in a strange relationship: Sometimes they irritated each other fiercely, while at other times they united to try to buck up their boss. Falls viewed Dimon as the brother she never had, and Dimon, who had no sisters, found himself living with strong-willed women at home and at work. But the most important bond developing in the office was between Sandy and the twenty-eight-year-old Dimon. The vibrant young man was a quick study on every prospect and showed complete devotion to his boss at the worst point in his life. Sandy admired Jamie's intelligence, confidence, and presence. Even though Sandy talked to his son, Marc, who was his Shearson stockbroker, twenty times a day about trades, he often yelled at him, criticizing his actions or abruptly giving orders. Jamie, on the other hand, would argue back at Sandy, somehow without being disrespectful. As the weeks in exile turned into months, Sandy's appreciation of and affection for his assistant, who could have had almost any job on Wall Street, grew. *Sandy loves Jamie Dimon like a son,* Falls thought.

Even as activity ebbed at the office, Sandy tried to keep alive some enthusiasm for other aspects of life. His fondness for and appreciation of fine wine inspired him to expand and improve the contents of his Greenwich wine cellar. He packed the cellar with top-of-the-line wines with an emphasis on his beloved Château Margaux. He also joined an elite and super-secret wine-tasting club. There were only nine members, and each had to pledge to keep the identity of the others secret. They met only once a year in a private room at Windows on the World, high atop the World Trade Center. Each member contributed a few of his prized bottles. At their 1985 dinner the members imbibed what one estimated to be $1 million worth of rare vintage wine.

When the British automotive manufacturer Jaguar unveiled in 1985 its sleek V12 Cabriolet, a two-seater with a convertible roof and a luxurious interior, Sandy decided to treat himself to one. "Find out how much it is and write a check for it," he commanded Falls. Because an American Express chauffeur took Sandy around Manhattan in his big Mercedes, the $40,000 Cabriolet spent most of its time in the garage of the Greenwich estate. Sandy would occasionally drive it to the nearby Century Club, the exclusive Jewish country club and the de facto golf course for Harmonie Club members, and he laughingly dubbed the Jaguar the most expensive golf cart in the world.

With his 14 handicap, he played more golf than he ever had before, mostly at the Century Club. He used the golf course as he used the Four Seasons and Carnegie Hall, as a place to reconnect with old colleagues and friends. But Joan's efforts to get Sandy to exercise more when they were in New York City met with much less enthusiasm. First she tried to get Sandy to take long walks with her in Central Park, but it was clear that he worried he might miss something if he was trudging around the park rather than sitting in his office. Then she hit on the idea of getting Jamie Dimon, a regular jogger who stayed trim despite frequent meals with his boss, to shepherd Sandy's exercise regimen. With Dimon at his side Sandy might think about the workout sessions as "business" rather than "exercise." When Dimon showed up for his first outing with Sandy he could barely restrain his laughter as his plump boss ambled out of his apartment in a brilliant neon orange sweat suit. But as the two walked—not jogged—around the Central Park reservoir, Sandy asked, almost pitifully, "Why isn't more happening?"

5

RIP VAN WINKLE INC.

As 1986 opened, Sandy resolved to make something happen. One of the many stocks he had tracked from the first day after his ouster was BankAmerica Corp. The largest bank on the West Coast, San Francisco–based BankAmerica had long been a paternalistic bureaucracy overseen by a notoriously conservative board and management, headed by CEO Samuel Armacost. The bank had suffered years of declining earnings, but the situation had become very serious early in 1986. The bank posted a massive loss of $337 million for 1985 and eliminated its dividend payment. Federal regulators were pressing the company to increase its capital base because of growing loan losses. The bank responded with hefty assets sales and boosted its provision for future loan losses. As Sandy read one news report after another about the bank's deteriorating situation, he hatched an audacious plan: He would provide BankAmerica with a $1-billion capital infusion in return for being named chief executive officer. To test the waters for his plan, Sandy called Charles Schwab, the famous founder of the discount brokerage firm that bore his name. Like Sandy, Schwab had been something of a renegade on Wall Street. And, like Sandy, Schwab had sold the firm he created to a bigger company— BankAmerica Corp., where Schwab was now a disgruntled director. Schwab loved the idea of Sandy Weill's coming in to shake up the moribund bank and urged him to make his proposal directly to Armacost and the board.

By coincidence Sandy was headed to the West Coast at the end of January anyway to participate in his second Pebble Beach National Pro-Am golf tournament, an invitation he had received because of his position at American Express and his deep affection for the game. With Schwab's encouragement, Sandy started laying plans. He called his old protégé Peter

Cohen, who was running Shearson. "Look, you have to come out here," Sandy said. "I have to walk in with something substantial to get the board's attention." His request: a commitment letter for $1 billion. "I'll call Jim," Cohen said. Despite the lingering ill will between Sandy and the two American Express executives, they were not about to turn down a chance to be involved in something as big as the takeover of BankAmerica. Cohen and Robinson flew to Pebble Beach, where they met with Sandy to draft the commitment letter, which Sandy intended to show the bank's board before their February meeting.

Sandy made his first approach to BankAmerica Corp. quietly, calling certain board members to inform them of his plan and the commitment he had in hand for the $1-billion infusion the bank so desperately needed. But the stuffy board wanted nothing to do with Sandy Weill and, with the exception of Schwab, all the board members he contacted were noncommittal or rejected Sandy's proposal outright.

Okay, if I can't do this quietly, I'll do it noisily, Sandy concluded. He would take his proposal public, hoping to bring sufficient pressure on the board from shareholders and regulators that they would have to accept his offer. On February 20, 1986 BankAmerica stock shot up 10 percent on rumors that Sandy Weill was pursuing a management shake-up. The bank confirmed the rumors and the stock went higher, eventually climbing 40 percent while Sandy's offer was on the table. Despite the stock market's endorsement of Sandy, the board remained unyielding. Board members branded Sandy's offer a blatant attempt by the unemployed executive to find a job. Rallying around Armacost, the board delivered an icy rejection: "The outside directors unanimously agreed that they have no interest in considering you as a candidate for the chief executive officer's position."

Ending speculation that he might mount a proxy fight to have shareholders elect him over the objection of the board, Sandy called off his effort. BankAmerica stock promptly plunged 10 percent in two days. (The bank reported a stunning $640-million loss in its second quarter, and the board finally ousted Armacost later that year, sending him packing with an extremely lucrative severance package.)

When Sandy arrived back in New York, Alison Falls saw a man in terrible pain. He was stung by the blatant rejection, particularly the board's attempt to paint him as a pathetic job applicant and a hostile suitor. Even worse, the rejection may have lain in the fact of his Jewish heritage. James Calvano told him as much during a golf game shortly after the failed bid:

"Sandy, I don't think the board was ready to have a Jewish person as the chief executive of BankAmerica."

"You may be right," Sandy acknowledged. "Other people told me that. They never let me in the door. They didn't want to hear what I could do. Time will tell."

Sandy's failed bid had longer-term repercussions for him and his wife, too. Joan Weill had been seeing a New York psychiatrist, Robert Willis. Willis, whose office was located near the Weills' Manhattan apartment, had been a sympathetic listener as Joan detailed the ups and downs of her husband's career and the strains that career inflicted on their relationship. She had relied heavily on Willis's counsel during the year that Sandy was in exile. And in the comfort of this confidential relationship, she also divulged information that Sandy had shared with her about his career plans. Weeks before Sandy went public with his intentions to take over BankAmerica, Joan had wondered in her sessions with Willis what would happen to her marriage and her children if Sandy really was able to pull off such a coup. Using the knowledge gleaned from their conversations, Willis quickly began buying BankAmerica Corp. shares and, after Sandy announced his intention to pursue the bank, sold those shares for a profit of more than $30,000. (Sandy and Joan did not become aware of Willis's dealings until shortly before the doctor was indicted in July 1989 on charges of insider trading. In December 1991 Joan Weill filed a $5-million lawsuit against her former psychiatrist in the U.S. District Court in Manhattan, seeking damages for breaches of fiduciary duty, confidence, and contract, as well as malpractice, fraud, and infliction of emotional distress. The suit was eventually settled for an undisclosed amount. In January 1992 Willis, who faced up to ten years in prison, was sentenced instead to five years of probation and three thousand hours of community service and fined $150,000. The judge reasoned that his long-term patients would be harmed if he were jailed and unable to treat them.)

In hindsight many of Sandy's acquaintances concluded that the Bank-America bid had been a long shot, at best. Joe Wright, a longtime friend, asked Sandy over dinner one night why, if the odds were so long, he took the chance on BankAmerica.

"I'm shooting across the bow of opportunity," Sandy replied. "I want everyone to know I'm still here. I'm a player, and I want back in the game."

If Sandy's sole purpose with his BankAmerica bid had been to attract attention, he succeeded thoroughly. The May 1986 issue of *Fortune* magazine featured a major article headlined SANFORD WEILL, 53, EXP'D MGR, GD REFS. *Fortune* described Sandy's unsolicited and spurned offer to head up BankAmerica as "the definition of chutzpah." But it went on to describe how he had transformed Shearson Lehman Brothers "from a minnow to a whale" and spoke glowingly of him as a "decisive, pragmatic, do-it-now manager." Despite the BankAmerica debacle, it said, Sandy Weill had a reputation for executing a "strong turnaround plan and a strong sense of urgency."

Fortune's clever headline caught the eye of Robert Volland in Baltimore, Maryland. Volland was the vice president for finance at Commercial Credit Company, a consumer-loan outfit owned by the struggling computer maker Control Data Corp. For months Volland had been watching his company and its parent firm sinking into increasingly dire financial straits. Control Data had once been the world leader in the manufacture and sale of computer disk drives, one of the few technology companies to prosper in the huge shadow cast by International Business Machines. Control Data had bought Commercial Credit in 1968, intent on using it to help finance the sale and lease of computer systems. But Control Data had begun to encounter fierce competition from the Japanese in the early 1980s. At the same time, personal computers were starting to supplant the big mainframes for which Control Data manufactured disk drives. The new PCs used smaller, cheaper "floppy" disks that Control Data simply couldn't manufacture cheaply enough. In the fall of 1985, Control Data defaulted on its bank loans and pledged the stock of Commercial Credit as collateral. The loss-plagued computer maker also borrowed heavily from Commercial Credit, creating concerns among the lenders who financed Commercial Credit. As Commercial Credit's cost of borrowing rose, it was becoming increasingly difficult to compete profitably with other big consumer lenders like Beneficial Corp. and Household International Inc. Control Data put Commercial Credit up for sale, but the finance unit's poor performance, high borrowing costs, and inefficient branch offices scared away suitors. With no takers, Control Data had begun paring away Commercial Credit's assets. Volland was fearful his company would be liquidated out of existence to keep its parent from bankruptcy.

Volland took a few minutes to read the article about the out-of-work executive. Of course, he had heard of Sandy Weill. But he hadn't realized that Sandy was basically unemployed and looking for work. He picked up the magazine and walked into the office next door where Paul Burner, Commercial Credit's assistant treasurer, was hard at work.

"Have you seen this?" Volland asked, tossing the magazine on Burner's desk. "This is the kind of guy we need. Let's see if he's interested."

Burner skimmed the article and was immediately skeptical. "This is a man of great accomplishments in New York," he told Volland. "What makes you think he'd even look at us down here in Baltimore?"

"But *Fortune* says he's not that busy," Volland replied.

"What could it hurt to call?" Burner agreed.

Before this moment neither Volland nor Burner had even entertained the notion of being negotiators of big deals. Indeed, they were initially surprised that they were even able to obtain Sandy Weill's phone number from directory information in New York. Surprise turned to shock when Alison Falls answered the phone. And the two nearly fainted when she said, "I'll put him on."

A moment later they heard a pronounced Brooklyn accent bark into the phone: "This is Sandy Weill."

Their voices shaking with nervousness, the two young executives huddled over a speakerphone to pitch Commercial Credit as a "great opportunity" for someone with Sandy's background and skills. He was just the kind of leader the company needed, they said. With little discussion of Commercial Credit's specifics, Sandy asked them to come to his office in two days. They hung up and looked at each other in stunned amazement. They were going to meet with Sandy Weill! *This man saved a dozen securities firms in the 1970s,* Burner thought. *Maybe he can save us.* The surge of adrenaline overpowered Burner's simultaneous queasiness about going behind his bosses' backs to appeal directly to Sandy.

When Sandy hung up, he briefed Dimon on the call and asked him to hunt down the latest SEC filings and other documents on Commercial Credit and Control Data. Sandy hadn't needed to ask his callers much about the company because he was already familiar with it. As president of American Express, Sandy had reviewed—and rejected—the Baltimore company when it was first being shopped around by Control Data in 1984. Commercial Credit simply wasn't in American Express's league; it was a messy mix of mediocre financial services peddled to a largely blue-collar customer base. Yet two years later the ailing finance company didn't seem so pedestrian to a jobless CEO desperate to get back into the financial-services industry. Given the trouble he had fitting into the elite management of American Express, maybe a more down-and-dirty business devoted to working-class families would be a better fit. At least it was worth a look.

As Volland and Burner set out from Baltimore to pay their visit to Sandy, they fretted that someone from Commercial Credit would discover where they were going and what they were doing. They worried about keeping the meeting a secret and feared they would be fired if anyone knew about it. But they also feared that their bosses would laugh at the idea of recruiting Sandy Weill to run the company. They convinced themselves that their mission was to save Commercial Credit. If they couldn't save it, they wouldn't have jobs anyway. And what the hell, they were going to meet Sandy Weill! The risk was worth it.

When they arrived at the Seagram Building a very nervous Volland and Burner braced themselves to meet a real power broker. But rather than the stern and forbidding countenance they expected, Sandy, puffing a cigar, greeted them warmly and ushered them into his office, where he introduced them to Jamie Dimon. He immediately got down to business: "Why do you think I should be interested in Commercial Credit?"

The Baltimore visitors acknowledged that their company didn't seem that attractive at first blush. It's saddled with several stray and underperforming businesses, they told Sandy and Dimon, including an equipment-leasing unit in Israel and a unit that leased cars to ex-convicts, some of whom made off with the vehicles without paying. It had a $316-million portfolio of questionable foreign loans, mostly to Mexico, Brazil, and Venezuela. And it had been losing money hand over fist in 1985.

But, Burner hastened to add, "it has some real jewels in its core business of consumer lending," and the company's financial performance had been improving in 1986, suggesting a turnaround was possible. "Come take over Commercial Credit," Burner pleaded. "We need a strong executive with your impressive background."

Finding hidden jewels, slashing unwanted assets, and being a strong manager—those were all things that Sandy Weill knew he did better than anyone else. He and Dimon bombarded the young Commercial Credit managers with dozens of questions, demonstrating a keen understanding of where the problems and the opportunities in a company like Commercial Credit could be found. Then Sandy assured them he would consider their proposal and walked them to the door.

All the way back to Baltimore, Volland and Burner marveled to each other about how "down to earth," "practical," and "just plain human" Sandy was. "He had no arrogance," Burner told Volland, "and *he* thanked *us* for coming!"

When Volland and Burner made their pitch to Sandy, they simply wanted him to be the president of their company and to turn it around. They didn't realize that just running a company like Commercial Credit wasn't something that interested Sandy. He not only wanted to run something, he wanted to be the absolute ruler of whatever he ran. Unless Sandy and Dimon could figure out a way to free Commercial Credit from Control Data and be in full control of the finance company, this prospect would join the three hundred or so other financial companies on the waste heap of rejected ideas.

Sandy and Dimon immediately began brainstorming ways to make Commercial Credit independent as they evaluated it as a stand-alone business. They were pleasantly surprised that it wasn't as dinky as they originally thought. The company had offices in twenty-eight states, annual revenues of $1.1 billion, and assets totaling $5.5 billion—"not much smaller than Shearson," Sandy observed. Dimon constructed a chart plotting the ten-year financial performance of similar finance companies. Every decent company had a return on equity in excess of 15 percent and an annual growth rate of 10 percent or more. Not surprisingly, Commercial Credit ranked near the bottom with a measly 4 percent return on equity. But that was okay with Sandy and Dimon. All they had to do was to manage Commercial Credit so that it reached the industry averages on growth and return on equity. That would produce a powerful surge in the company's earnings and, ultimately, in its stock price if it was independent. Dimon noted that Commercial Credit wasn't expanding the number of loan offices it had and seemed complacent simply to serve existing customers. That prompted Sandy to begin calling the company Rip Van Winkle. "It's been fast asleep," he said. "It has six hundred thousand customers, and I don't see why it can't have five million." What's more, Commercial Credit was in an unregulated and largely ignored industry that was highly fragmented. While there were big players like Commercial Credit and its chief competitors, Household and Beneficial, most of the twenty-eight thousand consumer-finance offices around the nation were parts of very small firms. That made the potential for acquisitions enormous, a substantial attraction to a world-class deal maker like Sandy. As the builder of Shearson, he could see that the current state of the consumer-finance business closely resembled the brokerage industry of fifteen years earlier.

Commercial Credit's string of some four hundred lending offices typi-

cally consisted of four employees each, made personal loans averaging
$4,000 and real-estate loans averaging $19,000, mostly at interest rates of
18 percent to 23 percent. "It's better than banking," chortled Dimon. "It's
a high-margin business with lots of small risks." He noted that unlike banks,
which borrow funds for short periods and lend them for long periods,
consumer-finance companies mostly made short-term loans at high rates
while borrowing for long periods at low rates. In practical terms, that
meant that rising interest rates, which hurt bank earnings badly, wouldn't
be a significant factor for a consumer-finance company.

Sandy agreed: "It's not the kind of business where you need big reserves to protect yourself from the unknown, because you write off a loan
in six months." In other words, Commercial Credit had the potential to be
an enormous cash cow as long as it could borrow low and lend high. Of
course, one of Commercial Credit's major problems was that it couldn't
borrow low, because lenders were afraid Control Data's cascading problems would mean any loans they made to Commercial Credit might not be
repaid. The debt-ratings agencies had downgraded Commercial Credit's
credit rating several times. Thus lenders demanded much higher interest
rates to make loans to the company, and those higher rates hurt Commercial Credit's profits. Fixing the company's credit rating was a must,
Sandy knew.

Alison Falls took in all this excited analysis from her vantage point in
the reception area. Finally, she couldn't restrain herself. These two men,
living in their pricey Manhattan apartments, driving expensive cars, and
eating at the best restaurants, didn't really grasp the essence of Commercial Credit and the exorbitant interest rates it charged borrowers who had
no other place to turn. "Hey, guys, this is the loan-sharking business," Falls
interjected. " 'Consumer finance' is just a nice way to describe it. My grandmother in Queens used to go there for a loan. My mother's first refrigerator was financed through Commercial Credit."

Immediately Sandy and Dimon leapt to the defense of their possible new
employer. "This is Main Street, America," Sandy scolded her, implying that
anyone who thought finance should be restricted to the august corridors of
Wall Street was a snob. Dimon, too, was indignant: "These customers are the
same ones McDonald's sells hamburgers to." Suddenly Sandy was comparing Commercial Credit's loan offices to Wal-Mart stores.

"That's our model," he told Dimon, noting that it was a huge company
with a 30 percent annual growth rate that was built on selling stuff mostly

to blue-collar workers in small communities. "Think of it as a platform," Sandy said. "We need a financial-services company to grow from."

Over the next several days Dimon and Sandy continued to analyze Commercial Credit, looking for any flaws that might make the company undesirable. Dimon placed numerous confidential calls to Volland and Burner, using their intimate knowledge of the company's finances to test hypotheses and develop more refined analyses. Falls nicknamed the Commercial Credit duo "Deep Throat." While the two men never disclosed inside information, they served an invaluable role in helping Sandy and Dimon identify which assets were vital to their developing strategy and which could be sold for cash.

Although Sandy had learned his lesson about keeping pending deals quiet after rumors spoiled his attempt to lead EF Hutton, he did want the input of one more person. Robert Lipp, one of three presidents at Chemical Bank, had been the architect of that bank's very successful retail banking strategy and had ambitions for a bigger role. But those ambitions were likely to be blocked at Chemical by the bank's chairman, Walter V. Shipley, who was only two years older than Lipp. When rumors about Sandy's behind-the-scenes efforts to take over BankAmerica had begun sprouting, Lipp, who knew Sandy casually through New York charitable circles, had requested a meeting with Sandy to tell him that he might be available to help him if Sandy's bold bid for the top spot at BankAmerica succeeded. Now Sandy wanted to hear what Lipp might say about Commercial Credit. He called Lipp and told him in confidence what he was thinking about and asked the banker to stop by the Greenwich house Sunday morning. When Lipp arrived, he was armed with several long sheets of yellow paper on which he had jotted notes and analysis while doing some independent research on Commercial Credit. Sitting on the back porch overlooking the garden, Lipp told Sandy and Dimon how Commercial Credit's branch system could be run more efficiently and effectively. Sandy surmised during their conversation that Lipp might be interested in—and, more important, extremely valuable at—helping run the consumer-lending outfit. If Sandy could win it.

Soon after the back porch meeting, the Weills invited the Lipps to dinner at the Greenwich mansion. Knowing full well what was happening, Lipp told his wife, Bari, a fashion industry executive, that the evening would be the "requisite dinner" to see if Sandy and, more important, Joan thought the two men could build a partnership. "With Sandy, it's not just business, it's a personal relationship," he told her. Dressed casually in sweaters and slacks, the two couples had drinks on the patio and enjoyed one another enormously. Lipp and Sandy shared the same hands-on, no-nonsense management style and a dry wit; Joan and Bari talked about their children—each couple had a son and daughter—and fashion. Bob Lipp passed the test.

Meanwhile, Control Data was running out of ideas on how to unload Commercial Credit. Security Pacific Corp. took a good, hard look at the company but walked away after doing due diligence. With its access to fresh capital choked off, Commercial Credit was having to sell any business it could to meet maturing debts, and Charles Prince, the company's lawyer, told his bosses there simply weren't any takers for the core consumer-lending business.

Then along came Sandy Weill. Flying on the budget-based airline People Express to Minneapolis, Sandy, Dimon, and Morgan Stanley investment banker Robert Greenhill, a longtime friend and advisor to Sandy, called on Control Data chairman Robert Price. The offer they made was a variation on Sandy's BankAmerica pitch: Sandy would become chief executive of Commercial Credit, and from that vantage point he would help Control Data spin off the company in a public offering. Under the plan the computer maker would sell an 80 percent stake in Commercial Credit, 70 percent to the public and 10 percent to the management group Sandy headed. Suddenly Price had a solution to the crushing problems facing his company. Desperate for the cash that the spin-off of Commercial Credit would make available, he agreed almost instantly to Sandy's plan.

Within days Control Data's board gave its consent to the deal and lawyer Chuck Prince was dispatched in utmost secrecy to thrash out the details with Sandy. Meeting in the conference room at Ken Bialkin's law firm, Prince was shocked at how aggressively Sandy negotiated. It was as if every dollar would be coming directly out of his own wallet. While that wasn't strictly true, it was a fact that Sandy would be putting up $6 million of his own money to buy Commercial Credit stock at a negotiated price of $18 a share. Dimon was included in the negotiations, too; he had managed to scrape together $425,000 to buy Commercial Credit stock. When Prince presented the entire agreement to Sandy, including the details of Sandy's employment package, he joked that "I know I'm making at least one good hire in my life." Despite the head-to-head negotiations they had just gone through, Sandy liked the young lawyer's humor and attention to detail.

The time came to get a closer look at just what he was buying and to see if he and Commercial Credit's current chairman had anything in common. He asked Falls to do a little research on Joe Minutilli, and as he prepared to leave the office for Baltimore he quizzed her about the man.

"Does he have a family?" he asked.

"No family," Falls replied.

"How long has he been married?"

"Never married," Falls said.

"Does he play golf?" Sandy inquired.

"Can't tell," she said.

"Do we have anything in common?" Sandy asked plaintively.

"He owns a restaurant somewhere," Falls volunteered.

"Great, I love to eat in restaurants," Sandy said on his way out the door.

Minutilli had not been informed of the negotiations between Sandy and Control Data until the deal had been agreed upon. At age fifty-eight Minutilli had already been planning to retire in the next few years after a thirty-five-year career at Commercial Credit that began as a repo man, chasing down deadbeats and repossessing their cars. With a partner Minutilli owned a fancy classic American restaurant called Kirby's in a historic mansion in Lewistown, Pennsylvania. One of Minutilli's hobbies was restoring historic buildings; the mansion that housed the restaurant had been one of his early efforts. He also owned a farm in Port Royal, Pennsylvania, and he had restored the large stone farmhouse that had been built in the 1820s. He loved fine wine and antiques.

Their meeting took place in a Baltimore hotel restaurant that Minutilli selected as a place where the two men wouldn't be seen by local notables. Sandy, who normally made the wine selection for a dinner, left it up to Minutilli, who ordered a fine red to accompany their dinner of red meat. Both smoked voraciously during the meal, Sandy puffing a cigar and Minutilli inhaling one cigarette after another. Minutilli, a reserved man, was surprised at how much he liked the candid man who would replace him. Sandy, in turn, found that he liked and respected Minutilli, both for their shared interests as well as Minutilli's grace in accepting the fait accompli presented him.

In subsequent trips to Baltimore in the early fall of 1986 Sandy and Dimon concluded that their ambitious plan to revitalize Commercial Credit would require more management horsepower than the company had available. The first call went to James Calvano. Sandy had first met Calvano in the summer of 1981 when the two were seated next to each other on American Express's jet en route to a golf outing that the company sponsored for its travel-related clients at the famed Augusta National golf course. Calvano was president of Avis Rent a Car, and during the flight Sandy peppered him with questions about Avis's staffing, expenses, and cost controls, interspersing his questions with grousing about American Express's high overhead costs. When, later that summer, Sandy read news accounts that Calvano was leaving Avis for "personal reasons"—he had lost a battle with a major shareholder over Avis's long-term strategy—he alerted his colleagues in American Express's travel-related business that they might want to talk to Calvano. Gerstner hired him in October 1981, and Calvano rose quickly to become a vice chairman. But after Sandy's departure, relations between Calvano and Gerstner deteriorated, and Calvano had resigned early in 1986.

"Meet me in Baltimore for lunch," Sandy told Calvano. "I've found a place with great crab cakes."

"Sandy, for Christ's sake, Baltimore?" Calvano replied. "Why? What are we going to talk about?"

"You'll love the crab cakes," Sandy demurred.

"I don't happen to like them," Calvano said, urging Sandy to spill the beans.

"I can't tell you until I see you in person," Sandy said. "Just get down here."

Assuming that Sandy had something cooking that might be worth talking about, Calvano drove from his New Jersey home to Baltimore. At lunch Sandy told him about his plans for Commercial Credit.

Calvano's initial reaction was laughter. "Who? What? Commercial Credit?"

For two executives who had been at the apex of the finance industry to be talking about making comebacks through a consumer-finance company at the bottom of the food chain struck Calvano as ludicrous. "Sandy, this just doesn't compute. Are you really serious?" he asked.

Wincing at the put-down, Sandy persevered. "Commercial Credit is just like any other financial-services business—you take care of customers, build distribution, cut costs, develop a brand." Calvano still didn't seem convinced, but Sandy kept pressing. "We can make money with this company. It can be a good platform." The rest of the lunch was spent discussing how they could build and grow the company.

On Friday, September 12, 1986, Control Data announced its agreement with Sandy Weill to spin off Commercial Credit. The computer maker's chairman praised Sandy's ambitious plan and his proven track record and predicted a great future for Commercial Credit. That forecast was endorsed by the bond ratings agencies: Both Standard & Poor's Corp. and Moody's Investors Service promptly raised Commercial Credit's debt ratings, making it instantly easier for the company to borrow much-needed cash to finance operations.

The press coverage of the announcement focused more on Sandy than on the ailing Control Data. "Top executives at Merrill Lynch & Co. and EF Hutton Group can breathe easier: Sandy Weill finally got a job," wrote *BusinessWeek*. The fifty-three-year-old wasn't returning to the business he knows best, the magazine noted, but rather the "comparatively unglamorous field of consumer finance."

The following Tuesday, Sandy, Dimon, and Bialkin swooped into Baltimore to meet Commercial Credit's managers, all of whom had been furnished a package detailing Sandy's background as "one of America's most distinguished financial-service executives." Chuck Prince, who was the only manager besides Minutilli and Sandy's two "Deep Throat" sources to have met the new boss, sensed his colleagues' excitement at being liberated from their overbearing parent company by this "A-team" from the financial capital of the world.

With the public sale of Commercial Credit stock pending, Sandy told his new staff that SEC regulations forbade him from giving out details about the plans he had for the company. "My lawyers told me all I can say is that I'm happy," he said. "I'm happy, believe me, I'm happy." Then he tried to convey some measure of how happy he was by recounting his management philosophy. "We're all going to have a heck of a lot of fun doing this and be proud of what we build," he concluded. "Let's not do this because we have to do it for the paycheck. Let's do it because we love it."

When Sandy returned to New York City, he found an office transformed from lethargic to lively. "The phone calls have started, baby," Falls chirped to Sandy when he walked in the next morning. Now that he was a fully employed executive again, Sandy was getting congratulatory calls from executives around the country. But the person he really wanted to talk to was the man who had sought him out when he seemed to have no friends: Bob Lipp. On the evening of Rosh Hashanah, Sandy called Lipp at home, where he was entertaining guests. "I just want to wish you a happy new year,"

Sandy told Lipp, "and to tell you how much I would love for you to join me at Commercial Credit." Lipp didn't have to be sold. He jumped at the chance to be downwardly mobile in return for the upside potential of helping build a financial conglomerate from scratch and reaping big financial rewards.

A public company with all its constituencies and regulations is a very different animal from the partnerships that Sandy used to run. Thus he wasn't able to offer Lipp, Dimon, Calvano, and others he quickly recruited to his management team huge stakes in the company, because the shares weren't his to offer. But he did try to create something like the entrepreneurial environment that can make partnerships so effective. He asked each of his new executives to take pay cuts, which could be offset by generous stock options potentially worth millions. "If we do this right, we will all do very well," Sandy cryptically told Calvano, who had agreed to join Sandy despite his early reservations. Sandy structured the spin-off so his executive ranks would own 10 percent of the company at a discounted price, a huge incentive to think like partners and work to increase the price of Commercial Credit stock.

In late October, 38 million shares of Commercial Credit were sold to investors in one of the largest offerings in the nation's history. Sandy and Joan Weill went to the floor of the New York Stock Exchange for the market's opening. At Sandy's insistence, Joan, for good luck, bought the first share of Commercial Credit stock, traded under the new symbol CCC. Sandy was giddy with excitement to once again be at the helm of a public company, and lots of other investors seemed giddy at the prospect as well. Many of the investors who placed orders for CCC that day knew little or nothing about the obscure lowbrow company. Instead, they were betting on Sandy Weill, roughly the equivalent of betting on a jockey rather than a horse. Many of the 5,700 brokers at Shearson Lehman, staunch believers in their former boss, bought millions of shares for the portfolios of their clients. The offering raised $850 million and, with the stock selling at $20.50, Sandy had an immediate paper gain of nearly $700,000 on the 273,733 shares he had purchased just a week earlier for $18 a share. But he wasn't thinking short term. He knew that with his options to purchase another 3.3 million shares in the future at $19.48 a share, he would make $3.3 million for every dollar Commercial Credit stock rose. As chairman, Sandy had the power to award options to his executives as well. Dimon, his loyal assistant through exile and the new chief financial officer of Commercial Credit, was given the second greatest number of options. Shocking the banking world with his departure from Chemical, Lipp took a 50 percent pay cut from his $680,000 salary to become Commercial Credit's executive vice president in charge of consumer finance. He received slightly fewer options than Dimon.

As the head of the newly public company, Sandy wanted to throw a party for his troops when he planned to visit the next week. He called the human-resources director, Barry Mannes, who recommended that the meeting be held in the cafeteria, the biggest room in the building. "Let's have it at five-thirty," Sandy suggested. "Then we'll have cocktails and have it catered."

"Sandy, five-thirty is too late," Mannes replied. "Baltimore is not New York. There's no subway system. If employees don't catch their bus at five, they might be here until nine o'clock."

Bewildered at this rush to leave work, Sandy agreed to start the party at four. But when he hung up, he knew that kind of clock watching would be a thing of the past for anyone who wanted to work under his regime.

The next week found Sandy nervously pacing the executive floor of Commercial Credit's 1950s-vintage headquarters in downtown Baltimore. The party would start in a few minutes. "I just want to make sure I say the right thing," Sandy muttered to no one in particular. Michelle Krabbe, the executive-office manager, overheard the remark and thought to herself, *My god, here is this man who just took us public and he's scared to death to speak.* She was relieved. *He's human after all,* she thought.

Many Commercial Credit employees weren't as sure as Krabbe that their new boss *was* human. All week long the workers had been circulating old press clippings about Sandy—the ruthless cost cutter, the hot-tempered tyrant, the insatiable deal maker. The rank and file were thrilled that Commercial Credit was getting a second chance under Sandy Weill, but overlaying the thrill was individual terror for their own jobs. The afternoon of the party a steady stream of employees found excuses to visit the executive floor, just to catch a glimpse of Sandy. With his portly profile, he didn't look too ominous; in fact, he wasn't very impressive looking at all, they whispered. Around the water coolers and in the bathrooms that afternoon, a consensus developed. "Commercial Credit is in desperate shape," George Hupfer, a tax manager, told his colleagues. "If we don't get behind Sandy, we're all cooked anyway. We have to throw in our fates with his."

When Sandy entered the bare-bones company cafeteria for the party, hundreds of employees gave him a hero's welcome. Because nearly every person at headquarters was crammed into the cafeteria and spilling out the doors, the Formica tables and chairs had been shoved against the walls, which were decorated with huge banners declaring INDEPENDENCE DAY. Minutilli, the previous chairman who would be put on the new board of directors, presented Sandy with a big black T-shirt with Sandy's face silk-screened on the front. Emblazoned around Sandy's smiling face were the slogans the Commercial Credit managers had discerned as Sandy's philosophy: WORK HARD! HAVE FUN! BUY COMMERCIAL CREDIT STOCK!

With the crowd cheering, Sandy pulled the T-shirt over his dress shirt and tie. Still a terrible and frightened speaker, he got out a few words. "I believe most of all we should be a team. We're working together," he said. "We're here to help each other, not to hurt each other." Then he told everyone, "Call me Sandy. No calling people Mr. This or Mr. That." The employees cheered. Trying to bring his speech to a close, Sandy asked if anyone had questions for him.

The head of the strategic planning department took the microphone and asked: "Sandy, can you share with us your philosophy of strategic planning?"

"I get up in the morning, I read *The Wall Street Journal,* and I make a strategic plan for the day," Sandy responded. The department head looked stricken. This was someone who created massive books of five-year plans, and it was painfully clear the new boss would have no use for all those plans. After several other questions, a longtime employee from the accounts-payable department took the microphone.

"Mr. Weill, tell us the truth. You've come here from New York to rape us," she said as everyone stood in stunned silence. "You will scrunch us down and then sell us to the highest bidder."

"That's absolutely wrong," Sandy snapped. "I have built one empire in my life—which was Shearson. And I want to do it one more time before I retire."

His forceful answer drew more cheers. He offered a toast to Commercial Credit's new status as a publicly traded and independent company. Then Sandy and Minutilli cut the three-foot-long "freedom cake," ending the official presentation. Employees began circling around Sandy to introduce themselves and shake his hand.

After a few hours of greeting and drinking, Sandy headed up to the executive floor. He just stood there for several minutes, looking at the offices and out the window at Baltimore's Inner Harbor. Rose Wilz, an executive secretary, ran into him as she fetched her bag to go home.

"Congratulations," she said. "It looks like everything is going well."

Sandy looked at her tentatively, still uncomfortable with small talk. "I have a job!" he blurted.

"Well, good night" was all Wilz could respond to such a curious statement.

CENTER STAGE

As the most tumultuous year in his life drew to a close, Sandy had the business title he craved: chairman. And he also had finally obtained the title that would mark his arrival among the cream of New York City's society circles: benefactor. When Sandy agreed to cochair with James Wolfensohn the $50-million effort to restore Carnegie Hall, he knew that he would have to put his money where his mouth was. He determined early on to make a bold statement about his intentions to be part of New York's elite. Wolfensohn had already contributed $1 million to the restoration fund. Social doyenne Brooke Astor had upped the ante to $2 million. Then Sandy Weill stepped forward and pledged $2.5 million, the single largest contribution to the hall since Andrew Carnegie had funded construction of the magnificent auditorium in 1891 with a gift of $3 million.

Sandy's contribution paid enormous dividends. The debut of the refurbished hall in a gala concert on December 15, 1986, also marked the debut of Sandy among New York society. On this crisp wintry night, Sandy and Joan, along with a distinguished group of New York dignitaries, arrived at Carnegie Hall in a parade of horse-drawn carriages. As they walked down the red carpet under the floodlit marquee of the newly resplendent hall, Sandy and Joan were greeted by television cameras and the blinding flash of strobe lights as photographers captured Manhattan's most prominent entertainers, moguls, socialites, and politicians. Once inside the glitziest social event of the season, the Weills sipped champagne alongside Rockefellers, Astors, Vanderbilts, and Kennedys. As the concertgoers made their way to the new red velvet seats, the Weills were shown to one of the prime locations in the hall—a first-tier box, front and center. Other titans of business and industry, including Armand Hammer, Rupert Murdoch, John Gutfreund, Carl Icahn, and William S. Paley, sat in boxes along the side. A glimpse around him told Sandy that his seats were even better than those of fashion designers Oscar de la Renta and Ralph Lauren (who designed the new red-and-black uniforms for the hall's ushers), actor Gregory Peck, *Dallas* star Larry Hagman, Maureen Reagan, Beverly Sills, and Mayor Ed Koch.

In the packed auditorium, Sandy and Joan Weill bumped into George Sheinberg, the former American Express treasurer who had rejoined Shearson after falling out with Sandy over the purchase of IDS. Sandy had cut off all contact with Sheinberg. Now they awkwardly stood face-to-face for a moment.

"I guess I should thank you for helping revive Carnegie Hall," Sheinberg stammered. Sandy gave him an icy stare and moved into the crowd. Turning to his date that evening, Sheinberg said, "I used to be that man's best friend."

With his newfound appreciation of classical music, Sandy thoroughly enjoyed the four-hour concert, featuring the New York Philharmonic under the direction of Zubin Mehta. The orchestra performed Wagner, Haydn, and a new piece written especially for the event by Leonard Bernstein. Pianist Vladimir Horowitz gave a surprise performance, followed by cellist Yo-Yo Ma, mezzo-soprano Marilyn Horne, and virtuoso violinist Stern. After the intermission, Frank Sinatra, accompanied by the Peter Duchin Orchestra, sang crowd favorites including "Mack the Knife" and "Theme from New York, New York." But not even such bountiful and beautiful music could compare with the thrill that Sandy had felt when the concert opened with "The Star-Spangled Banner" and he was brought to center stage and publicly thanked by Isaac Stern for heading the effort to restore the hall to its former splendor.

After the concert, the Weills were guests at Petrossian restaurant at a small, exclusive supper for the celebrity performers. Dining on caviar, smoked salmon, medallions of veal, and French pastries, along with plenty of Veuve Clicquot champagne, Sandy relished his star treatment until three o'clock in the morning.

With $2.5 million, Sandy had secured the recognition usually accorded Brooke Astor and David Rockefeller. Carnegie Hall even named the restored and smaller recital hall for Joan and him. His gift had purchased a significant niche in the upper reaches of the New York philanthropic and cultural world. From now on, references to Sandy wouldn't include solely his Jewish and Brooklyn roots, but also his new place in New York's establishment.

A media hound, Sandy was thrilled to see his photograph in New York's *Newsday* the next morning. But when he read the caption, he realized he still had a way to go in gaining the recognition he craved from the press. The caption mistakenly identified him as the opera singer Sherrill Milnes. But then he read something even better than he could have imagined. The *Chicago Tribune*'s article on the gala mentioned him in the same paragraph with the Rockefellers and Astors! Sanford Weill was identified as one of the "modern-day equivalents of Carnegie, Mellon, and Morgan."

He knew he had better work miracles at Commercial Credit to live up to that billing.

6

BACKWATER MOGUL

S andy Weill hated waiting, and it was especially vexing to be waiting today. As he plowed through a stack of newspapers, he kept glancing up at the hurried throng of early passengers sweeping past the Piedmont Airlines gate in New York's LaGuardia Airport. Dawn was creeping across the New York skyline on this first Monday of 1987, and business travelers were getting back into the swing of things after the holidays. In their hurry to return to business, none of them could appreciate that the pudgy man fidgeting in the Piedmont gate area wasn't waiting just for his flight to begin. Sandy Weill was waiting to start his longed-for comeback.

Perennially ahead of schedule, he was also waiting for his staff of newly appointed senior executives to join him for the flight to Baltimore. Although Sandy had made several treks to Baltimore to survey the territory at Commercial Credit, today would be the first time that the new management team would take full command of the company.

Excited and apprehensive, Sandy welcomed each member of his new team as they arrived at the gate for the 7:10 A.M. flight. As always, Jamie Dimon was there, on his way to take up his post as a senior vice president and the chief financial officer of Commercial Credit at the tender age of thirty. There was Bob Lipp, the former president of Chemical Bank who would be Commercial Credit's executive vice president in charge of consumer financial services. James Calvano joined the entourage to serve under Lipp as senior vice president of the consumer group. Joseph DeAlessandro, who had made millions in salary, bonus, and stock grants as a corporate vice president at American International Group, had left that post to become Sandy's senior vice president of insurance services. John Fowler, formerly an executive vice president of Warner Amex Cable Communications, was heading to Baltimore as Commercial Credit's new senior

125

vice president of corporate development. F. Gregory Fitz-Gerald, formerly the chief financial officer at Merrill Lynch, would be executive vice president in charge of Commercial Credit's corporate staff and services, and John R. Edds, formerly a vice president of Citibank, would be senior vice president of international and commercial services and corporate credit. John Hsu, who had left his post as managing partner of Greenspan O'Neil Inc., an economic consulting service, would be senior vice president in charge of running Commercial Credit's investments.

The nervous energy of all that high-powered talent crackled in the gate area, and the jokes flew fast and furious. Sandy recalled for them the reaction of his longtime friend Arthur Zankel when Zankel first heard about the high-powered talent who had agreed to leave their posts in fast-paced New York to join Sandy in the city of Babe Ruth and H. L. Mencken.

"Sandy, why are you laying all this talent on this little company?" Zankel had asked.

"You'll see in a year," Sandy had told him.

Toting expensive suit bags filled with enough clothes for a week's stay in Baltimore, the executives laughed about leaving their women and children behind as they set out on their "rescue mission." It was like going off to camp, they joked, little knowing how apt the comparison would become as they embarked on a regimen that would throw them together day in and day out in an intense bonding process with their fellow "campers."

Accustomed to private jets or at least first-class seating, the Maryland-bound New Yorkers took the no-frills accommodations on the all-coach Piedmont jet in stride. Making his way down the narrow aisle, Bob Lipp swiped a stack of plastic foam coffee cups. When the executives were seated, he took out a pen and scribbled "First Class" on them before handing them out to his new comrades. "I'm doing my part to upgrade the service here," he quipped.

Jim Calvano sat down next to Lipp, his new boss, for the thirty-five-minute flight. The commuting executives had been given the choice of two Baltimore hotels: the new Harbor Court luxury hotel with every amenity but a ten-minute walk from the office, or a converted apartment building with meager kitchens and utilitarian bedrooms located next door to Commercial Credit. Lipp casually asked Calvano where he would be checking in that evening. Calvano startled him by moving in close over his armrest to answer.

"Look, you don't know Sandy like I do," Calvano whispered. "One of the great things I can do for you is help you live with Sandy."

Lipp looked around nervously and giggled. "What are you talking about?" he inquired sheepishly. "I'm not living with Sandy; I'm working with Sandy."

Calvano laughed at Lipp's naïveté. Clearly he didn't fully appreciate Sandy's all-consuming passion for work, especially now that their boss had so much to prove or to lose.

"Number one, don't stay in the same hotel with Sandy, because you'll never get a moment's peace," Calvano warned Lipp. "Do you want to be there with Sandy when he lights a cigar at six-thirty in the morning and doesn't put the last one out until midnight?"

Calvano paused for effect. "Number two, don't ever object to going to dinner with Sandy, unless it's vitally important *for business* to do something else. Meals are mandatory."

After landing in Baltimore, the New Yorkers got another dose of budget reality: The "company cars" that met them were two aging blue Ford station wagons driven by garage attendants.

"Toto, we're not on Wall Street anymore," mused Jamie Dimon.

The "drivers" offered to give the New Yorkers a quick tour of the city and its revitalized waterfront, the Inner Harbor, on the way to Commercial Credit, but Sandy vetoed their offer. "It's already past eight o'clock," he grumbled. "We're here to work."

"That's right," echoed Lipp. More relaxed than his new CEO, Lipp tried to laugh off the pressure they all felt. "After the important companies we left behind and the pay cuts we're taking to come down here," he chuckled, "if we don't succeed, we're going to look really stupid."

The others laughed, but they all recognized the essential truth of Lipp's remark. Sandy and his band of corporate crusaders were attempting to make Main Street the route back to fame and fortune on Wall Street. Baltimore was simply a detour, just as Commercial Credit was simply the vehicle. Yet, in their hearts, the affable group jammed in the station wagons this frosty morning knew that a failure to negotiate their way through this detour could put their careers on the scrap heap.

The station wagons pulled up in front of Commercial Credit, a boxy eighteen-story aluminum structure, at 300 St. Paul Place. General Counsel Chuck Prince was in the lobby when the New York contingent swept in, wearing dark suits and power ties and clutching leather luggage. A palpable wave of energy surged through the lobby, and Prince suddenly thought of what it must have been like for the British soldiers trapped on the beaches of Dunkirk. A motley assortment of rescue vessels had arrived from England to rescue them in the nick of time from the advancing Germans. Now this odd assortment of powerful men was here to save Commercial Credit.

As the New Yorkers came spilling out of the elevator on the executive floor, their loud voices and New York accents pierced the air, abruptly ending the languid start of Baltimore's first business day after the holidays. Commercial Credit staffers were ambling to their offices, pausing to chat about their Christmas vacations and New Year's parties. Drained by Control Data's efforts to save itself at their expense, the employees had long ago lost any remnant of enthusiasm for their work. Many of the managers had been at Control Data in the past and had been booted down to Commercial Credit after losing their posts at the parent company for one reason or another. With no hope for promotion, they were simply biding their time until retirement. The chatter came to an abrupt halt as the A-team fanned out across the floor.

"You're in business again," Sandy told the employees hovering around his office. "Let's get to work."

Entering the chief executive's corner office, Sandy promptly ordered Dimon to help him turn his desk to face the door and his staff, not the scenic view of Baltimore's Inner Harbor as his predecessor had. He reeled off names to Michelle Krabbe, the assistant to the previous chairman, to get on the phone. When she hadn't gotten back to him in five minutes, Sandy was beside himself. He called Alison Falls, who had remained in the Seagram Building office in New York.

"Come down here, at least for today," Sandy whispered to his assistant. "Get on the train now." When she arrived three hours later, Falls saw the New York executives running in and out of Sandy's office. When he spotted her, he yelled, "Okay, Al, let's show them how it's done! I need to talk to Sam, Ed, and John."

Falls dropped her bag at Krabbe's desk. "This isn't as bad as it looks," Falls told the cowering office manager. "This is the order he wants them. Here's his Rolodex. He'll never make his own phone calls, because he doesn't like to wait," Falls quickly explained. "Does he have coffee? Bring him a cup of coffee." To teach the secretaries to work at Sandy speed, Falls decided to stay the week, even though she had brought only the clothes she was wearing.

To put his turnaround in motion, Sandy had set three priorities for his new executive team. First, cut costs aggressively to stem the flow of red ink and give Commercial Credit a chance to become a low-cost provider of financial services. Second, undertake a massive restructuring aimed at selling any parts of the company that didn't complement its consumer-lending and insurance businesses. Third, transform branch managers from complacent paper pushers and application takers to motivated salespeople and thrifty proprietors. All those wheels were set in motion before any of the New Yorkers left the office that first chaotic day.

Without the benefit of the advice Calvano had given Lipp, the rest of the New Yorkers followed Sandy to the Harbor Court Hotel that night. Its gracious lobby boasted a grand winding staircase with golden oak woodwork, Oriental rugs, multi-tiered crystal chandeliers, and high, arched windows offering panoramic views of the seaport. At check-in, Sandy insisted that Dimon, as his right hand, be permanently assigned to the room sharing the hallway to his suite. John Fowler, the only other officer in his thirties like Dimon and somewhat competitive with him, took a room next door to Sandy's. Joseph DeAlessandro was pleased with the hotel choice, mostly because of its restaurant's reputation for distinctive cuisine. A lover of fine food and wine who had come to know Sandy through their membership in the secret wine society, DeAlessandro preferred staying in five-star accommodations. If they were going to spend a lot of time in this backwater town, DeAlessandro decided, at least they could stay at Baltimore's only luxury hotel with rooms filled with antiques, four-poster beds, six-foot marble soaking tubs, televisions in the bathrooms, and fully stocked minibars.

Several blocks away, Bob Lipp and Jim Calvano checked into the budget-priced hotel right near Commercial Credit. Their colleagues had questioned their choice; before Lipp could answer, Calvano had jumped in and said, "Bob and I want to stay close to the office. We'll get more done." Sandy, pleased with the early demonstration of work ethic, added approvingly, "And it's cheaper." The lobby looked pretty grim, but Lipp figured they would just be sleeping in the hotel. When the men turned on the lights as they entered their adjacent rooms, cockroaches darted for cover. Unpacking his toiletries in the bathroom, Lipp spotted silverfish scurrying across the tub. Just then, a gray mouse raced across the stained carpet.

"Jim, come in here," Lipp yelled to Calvano. "Are you telling me you'd rather room with mice than Sandy Weill?"

"Trust me, this is an acceptable trade-off," Calvano replied.

After checking to be sure there were no bugs or other creatures in his sheets, Lipp crawled in and resolved before going to sleep, "If my wife visits, I've got to move to Harbor Court."

On Tuesday morning, Dimon awakened at 6:15 A.M. to the smell of cigar smoke wafting under the door from Sandy's room. *Damn, Sandy's already up and working,* he thought as he jumped out of bed. He showered and shaved in record time. He *had* to read the newspapers before Sandy beckoned. Sure enough, at ten minutes before seven o'clock, Sandy knocked on his door with a couple of questions about the morning's news.

Within an hour, Sandy and his handpicked team stormed into Commercial Credit's lobby. The new CEO stopped abruptly at the stacks of *The Wall Street Journal* and Baltimore *Sun* awaiting distribution. "See if these papers are paid for by Commercial Credit," he instructed Dimon. "Cancel all subscriptions. If employees want a *Wall Street Journal,* tell them 'pay for it yourself.'"

When Sandy got off the elevator, he noticed that the few employees already there at eight o'clock were filling up coffee pots. "Take the coffee pots away. We aren't going to pay for anybody's coffee pots in their offices." Spotting a plant-service contractor watering the potted trees outside his office, Sandy scowled. "No more watering plants." Then he turned to the secretary closest to the ficus and snarled: "Water your plant yourself."

The reign of Sandy Weill, brutal cost cutter, had begun. Commercial Credit was about to learn a hallmark of Sandy's management style: an almost draconian single-mindedness on expense control.

By 9:00 A.M., Dimon, implementing Sandy's fervor to slash expenses, fired off a memo to all managers announcing Commercial Credit's new policy on company cars. In the past, managers could lease any car they liked, be reimbursed $500 each month for the car payment and insurance, and then be allowed to purchase the vehicle for a "sweetheart" price after two years. Under the expensive plan, several managers had four or five cars for their wives, children, and other relatives. The memo stated: "You have three days, no later than this Friday, to do one of the following: (1) turn in your company car, or (2) deliver a certified check for the fair-market value of your company car."

Chuck Prince had just leased a big Oldsmobile station wagon with fake wood side panels and a roof rack, a good family car for his two children. Barry Mannes, head of personnel, was driving a company-subsidized Mercedes. Immediately barraged with complaints and indignation, Mannes headed straight to the CEO's office for an explanation. "We don't give cars," Sandy said matter-of-factly. "We don't give memberships to clubs. If people make enough money, they can live whatever lifestyle they want." When Mannes protested that current salaries couldn't absorb the costs of the perks, Sandy reminded him of what he'd said from Day One. "If everyone works hard, we'll all share in the company's success with stock options."

A shell-shocked Mannes knew he had better tell his wife that their new Mercedes would be gone by week's end. "I have good news and bad news," he informed her that evening. When she asked for the bad news first, he replied, "We're losing the car. But the good news is we're getting options."

"What's an option?" she asked.

While dozens of managers lost their cars that week, hundreds of Commercial Credit employees lost their jobs over the next month. Control Data had already begun the process of slashing 2,000 jobs at Commercial Credit. But when Sandy arrived he immediately ordered that 125 more jobs be cut. Then he turned his laserlike focus on the department he disliked most at any company he had ever run: human resources. He slashed its 100 employees to 35. When Mannes got the order to issue pink slips to 65 of his staff, he marched into Sandy's office.

"The bodies out the window show you don't value the human-resources department," said Mannes, usually an unassuming and solicitous executive. But he was floored that the department he had built so carefully was being dismantled wholesale. "You're firing all of HR's field people."

"What do they do?" Sandy asked, setting up Mannes for the kill.

"They help our branch managers to recruit, hire, train, and discipline their staff," Mannes replied proudly.

"Why can't managers do that?" Sandy asked. "Your field staffers are holding the hands of my managers, and I want you to train my managers to do it themselves."

Mannes struggled to raise concerns about compliance with employment laws, but Sandy cut him off. "My managers should pick their most important assets—their people—themselves, and learn to operate more cheaply."

"But human-resources staff can help find the right people," Mannes countered.

"If I have managers who can't handle this," Sandy said, "then I have the wrong managers."

In a state of shock, Mannes turned to leave, but Sandy stopped him. "See this?" Sandy held up the ten-inch-thick Commercial Credit policy manual. "This is why managers have trouble following the policies." With his cigar clenched between his teeth, he tossed the huge binder into the garbage, where it landed with a loud thud. "Tomorrow I want one-page guidelines for my managers on the most important policies so they can operate on their own."

Thinking his life couldn't be more miserable and he should prepare his resumé, Mannes, along with his assistants, that day cranked out seventeen single pages dealing with significant policy questions. He even took out a ruler to make sure the binder was no more than a half-inch thick.

But Sandy wasn't finished with HR. A few days later he summoned Mannes into his office, where spreadsheets were laid out on the CEO's desk. "What's this?" Sandy asked, pointing to a line called "Earned Vacation Bank." The HR director explained that many employees had been saving their vacation each year to use for early retirement. Consequently, Commercial Credit was carrying the amount on its books and had to reserve against the future costs.

"I want to get rid of this," Sandy said. "I believe in 'use it or lose it.'"

"People earned this," Mannes countered. "They'll want money if they don't get the time off eventually."

"Fine, we'll buy them out at 25 percent of the value," Sandy concluded.

The Commercial Credit CEO next honed in on a large amount reserved for "retiree medical." He asked Mannes, "How much does a retiree pay for medical?"

"Nothing," Mannes answered. "Commercial Credit pays their medical costs for life."

Sandy recoiled violently. "What?" he snarled. "We're changing that right now. Retirees will pay one hundred percent of their own medical costs."

The HR director hated to defend more costly expenses to his frugal boss, but he knew he had to try. He pointed out that many of the retirees weren't eligible for Medicare, because they weren't yet sixty-five years old.

Sandy couldn't believe his ears. "Why are they retiring so early? If they make a life choice, why should the company pay for it?"

Mannes warned that such a move would subject Commercial Credit to bad publicity and lawsuits and finally persuaded Sandy to phase out the coverage of retiree medical costs over four years, a move that didn't, in the end, prevent either the bad publicity or the lawsuits that Mannes had predicted.

During their first full week in Baltimore, Sandy and his executives worked practically around the clock to learn Commercial Credit's business from top to bottom. "Let's understand, deep down in the organization, how the thing really runs, where the profits come from," he urged his colleagues. Dimon pored over the balance sheet, demanding to see an itemized list of all expenses for the last year. He was ably assisted by the "Deep Throat" pair, Volland and Burner, who had first alerted Sandy to Commercial Credit. Joe Minutilli, the former chief executive officer who remained a director, had wanted to fire them both when Sandy told him how Commercial Credit had come to his attention. But Sandy had instead promoted them both, giving Volland the post of treasurer and Burner more responsibilities working directly for Dimon. Joe Minutilli eventually got a small measure of revenge by not inviting the two executives to his going-away party that month.

Lipp and Calvano, the branch management team, began setting up meetings with all regional managers to get detailed information on the branches' performance. They were shocked to find that there was no way to know which branch offices were profitable and which were losing money. Equally appalling, they found that the senior vice president in charge of branches did not like to visit them, preferring to summon regional managers to headquarters. "Who are our strongest managers?" Lipp wanted to know. The senior executive had no clue.

Meanwhile, DeAlessandro sized up Commercial Credit's meager insurance offerings and began to plan new products, such as unemployment insurance, that would be appropriate for the company's blue-collar clientele. John Fowler tried to provide Sandy with more information on the stray units of Commercial Credit, and Sandy quizzed longtime managers about their businesses to determine which units could be sold to raise cash. Most of all, Sandy wandered the halls, a thick haze of cigar smoke trailing him. "What do you do?" he would demand of anyone he encountered.

While the New York contingent worked hard that first week, none worked harder than Michelle Krabbe, the only assistant in the chairman's office. With Alison Falls coaching her, Krabbe was suddenly rushing to meet not only Sandy's many demands but also the requests of all the other new executives who were taking over the floor. She frantically tried to answer their nonstop questions and retrieve the financial and accounting records they sought. And while Krabbe did all she could, it often wasn't enough. Sandy, Dimon, Lipp, Calvano, or DeAlessandro, accustomed to New York's long hours, frequently complained about the absence of staff after five o'clock. Then one day Sandy brought it all to a screeching halt. In the midst of a meeting with Sandy, several managers jumped up at precisely 4:57 P.M. "I have to leave for my car pool," they said almost simultaneously. Before Sandy could launch into one of his tirades, they were out the door. When he found one stray employee still in the office, he angrily demanded an explanation. Not only were employees leaving before the day's work was done, Commercial Credit was subsidizing the departures with car and van pools. Sandy exploded. "No more car pools!" he screamed. "No more van pools!" The caravans ended the next day.

Sandy and Jamie desperately searched for ways to bolster Commercial Credit's bottom line, the profits it would report at the end of the year. Only by showing a healthy gain in profits would Sandy be able to build credibility on Wall Street. When he and Dimon discovered a $50-million surplus in the company's pension plan, Sandy's eyes lit up. He summoned his favorite whipping boy on costly benefits, Barry Mannes.

"I need that fifty million dollars," Sandy stated. He told Mannes he intended to terminate the current pension plan in order to put its cash surplus into the company's coffers.

"Doesn't that surplus belong to the participants?" Mannes asked, indignant that Sandy would even contemplate such a drastic move on a pension plan held sacred by employees. The surplus had accumulated from good investments that the pension plan had made, and most companies preferred to keep any surpluses as a cushion against times when investments might not perform well.

"I need that fifty million dollars, and I need it now," Sandy stated urgently. It was clear to Mannes that the CEO and CFO had already calculated the numbers they needed to achieve for 1987, and the pension surplus would get them a lot closer to hitting those numbers. Suddenly the gravity of Sandy's mission sank in. Mannes, who had tangled with the new CEO from the day he arrived, saw that all the costs of benefits, all the salaries paid to employees who had been working halfheartedly, even the human-resources staff that he thought had been such a help to branch managers, all had been piling up to suffocate the company. Nobody had the courage to say so until Sandy, he realized.

Suddenly apologetic, the forty-seven-year-old Mannes blurted, "I feel like a parasite that keeps eating the money you need to save the business." From that moment on, Sandy, who had considered sending the HR director packing, knew he could count on Mannes as part of his turnaround team.

The slash-and-burn tactics, however, were taking their toll on the employees' morale—and their view of their new commander in chief. After the hero's welcome accorded Sandy, his efforts to be genial in the halls were no longer reciprocated by the employees. He worried they misunderstood his cost cutting as mean-spirited rather than fiscally prudent. There was lots of grumbling: Unused vacation time had been erased, employees' health insurance costs were going up, company contributions to 401(k) plans had ended, and a new, less lucrative pension plan had been put in place.

"Al, go ride the elevator and tell me what people are saying about me," he directed his assistant. Falls refused.

"I'll do it," volunteered Michelle Krabbe, trying hard to please her new boss.

"Are you nuts?" Falls snapped. "Sit down, Michelle. Sandy, we won't do this for you."

But Krabbe snuck off later and spent some time talking with employees around the building. She came back to her desk in tears, shocked at the depth of pain and anger among so many of her colleagues. After wiping away her tears, she timidly entered Sandy's office. But she was able to murmur only two words before tears again overwhelmed her: "It's bad."

Dejected and chewing his cigar, Sandy walked down to Mannes's office and plopped down.

"What's wrong?" asked the HR director, sensing that Sandy was on the verge of tears.

"Nobody is speaking to me on the elevators anymore," the CEO said haltingly.

"Sandy, you just laid off half the people in the building," Mannes explained. "These are the other half; of course they aren't going to look you in the eye."

"Don't they understand that if I hadn't come in and taken Commercial Credit public, there probably wouldn't be a Commercial Credit?" Sandy asked sadly.

"No, they don't understand," Mannes told him softly. For the first time since Sandy's takeover, Mannes saw a very human CEO grappling with the fallout of his drastic measures and distressed at being shunned by his own troops.

FEEDING FRENZY

By the end of January, Sandy and his associates had settled into a routine centered around working in Baltimore from Monday morning until Thursday night. And, of course, "working" with Sandy Weill also meant eating with him. Sandy made it a point in that first month to hit nearly every one of the city's nicer restaurants for lunch, typically dragging along one or more colleagues so they could discuss business. Chuck Prince, Commercial Credit's thirty-seven-year-old general counsel, wasn't accustomed to talking about nothing but business even in the office. Now he found himself in ceaseless discussions about Commercial Credit at lunch and thought to himself that he had somehow become a member of "workaholics anonymous." But he admired the energy and the intelligence of Sandy's colleagues and wasn't averse to putting in long hours as well, a trait that endeared him to Sandy.

Bob Lipp hadn't known Sandy well before leaving Chemical Bank, and he was struck by how much his new boss enjoyed food, drink, and the ritual of dining. Although Sandy's fondness for food was amply evident in his girth, Lipp could also see that Sandy felt not the least bit guilty about indulging his passion. Lipp's lanky build tended not to show excess weight, but he nevertheless felt obliged to rise early in Baltimore for a jog to keep his weight under control. One of his first lunches with Sandy was at a fish restaurant up the street from Commercial Credit. As Sandy tore into his fish, he suggested that Lipp take a close look at the branches' loan portfolio.

"Sandy, I'm already looking at it," Lipp began, "and the delinquencies are edging up."

"What?" Sandy nearly choked on his bite. His face flashed red, and he raised his voice at Lipp for the first time. He insisted on hearing exactly how Lipp determined delinquencies and what the trend lines were for the branches. Lipp, unable to finish his own lunch after the outburst, gave Sandy the facts as calmly as possible, trying not to disturb diners at nearby tables.

Back at the office, Lipp sought out Jamie Dimon, everyone's expert on Sandy Weill. He recounted how Sandy blew up over something as "irrelevant" as a slight increase in loan delinquencies. "He got very, very upset," said Lipp, looking for a rational explanation from Sandy's protégé.

"Never give him bad news when he's feeding," Dimon counseled matter-of-factly. Lipp snickered—until he realized Dimon couldn't have been more serious.

Dinner became the main event for the New Yorkers, stuck in Baltimore without families or other diversions. Dinners with Sandy were both a command performance and an elaborate feast, held nearly every evening in a private dining room at the Harbor Court Hotel. As part of Baltimore's effort to shed its reputation as a shot-and-beer town, the newly opened Harbor Court was valiantly offering culinary fare associated with more sophisticated cities. The hotel and restaurant staff worked especially hard to please Sandy Weill, their new "permanent" guest.

The "dirty dozen," as some at Commercial Credit had dubbed Sandy and his New York associates, left the office together between seven and eight o'clock each evening, then walked ten minutes to the Harbor Court. The evening always began with rounds of cocktails; Sandy, of course, had his beloved Gibson made with Tanqueray gin and cocktail onions. Dinner began with massive platters of seafood containing cold lobster, shrimp, and clams on the half shell, accompanied by white wine. Around a large oval oak table, the gregarious and boisterous men recounted the day's events. When they moved to the main course, they switched to red wine. Sandy loved selecting his entrée from among the restaurant's offerings, which ranged from delicate seafood with rich cream sauces to large rare steaks or seasonal game. And partly because he could afford to and partly because his ego demanded the biggest and the best, he did it all to excess. If two seafood platters were sufficient as appetizers for the men, he would order five. If a twelve-ounce steak was on the menu, Sandy ordered a twenty-ounce steak.

Irwin Ettinger, recruited by Sandy from his position as the head of Arthur Young & Co.'s tax department, loved eating every bit as much as his new boss but was unsettled by the gluttony. The forty-nine-year-old accountant had undergone two angioplasty procedures in recent months to open clogged arteries. But since he had nothing else to do in Baltimore at night, he went along to the dinners and tried not to overindulge. Best of all, he found the group's discussions—always about business, never about sports or families—lively and informative as they tried to unravel Commercial Credit.

As the alcohol and camaraderie lowered their guards, the men also learned about one another. Soon Sandy knew each man's traits, strengths, weaknesses, and spirit. The Commercial Credit CEO, for whom business and personal lives were completely interrelated, used the dinners as a tool to meld his core team together in preparation for taking their dinky consumer-loan company to another level. Sandy clearly wanted to work with people who were his friends and who viewed their work as much more than a job.

"Let's go around the room," Sandy announced on the group's first night out, after the dishes were cleared. "What's on everybody's mind? How are you feeling about things?" He brought out his trademark cigar and ordered a bottle of his favorite after-dinner drink, Calvados, an apple brandy, for the table. Cradling a snifter in his hand to warm the expensive brandy, Sandy encouraged his cronies to join him in lighting up and drinking. "What's on your mind?" he asked, calling on Lipp to begin the discussion.

Nervous that Sandy might still be "feeding," as Dimon had described it, the ex–Chemical Bank president began blandly recounting some of the meetings he had that day.

"No, no, no," Sandy interrupted. "This isn't a business report. I want to hear how you're feeling about things. Where do you think we are?"

The conversation went around the table. When it was finally Chuck Prince's turn, he started to agree with one of his new colleagues. Sandy stopped him. "You can't just agree or disagree," the CEO said, as he was setting the rules for the table talks. "You have to come up with something new." Prince, who was the last this evening in the round-robin, prayed that next time he would be first so all the obvious topics wouldn't have already been taken.

Except for interruptions to make the rules, Sandy just sat, drinking his apple brandy and smoking his Te-Amo cigar, occasionally chuckling at his associates' comments. Even with a significant amount of alcohol, Sandy was taking it all in, enjoying putting his people on the spot, spurring the group interaction, and building camaraderie. Sandy was so delighted by the information that flowed that night, he decided on the spot to make it part of a nightly ritual. But the evening still wasn't over. The executives felt they couldn't retire to their rooms until Sandy determined it was time for bed, and often that was long after midnight and long after the conversation had turned from entertaining and enlightening to tedious and tiring. After a few weeks, Calvano and Lipp found yet another feature of their sordid hotel rooms: They could use the excuse of the long walk home to bow out of the conversation immediately after the nightly round-robin discussion. The others paid a huge price for the comparative luxury they were enjoying.

On one of their walks back to their shabby hotel, Lipp thanked his roommate for sparing him that nightly ordeal. "This walk lets me clear my head so I can sleep," Lipp told Calvano. "And eating like this, more than ever, I want my morning run."

"I told you this would be just like summer camp with Sandy," Calvano replied. "Boys' night out is fun—to a point."

"The dinners together are a lot of laughs," Lipp agreed, but he confided to his new friend, "It's taking me a while to get used to Sandy. This isn't exactly the Harvard Business School model here." Lipp, who had earned his MBA at Harvard before spending more than two decades at Chemical Bank, added, "You know what Sandy's doing, don't you? He's deprogramming us from all the bureaucratic ways we've learned."

"While he's whipping Commercial Credit into shape," Calvano said, "he's also whipping us into a cohesive unit that operates his way."

"He's giving us his habits—cutting through the layers of organization, spending money like it's your own, acting like a small business owner . . ." Lipp trailed off.

"And eating and drinking too much," Calvano added. They laughed as they arrived at the bug-infested hotel they were happy to call home.

But it didn't take many feasts before several of the executives got sick of the rich and complicated entrées. One night Lipp tried to order something not on the menu. "I just want a baked chicken breast," he told the waiter. Appalled at such a lowbrow request, the waiter tried to steer him back to the menu. "But I'm sure the sir would be quite pleased with the delicious pheasant under glass—"

"What about French fries? Why can't we ever have French fries?" Dimon blurted out. Sensing a strategic moment that could change the course of dinner history, the young executive demanded: "I just want a hamburger and French fries." Prince added quickly, though more politely: "I would like a basic salad with lettuce and tomatoes, please."

The onslaught flustered the waiter, who insisted that the esteemed, awarding-winning chef would prepare only the "creations" on the elaborate menu. Then Fitz-Gerald had an idea. He quickly darted out during the haranguing and returned with his room-service menu. Dimon ordered his hamburger, and soon several others at the table were ordering sandwiches and potato chips or soup and salad—all from the pedestrian room-service menu. Sandy stuck with the chef's "creations."

After bunking together from Monday through Thursday, the crew would return home for the rest of the week. But being home didn't mean being off work. On Fridays the executives packed into Sandy's Seagram Building office, where Falls still held down the fort. With offices only for Sandy and Dimon, as many as ten others crammed into the small conference room equipped with only one telephone, one table, and four chairs.

Sandy and Dimon used their Fridays to meet with investment bankers and other businesses to sell off operations that made no financial or strategic sense. In the first quarter of 1987, they quickly negotiated the sale of Commercial Credit's vehicle-leasing operations in Canada and the United States for about $77 million in cash, plus payment of liabilities totaling some $250 million. With the company's new investment-grade rating, Sandy also arranged to issue some $500 million in new debt in order to better match assets to liabilities and to prefund its consumer-finance business for the year. Sandy urged Dimon, who loved working the numbers, to try every conceivable way to clean up Commercial Credit's balance sheet. As the consummate deal maker, Sandy would keep his eye out for acquisitions.

During weekends, the men often gathered at the Weill home in Greenwich to discuss plans for the next week and occasionally played golf at the Century Club. Come Monday morning, they reassembled at LaGuardia Airport for the 7:10 Piedmont flight to Baltimore.

As winter set in, a snowstorm hit the East Coast, but Sandy and his executives braved the weather and made it to the airport from their homes in New York, Connecticut, and New Jersey. With Baltimore blanketed under about four inches of snow, only one station wagon appeared to pick them all up. When they arrived at Commercial Credit's headquarters, the offices were empty.

"What the hell!" Sandy screamed, as he madly paced up and down the halls. "What the hell! If I can get here from New York by eight-thirty, why can't these people who live ten miles away get here?" The chief executive ranted and raved as he visited every floor. "This is never going to happen again!" he yelled. In a rage, he ordered the scared garage attendant to take the station wagon to pick up his secretary. When she arrived, she tried to explain that her bus didn't run that morning. "Fine, get Governor Schaefer on the phone," he barked. Trembling, she got the Maryland governor on the line.

"If you want Baltimore to be a big town and attract industry, fix your public transportation system," Sandy yelled to Governor William D. Schaefer. Listening only perfunctorily to the governor's excuses, Sandy slammed down the phone. Then, pounding his desk, he ordered up a new policy to be announced the following day: "If you don't show up for work, you don't get paid."

The next morning when the snow had melted, employees found the new memo on their desks. As usual, it was up to HR director Barry Mannes to try to appease Sandy. What angered Sandy more than the lost snow day, Mannes discerned, was his growing frustration with Commercial Credit's lazy workforce. To a hard-charging New Yorker, the snow day—like the 5:00 P.M. car pools—was symptomatic of the unacceptable work ethic. Sandy told Mannes, "We aren't going to get better if people don't work harder."

Then it dawned on Sandy. As the new CEO of Commercial Credit, he had been so caught up in buttressing the balance sheet and selecting the right executives to mount a turnaround, he had forgotten to inspire his workforce. What his troops needed was some good old-time religion on the value of stock options. That will make them *want* to work harder, he thought. Sandy called an employees' meeting in the cafeteria, the scene of the "Independence Day" party when he first took the company public a few months earlier. Of course, Sandy wanted a full day of work first, so he called the meeting for five o'clock. With their benefits cut to the bone, the employees, now a smaller group after the layoffs, faced their boss with trepidation.

"I want every one of you to become a shareholder in this company," Sandy began. "With stock options, you are an owner in Commercial Credit just as I am." (Mannes had warned Sandy that he would have to "educate an entire population about stock options.") Accustomed to paychecks and bonuses, the employees were unsure what Sandy was talking about.

"Do we buy the options in the stock market?" one middle manager asked. Sandy explained that options were given by the company to its employees. They enabled the employees at some future date to buy the company's stock at a certain price which, if they worked hard and the company did well, would be less than what outside investors would have to pay to buy the stock on an exchange. Options would soon become part of the compensation and retirement package for most employees, he promised. "Your options are really going to matter," the CEO said. "I want you to get wealthy on this, too. We are all in this." He noted that even Commercial

Credit's new board of directors, including former president Gerald Ford, was paid in stock alone.

"Can I take an option to the grocery store?" asked another employee. Sandy tried to explain that an option isn't money that can be spent.

"I would rather have the money than a stock option," the employee retorted.

"You think that now," Sandy countered. "But your options one day could be worth a lot more than any money you would be given today. Trust me when I tell you I'm putting in place an environment where you will want to succeed." He tried another explanation: "You have to reap the benefits not just of what you earn for a salary, but also in how well the company does. Remember, you're not just an employee, you're an owner just like I am. Let's work like owners."

Most employees, even an operations manager like Herb Seligson, still didn't grasp what Sandy was promoting. "I just don't understand him," Seligson told a colleague as they were leaving the cafeteria. "He's keeping our salaries low but telling us we'll still do well. How can we create our own wealth by working hard?"

"All I know is that stock options must not cost him much to give, because he won't give us the cash," his colleague replied.

The offer of options might not have turned sentiment back in Sandy's favor, but his continuing and obvious dedication to the company had a beneficial effect on morale. The long hours and his deep and intimate knowledge of the company and its people made lasting impressions on the employees who came in contact with him, no matter where that contact occurred. Shortly after the employees' meeting on options, Seligson was in the men's bathroom. Suddenly Sandy burst in and stood at the urinal next to him. "I got the numbers on your region," Sandy said. "Your numbers look good." A startled Seligson glanced around to see if anyone else was in the bathroom but found Sandy looking at him. He barely muttered, "Thanks," but inside he was aglow that this big-time CEO had seen his region's results that morning just as he did and had noticed him. Seligson hadn't even been sure Sandy knew who he was. But embarrassment quickly got the better of Seligson; he zipped his fly the moment he was finished and practically ran out of the bathroom.

While morale began to improve, Sandy's unusual and restless management style continued to perplex his employees. He was accustomed to roaming the halls of his brokerage house, from the mail room to the trading floor. Commercial Credit folks, on the other hand, were accustomed to an aloof CEO who stayed in his office or met with other CEOs at the Center Club. During a meeting of middle managers in the executive floor's conference room, called "the fishbowl" because of its glass walls, Sandy walked in and sat down. The managers stopped midsentence. "Can we help you?" one man asked.

"No, just continue," Sandy replied, as he puffed on his cigar.

They tried, but were thrown off balance. "Did you want to tell us something?" another manager asked.

"Nope," Sandy said as he leaned back in the chair.

Uncertainly, the men resumed their meeting. As quickly as he entered, Sandy was gone. They stopped again. "Why does he just want to listen?" one manager asked. "That's weird."

Another worried, "He's trying to scare us or intimidate us."

Sandy's drop-ins were becoming commonplace; no one was safe from them. Mannes was meeting in his office with benefits consultants from Towers Perrin. Sandy walked into Mannes's office without so much as a knock or hello. "Who are you?" the CEO asked the visitors. The HR director quickly introduced them. "I just want you to know I don't like consultants," Sandy stated matter-of-factly. Looking at his uncomfortable guests, Mannes tried to explain that they were considering a flexible-benefit program. "I don't like flexible benefits," Sandy interrupted. The consultants uneasily began gathering their materials; Sandy stood still. As they filed out of the room, Sandy abruptly turned and left. Mannes, suddenly paranoid, wondered: Was that a coincidence, or did Sandy Weill know they were here and want to get rid of them?

Rumors about Sandy's "sixth sense" picked up steam at the Baltimore headquarters. The CEO seemed to have a nose for who was lying or who didn't know what he was talking about. "He can pick up the vibrations in the air, like a lie-detector test," Prince marveled to a colleague. "Your heart rate goes up and he senses that there's one person in the room who doesn't want his attention."

Watching colleagues squirm in the face of Sandy's wrath, Prince decided that a mistake was better volunteered to Sandy than detected by him. The general counsel had listed the wrong record date on a dividend declaration and wanted to tell Sandy as soon as he realized the mistake. "I am really sorry," Prince said. Sandy exploded. He screamed at Prince for three or four minutes, his ranting overheard by everyone on the executive floor.

When Sandy finally noticed the horror on Prince's face, he abruptly stopped. "I guess now you know you're part of the team," Sandy said, and waved him out.

When Sandy and John Fowler were preparing to meet with Morgan Stanley about an insurance unit they wanted to sell, Sandy asked questions that went beyond Fowler's knowledge. Fowler tried to bluff his way through them. Sandy glared at him. "You don't know what you're talking about," he yelled. "Go find Jamie."

Life under Sandy Weill certainly wasn't easy, but it sure was interesting.

7

BRANCHING OUT

As the headquarters staff learned to live the Weill way, the time came to give the more than four hundred branches a crash course in performance-based management. That difficult task fell to Bob Lipp and Jim Calvano, under Sandy's watchful eye. When the pair had first tried to evaluate the branches, they found there were no performance statistics on individual offices, just by large regions. They also discovered a complete lack of personnel turnover. Managers left only when they retired or died. No one had ever been fired; the average branch manager had been with the company for twenty-five years. Branch managers had no idea about their unit's profitability, expenses, or growth rates. The big distribution system basically offered only two products, an unsecured personal loan or a second mortgage. Every branch manager got a 5 percent bonus as long as he was still alive at the end of the year.

"These aren't good signs," Calvano told Lipp dryly.

Their first order of business: put in place a method to measure each branch's performance on criteria such as the volume, quality, and average rates of loans. Also, each manager would prepare a "controllable income statement" to track income and expenses. That would provide a clearer picture of the office as a stand-alone business. Then branch managers' results could be evaluated and their compensation adjusted accordingly. Sandy further insisted on an incentive system, similar to what he had put in place in the securities business.

"The top ten percent of managers will receive a bonus equal to their salary, doubling their compensation," Sandy proposed, a system unheard of in the consumer-finance industry. "The bottom ten percent will be out of a job."

Realizing that they needed someone who could train the managers under the new regime, Lipp suggested Robert Willumstad, a Brooklyn man who had worked with him at Chemical Bank for twenty years. They asked Willumstad, a sturdy six-foot-three-inch Nordic, to fly to Baltimore. Reluctant to consider such a "ratty consumer-finance company," Willumstad made the journey as a favor to his old boss, Bob Lipp.

Picked up in one of the blue station wagons, Willumstad was taken to the Prime Rib, a dimly lit restaurant with plush banquettes, black walls trimmed in gold, and leopard-print carpeting. Sandy and the others were waiting to have dinner. "What are you drinking?" Sandy asked after the introductions. "Order the ribs; they're great," he added. The tall, handsome Chemical operations executive looked around the table. *Here are a lot of big egos,* he thought, *but they seem to be getting along and having fun, after only a couple of months of working together.* Their conversation reminded him of proprietors or partners in a small business. *It's as if they're the owners, and the fact that Commercial Credit is a public company is almost secondary,* Willumstad reflected as he gnawed on his ribs. Still, he wasn't convinced, worried that the place had "more chiefs than Indians," and he returned to New York without making a commitment.

Back in the hierarchical confines of Chemical Bank, however, Willumstad remembered how much fun the anti-bureaucrats were having. He agreed to join Lipp at Commercial Credit to transform its stale branch network into an entrepreneurial money machine. His first day coincided with a branch-manager conference in Boca Raton, Florida, that previous management had planned as a boondoggle at the opulent Boca Raton Resort and Club. Sandy decided not to cancel the meeting; it would give him a chance to meet seventy-five branch managers from the Midwest to the Deep South at once. He did, however, cancel the appearance by the singing group the Pointer Sisters, who had been scheduled to perform for Commercial Credit for $50,000.

When Willumstad arrived at the conference's opening night, he badly wanted to turn back. The branch managers, many dressed in polyester leisure suits or open shirts that had long been out of fashion, were a bunch of older men knocking back the free booze amid a dense cloud of cigarette smoke.

What have I gotten myself into? he wondered.

Branch managers soon had a similar reaction. Their plans to spend the next two days playing golf or lounging on the beach were shattered when they awoke to find their schedules full of group meetings and work sessions.

At the morning welcome session, Sandy, nervous and sweating, wanted to rouse this grumpy group of middle-aged men and remake them into hungry salesmen pitching Commercial Credit loans to Middle America.

"We want to be the company of first choice by consumers, rather than the eighth or ninth," he declared. "Get out of the office, meet new people, and begin offering the new services and products we have."

To give the branches greater product offerings to attract more customers, Commercial Credit was establishing different loans with variable rates and structures, as well as certain forms of insurance. "Eventually we want to grow with the customer, where we can offer him some investment and savings products instead of turning him over to a bank or brokerage," Sandy said, foreshadowing his ultimate plan to use the storefront offices as a distribution network to become a big financial-services provider.

The same strategies that worked at Shearson to get each branch to increase its production and improve its profitability would be executed at Commercial Credit, he told them. Most important of all: "Think and act like you own your own branch. You are now president, Commercial Credit, in your town."

That set off cheers. The managers clearly liked their new titles. Still, they weren't sure exactly what acting like an owner meant. Sandy explained that each branch manager would receive options for two hundred shares of stock. "Work hard, and these options will be worth something!" Sandy proselytized. But to these men from some of America's smallest communities, their CEO was speaking Wall Street–ese, essentially a foreign language.

Sandy assured the managers that he and his team were there to help. "Phone me any time you want," he said, "and I promise I'll return your call within twenty-four hours." Then the CEO introduced the men overseeing the branches: Lipp, Calvano, and Willumstad. When Willumstad shook Sandy's hand, he noticed it was soaking wet. "This guy's not as slick as I thought," Willumstad told Lipp with admiration, not disdain. "He didn't try to impress anyone by being elegant, articulate, or moving," Willumstad observed.

Enveloped by cigarette smoke and surrounded by leisure suits, Willumstad somehow felt calmer about his career change.

At the conference, Lipp and Calvano held sessions to introduce the new culture of "monthly business reviews." Using an overhead projector, Lipp displayed a transparency as he explained the precise reporting system used to calculate the profitability of each individual office. The reaction: deafening silence. The branch managers had never been held accountable and weren't sophisticated enough to grasp the grid of performance statistics. Calvano and Lipp gallantly tried to clarify how results would be reviewed so that branches could be compared against one another. They explained that the monthly standings represented refinements on the methods they had devised at Chemical and Avis.

The conference's break-out sessions were designed to teach the managers how to drive profitability, which they took to mean make more loans. Willumstad tried to improve their business sophistication with a basic primer on income and expenses. "You can also drive income by controlling expenses and pricing the products properly," he explained. Calvano echoed the same principles in his sessions, trying to reverse the long-held views that the biggest offices were the best. "A large office can have inferior results," Calvano told the local officers. "It can have more loan defaults or more monthly expenses—all driving down its return."

After the Boca Raton conference, word trickled back to Baltimore that the branches didn't buy the new act. The novel performance and incentive systems would be more work with no guaranteed payoff. Of course, that was Sandy's point—no more guarantees; either shape up or ship out! Calvano and Lipp knew that a thorough housecleaning might be in order and prepared to tour many of the branches. "Let's see if any of these managers pack the horsepower," Calvano told his colleague.

Over the next several weeks, Calvano, Lipp, and Willumstad made personal visits to dozens of Commercial Credit offices in twenty-eight states to size up their managers' ability to meet the new standards of performance and profitability. Many were eager for a shot at doubling their salaries. Others were set in their ways and had no interest in changing for the slick city boys.

The New Yorkers soon found themselves in the small towns where Commercial Credit storefront offices provided loans to blue-collar customers, from Selma, Alabama, to Wapakoneta, Ohio. With a *BusinessWeek* reporter documenting his unorthodox travels, Lipp drove through the twisting roads of the Appalachian Mountains to the tiny town of Hazard, Kentucky. It was the first of the month, and borrowers were lined up around the block to make their Commercial Credit payments with Social Security checks, paychecks from the United Mine Workers of America, or checks that represented compensation for the black lung disease that they had contracted working the deep coal mines that tunneled all through the mountains. The office was run by Henry Smith, a devout Christian with one year of college, who judged a potential loan based on the borrower's character rather than on any red tape. Smith invited Lipp to join him for lunch at the counter at Bailey's, a popular hangout adjoining a gas station. Over chicken-fried steak, pimento cheese sandwiches, and fluffy coconut cream pie, Lipp explained to Smith how he could be rewarded for improved performance.

"You make thirty-two thousand dollars a year," Lipp observed. "How would you like to double that, to make sixty-four thousand?" That's a lot of money in Hazard, Smith said. He eagerly agreed to use his lifelong contacts around the hills and hollows of Hazard to bring in new loans.

"If a man comes in dirty and all, we talk to him same as if he has a suit and tie on," Smith explained. That kind of treatment, far better than the two big banks in town, will lead to good referrals, even with Commercial Credit's steep interest rates, from 18 percent to 23 percent, he predicted. "These are country people; they're God-fearing," Smith said. Lipp liked the sound of that: His customers wouldn't wind up as deadbeats. "Bring in as many as you can," the Baltimore executive urged.

In a swing through the Florida offices, Willumstad painstakingly laid out the "better products, pricing, and efficiency" that would help managers grow their businesses.

"I'll need to hire a new person to do all of this," one Florida manager groused.

"Fine, you're in charge. We trust you. We'll treat you like adults," the executive said. "But remember: You will be held accountable for the total performance of your office. Extra expenses will hurt your profitability." Before Willumstad's departure, the manager had already determined that a part-time employee would be a better option.

The New Yorkers knew they would have to make this "real easy" for the managers in the hinterlands. The solution: set up each branch almost as a franchise, automate procedures so that all credit decisions and product offerings would be uniformly handled, and provide management direction for consistent execution of strategy. Only then could each branch be held accountable based on the same standards, particularly with new technology delivering timely data, rather than the existing hodgepodge of assorted paper reports and ledger cards haphazardly sent to headquarters.

For this gargantuan task, Lipp and Willumstad wanted one of their brightest—and most patient—colleagues from Chemical Bank, Marge Magner. Married with a young son, Magner jumped at the chance to work with her mentors. Her cheery demeanor would be just the ticket to smooth out the transition for many of the stubborn, unsophisticated branch managers and their employees. Moreover, the "two Bobs," as she called Bob Lipp and Bob Willumstad, knew she could be just as focused on bottom-line results as her male counterparts and do the kind of hand-holding the outlying offices needed to turn them around. Magner, at her own suggestion, began working at Commercial Credit by spending two weeks in a branch in Waterbury, Connecticut. Alongside the employees, the thirty-six-year-old Magner took loan applications, talked to customers, and did collections—all the while determining how to automate the procedures companywide.

A psychology major with an advanced business degree, Magner had been recruited by Chemical Bank to bring diversity to its management-training program. The daughter of a Brooklyn policeman, Magner desperately wanted to get ahead in banking, a field dominated by men. She began wearing dark suits and silk bow ties. She even joked that if she could pee standing up, she would in order to fit into this macho environment. But unlike the men, she was a good listener and disarmingly down to earth. Sandy liked her spunk as soon as he met her. He asked her lots of questions about her stint at the Waterbury branch and pressed her to make changes that would produce results—fast.

With Sandy breathing down their necks, Willumstad and Magner quickly implemented the new system measuring each office's monthly results. They also gave hokey incentives: Branches in one region that booked $1 million in new loans in a given month would win an expense-paid weekend at Cincinnati's Omni Netherland Plaza for the office staff and spouses. The branch managers soon discovered that simply making sure that existing customers were making their payments on time was no longer good enough. New loan production and cost control would be rewarded, and that would be especially true at the end of the year, when bonuses were distributed. With branch rankings, everyone knew who was doing well and who was doing poorly. Suddenly, employees were coming back to the office after dinner and working on Saturdays to get new business.

WARM WELCOMES, COLD SHOULDERS

While Sandy and his band of New Yorkers still joked about Baltimore's lack of sophistication, the city itself couldn't have been happier to have them. The increased attention that the business press gave Commercial Credit reflected well on the city. A few months after the rescue team first swept into town, the mayor threw a gala reception for them, taking over the entire Baltimore Museum of Art. All the important city officials and many of Baltimore's corporate chieftains and society grandees were there to welcome Sandy and his crew. As the New Yorkers circulated among the well-wishers, the same question kept recurring: When are you moving your families to Baltimore? Implicit in the question was the assurance that the new executives wouldn't up and move the finance company to Manhattan. Of course, none of the Commercial Credit team expected to stay very long in Baltimore; they knew this was just the first step in building the company. Only Jamie Dimon had decided to look for a house; with his wife, Judy, expecting their second child in the spring and a toddler at home, he wanted his young family with him. When nearly every Commercial Credit "import" was asked about moving, Dimon's plan suddenly came in handy. "Oh, our CFO is moving down with his family," became the standard answer to the question. Until Jim Calvano surprised his colleagues with a different response. When a city official asked, "When are you and your family moving to Baltimore?" Calvano replied, "I'm looking." The delighted official said, "Oh terrific," and left him alone. Joan Weill was standing near Calvano. "I didn't know you were looking," she said.

"Joan, what I'm looking for is a good answer to that question," he replied, chortling. "There's no way in hell I'm moving down here."

Yet all the warmth and attention from the Baltimore leadership made Sandy rethink his decision to commute back and forth to New York. Clearly he was a very big fish in this much smaller pond, and he relished the star treatment. After talking it over with Joan before she returned to Manhattan, Sandy asked the Baltimore boosters to arrange for real-estate agents to show him prime estates in the area. He was especially interested in the rolling farmland and woods directly across Chesapeake Bay from Baltimore.

"Joanie and I might move to the Eastern Shore," he announced to Chuck Prince one afternoon. Spread out all over Sandy's desk were aerial photographs of farms, as well as color photographs of chateaux and estates on the other side of Chesapeake Bay.

"And we thought we were being taken over by a Wall Street mogul," Prince said, chuckling.

When Dimon breezed in, Sandy pointed to one farm. "Here's where the boats and geese are, and the corn would go here." Dimon and Prince glanced at each other in amusement. "Sandy doesn't *look* like a gentleman farmer," Dimon quipped. "Sandy doesn't *act* like a gentleman farmer," Prince echoed, laughing. When the other New Yorkers got wind of Sandy's farming fantasies, they decided among themselves to stall any real effort to relocate until Sandy got over "this fascination."

Baltimore's warm welcome also persuaded Sandy to join a local country club. Soon after setting up shop in Baltimore he had played golf at the elite Five Farms Club as the guest of Reg Murphy, publisher of the Baltimore *Sun*. Shooting a terrific score of 79, he wanted to have access to the course—and its prestige. Sandy never applied, however, once he was informed that there was a five-to-ten-year waiting list for membership. The real reason, old-timers gossiped, was that Five Farms admitted blue-blooded WASPs, not Jews from Brooklyn.

Not to be deprived, Sandy told his fellow CEOs in the area that the lack of country club availability was "pretty bad for a city like Baltimore." He persuaded other executives of large Baltimore companies, including Black & Decker, Alex. Brown, and U.S. Fidelity and Guaranty Co., that the harbor city needed to offer more choices than Five Farms. Soon he was leading the charge to raise $40 million for a new private golf club called Caves Valley, where businesses could purchase memberships and have their own cabins built on a course to be designed by architect Tom Fazio. At the same time, Sandy, with the exclusive Five Farms inaccessible to him, quietly dropped his banter about becoming an Eastern Shore farmer and threw out the real-estate listings.

There were other disappointments about living in Baltimore. Marconi's, a classic Italian restaurant three blocks from Commercial Credit, quickly became one of Sandy's favorite lunchtime destinations. In an old restored town house painted white with black-and-white-striped awnings, a gaunt, elderly doorman nearly seven feet tall greeted the "regulars" entering the classic Italian eatery, a fixture on Saratoga Street since 1920. With gleaming teardrop chandeliers, ornate moldings, and starched linen tablecloths, Marconi's dining rooms had an old-fashioned atmosphere that made it a noontime institution for the salt-and-pepper-haired businessmen accustomed to their favorite tables. Sandy liked the deference of the headwaiter, who quickly learned his name and drink order, and soon established his "usual" order of Marconi's Italian salad, crab cakes, and French vanilla ice cream with homemade chocolate sauce.

Then one Monday after returning to Baltimore from New York, Sandy directed Krabbe, the executive assistant, to make a reservation for him at Marconi's.

"I can't," she said meekly.

"Why not?" he snapped.

"They're closed," Krabbe said.

"What do you mean, they're closed?"

"It's Monday," she offered, as if he would understand that notion.

"What do you mean they're closed?" he repeated, unwilling to register her explanation.

"They're always closed on Monday," she explained.

Sandy ranted that a city that wants big business can't let its restaurants close on Mondays, and he continued for many Mondays to demand a reservation at Marconi's. Finally, Krabbe, whose politeness and sense of decorum would never allow her to talk back to Sandy as Falls would, made a suggestion. "I know you're having a hard time accepting the fact that they're closed on Mondays, but they are," she said. "Why don't I make your Monday reservations at the Center Club?"

Sandy nodded in annoyed agreement. Of course, he had dined at the Center Club, a private club for business leaders, several times, because Commercial Credit was a member at the city's "power lunch" spot. But damn it, if he wanted Marconi's crab cakes on Mondays, he should be able to have them.

A DREAM DEFERRED

With Sandy's plans to reinvigorate Commercial Credit coming to fruition, he began preparing in April 1987 for the spring ritual that so many CEOs despise: the annual meeting of shareholders. John Fowler worked with Sandy on his speech, rehearsing it several times with him. On April 22, the day of the meeting, the cafeteria tables were pushed aside so that hundreds of chairs could be set up in a semicircle. Then Sandy's new board began arriving for their first look at the headquarters of the company they governed. Ex-president Ford caused a sensation when he entered the building with his Secret Service entourage. He had never heard of Commercial Credit when

Sandy invited him on the board but had accepted based on his earlier association with Sandy as a director of Shearson. Ford was dismayed when he entered the plain cafeteria with its linoleum floors and tacky orange-and-blue plaid curtains. *Sandy's no longer the "big leaguer,"* Ford thought.

Another new board member, Andrall Pearson, reacted similarly. Pearson had been the longtime president of PepsiCo, Inc., until 1984, when he became a professor at Harvard Business School. Pearson had gotten to know Jamie Dimon through his daughter, who had studied at Harvard Business School at the same time as Dimon and his wife, Judy. When Sandy was looking for directors, Jamie had recommended Pearson, a highly respected business leader. Now, after being picked up in the station wagon, the former Pepsi president remarked, "Jesus Christ, this is a real barebones operation."

To make matters more embarrassing, only fourteen outside shareholders and several dozen employees showed up in the room prepared for hundreds. As usual, Sandy was nervous about making a speech; he stumbled and sweated his way through the prepared remarks, explaining how he was attempting to turn the company around. After the perfunctory meeting was adjourned, Sandy hosted the board members at lunch. Pearson, who barely knew Sandy, was mildly disturbed to see him drink a gin martini before noon. But once Sandy began talking about the company in the more intimate setting, Pearson's opinion of the Commercial Credit CEO improved dramatically. Without prompting or notes, Sandy ticked off the company's average loan rates, branch activity, loan volume by type of loan, line-item expenses, loan-loss reserves—the kind of detail most chairmen either read from a report or have an underling recite. Even more amazing, Sandy made the humdrum business of consumer lending sound as exciting and promising as high finance. Sandy, who had a prior reputation as heading the best-run firm on the Street, told his directors that he would now take that credibility to improve Commercial Credit's stature in the market. He planned to go on the road to solicit support for the stock because consumer-finance companies fell between the cracks of securities analysts' industry groupings. "We are going to be a much more visible player," Sandy assured the directors, whom he was paying $50,000 each in Commercial Credit stock.

"Wow, this guy knows his stuff," Pearson told Dimon after the board meeting. "And he's got guts."

By summer, it was becoming clear that Sandy's Herculean efforts were paying off. Securities analysts from firms like Oppenheimer and Furman Selz began to write research reports on Commercial Credit and to recommend investors buy the stock. Quarterly earnings were expected to shoot up 100 percent. The stock price climbed 40 percent; from its initial offering price of $20.50, the stock closed in July 1987 at $29. The *Wall Street Journal*'s "Heard on the Street" column heralded Sandy's return: "Disproving the adage that there are no second acts in American lives, Sanford Weill is bringing Commercial Credit to glory after his first-act success with Shearson Lehman Brothers."

Sandy was on the way back! And now he wanted to return to New York, where the action was. Commercial Credit headquarters would remain in Baltimore, where rents were cheaper. Besides, few employees wanted to make the move to New York. But Sandy and his executives needed more room than was available in the Seagram Building. His search for new quarters took him to the Park Avenue Tower, a flashy new Helmut Jahn–designed building between Fifty-fifth and Fifty-sixth streets, west of Park Avenue. It had a three-story marble lobby with vaulted ceilings and a huge lighted pyramid on top. Sandy fell in love with the building and leased the top two floors. The new building didn't have a five-star restaurant on the ground floor, but Sandy's beloved Four Seasons was only four blocks away. He took great pains to design the floor plan and décor, employing his son-in-law Natan Bibliowicz, an architect. They designed the executive floor, a fourteen-foot-high penthouse with a brick walkway along the perimeter, creating a greenhouse effect with tall, sloping windows. The offices were placed on the inside with French doors, so that each executive could see what was going on inside as well as outside the office. For a busybody like Sandy, it was a perfect plan to keep tabs on everyone. He also ordered that a working fireplace, in white marble, be installed in the library, which had red walls, a pair of black leather Chesterfield sofas, and a large pantry equipped with a wine cooler, well-stocked liquor cabinet, and a drum of peanuts.

When the space was ready for occupancy, many of the New Yorkers began spending much more time there. Their deal with Sandy from the outset called for them to help turn around Commercial Credit and then use it as a platform to get back into the securities business. Willumstad and Magner, immersed in overseeing the branch network, spent more time in Baltimore, as did Jamie Dimon, who had rented a house in Baltimore. He found that he enjoyed being the senior executive in the headquarters building, and he relished Sandy's dependence on him. No longer able to wander the corridors, Sandy called Dimon several times a day to ask, "What's going on down there?" Dimon loved that Sandy could no longer yell at him; he needed his CFO to provide vital information.

Back in New York where he belonged, Sandy began laying the groundwork for his next move. He brought back Mary McDermott, who had originally joined him in 1965, to head up a new investor-relations and corporate communications department. McDermott, the early firm's first gal Friday, had risen to become Shearson's executive in charge of corporate communications, including chief spokesperson. She had recently quit the brokerage after twenty-one years, tired of the guerrilla warfare at Shearson following its acquisition of Lehman Brothers. McDermott, single and forty-four, took the job only after Sandy agreed to award her the lucrative options she was never given the first time around.

"I'm not that twenty-one-year-old girl you hired for eighty-five dollars a week," she told Sandy. "Girls need options, too. Not all of us will be swept off our feet by a knight in shining armor."

In September Sandy bought out Control Data's remaining 18 percent stake in Commercial Credit for more than $300 million, freeing him to move Commercial Credit in whatever direction he chose. He sniffed around for possible acquisition targets but concluded that most financial companies in mid-1987 were simply too expensive. But, he told Dimon, "usually things get corrected, and we'll be set up to exploit it."

Then, on October 19, 1987, that correction came with a vengeance. The Dow Jones Industrial Average plunged from the outset of trading. Wall Street reeled under the impact of what quickly became known as Black Monday. Sandy, who was out of town at a meeting, nearly went berserk. Like every American who owned stocks or equity funds, he reacted in horror as the market spiraled downward despite President Reagan's effort to tell the country that the economy remained strong. "Goddammit!" he yelled over and over as Dimon gave him updates on the stock market about every three minutes. At the end of the day, the stock market's 22.6 percent plunge dwarfed the crash of 1929—the worst day at the outset of the Depression saw stocks down 12.8 percent—and sent shock waves around the world. Investor confidence in stocks vanished as securities companies struggled to keep up with the huge influx of "sell" orders. Some firms simply stopped answering their phones, leaving terrified investors helpless in the face of the tumble.

On Tuesday, Sandy barreled into his New York office and watched Commercial Credit's stock continue to fall.

"I'm losing my whole life," Alison Falls moaned. After indulging her passion for shoes, she put her money into stocks.

"Your whole life?" Sandy sputtered. "What about mine? Millions and millions of dollars—gone!"

"Everything is relative, Sandy," retorted Falls, who mirrored the gloom of hundreds of Commercial Credit employees who had followed their CEO's directive to invest in the company's stock.

Several of the shell-shocked executives gathered in the library that evening, drank gin or vodka on the rocks, and commiserated. Commercial Credit stock closed at a new low of $17 a share. Even their discounted options, from $20 to $25 a share, were underwater and therefore worthless.

"My net worth is cut in half," John Fowler complained. "What are we going to do?"

No one answered what seemed a rhetorical question. Sandy, chewing his cigar and his fingernails, however, was deep in thought.

"Buy our stock!" he suddenly shouted. "We're going to buy our stock."

The executives stared at Sandy. No one said a word for several seconds until Bob Lipp spoke up. "It's the right thing to do. I'm buying." Soon everyone agreed to go into the market the next morning and buy as many Commercial Credit shares as they could afford.

"We believe in our company and ourselves," Sandy said enthusiastically. Black Monday would cause most of Wall Street to lose its financial nerve. Not Sandy Weill. Not Commercial Credit. As Shearson's CEO a decade earlier, he had used the bear market in the 1970s as an opportunity to buy cheap. This crash marked the end of a five-year bull market that had seen the Dow Jones Industrial Average rise from 777 in August 1982 to a high of 2,722 in August 1987. Just as bloated securities firms in the '70s were self-destructing, Wall Street houses now would feel the pressure as well. Sandy had been waiting for a market correction to bring down the prices of possible acquisitions, he told his associates. He admitted, of course, that he hadn't expected such extreme downward pressure.

"Look, we're tiny Commercial Credit," Dimon jumped in. "We aren't going to get invited to the dance by the prettiest girl. We need to find a firm in enough trouble to want us."

If other companies were going to suffer, then the man who had built a brilliant empire by snapping up troubled companies on the cheap was ready. "It's time to make our next move," Sandy stated.

The next morning, the senior executives bought more stock and tried to shore up morale among the troops. Sandy worked his Wall Street contacts to find vulnerability—and opportunity.

EF Hutton, which he had considered during his exile, was in even worse shape after Black Monday. Still plagued by doubts about its future in the aftermath of the check-overdraft scandal and a management shake-up, Hutton was hard hit by the stock market crash. It desperately needed a merger partner or substantial cash infusion.

Sandy approached Robert Fomon, who as Hutton's chairman had publicly snubbed him a year earlier. Now Fomon, pushed out in the firm's attempts to try new management, was nevertheless working with some Hutton directors who wanted to orchestrate the sale of the firm.

"Yeah, I could merge Commercial Credit with Hutton, maintain the Hutton name," Sandy eagerly told Fomon. "I'll move into the Hutton building as CEO."

Unbeknownst to Hutton president Robert Rittereiser, who was struggling to stay in charge, Sandy began meeting with some of the Hutton directors. The board members, losing confidence in the current management, showed keen interest in the Commercial Credit chairman. One Hutton director, Major League Baseball Commissioner Peter V. Ueberroth, talked several times with Sandy about his takeover of the brokerage house. Excited that her boss might be back in the big time, Alison Falls would announce, "The commish is on the line." The talks progressed to the point that Sandy secretly flew to California to meet with a very important Hutton director, actress Dina Merrill, E. F. Hutton's daughter.

At Hutton's next board meeting in November, the directors informed Rittereiser about their discussions with Sandy. Distressed and humiliated, Rittereiser convinced them to bring in investment bankers to find other potential bidders. That forced the board, under pressure to extract the highest possible price, to reject Sandy's request for an exclusive right to negotiate and instead to open up the bidding.

What Sandy had started—getting the board to actually examine a sale of Hutton—suddenly became a bidding war, with Dean Witter, Merrill Lynch, and Sandy's own creation, Shearson Lehman Brothers, entering the fray.

Sandy was considering an offer of $21 of Commercial Credit stock for each share of Hutton. Sandy and Dimon felt this amount would give them enough leeway to handle unforeseen problems at Hutton; besides, that was the most the Baltimore company could afford with its capital base. Suddenly, Shearson offered a startling bid of $29, nearly all cash. Led by Sandy's onetime protégé Peter Cohen, Shearson emerged victorious, backed by the deep pockets of American Express. Sandy's much smaller Commercial Credit couldn't compete with the firepower of his previous empire. Though he had entertained visions of himself running Hutton, Sandy reluctantly bowed out.

His pride demanded a win, but price mattered more. He couldn't risk Commercial Credit's survival to one-up Peter Cohen's higher bid from Shearson. When the newspapers reported the giant merger on December 15, 1987, the articles heralded Cohen for daring to create a financial juggernaut. *USA Today* noted the recent disappearance of the oversized shoes that had been in Cohen's office to symbolize the big shoes he had to fill when assuming the helm from Sandy Weill. The forty-one-year-old Cohen, Wall Street's youngest executive, "is tired of living in Sandy's shadow," the article continued, and was leaving "not a shadow of a doubt who's in charge of Shearson."

Sandy's dream of returning to conquer Wall Street would have to wait.

8

FAST JETS, GOLDEN PARACHUTES

The smell of blood was in the water, and Sandy Weill was a hungry shark. It was January 1988, and investors—still reeling from the October stock market crash—had abandoned stocks in droves. Brokerage firms that had been busily executing buy and sell orders for millions of individual investors before the crash found their phones silent. Branch offices were shuttered, and thousands of brokers laid off. The mergers-and-acquisitions business, another of Wall Street's long-running gravy trains, had come to a screeching halt. And to further test everyone's stamina and fortitude, the lingering savings-and-loan crisis, a scandal of enormous proportions, was intensifying. It all meant just one thing: It was Weill time on Wall Street.

Sandy's finely honed sense of trouble—and the opportunity such trouble presented—drew him to his favorite kind of prey: beloved, bloated, and bleeding. It didn't take long to home in on a target. For most of its one hundred fourteen years in business Smith Barney Inc. had catered to the so-called carriage trade, wealthy individuals who appreciated the coddling and deference the firm was accustomed to showing its customers. Its reputation was deeply embedded in the investing public's mind by an advertising campaign featuring the distinguished actor John Houseman intoning, "They make money the old-fashioned way. They earn it." The highly conservative firm ran its business in an old-fashioned way, too. It had come late to the mergers-and-acquisitions game, and its close attention to its clients had left Smith Barney with an expensive branch network of 2,100 brokers who were generating far fewer trades after the October crash.

But something else made Smith Barney even more attractive to a killer deal maker like Sandy. The securities firm had been purchased less than a year earlier by a high-flying Wall Street player that Sandy knew from an earlier time: Gerald Tsai Jr. Gerry Tsai had made his name in the early 1960s as a gunslinging manager of mutual funds, first at Fidelity Investments and then for his own flagship Manhattan Fund. Tsai's stock picks, including such glamour stocks as Polaroid and Xerox, made him rich and famous. During his heyday, a stock price would move merely on the rumor that "the Chinaman's buying."

Nothing if not opportunistic, Tsai in the early 1980s had begun assembling a massive conglomerate built around the core of American Can Co., an old-line manufacturer of tin cans that nevertheless was prestigious enough to be one of the thirty stocks that comprised the Dow Jones Industrial Average. Under Tsai's management the company had sold off its container-manufacturing businesses to focus on retailing and now owned such companies as the Musicland/Sam Goody chain of retail record stores, the Fingerhut mail-order operation, and San Diego's landmark Hotel del Coronado. But Tsai's real focus was on turning American Can—recently renamed Primerica—into a financial-services conglomerate. Smith Barney was the crown jewel sitting atop such other businesses as mutual funds and insurance.

But Tsai had made one big mistake, a shocking miscalculation for someone with his reputation for financial savvy: He bought the brokerage firm at the peak of a bull market. Not only that, he had paid dearly for it. The $750 million Tsai had paid was twice the firm's book value and, to make matters worse, he had borrowed heavily to finance the purchase. Now with business at an ebb and the weight of those loans pressing down on him, Tsai knew something had to be done. Sandy knew it, too.

Sandy's first opportunity to sound out Tsai came from an unexpected quarter. John Hsu, Commercial Credit's investment officer, was, like Tsai, a Chinese American, and the two men met occasionally to compare notes. Tsai had invited Hsu to dinner to meet Tsai's new wife—the third Mrs. Tsai—and Hsu, still struggling to cope with Sandy's volatile mood swings, made sure his boss knew the meeting was social and nothing else. God forbid Sandy should find out via Wall Street's hyperactive rumor mill that his chief investment officer was dining with Gerry Tsai.

Sandy seized the moment. "Tell him we have a lot of capacity and a lot of talent here," he told Hsu. "We have a heavyweight team who is very familiar with the brokerage business." He added that Tsai's talents ran more toward analyzing stocks and the market, not managing complex operations.

"Okay, I'll mention that," Hsu said, uncertain whether his mercurial boss was merely offering a helping hand or making the opening move in a gambit to take over Primerica.

If Smith Barney's problems were weighing on Tsai, the cocky Primerica chairman gave no sign of it at dinner with Hsu. Instead, he chatted about his two new loves—his wife, a broker at Kidder, Peabody, and his new 120-foot motor yacht on which he and his bride had recently toured the Mediterranean. He regaled his guest with descriptions of his luxurious Fifth Avenue duplex apartment overlooking Central Park and its specially designed room for his gleaming white Steinway grand piano. When Hsu passed along Sandy's message, Tsai seemed nonplussed by the offer and went on to other topics.

Now it was Sandy's move again. Was Tsai bluffing, too proud to show his friend John Hsu any hint of trouble? At some point Tsai would feel the noose around his neck getting tighter, and then he would go to Wall Street to raise more money. And he would surely go to J. Ira Harris, one of the country's preeminent deal makers and one of Sandy's old friends. Harris had recently joined the prestigious firm of Lazard Frères & Co., recruited by its chairman Felix Rohatyn. But Harris and Sandy came from similar backgrounds. Harris had been a poor kid in the Bronx and, like Sandy, had suffered early rejection from Wall Street's "club." Indeed, Harris had thirty-two rejection letters from investment firms that he kept in a scrapbook in his Chicago office. He and Sandy, their waistlines betraying their love of food and drink, had dined together occasionally at the Four Seasons and loved to gossip about business over a game of golf. Harris wasn't entirely surprised to get a call from Sandy.

"Everybody knows you want Smith Barney," Harris said, during one of his periodic chats with Sandy. But the investment banker had nothing to offer, at least not yet. Harris knew his old friend from Brooklyn would relish tackling the operational problems plaguing Primerica. *Deep down, Sandy is a salesman,* Harris thought to himself. *He could work wonders with Smith Barney's brokers, who would regard him as one of their own.*

True to Sandy's mental script, in early 1988 Tsai arrived in his black Cadillac stretch limousine for a breakfast meeting with Harris and Rohatyn at New York's Regency Hotel. Tsai asked the investment bankers to look at "all options" for the company to raise more cash. Harris suggested selling Smith Barney—albeit at a considerably lower price than Tsai had paid for it—and concentrating on the remaining businesses. But Tsai wanted to save face. He couldn't accept selling the troubled brokerage for half of what he paid. Besides, his growing insurance business needed money, too. While the insurance business was booming, the way in which insurance was sold required that agents be paid a fat commission that often exceeded the amount of the premiums that customers paid in the first few years of a policy. Just as Sandy predicted, the noose was tightening.

Harris began examining a number of options that Primerica might pursue to extricate itself from its troubling situation. Then in April *Barron's* ran a lengthy story entitled "The House That Gerry Built—How Solid Are the Foundations of Primerica's Growth?" The critical piece tore apart Tsai's rosy spin on the company's finances, pointing out that Smith Barney's balance sheet valuation had been halved in the aftermath of the October crash and revealing the "telltale signs of the company's growing cash bind." Now the noose was *really* getting tight. Harris, whose long-term relationships with clients gave him extra credibility with them and deep insight into them, gently suggested to Tsai: "Maybe Primerica should become part of a bigger company." He chose his words very carefully to avoid any hint that Primerica had to be "saved" or "taken over," anathema to the image-conscious Tsai.

Reluctantly, Tsai authorized Harris to investigate the possible sale of Primerica. Around the same time, Tsai quietly put into place addenda to existing severance agreements that would give him and his key managers lucrative payments if they lost control of Primerica in the event of a takeover. The existing agreements had protected the executives in the event of a hostile takeover; the addenda protected them even if the deal was friendly. Carefully avoiding any mention of "golden parachutes," the executives told Primerica's board that the new agreements would enable management to get the best possible price for the company because they wouldn't have to be worried about their jobs or financial well-being.

At Lazard Frères, Harris, true to his duty as an investment banker to do his best for his client, considered various possible buyers, including European firms that might want a foothold in the U.S. financial-services industry. But he kept circling back to Sandy and Commercial Credit. *He's just such a logical choice,* the banker thought. *He's a guy with a base, solid assets, a good balance sheet, and Wall Street savvy.* Comparing Commercial

Credit and Primerica, Harris saw that putting the two companies together created an "overlay" of complementary financial products. Still, there was a tremendous obstacle standing in the way of such a deal: Sandy and Gerry Tsai. The two powerful CEOs had too much at stake for either to come out a loser, yet their personalities would demand that only one could be the boss in the end.

In late spring Harris called Sandy. "What about the whole thing?" He didn't have to spell out that he meant all of Primerica—the insurance operations, the mail-order unit, and other stray segments in addition to the real prize Sandy sought: Smith Barney.

"I have a big appetite," Sandy replied.

In a few days a huge package labeled GREENWICH arrived on Sandy's desk. The collection of Primerica's financial data was code-named for the town in which the company was based. Similarly, Commercial Credit would be known as "Baltimore." Sandy forwarded a copy of the Greenwich package to Jamie Dimon in Baltimore and told him to "read it on the train. We'll talk about it when you get here."

When his young protégé arrived in Sandy's office, the two men could barely contain their excitement. "Fascinating!" Dimon exclaimed. "If we only had the money for it."

Here, at last, was their chance to prove how wrong American Express had been about their abilities. But it would take guts and more to accept this challenge. With annual sales of $912 million, Commercial Credit was only one-fourth the size of Primerica, whose sales were $3.8 billion. Head counts were even more disparate: Commercial Credit had 3,700 employees compared to Primerica's 22,000. But Sandy wasn't one to be deterred by such statistics. After all, he had started his initial acquisition binge in 1970 when tiny Corned Beef With Lettuce took over the much larger Hayden Stone.

"This one is a stretch," he conceded while salivating at the prospect of getting his hands on Smith Barney—his vehicle back into the business he knew so well.

Sandy and Dimon quickly mapped out a plan for doing the necessary due diligence. Dimon would scrutinize Primerica's dicey balance sheet to formulate a strategy of divestitures and write-offs that would win the approval of the ratings agencies if the deal was done. Sandy activated his old friend, Robert Greenhill, the Morgan Stanley investment banker, to build extensive models on each Primerica business and its cash flow. Then he briefed his top executives, the core group that Sandy now called the "planning group," basically the men who had endured the interminable dinner ritual in Baltimore.

"We can take this and turn it into something big," he told his managers. "We can't move up if we stay at Commercial Credit. It just doesn't have the sexy businesses."

Gathered in the office's "library" with its blazing fireplace, the men exchanged excited glances. After whipping Commercial Credit into shape, Sandy's associates were starting to feel all dressed up with nowhere to go. Suddenly they had a destination.

One executive asked about valuation. "I'm not known for paying too much," Sandy told him. Another raised questions about one of Primerica's insurance units, a company called A.L. Williams & Associates, that infuriated other companies in the insurance industry by attacking their products while selling its own kind of insurance called "term life." Sandy agreed it needed further study, although he noted it was growing very fast and, more important, had a sales force of two hundred thousand.

"To Sandy, that's like candy to a baby," said John Fowler of the immense sales force.

Before leaving for the night, the colleagues agreed to ramp up an intensive analysis of Primerica. Harris told them Primerica's records in Greenwich would be open to them on weekends, when employees weren't around. Sandy could speak confidentially to the heads of Primerica's business units and to the company's chief financial officer, Mike Roth. But he couldn't meet with Gerry Tsai. Harris knew these two strong personalities would wind up clashing if they were brought together before the deal was negotiated. Harris told them both that he would spend whatever time was necessary shuttling between their Manhattan offices. He also told each that the deal would get him what he wanted. Tsai would be saved the embarrassment of having Primerica perhaps blow up in his face, and he would walk away with plenty of money to indulge his exorbitant lifestyle. Sandy would get a financial platform much bigger and more prestigious than his dowdy little consumer-finance company. "The Smith Barney name will get you back in the game," Harris assured him.

As the other executives undertook their various assignments, Sandy decided to take a closer look at the A.L. Williams insurance operations. For one thing, it was an important piece of Primerica, accounting for about a third of the parent's profits. For another, it was constantly under attack

from other insurance companies for its aggressive and sometimes misleading tactics to persuade customers to switch from the "whole-life" policies
that the other firms peddled to its own lower-cost "term-life" policies.
Founded eleven years earlier by a former high school coach, Arthur L.
(Art) Williams, the company employed a part-time army of two hundred
thousand welders, teachers, truck drivers, and other working-class agents
to sell the term-life policies, which basically provided only a stated payout
and were in effect only for a stated period of time. Whole-life policies, on
the other hand, were held until the owner died, and part of the higher premiums the policy owner paid were invested. Art Williams knew from bitter
experience, though, that the investment results of such policies were often
lackluster and that a typical insurance buyer would get a much bigger bang
for his buck from a simple term-life policy. Despite the Williams company's renegade image, Sandy hoped that it might be like IDS, the financial advisory firm for the middle class that he had championed at American
Express.

Gerry Tsai called the Williams company's chief executive, Treacy
Beyer, to tell him that a secret visitor would be arriving at Williams's Atlanta headquarters in a few days.

"Smith Barney is in big trouble," Tsai told Beyer. "Nobody's supposed
to know, but a man named Sandy Weill wants to visit your office. Just
make sure he's happy; he may want to buy the whole company."

Expecting the usual entourage that accompanied Tsai on his visits to Atlanta, Beyer was startled when a short, pudgy man with a red face and
someone who looked like a teenager showed up a few days later. They introduced themselves as Sandy Weill and Jamie Dimon. "I just want to kick
the tires," Sandy said casually. As Beyer set out to take the two on a tour of
the offices, Sandy stopped to shake hands with employees.

"Hi, I'm Sandy Weill," he said. "Who are you? What do you do? Do
you like it here?"

If this is supposed to be a big secret, it won't be anymore, Beyer
thought.

From Atlanta, Sandy and Dimon flew to Amelia Island, Georgia, to
meet the company's founder, Art Williams. Sandy and Williams fell for
each other instantly. Both had come from nothing to create huge companies and make themselves millionaires many times over. Both were emotional overachievers striving constantly to prove their worth. And they
both had a deep respect for salespeople. Yet they had their differences. A

true son of the South, Williams had a deep disdain for doing business with Yankees, and Sandy was nothing if not a New York Yankee. While Sandy now wore suits tailored for him on London's Savile Row, Williams typically was attired in shorts and golf shirts straight from the JCPenney catalog. Williams, a fundamentalist Christian, regarded alcohol as sinful, while Sandy loved quaffing cocktails and wine. Nevertheless, when Sandy rose to leave, he and Williams embraced.

Winging their way back to New York, Sandy and Dimon agreed that Williams & Associates' sole product, term-life insurance, worked for a large class of consumers, even though its distribution through part-timers was unorthodox. "Every person who bought that insurance is probably better off," Dimon said.

Sandy, with his keen eye for sizing up potential partners, focused on Art Williams. "Art is real," he said. "Art is down to earth and honest. I feel good about Art." Nevertheless, he instructed Dimon to investigate the details of term-life insurance. It was so cheap; he wanted to be sure the product was really profitable. Sandy wasn't worried about how it was sold. He intended to take a much firmer hand than did Gerry Tsai, and he was certain he could get Art Williams to tone down his attacks on the other insurance companies.

THE ULTIMATE BARGAINING CHIP

By early summer, negotiations were going full tilt. Jamie Dimon left Bob Lipp and Bob Willumstad to run Commercial Credit while he spent more time poring over Primerica's financial data. "Work the upside, work the downside," Sandy kept telling him. From the start, they decided the purchase would be made mostly with stock, with a small cash sweetener, to avoid burdening the deal with debt. Sandy was determined that Commercial Credit's debt rating stay at its current level, and that limited how much he could pay for Primerica. Dimon was charged with figuring out the cost down to the last dollar.

Then Dimon began coming across the severance agreements. First one, then another golden parachute popped up. He couldn't believe it. Their complexity struck him as designed to hide their true cost. The agreements had been approved by Primerica's board in segments and had many complicated components, including pension plans, tax rebates, bonuses, stock, options, and assorted "enhancements."

Sandy exploded when Dimon told him what he had found. "How much? How much?" Sandy screamed. Dimon said he didn't know, and that drove Sandy into a further rage. "There's absolutely no way even Primerica's board knew what all this added up to," Dimon explained to Sandy, trying to calm him. Under Sandy's relentless pressure to come up with a figure, Dimon finally estimated that the assorted severance agreements for Primerica's top ten executives could cost more than $60 million.

"What?" Sandy shouted. "Sixty million! That's it! It's over!"

He summoned Ira Harris from Chicago. When the investment banker walked into his office, Sandy launched into another tirade, fulminating about the "greed" and "sleaziness" of the golden parachutes. "The Primerica board should never have let this happen!" he screamed. "They add millions of dollars to the price tag. They'll kill the deal!"

"I know the parachutes really stick in your craw," Harris responded, but added firmly, "Sandy, it's very simple—it's part of the transaction. It's part of the cost of the deal."

"Hell, I know it's customary to give the acquired CEO certain perks, like office space and consulting agreements, for a period of time," Sandy snarled. "But this is extreme. It's robbing the shareholders of part of the purchase price they would get." Then he stormed out of the office.

Harris hurried down Park Avenue to Gerry Tsai's office on the thirty-first floor of the Pan Am Building. He knew that he and Tsai had to come up with something fast to lure Sandy back to the table. Several companies had expressed interest in acquiring bits and pieces of Primerica, but only Sandy Weill was daring enough or dumb enough to consider buying the entire company.

The bait was hand delivered by messenger to Sandy's office a few hours later. The large envelope from Harris was marked PHOTO: DO NOT BEND. Inside was a color photograph of the hottest and latest status symbol for powerful and pampered CEOs: the new Gulfstream IV private jet. Harris had placed before Sandy the ultimate bargaining chip with the attached note: "This could be yours."

Since leaving American Express, Sandy had sorely missed the prestige and convenience of having a private jet at his disposal. The Gulfstream IV was the largest business jet on the market, a technological marvel capable of carrying twenty passengers anywhere in the world at high speeds, high altitudes, and in great comfort. Even with its price tag of more than

$20 million, CEOs were fighting to get on the waiting list for their own G-4, which took nine months to build.

Soon the portly and jovial investment banker was back in Sandy's office. "I know how much you would love to have your own corporate jet," Harris told Sandy. "You and I both know it's a lot easier for a CEO to get a plane when it comes along with an acquisition than to go to your board and say, 'I want to spend twenty-two million dollars for a plane,'" he said. "Look, you're full of crap if this doesn't get you back to the table."

Harris didn't know it, but Sandy was fully aware of the logic behind his argument. He had earlier asked the Commercial Credit board for permission to buy a much smaller, less costly plane and had been denied. And Harris didn't tell Sandy how much pressure he had put on Tsai to include the G-4 in the deal. "Gerry, goddammit, you better wake up to this," Harris had warned him. "You're going to have a real mess on your hands, and you need somebody to help fix it. You need Sandy Weill."

With negotiations back on track, Harris returned to Chicago, content in the knowledge that few other investment bankers could have saved the deal. A throwback to the days when relationships mattered, Harris felt his intimate knowledge of both men gave him ways to keep the parties talking and help them do what was best for their companies. And he suspected that those skills might be tested again before this deal closed.

He was right.

The Commercial Credit team struggled through the summer to understand Primerica and how its many disparate parts fit—or didn't fit—together. By the second week of August the final details of the deal were beginning to come together. Primerica's main liaison throughout the summer had been Mike Roth, its chief financial officer. Accustomed to Gerry Tsai's hands-off management style, Roth had been surprised at Sandy's aggressive, nit-picking approach to the negotiations. Now Roth had to fill in the details of the complex golden parachutes, putting real numbers into the formulas where only "assumptions" had been used earlier to calculate the various benefits the senior Primerica executives would collect. He turned over his final calculations to the Commercial Credit team on Friday, August 19, 1988. His estimated total cost: nearly $90 million.

On Saturday morning Roth received a summons to Sandy's Greenwich estate. He drove to Connecticut from Manhattan expecting to explain the various provisions in the contracts to Sandy. But when he walked into the room and faced a glowering Sandy and half a dozen Commercial Credit executives, he realized that he had stepped into a lion's den.

"Where's Gerry?" Sandy snapped, as if Tsai's presence were required as well.

"I told Gerry I was stopping by, but he's on a trip on his yacht," Roth responded.

Sandy erupted. "What's going on here?" he bellowed. He threw the documents containing Roth's complex calculations at the startled financial executive and continued to rage about the huge increase in costs over Jamie Dimon's $60-million estimate of the golden parachutes.

But Roth held firmly to his calculations. "My job is to do the best for us," he retorted. "If that pisses you off, tough." Driving away from Sandy's mansion, Roth was convinced the deal was dead.

Ira Harris was playing golf that weekend at the majestic Castle Pines Golf Club near Denver. He had been invited by F. Ross Johnson, the president and chief executive of RJR Nabisco, to discuss strategies for boosting the company's stock price. When Harris got word of the confrontation between Sandy and Roth, he told Johnson he was needed urgently in New York. An RJR jet was put at his disposal. As he boarded the plane, Harris noticed its registration number contained a 13 and he suddenly felt better about the deal. Harris, an admitted triskaidekaphiliac—one who has an uncommon attraction to the number 13—was born on April 13 and makes sure that the number 13 is part of his phone numbers and license plate. As he winged his way eastward he found another reason for comfort: "Sanford I. Weill" had thirteen letters.

Back in New York on Sunday, Harris called both Sandy and Tsai to assure them "everything is going to be fine." He then scheduled a meeting with the Commercial Credit team and their investment banker, Bob Greenhill, for the next day.

On Monday, August 22, Sandy was still seething. Harris took him aside before the meeting. "Sandy, the golden parachutes are part of this deal—a deal that makes too much sense for both sides to come apart now," he told his old friend. When Sandy continued to rant about the excesses contained in the golden parachutes, Harris took aim at his weak spot—the Gulfstream jet.

"Fine. Gerry will put the plane up for sale tomorrow," Harris shot back. He indicated that bids would come in immediately from chief executives all over the world eager to step up in the queue for one of the prestigious planes. The proceeds of the sale would be used to offset some of the expenses of the golden parachutes. "You know I'll do it," Harris threatened. "I'll take the plane away."

If Sandy was going to take over Primerica with all its problems, he damn well wanted that jet as part of the package. Begrudgingly, Sandy suggested they look over the numbers one last time. "We'll be leveraged to the teeth to do this," he complained. "We can't negotiate past a certain point. There's only so much we can pay."

The negotiators around the table knew Sandy was approaching his limit. As much as he wanted Smith Barney—*and* the G-4—they knew he wouldn't swallow the golden parachutes if the total price tag for Primerica threatened Commercial Credit's credit ratings or its stock price. He had agreed to concessions to Gerry Tsai that didn't pose any risk, such as a seat on the board and a face-saving title of "chairman of the executive committee." Now Greenhill demanded that Tsai and Primerica reciprocate by shaving a few million dollars off the exorbitant golden parachutes.

Sandy, drained by the incessant wrangling and tension, looked physically ill. Dimon thought his boss was nauseated at the prospect of yet more tense arguments about the golden parachutes.

Sandy sighed disgustedly. "I can't do this," he said. No one knew if he was referring to the entire deal or just the discussion of golden parachutes. Then he turned to Greenhill and said, "Bob, you do it." The tension eased palpably—the deal was still under negotiation.

At that moment, Harris popped out of his chair to announce he was going to the bathroom. He looked pointedly at Greenhill and said, "Greenie, do you have to go to the bathroom, too?" Greenhill followed him through the door. Veteran investment bankers opposing each other across a conference table can sense when negotiations are at the critical stage that only they, talking candidly and confidentially to each other, can push beyond. In the restroom the two quickly worked out a compromise: If Tsai would forgo some of his $30 million in severance payments, Sandy would give the Primerica chairman two hundred hours a year on the Gulfstream jet and cover some of his travel and entertainment expenses. Sandy would see that he was saving millions in up-front cash, while Tsai would see that this was a way to preserve his extravagant lifestyle.

Greenhill returned immediately to the conference room and told Sandy, "It's done." Harris meanwhile detoured to another office to phone Tsai with news of the compromise. When his client resisted giving up any of his

$30 million, Harris stopped him abruptly. "Gerry, don't push this," he warned. "One more dollar either way, and we've blown it."

When Harris returned to the conference room he sat down beside Sandy and Greenhill while signaling the others to beat a hasty retreat. "Sandy, this is it. Make your decision," Harris told the Commercial Credit chairman. "If you don't think this is right, don't do it. Either way, we're all going to be good friends and we'll go from there."

Sandy nodded. They had a deal!

According to Dimon's calculations, Commercial Credit would pay one share of its stock and $7 in cash for each share of Primerica, giving the transaction a value of $1.7 billion. The 1.5 million shares that Tsai and his family owned would make the outgoing chairman the company's biggest shareholder. There was no doubt, however, that Sandy would be the new company's chairman, chief executive officer, and president. Primerica shareholders would end up with 54 percent of the new company, but only four of the fifteen directors' seats. And Sandy insisted the company slash its $1.60 dividend to 20 cents to conserve cash.

Now Sandy and Tsai had to persuade their respective boards that the deal was the best for each company. With board members vacationing around the world, much of the persuasion had to be done by phone. Andrall Pearson, the Harvard Business School professor, took Sandy's call at his daughter's rented home on Martha's Vineyard.

"We have a great deal," Sandy began. "It includes Smith Barney, insurance companies, mutual funds, a bunch of stuff—"

"Commercial Credit is doing well now. Why would you put it at risk?" Pearson interrupted. He also criticized Primerica's disparate assemblage of companies, the result of Tsai's opportunism rather than a disciplined growth strategy. "How are you going to run it?" Pearson asked. "You're taking on a lot of unwanted and unknown types of businesses."

But Sandy countered that acquisitions rarely come neatly packaged. "It's as if you want a turkey sandwich, but the menu only offers a club sandwich," he explained. "You have to order the club sandwich and toss the tomato and bacon to end up with the turkey sandwich you wanted."

Pearson laughed at Sandy's apt food metaphor. Sandy offered good reasons for the combination, and Pearson knew he was a savvy, rational operator. "It's a big move," he said, but gave his approval, as did every other Commercial Credit director.

A thoroughly defeated Gerry Tsai met his board on Monday morning,

August 29. He sat quietly as Felix Rohatyn presented the case for merging and the directors approved it. The deal was announced just before 10:00 that morning.

That afternoon Sandy and Dimon headed for Smith Barney's headquarters at 1345 Avenue of the Americas to meet the partners. Sandy had already met George Vonder Linden, the forty-seven-year-old president of the firm, during the due-diligence period and had grilled him thoroughly about the business. Vonder Linden had come away from that first meeting recalling what one of Sandy's earlier colleagues said about the experience of working with Sandy: "Sandy makes you money, but you hate it all the time you're getting rich."

Vonder Linden knew Sandy's reputation as a ferocious cost cutter and had warned him before the partners' meeting not to bring up the touchy issue of the partners' high compensation. Many of Smith Barney's top managers had lucrative five-year contracts that had been put in place when Primerica bought the firm a little over a year earlier. But after some short introductory remarks to the partners, Sandy called for questions, and one of the first was about the contracts. "Don't expect to make that much money now," Sandy responded. "Most of you guys are overrated." The stunned managers could think of little else to ask their new boss, and the meeting soon ended. In that one short meeting, Sandy had shattered the morale of the Smith Barney executives. Vonder Linden was besieged by complaints from them as he returned to his office, and he was extremely irritated that Sandy had done exactly what he had advised him not to do. As he entered his office, his secretary said Sandy Weill was on the line.

"How did it go?" Sandy boomed into the phone.

"Not great," an annoyed Vonder Linden answered. "You cut them down the first thing."

Sandy nearly went berserk and began screaming over the phone. Unaccustomed to such uncivil behavior, Vonder Linden held the phone away from his ear but could still catch snatches of the tirade, including the words "bunch of goddamned babies."

It was bad enough that Sandy had run afoul of Smith Barney's top managers on what should have been his triumphant return to the brokerage business. But much worse was the sour welcome investors gave him that Monday. The stocks of both Commercial Credit and Primerica fell on news of the deal. Investors in Commercial Credit didn't like all those new shares the company was issuing to buy Primerica, since the new shares would dilute their own holdings. Meanwhile, analysts were sniping at Primerica, noting that it was obviously in trouble and wasn't dominant in any of its businesses.

The second day after the announcement was little better. *USA Today* wrote: "Wall Street is giving Commercial Credit chief Sandy Weill a rude homecoming." *The Wall Street Journal* was equally downbeat: "Many in the financial services industry are wondering if Sanford Weill knows something they don't." The stocks of both companies slipped again that day.

Later that week, Sandy was slated to meet with securities analysts, a meeting that had been scheduled long before the deal to buy Primerica had been finalized. Mary McDermott greeted the arriving analysts at the Metropolitan Club and was shocked at the questions they posed as they entered. "Is he giving away the store?" one queried. Another analyst was painfully blunt: "Has he lost his fucking mind?"

McDermott warned Sandy before he went into the meeting that the analysts were after blood. "They already know about the golden parachutes," she warned him.

Without pleasantries, Sandy opened his remarks: "Before anyone asks, I don't like the golden parachutes any better than you do, but they are contractual obligations that must be honored."

Sandy stayed angry much of September, but that proved a powerful motivator for him. He had proved his critics wrong at nearly every juncture of his career. Now he would have to do it again.

9

A SPLENDID BALANCE

While Sandy had little use for Gerald Tsai, he wanted to nurture his relationship with one of Primerica's most important assets, Art Williams. The ex–football coach was single-handedly shaking up the insurance industry and making a fortune for himself selling term-life insurance. Sandy wanted to ensure that Williams's working-class army of 200,000 part-time agents, who called themselves "term-ites," would do the same for Primerica. Sandy had heard of Williams's revival-like "superseminars," in which the forty-six-year-old Georgian fired up the huge sales force that loved him as much as traditional-life insurance agents hated him. When Sandy told Williams he would like to attend the upcoming event in Detroit, the insurance renegade promptly asked him to speak to his loyal flock. Sandy accepted, not knowing exactly what he was getting into. He asked Mary McDermott to work on a speech that would appeal to the Williams agents. To prepare, she viewed videotapes of past superseminars, which left her repeating, "Oh my god, oh my god, oh my god." In the tapes the audience would go wild after Williams's every word, thundering "Right!" and clambering to their feet for standing ovations. McDermott's first thought was how much Williams resembled the televangelist Jimmy Swaggart: persuasive and emotional at the same time. She knew she couldn't turn Sandy into a Bible-thumping crusader, but she did manage to craft a kind of down-home speech for her boss, who had never given a down-home speech in his life.

The October morning of the event, Sandy had use of the existing Primerica jet, a Gulfstream II. (The Gulfstream IV was still on order.) Since he could fill up the plane without any extra cost, Sandy cajoled several executives on his floor to come along for the ride, including Chuck Prince, Joseph DeAlessandro, John Fowler, McDermott, and Dimon. When they landed, they were whisked into limousines and ferried into the underground bowels of the huge arena in Detroit where the Pistons basketball team played.

Like a rock star, Sandy, accompanied by Joan, was escorted to VIP seats at the front of the stage. He was stunned at the cheering throng of more than ten thousand "term-ites." Treacy Beyer, who had shown him the Atlanta offices in the summer, introduced him to his wife, Darcy, who would sit with him until he was introduced to go on stage. Joan was escorted with the other executives to another area of the stadium.

Sandy was terrified. When Darcy Beyer patted his knee to tell him he would be fine, the CEO unconsciously grabbed her hand in a tight grip. His hand was ice cold.

On the stage before them was the emcee, a short, balding, chubby man in flaming red shorts and a bright yellow "Do It" T-shirt. Behind him on a large screen, a huge rock symbolizing Prudential Insurance Co. was being beaten and blasted to the theme music from the movie *Ghostbusters.* "Who ya gonna call?" the soundtrack blared. "ROCK-busters!" the crowd screamed.

With the audience in a frenzy, Williams sprinted to the podium. "Folks, how bad do you want to be somebody?" he shouted. "Bad!" came the raucous reply. Nearly each person clung to a copy of Williams's best-selling book *All You Can Do Is All You Can Do, But All You Can Do Is Enough!* They cried when Williams reminded them in his Southern drawl of why he got into the insurance business in the first place. The sudden death of his father, whose whole-life coverage couldn't support the family, led him to discover a better product. That's when he realized that a policy that cost less but paid out more because it lasted for a certain term was the answer for middle-class America. More cheers and tears.

Still holding Darcy Beyer's hand in a death grip, Sandy was mortified. Then, to much fanfare, including bullhorns and balloons, Williams introduced Sandy as virtually the new savior of the corporate world. The insurance crusader in shorts embraced Sandy in his dark, sweat-soaked suit, crushing the two cigars in his pocket.

Standing stiffly with his prepared speech, Sandy started to read. His lips twitched so much from nerves that he had trouble getting the words out. When he read one of the first sentences that ended with "Right?"—a device McDermott had inserted to match Williams's knack for getting the audience to respond—Sandy was about to read the next sentence when thousands jumped to their feet and yelled "RIGHT!" The Commercial Credit CEO looked up, stunned, until he realized they were responding to him. He liked it, so he yelled again, "Right?" The thundering response: "Right!"

Despite the sweat running down his cheeks, somehow Sandy managed to read through his hokey speech about his "F-E-E-L"—Fun, Energy, Enthusiasm, and Love—management philosophy. His performance was awful, but the crowd didn't care. They loved him. "Stud! Stud! Stud!" they chanted, a favorite term of endearment in Williams's athletic model. They could relate to someone who was scared of public speaking. After a standing ovation and a bear hug from Williams, Sandy walked into the arena, where agents surrounded him, trying to touch his sleeve and get his autograph.

When the Commercial Credit crew boarded the plane for New York, no one said a word at first. Only after everyone had a stiff drink did they talk about what just happened. "Can you imagine those lunatics going after Middle America peddling financial services?" someone asked, amazed.

Sandy looked blissfully happy. "Yeah, I can."

Sandy returned from Detroit on an emotional high. "I'm truly happy again," he told Dimon one evening when they were worrying how they could manage such a far-flung empire.

When he heard that Smith Barney was holding its President's Council meeting of top brokers later that month, Sandy instantly wanted to be part of it. Maybe they would show him the same adoration. He was disappointed, then, when the firm's president, Vonder Linden, respectfully asked his soon-to-be new boss to stay away from the Pebble Beach resort until the conference's second day: "I want to calm the troops," he explained.

Not one to be denied, Sandy appeared on the first day, as Vonder Linden was opening the conference—to the Smith Barney president's complete surprise. When Sandy picked up an agenda, he angrily noticed that he wasn't one of the speakers.

Sandy's countenance flashed angry red. No one would keep him away from the company he'd just sweated blood to buy. Besides, he planned to have drinks with the brokers and pick their brains. The Commercial Credit executives who had traveled to Pebble Beach with Sandy were certain of one thing as they left the conference: Vonder Linden's days were numbered.

Once the transaction was set for closing, the companies released the prospectus, which included details about the golden parachutes. By early December, many shareholders were protesting the change-in-control agreement and threatening lawsuits to halt the payments. Angry shareholders complained that 6 percent of Primerica's $1.7 billion value was being paid to ten executives. They singled out Tsai's cash payment of $30 million, as well as other benefits such as unspecified "business and personal travel."

During Primerica's shareholder meeting on December 15, at the Sheraton Hotel in Stamford, a besieged Tsai wore a bulletproof vest concealed under his suit. Commercial Credit held its shareholder meeting on the same day. Both companies approved the merger, and it officially closed that day with Sandy taking the better-known Primerica name. That night, Sandy hosted an elegant dinner at Le Cygne, a fancy restaurant in a two-story town house off Madison Avenue. In the private dining room next to the wine cellar, Sandy welcomed his senior executives and the new board members, which now included Gerry Tsai. Despite the gastronomic delights for which Le Cygne was famous and excellent bottles of 1979 Château Talbot, Sandy didn't seem to enjoy the meal, a rare event for him. Dimon, seated next to Sandy, could see that Gerry Tsai's presence put his boss in a foul mood.

Halfway through the meal, a Primerica accounting manager tried to speak discreetly to Dimon about authorization for a wire transfer before midnight. The CFO whispered to Sandy, "They want my permission to wire the parachute money."

Sandy tensed up. He glared at Tsai and then blurted out in front of the guests, "It's just not right, Gerry. It's just not right."

Dimon noticed that Sandy seemed flushed and sick to his stomach. Sandy pushed away his plate; his face grew dark and menacing.

"Sandy, should I sign the wire authorization?" Dimon repeated.

With his teeth clenched, Sandy barely spit out the words: "Just do it."

GETTING UP TO SPEED

Now that Sandy had Primerica firmly under his control, he surveyed his new empire and liked the potential of what he saw. Certainly there were plenty of entities he would want to get rid of, not least the Fingerhut catalog operation. But the three major units at the core of the company—Commercial Credit, Smith Barney, and A.L. Williams—provided a splendid balance between the cyclicality of the brokerage and investment-banking business and the steadier cash flow produced by insurance and consumer loans. They also gave him entrée to every stratum of the American economy: Commercial Credit catered to blue-collar workers hard-pressed for other sources of money; A.L. Williams sold insurance aimed squarely at the middle class; Smith Barney offered brokerage and money management services to the wealthy while also providing investment-banking services for companies seeking to raise capital or do mergers and acquisitions.

The challenge, of course, was to see that each of the three core units realized all that potential. Not surprisingly, the former stockbroker gravitated first to Smith Barney, the prestigious firm that originally attracted him to Primerica. His strategy to reverse the brokerage's slumping fortunes was, as always, stunningly simple: boost revenues and cut costs. But to do that he needed leadership that reflected his own personality. Just as Sandy's colleagues had sensed, George Vonder Linden's early missteps would prove fatal to his career at Smith Barney. To replace the ousted executive, Sandy recruited Frank Zarb, the man who years earlier had been instrumental in setting up the back office at Corned Beef With Lettuce. Sandy and the fifty-three-year-old Zarb had remained close since their days together at CBWL–Hayden Stone. Zarb had left the firm in 1971 to go to Washington, first serving as an assistant secretary of Labor in the Nixon administration and then taking the high-profile position of "energy czar" in the Ford administration during the energy crisis. He had returned to Wall Street in 1978 as a partner with Lazard Frères & Co. Sandy had named him to the board of Commercial Credit in 1986, and Zarb now joked that turning around Smith Barney would be as much work as dealing with the long lines of cars at gasoline stations during the oil embargo.

Backing up Zarb would be Lewis L. Glucksman, the savvy stock and bond trader who had stunned Wall Street when he seized the management reins at Lehman by pushing aside his then cochairman Peter Peterson. The brokers at Smith Barney had heard the horror stories about how Glucksman and the rough-and-tumble traders he oversaw had executed the coup that put them in charge of the old-line firm at the expense of their more gentlemanly investment-banking colleagues. Now the prospect of Glucksman's stern management oversight sent tremors through the Smith Barney brokers.

Both fond of a drink at the end of the day, Sandy and Glucksman soon found themselves meeting in Glucksman's office in the early evening to review the day's events. The former Lehman trader kept a small icebox in his office, and most evenings he would take two glasses from the counter, add ice, and pour vodka for himself and Tanqueray gin for Sandy. Over their "extra dry" martinis—they were not martinis at all, but straight vodka and gin—Sandy and Glucksman often set policy for the firm.

It soon became apparent to Sandy and Glucksman, two of Wall Street's most deeply addicted workaholics, that much of the problem at Smith Barney could be attributed to the lax working environment. When Glucksman arrived at 6:30 every morning, the office was empty; most brokers strolled in some three hours later, just before the 9:30 opening bell on the New York Stock Exchange. Sandy noticed the same emptiness when he toured Smith Barney, his new prized possession, at 5:00 P.M., an hour after the exchange's closing bell. This "trading hours only" work schedule infuriated both men. Exacerbating that anger was the fact that many of the traders and brokers weren't ready to get down to business once they got to the office.

"They haven't even read the newspapers before the market opens. They can't hit the ground running," Glucksman complained to Sandy, who had his own habit of reading the morning papers at dawn.

That kind of nonchalance had to end. A few weeks after the new management team settled in at Smith Barney, Glucksman took over the intercom broadcast to all branches. "We've been observing the way you operate here," the Smith Barney vice chairman growled. "We expect everyone to be here at seven o'clock in the morning. If you can't get here by seven A.M., you should move or quit." And, he barked, "Have the papers read before you walk in the door."

The workforce was stunned and resentful. To protest being treated like a scolded child, the head of taxable fixed-income trading, Stephen Maher, didn't come to work for several days. When he realized the new regime wasn't backing down on its work rules, he resigned.

Now that they were in the office longer, Smith Barney brokers were given a simple message: produce more or leave. The stockbrokers were bringing in average gross commissions of $270,000 a year, which was higher than the 1988 industry average of $190,000. But Weill and Zarb were far from satisfied. In three years, Zarb told the troops, Smith Barney producers would be expected to bring in commissions averaging double current levels, to at least $500,000.

Next on Sandy's agenda: maximize profit. Sandy had been shocked to find that only one third of Smith Barney's retail customers bought stock "on margin," that is, borrowing money from Smith Barney to buy securities, which became the collateral for the loan.

"That's what I want—margin," Sandy told a group of executives. "I can lend them money, be the bank, and have the best possible collateral—their stock portfolios." Interest generated on margin debt would increase profitability. If the value of the customer's portfolio declined and a margin call wasn't met, Smith Barney made itself whole by liquidating the assets in the customer's account to pay the debt. At Sandy's behest, Smith Barney launched a marketing campaign to encourage customers to borrow money against their portfolios not just to buy securities, but also to buy consumer items—"anything you normally get through a bank." Brochures went out in monthly statements, demonstrating Sandy's zeal for the retail side of the business.

One of Sandy's tried-and-true methods of adding revenue—picking up other brokers' businesses when their houses were on the skids—presented itself within a few months. Drexel Burnham Lambert was crashing after having to fire its most indispensable employee, junk-bond chief Michael Milken. The company had pleaded guilty to felony crimes and paid a fine of more than half a billion dollars. Drexel, which had merged with one of Sandy's earliest employers, Burnham & Co., was headed by Fred Joseph, who put the retail division up for sale in April 1989.

Even though Primerica was short on cash, Sandy recognized a bargain and snapped up sixteen Drexel branch offices for a mere $4 million, just enough to cover Drexel's costs for rent, furniture, and fixtures. The transaction, which added more than 500 brokers to Smith Barney's 2,100, was Sandy's second bargain-basement purchase from Joseph, who had been a top Shearson official when Sandy so shrewdly bought its troubled retail network in the 1970s. "We have a twenty-five percent increase in our sales force—poof!—for nothing," Sandy crowed. Indeed, the offices, which filled certain geographic holes in Smith Barney's network, brought in annualized revenue of about $100 million that first year and profits of $20 million.

A little later that year another opportunity to add branch offices—this time in Commercial Credit's consumer-finance operations—arose when Britain's Barclays Bank PLC, saddled with too many troubled auto and mobile-home loans, put its U.S. consumer-loan division on the block. Sandy dispatched a group of Primerica executives to spend a week investigating the finances of the 221 Barclays branches, then flew to Barclays' Charlotte, North Carolina, offices to hear their report and to meet with Barclays officials. As soon as he arrived, he began grilling his team: "What are the systems like?" "What about the people?" He quickly found one subject that his executives had overlooked.

"How long is it going to take to convert Barclays' systems to match ours?" Sandy barked. Without responding, the executives just shuffled through papers. Reflecting his irritation that such a basic issue in a take-over hadn't been analyzed, Sandy's face grew so red and swollen that at least one new Primerica executive, Jay Fishman, thought he might have a heart attack if someone didn't speak up, so he did.

"Six to nine months," Fishman blurted out, making up an answer.

Sandy looked askance at Fishman and then realized Commercial Credit's systems manager wasn't in the conference room. He had already left for New York. Sandy exploded. "What do you mean he's gone back to New York? We have work to do! What the hell is he doing leaving? Get him back here right now!"

As soon as the systems manager got off the plane at LaGuardia Airport, he was paged to return to Charlotte immediately. He walked to another gate and boarded the next plane to Charlotte. By the time the frazzled manager arrived, of course, Sandy was immersed in other issues.

At dinner that night with Barclays officials and their investment banker, Sandy began grilling them. "Tell me how you're paid," he asked one executive. The investment banker told the Barclays executive not to answer.

"What do you mean he can't talk about that?" Sandy fumed. "This is normal due-diligence stuff here."

When the investment banker refused to acquiesce, the Primerica chief stood up from the table, yelled, "Why the hell did I come down here?" and stormed out of the restaurant. Dimon and Lipp, who also attended the dinner, warned the banker that either he would give Sandy the information the next day or the deal would be off.

Ultimately Sandy was satisfied with what he saw. In November 1989, Primerica bought BarclaysAmerican/Financial for $1.35 billion cash, only a $50-million premium above the book value of the assets being purchased. The acquisition boosted Commercial Credit's loan portfolio by 40 percent, fortifying its position as a major consumer lender in the United States and increasing its presence in the western states, where Commercial Credit was weak.

With geographic expansion for Smith Barney and Commercial Credit under way, Sandy could begin to experiment with one of his fondest concepts: cross-selling. He had long believed that various financial companies could sell one another's products. He had envisioned that kind of "synergy" when he sold Shearson to American Express, but the credit-card executives had adamantly refused Sandy's brokers access to their coveted customer list. Now that he was in charge, the Primerica CEO was determined to prove that cross-selling could work.

The test vehicle was a popular product offered by Commercial Credit called the $MART LOAN, a home-equity loan designed to "Save Money And Reduce Taxes." Sandy wanted the A.L. Williams sales force to offer $MART LOANs to their hundreds of thousands of clients. Marge Magner, the hotshot overseer of Commercial Credit's branch network, took on the task of training Williams's part-time insurance agents to sell the $MART LOAN across the kitchen table to their friends and family. She spent three months in 1989 with one of Williams's star agents in Birmingham, Alabama, to fine-tune the product, position it properly for Williams's middle-class customers, and determine a commission structure sufficient to entice the agents. She also had to formulate the promotional materials to show how the $MART LOAN could consolidate debt and allow the interest payments to be deducted by securing it with real estate.

Sandy kept almost daily tabs on Magner's progress. He didn't just call, he walked into her office any time the thought crossed his mind. "How is it going? What do you see? Are they working with you?" he routinely queried. He fumed when Williams's agents didn't give Magner their cooperation, but she continued to plug away in her own sweet, steely fashion. The first time Williams agents sold a total of $1 million in $MART LOANs in a single day, Sandy knew about it almost instantly. He practically bounced into Magner's office to celebrate the burgeoning success of his cross-selling philosophy.

To reward the hundred leading salespeople at Williams, Sandy invited them and their spouses to New York. Many of them had never been to the Big Apple and toured the city with stars in their eyes. One night, Sandy gave a dinner at the opulent '21' Club, where he handed out T-shirts that read PRIMERICA & A.L. WILLIAMS. As he often did with his senior executives, he urged them to go around the table and "tell your story." When a large black woman detailed her struggle to pull herself out of poverty, she cried, as did Sandy. "I love these people," he whispered to Treacy Beyer, Williams's CEO, who observed his new boss's weakness for up-by-the-bootstraps sob stories.

Amid the successes enjoyed by Primerica's three core units, the Fingerhut catalog merchandiser was a growing sore point. Based in Minneapolis, Fingerhut was the nation's fourth-largest direct-mail marketer, peddling brands like Duncan Hines cookware and Samsonite luggage, as well as specialty gifts and foods like cheeses and nuts. Sandy had no use for selling anything other than financial products, so he had immediately put Fingerhut up for sale.

During negotiations, Primerica officials had told Sandy that Fingerhut could be sold for nearly $1 billion, but he and Dimon had counted on only $600 million in their calculations, and they needed that $600 million to reduce debt and to expand in financial services. But buyers were scarce. Even Sam Zell, the Chicago investor dubbed the "Grave Dancer" for his concentration in distressed companies, turned a cold shoulder to Primerica's efforts to rid itself of Fingerhut. A division of Shearson Lehman Hutton did due diligence on Fingerhut, and for a time it looked as if a deal might be done, but ultimately Shearson balked.

As months passed and Fingerhut languished, Sandy put Bob Lipp in charge of keeping an eye on the unit, which had been without hands-on management since its executives resigned after Commercial Credit's takeover of Primerica. Then Sandy got a call from Ted Deikel, who had just sold his TV-merchandising company to QVC. Deikel, who had sold mail-order monkeys to work his way through college, had married the daughter of Fingerhut's founder and had transformed the company from a manufacturer of plastic seat covers to a direct marketer before selling it to American Can, the forerunner of Primerica. Now he had a proposition for Sandy.

"You're having trouble selling Fingerhut because the market has trouble understanding the company," he told Sandy. "I'll buy the company with financing from venture people."

Sandy skimmed Deikel's poorly constructed proposal. Working the projections in his head, Sandy quickly concluded it probably wouldn't produce sufficient cash flow to carry the debt. He started laughing at Deikel's shaky effort to take Fingerhut. "Get the hell out of here," Sandy said. "This doesn't work."

Then he had another thought: get Deikel to run Fingerhut until he could sell it properly.

"No, you don't get to hire me," countered Deikel, who was comfortably wealthy from the first sale of Fingerhut. "Instead, I'll do what you guys did with Commercial Credit. I get ten percent of the business, and I'll turn it around so we can take it public." The Minneapolis visitor had obviously done his homework on Sandy.

"Okay, now I have one for you," Sandy said. "I want you to put your own money in here, too. And I want you to buy stock in this thing. Let's see how serious you really are."

To work out a possible alliance, Sandy invited Deikel, a trim fitness buff, to lunch at the Four Seasons. Sandy had his usual martinis and crispy duck. Deikel opted for the day's "spa cuisine" but drank along with the Primerica chairman. The two men agreed that Deikel would invest $3 million, giving him a 1 percent stake in the Primerica subsidiary. He would have an option to buy another 11 percent when Fingerhut was taken public in the next year. After the long lunch, Deikel could barely walk back to his hotel from the alcohol's effect. As they parted, he noticed the excessive lunchtime drinking seemed to have no effect on Sandy.

Before the end of Sandy's first year at the helm of Primerica, investors realized that Mr. Fixit still worked magic. In 1989 Primerica stock rose from $21 to $28. Institutions and mutual-fund managers had been big buyers of the stock, including the Oppenheimer Equity-Income Fund. The fund manager complained that he didn't like the "grab bag" quality of Primerica's disparate holdings, but acknowledged that his fund owned 410,000 shares because "my job is to make money any legal way I can."

During Sandy's first year, earnings per share rose from 53 cents in the first quarter to 65 cents in the second and 80 cents in the third. By the fourth quarter of 1989, the business magazines started giving Sandy the credit and limelight he craved.

PLAY IT AGAIN SANDY was the headline on the October issue of *U.S. News & World Report*. "Like Rodney Dangerfield, all Sanford Weill seems to want is a little respect," the article noted. In December, *Fortune* magazine touted the "turnaround at Primerica," adding, "Weill's thumb is still green, as in the color of money."

But the best of all was Sandy's first solo appearance on the cover of

BusinessWeek magazine. With a color photograph of the tan Primerica chieftain in a purple sweater, the December 4, 1989, cover proclaimed THE RETURN OF SANDY WEILL. The article inside showed another photograph of a peaceful Sandy standing on his Fifth Avenue terrace with a dainty floral china coffee cup on the ledge as he looked across the Central Park reservoir. Despite the placid setting, the headline told the real story: SANDY WEILL ROARS BACK.

THE GUEST HOUSE

After a year-end vacation with Joan in Puerto Rico, Sandy started 1990 with high hopes of expanding Primerica's financial businesses and selling off the outcast Fingerhut with Deikel's help. It was time for another meeting of his "planning group" at the "guest house."

Attempting to replicate the camaraderie and exchange of ideas that took place at the Baltimore dinners, Sandy established a monthly two-day retreat with his senior executives. The retreats had become among his most important tools for keeping tabs on his expanding empire. The spot Sandy selected for the retreat was an old stone mansion on the hundred-acre property in Greenwich, where American Can, Primerica's predecessor, had built a monstrosity of an office. From the start of the Primerica negotiations Sandy had no interest in relocating outside Manhattan, so he put the headquarters up for lease. But he fell in love with what had been the original manor house when the land had been a pastoral estate. Shrouded from the road by aging trees and situated atop rolling hills, the mansion had been used occasionally by Primerica for important visitors; hence the name the "guest house."

The mansion, which had never been updated with air conditioning or modern plumbing, had an aging but elegant feel to its high-ceilinged grand rooms on the main floor. Deer often ran across the lawn. Sandy loved to meet with his executives in the living room, where he would plop on the down-filled sofa, often reclining with his shoes off, while the other men lounged in overstuffed armchairs and love seats. Although the executives had collected around the Harbor Court Hotel's dining room table in Baltimore, Sandy found the "soft seating" far preferable—not only was it immensely more comfortable for a man who liked his feet up, but it also lent a relaxed atmosphere. He liked the living room so much that even during the sweltering summer heat, he refused to move to the house's only air-conditioned room, the library, which held a large conference table and chairs. Determined to remain on his couch, Sandy ordered large fans brought in, even though they were so noisy the men could hardly hear one another as their papers blew around.

The executives on the house's third floor, with its eight bedrooms and five baths, had to share bathrooms. Sandy took the biggest bedroom/bath suite with its own entrance up the back staircase; Dimon, Lipp, and Zarb typically occupied the other second-floor bedrooms with private baths. Prince and Ettinger shared a bath, as did Willumstad and Beyer, who was asked to join the planning group as the CEO of A.L. Williams. At his first retreat, Beyer confided in Zarb that his wife thought the getaways were some kind of "weird male bonding with no useful business purpose."

"No, it gives Sandy a good excuse to eat and drink with us," replied Zarb.

In typical Sandy style, the retreats included several elaborate meals and significant alcohol consumption. He had discovered a young, talented chef named Rebecca Kirhoffer, who was the caterer for Greenwich's upper crust. At the guest house, she and her staff catered to Sandy's every gastronomic whim. The Primerica CEO directed every detail. He picked the menu, the wine, the time for cocktail hour. And because he rose each morning at dawn before everyone else, she knew to prepare a "pre-breakfast," including three cups of coffee, for Sandy to inhale while he read the newspapers.

Kirhoffer, very observant of and responsive to her prestigious client, quickly adapted to Sandy's ways. Although Kirhoffer trained her staff that protocol dictated the host be served last, she instructed them to do the opposite with Sandy: Always make sure he is served and happy first. Another special rule: place Dijon mustard and jalapeño peppers at Sandy's place at the table, no matter what was served. Lunches and dinners featured lobster, steak tartare, homemade chicken potpie (dark meat only, one of Sandy's preferences), Maryland crab cakes, and other Sandy favorites.

"Can we have something to put ketchup on?" Lipp asked after several gourmet meals. He was hoping for something down-home and plain, maybe meatloaf and a baked potato. "Of course," Kirhoffer replied, knowing that whatever she prepared still would have to meet the test of Sandy's refined palate. That evening, she prepared meatloaf, but instead of using hamburger she made it with ground veal imported from France. And instead of good old Heinz ketchup out of a bottle, she whipped up a home-made ketchup.

"This isn't exactly comfort food," Lipp remarked of the elegant dish set before him.

Sandy set the pace for the meals, starting with cocktails: two martinis for Sandy. Then he led the way to the dining table. Kirhoffer, watching from the glass window in the door of the butler's pantry, would catch Sandy's nod, the signal to clear the dishes for the next course. Chintzy to a fault, the Primerica chief gave minimal tips to the catering staff (Kirhoffer supplemented the tips from her own pocket), but the servers enjoyed Sandy's meticulous attention to all facets of a meal and his obvious love of good food. They also learned quickly that when Sandy's temper flared or the table discussions became tense, they were to make themselves scarce.

Gallons of wine were quaffed at each meal. Sandy himself typically consumed nearly a bottle in the course of dinner and the discussions that followed. The guest house had come with its own well-stocked wine cellar, including dozens of bottles of 1959 Château La Tour, a world-class red from a French vineyard that had been operating since the Renaissance. Some of the private stock had no labels, and Sandy delighted in sampling the bottles.

In the spring of 1989 Sandy invited seventy-five top managers to the guest house for a pig roast and to play softball on a nearby field. The day of the gathering Kirhoffer asked Sandy if he was really going to play softball.

"Absolutely," Sandy said.

Once the pig was roasting, Kirhoffer made her way to the field to see for herself if Sandy would actually engage in such strenuous activity. She found him standing on the field, sure enough. But it wasn't a glove or bat in his hand, it was a martini.

"I thought you were playing," she called to Sandy.

"I'm supervising." He laughed and continued to make fun of his executives as they swatted feebly at the ball and missed easy catches.

Despite all the food and alcohol that flowed at the retreats, no one doubted Sandy's penetrating focus on business. The agenda called for each executive to talk about his business for an hour, which would fill an entire day. The intention wasn't to hear a review of each unit's budget and operations, but to get each executive involved in managing *all* of the businesses, not just his own division.

"We're all in this together," Sandy told them at one of the first retreats. "We're all going to make our fortunes together. Everybody's opinion counts."

Every person was expected to ask questions, point out problems, or offer suggestions about others' units. "If you can't participate," Sandy said
early on, "we don't need you." The forced participation required the executives to really learn all the businesses and brainstorm together about strategy and problem solving. A manager couldn't simply nod, sit quietly, or
agree. Compliments were forbidden, as one participant found when he
praised Zarb at an early meeting: "Frank, great job at Smith Barney."

"There's nothing you can add?" Sandy snapped.

Treacy Beyer, the newest addition to the planning group, at first felt
very much an outsider to the group, many of whose members had known
Sandy for years or had bonded with him in Baltimore. Never before exposed to such rigorous review, Beyer felt undressed at the end of his first
presentation. Sandy demanded that the group look only at operating results
and ignore such additions to income as investment returns, which didn't
really tell how a business was doing at its core.

No one could hide anything. Sandy constantly repeated that mistakes
were part of trying to be the best. "The only mistake you can make that's
unforgivable is if you make a mistake and hide it," Sandy told the group.
"If you have a problem, say so and we'll help you."

Beyer quickly learned that Sandy was right. "An insurance commissioner is on our case," Beyer once commented in a presentation. One of the
executives had scores of political contacts and volunteered, "I can help you
with that."

Of course, candor could be pushed only so far. Shortly after Primerica
had taken delivery of its fabulous Gulfstream IV jet, the executives attending a monthly retreat were set to review Primerica's various expenses.
"Good times are the best time to screw everything down," Sandy said. He
urged them to be brutal with each unit's head count and pare every expense. "We'll never have a quarter when we'll feel free to blow money
away," Sandy assured them. "Be disciplined."

Jamie Dimon, who was responsible for reviewing headquarters' expenses, then came to the front and placed on the overhead projector
a transparency that listed alphabetically each department's head count,
budget, and actual cost to the parent company. The first item on the list:
Aviation.

"Wow, that's far over budget," one executive said. "Too many people," chimed in another.

Sandy came flying off the sofa.

"Goddammit! Goddammit!" he screamed. "I need that many people to fly the plane. If I don't have that many people, the plane will crash!" Turning fiery red and spitting out his words, Sandy roared, "Why do we have to pick on aviation?! Why?!" He glared at Dimon.

"Sandy, because aviation starts with an 'A,'" Dimon calmly responded. "It's the first one on the list because it's the first letter in the alphabet." No one dared laugh; Sandy's tortured breathing didn't slow for several minutes. Later that night, the executives got a big kick out of noting that while they were forbidden to fly first-class, their boss, the "imperial chairman," got to go everywhere in his G-4.

The guest house sessions produced an entrepreneurial spirit of partnership among the executives who regularly took part, something rare in a sprawling corporation the size of Primerica. To drive that spirit further down the management ranks, Sandy unveiled a "capital accumulation plan," or CAP, to make restricted common stock a sizable component of the compensation for 1,400 lower-tier managers. To encourage key managers to stay, the stock issued to them would not become theirs to take for two years, and it couldn't be sold or transferred.

With his kinship to brokers, Sandy wanted to include them in the restricted-stock plan. He decided that year-end bonuses would consist of 30 percent cash and 70 percent restricted stock. "I believe it's important for people to invest in the company, to think like an owner," Sandy said in announcing the plan over the Smith Barney squawk box. "This is a wealth-accumulation concept. If we all pull together and the stock performs well, the company and employees gain."

Despite Sandy's cheerleading for his beloved stock-based incentives, many brokers didn't like the idea that their big cash bonuses were going to be in stock they couldn't sell. When department heads for government-bond and fixed-income trading complained vociferously, Sandy told them to take the stock bonuses or leave. They left.

The Primerica chief was disappointed that certain key employees didn't believe enough in the stock to recognize its value over cash. But he was absolutely livid when the biggest shareholder of all, Gerald Tsai, dumped most of his stock. On March 6 and 7, 1990, Tsai sold one million shares of

Primerica, representing 85 percent of his stake in the company he once ran, at an average price of $26½ a share, for $26.4 million.

Tsai, who was a Primerica director, didn't inform Sandy of his decision to sell the stock until he was on the verge of executing the sale from Asia. "I've been in Japan, and I'm very nervous about the world," Tsai told Sandy on the phone. "I'm pessimistic, and I really think I should sell my stock."

Sandy couldn't believe his ears. "You have to do what you have to do," the new Primerica chief said angrily. Sandy then called Ira Harris, Tsai's investment banker.

"I can't fucking believe that Tsai sold his stock—and didn't even tell me until this minute!" Sandy yelled on the phone.

"Sandy, don't look at me," Harris said. "I didn't know anything about it, either. I haven't really spoken to Gerry in a while."

Sandy was livid that Tsai, the onetime star money manager, was betting the stock would decline. Whatever the reason, Sandy vowed that Tsai would not return to the board after the next election of directors. He wasn't needed and, besides, Sandy had successfully neutered Tsai by making certain that the executive committee, of which Tsai was chairman, never met. And it wasn't long before Sandy's furor turned to sweet revenge. In the month following Tsai's sale, Primerica reported a 62 percent increase in first-quarter earnings, and the price of the stock shot up from the $26 a share that Tsai had been paid to $31.

"Do you know how much money Gerry left on the table?" Sandy crowed to Harris after the stock's climb. Tsai, whose reputation was built on his supposedly savvy market timing, had lost millions by selling when he did.

REINING IN THE RENEGADE

Once he had Smith Barney under control and Fingerhut on the way out the door, Sandy's next challenge was to get better control of A.L. Williams, Primerica's insurance unit. Sandy and Art Williams had gotten along famously during the negotiations to buy Primerica, but since then their relationship had grown increasingly strained. Williams, who made millions of dollars a year by getting a piece of every commission earned by his 200,000 agents, was as successful, controlling, and egocentric as Sandy. The man called the "P. T. Barnum of the insurance world" delighted in standing up to

Sandy. "We don't have to attack the other insurance companies and make them enemies," Sandy told Williams more than once. Yet even as insurance commissioners and competitors such as Metropolitan Life and Prudential took aim at Williams, he continued to thrill his zealots by screaming "Wet the Met" and "Screw the Pru." And if Sandy was in the audience, so much the better. "Oh my goodness," Williams said in mock concern at one rally. "Sandy's here. I shouldn't say that!"

In an expensive effort to convert Williams into an employee rather than a free agent, Sandy paid $470 million in Primerica shares to buy out the 30 percent of A.L. Williams stock still held by the public and to buy Art Williams's own separate insurance agency. Sandy justified the hefty price tag on the grounds that he needed to gain sole authority over the insurance empire because it accounted for one third of Primerica's profits. Not only was the Primerica CEO worried about Williams's take-no-prisoners antics; he also abhorred the risk associated with 200,000 independent agents operating under minimal control.

There was only one problem: The deal gave Art Williams more Primerica stock than even Sandy held, and he still refused to take orders from anyone, most of all Sandy. Instead of getting better, the insurance renegade's behavior got worse.

On July 9, 1990, Sandy was on his annual vacation in the south of France with Joan when he received a call from the Federal Bureau of Investigation and the U.S. Attorney's office in Florida: Art Williams was under investigation. Sandy promised to send his lawyers to meet with the authorities immediately. He ordered Chuck Prince, who was vacationing in Vermont, to go with Ken Bialkin, Sandy's longtime outside corporate lawyer, for a meeting with the FBI and U.S. Attorney. The two lawyers flew to Atlanta for a briefing on the allegations. On the flight back to New York, both men, sharp thinkers devoted to Sandy, were in such shock that they sat in complete silence all the way home.

When Sandy returned to New York, Prince and Bialkin recounted the gist of the allegations of white-collar crime. Art Williams was being investigated for allegedly having masterminded a "dirty tricks" campaign to drive a former employee's insurance company out of business by burying it with hundreds of bogus life policies. He allegedly ordered certain loyal agents, whom he dubbed his "spy teams" and "hit squads," to infiltrate the competitor's organization, Amerishare Investors Inc. of Jacksonville,

Florida, and attack it from within by writing fictitious life policies and receiving generous commissions.

"Art has to go," Sandy said simply.

Prince called Treacy Beyer, the Williams CEO who was with Williams at an incentive boondoggle for agents in Bermuda. "The FBI is investigating Art Williams's 'spy team,'" Prince told Beyer. "Sandy wants to meet Williams at the guest house as soon as possible." Williams was about to go on stage when Beyer rushed to break the news about the FBI. Williams burst into tears. Too distraught to appear before the crowd, he secretly left Bermuda without any explanation to the agents waiting to see his act.

On Friday, July 13, Sandy, Prince, and Bialkin were waiting for Williams, who arrived with his lawyer and Beyer. They sat down in the guest house living room.

"My first responsibility is to the company and its shareholders," Sandy said, opening the meeting. "We are a public company. You have to step aside."

"I can't step aside," Williams shot back. "It will ruin the sales force. They won't work for anyone but me." Fighting back tears, the black knight of the insurance industry continued. "You'll ruin everything. You'll precipitate a disaster. I can't do that."

"You have to do that," replied Sandy, remaining icy cold as Williams began to fall apart. "It's just not going to get any better until you're no longer directly involved. You have to take time to focus on your defense and your personal issues."

"No, no, no, I won't leave," Williams repeated. "I want to stay and defend against this. I want to be part of the defense."

"Art, you will deal with your problems," Sandy remained firm. "There are criminal implications, and the company must focus on the issues separately."

Williams broke down. His whole life, his company, his world were under attack, and he couldn't fight the way he wanted. Williams, who recently had a pacemaker installed at the age of forty-eight, had survived as the oldest living member of his family after the premature deaths of his father and uncle from heart attacks. The men gathered in the house's living room watched in horror and fear as Williams unraveled.

On the other side of the room, Sandy, typically the man with the hair-trigger temper prone to high-volume outbursts, retained his steely composure. Prince had never been more impressed with his boss than that day. Any notion that Sandy would protect a heavy hitter was out the window, Prince thought, because Williams's departure would certainly be regarded as a negative for the company's finances. Even Beyer, who had a much closer relationship with Williams than Sandy, admired the Primerica CEO's calm, ethical stance. *Sandy had just paid in spades for this organization,* Beyer thought to himself, *and now he's going to face not only lost revenue but also public embarrassment for having backed Art Williams.*

"We have to do it; you have to go," Sandy concluded. "There is just no other way."

Williams ran out through the living room's French doors to the stone patio. Outside, between sobs, Williams conferred with his lawyer. By exchanging his A.L. Williams shares for Primerica shares, Williams had ceded final authority to Sandy. He didn't even have a contract that specified he would run the insurance company. Dejected and demoralized, Williams returned inside.

"We have to issue a press release that you're stepping aside," Sandy continued. "We have to issue some kind of statement."

"Why do you have to say it publicly, as long as I take a leave of absence?" Williams countered. "You're humiliating me! You're just adding salt to my wounds—"

Bialkin, one of the country's leading securities lawyers, weighed in. "We have to issue a statement. It's a significant event. It's an SEC issue. We have no choice."

The Williams company's founder and driving force left that day for an indefinite "leave of absence" from which he would never return. And, as he predicted, the insurance company's part-time "term-ites" reacted with anger and sorrow. Nearly 100,000 of the sales force, or about half, quit the business in the next few months. Suddenly Treacy Beyer, an astute business executive but not an inspirational leader, was in charge of a declining business. Lipp came down to help out but quickly saw that his performance-based system with goals and budgets was ineffective with agents who sold to family and friends when they were "inspired" to. In an effort to give the Williams agents someone who would excite them to sell policies again as much as their ex–football coach, Sandy named Peter Dawkins, the former West Point football star, retired brigadier general, and former Shearson officer, its new chief executive.

At the same time, Prince started working at the Williams headquarters four days a week to defend the company in the FBI probe and to resolve several compliance actions brought by state insurance commissioners alleging misleading or inaccurate sales pitches. To remove any remnant of controversy from Williams and to reflect Sandy's imprint on the business going forward, the company was renamed Primerica Financial Services. After all the turmoil and probing, neither Williams nor the company was ever charged with any wrongdoing. And Williams's guiding philosophy about life insurance—"Buy term and invest the difference"—was ultimately vindicated. It *was* a better product, and to prove the point, many of A.L. Williams's competitors were soon offering their own versions of term life.

Amid all the turmoil of 1990, Primerica stock hit an all-time high of $37. It suddenly struck Jamie Dimon to compare Primerica's market value to that of the ultimate financial-services company, Citibank. He was delighted to discover that Primerica had a larger market cap than the prestigious bank. Since their days in exile, Sandy and Dimon had monitored the stock of Citibank, the company they always held up as a model for the kind they wanted to build. Having transformed little Commercial Credit into a $3-billion company in just three years was an awesome enough achievement, but to be as big as Citibank, "that's kicking butt!" Dimon exclaimed. Never mind that the renowned bank was taking a beating in 1990 and 1991 from huge Third World and real-estate loans that were going bad.

Sandy, puffing his cigar, took a moment with his protégé to relish the thought of taking on Citibank. Then they both looked at each other with the biggest thought of all: Take on Citi? "Hell, we're thinking big," Sandy said, laughing. "We're big enough to take over Citibank."

"Wouldn't that be the mother of all deals?" Dimon enthused.

The phone interrupted the reverie, but neither ever forgot the feeling that came over them at the thought of owning Citibank.

If they couldn't realistically consider taking over Citibank, they could at least buy some of its stock. When Citibank stock hit an all-time low of $8.50, Dimon bought $50 million for Primerica's investment portfolio (and, with his own money, bought some for his three daughters as well).

As Citibank recovered from its problems, the shares rose in value. That was fine with Sandy at first, but he soon began to get nervous about the investment. He pestered Dimon frequently to sell Primerica's stake. "Take some money off the table," he said.

Lipp, who overheard Sandy's badgering and assumed the worst, finally went to Dimon: "Jamie, why don't you just sell it? Sandy is beating you up. How much have you lost anyway?"

"We're not losing." Dimon grinned. "We're making a shitload of money!"

Lipp and Dimon laughed about their boss's ability to find something to worry about in the best of circumstances, but finally Dimon relented and sold the Citibank stock for a $30-million profit.

While Citibank stock was rising, the stock that mattered most of all to Sandy and his Primerica team was headed down. Primerica's share price hit a new low of $16.875 in October 1990, largely the result of the continuing slump on Wall Street and investors' growing concern about the turmoil at A.L. Williams following its founder's departure. The crew at Primerica's midtown headquarters gathered in the library to drown their sorrow over their losses. A few months earlier, they had calculated that their options were worth several million dollars each. Now the stock was nearly four dollars lower than when they took little Commercial Credit public.

"Three years of toiling away," Dimon lamented. "Killing ourselves, backbreaking deals . . . for what?"

Sandy didn't respond. He just quietly sipped his gin. He had been at this game longer than any of his executives. He'd seen worse markets before. In a cloud of cigar smoke, he didn't panic; he plotted.

10

HOMECOMING

In the years since Sandy Weill had been forced to resign from American Express, Peter Cohen, his former acolyte, had been moving aggressively to put his own stamp on the credit-card giant's Shearson Lehman Hutton subsidiary. His biggest triumph, of course, had been beating out Sandy and Commercial Credit in the bidding war to buy EF Hutton. That acquisition put Shearson in a position to challenge Merrill Lynch as the nation's largest retail brokerage firm.

But the triumph also carried the seeds of Cohen's destruction. Hutton had cost Shearson $1 billion—a sum that Sandy felt would have risked Commercial Credit's very existence—and Cohen had borrowed heavily to pay for it. Shortly after Shearson had taken on the huge debt, Wall Street slipped into another of its periodic funks. Investors drew in their horns, and the phones that had been ringing with buy and sell orders once again fell silent. At the same time, both the real-estate market and the market for junk bonds—the risky borrowings that had financed much of the mergers-and-buyouts boom—slumped, leaving Shearson holding millions of dollars of bad loans.

Although he had been brought up at the feet of the master of cost control, Cohen got caught up in the quest for power and fame. Encouraged by his American Express bosses, Cohen built a new company ski lodge in Vail, Colorado. At the same time he managed the firm's various departments and branches, he took on the role of Shearson's jet-set investment banker. In doing so he was challenging such established and powerful Wall Street figures as Bruce Wasserstein and Henry Kravis. When Cohen won the post of advisor to the management of RJR Nabisco Inc. in its fight against the powerful leveraged buyout firm of Kohlberg Kravis Roberts & Co., he found out just how cutthroat and arduous battle was on that level.

The $25-billion fight, chronicled in the best-selling book *Barbarians at the Gate,* became symbolic of Wall Street's unprecedented greed and ego and the disdain with which investment bankers and corporate chieftains regarded employees and investors. At the end of all the name-calling, mudslinging, lawsuits, and press leaks, Cohen and Shearson were beaten. Sandy's former protégé emerged in the popular press and in the book as a tough-talking arrogant bully who lacked the skills to back up his braggadocio. Even the close relationship between Cohen and American Express chairman James Robinson unraveled as each blamed the other for Shearson's decline. Cohen insisted that the firm's balance-sheet problems were due to American Express management's directive to pay cash for Hutton, and that he nevertheless had maintained Shearson's earnings during difficult times. But not long after, with American Express reeling under the impact of a $1-billion loss, Robinson fired the forty-three-year-old chief executive.

Sandy, of course, had sources and spies throughout Wall Street, and he kept close tabs on his former empire. He was horrified at how Cohen and American Express had run Shearson in a futile quest for glory. But he also made no secret that he coveted regaining that old empire. Apart from its sentimental value, Shearson had two qualities that Sandy found nearly irresistible—it was very big and very troubled.

At home the night he was fired, Cohen was humiliated and despondent. He refused all calls, particularly from the press reporting on his ouster. Then came the phone call he least expected: Sandy Weill was on the line. That was a call he would take.

"You're better off," his old boss told him. "The people at American Express are really horrible." Sandy offered to take Cohen to lunch "as soon as possible." Stunned by the call, Cohen hung up the phone and thought to himself, *There's a decent side of Sandy. He's been through this, and he's extending his hand to me.*

Two days later Sandy and Cohen met at the Four Seasons for lunch. Over cocktails, fine wine, and plentiful food, Sandy grilled Cohen for hours, probing for every detail about Shearson's operations and financial situation. Cohen's heart sank. Sandy wasn't commiserating with him; he was using him to find out everything he could about his next target.

Cohen was right. Within weeks Sandy had begun informal talks with Robinson about the possible purchase of Shearson or, as an alternative, a possible joint venture with American Express. Robinson, whose courtly demeanor and youthful appearance masked a driving ambition, was feeling tremendous pressure from American Express directors. His dream of creating a "financial-services supermarket" wasn't working. The directors were concerned that the American Express card was losing its cachet under a brutal assault from banks issuing millions of Visa cards and Master-Cards and that American Express was losing its focus as a company. Eager to be rid of the brokerage albatross hanging around his company's neck, Robinson seemed receptive to some kind of deal. But before anything could be concluded, someone privy to the talks leaked. There on the front page of *The New York Times* was an article extolling Sandy's possible return to Wall Street's big leagues. It was one thing for Sandy and Robinson to quietly negotiate a deal that solved Robinson's problem while salving his ego; it was quite another to be heralded as the savior of Shearson, pulling a fast one on the image-conscious American Express chief. "There goes that deal," Sandy told his executives when he saw the *Times* that morning. Sure enough, Robinson promptly called off the talks.

Okay, as long as Robinson was running American Express, Sandy probably couldn't get his hands on Shearson. But in his long career Sandy had always found ways around roadblocks. If he couldn't have Shearson outright, maybe he could have the next best thing: Shearson's people. One of his first calls went to Robert Druskin, Shearson's chief financial officer. Druskin had been a valuable resource in building a framework that enabled Sandy to create the "salami slicer" back office at Corned Beef With Lettuce. The modern and efficient back office had been a key factor in Sandy's ability to take over bigger firms that were in trouble. Sandy wanted Druskin to leave Shearson and come to the much smaller Smith Barney to oversee the development of an infrastructure that could handle thousands more daily transactions, all part of Sandy's plan to get bigger and better. "Let's build a system that can double our capacity within thirty days of making an acquisition," Sandy told Druskin. Excited at the prospect of working once again with Sandy, Druskin accepted on the spot. When he arrived home that night, his wife was admiring a magnificent flower arrangement. "Welcome back to the family," read the card, signed, "Sandy."

"It's classic Sandy," Druskin told his wife. "He's ready to build another family, another financial powerhouse."

Many calls followed, and a steady stream of Shearson employees left their jobs to join Sandy at Primerica. Wall Street veterans, noting the parade of executives from Shearson's downtown Wall Street offices to

Smith Barney's midtown headquarters, called the Smith Barney building "Shearson North."

But Sandy wasn't able to lure away every Shearson employee he wanted. There was, for instance, his thirty-one-year-old daughter, Jessica Bibliowicz, who had continued working in Shearson's asset-management division despite her father's resignation from American Express. Vivacious and attractive, Jessica had two young children. When her father offered her a job at Smith Barney, the ambitious young manager decided to explore her options. A graduate of Cornell University like her father, Jessica called on Hardwick Simmons, whom she had gotten to know when her father took over Hayden Stone, Simmons's family firm. Now the head of Prudential Securities, Simmons knew talent when he saw it. Rather than offer Jessica advice, he offered her a job. She could head up sales and marketing for Prudential's mutual funds. Teasingly, she called her father to tell him that his offer was "too low" and took Simmons's offer

Sandy also wanted to promote his thirty-four-year-old son Marc, whom he had wooed away earlier from Shearson with an offer to become an investment banker at Smith Barney. Marc had excellent credentials: an economics degree from Vanderbilt University and an MBA from Columbia. And while he was known around Smith Barney as a likable sort, colleagues considered him too prone to engage in youthful pursuits and lacking his father's shrewd mind and forceful will. Nevertheless, Sandy elevated him to the high-level post of vice president of investments for the parent company.

But by far the most important relationship within Primerica was between Sandy and Jamie Dimon. Over the years Dimon had gone from being Sandy's understudy to his full-fledged alter ego. Had the pair been painting a mural instead of building a company, Sandy would be making the broad brushstrokes to set the theme; Dimon would fill in the details with perceptive and precise specifics. When Sandy had an idea, he would turn to Dimon: "What numbers are we talking about?" Dimon, capable of calculating several transactions in his head simultaneously, would quickly give Sandy the exact answer he wanted. In their rapid-fire banter, the two executives frequently would complete each other's sentences. They even developed their own unconscious forms of verbal shorthand. One needed to speak only a few words of a sentence for the other to understand completely what was left unsaid. When Sandy and Dimon were firing on all cylinders, the other Primerica executives could only listen in baffled silence and wait for Dimon to explain it all later. Dimon also served the other executives well by being confident enough to stand up to Sandy's wrath, even to the extent of engaging in extended shouting matches with his boss.

"You're a fucking asshole!" Sandy screamed at Dimon one day.

"No, you're the fucking asshole!" Dimon shouted back.

The fiery exchange echoed down the corridors, causing visitors in Treacy Beyer's nearby office to wince. "That's just our chairman and CFO having a meeting," their host explained with a shrug.

Dimon traveled nearly everywhere with Sandy, providing on-the-spot commentary and analysis in business meetings. At public meetings or in front of employee groups, Dimon served as an effective warm-up act, regaling the audience with funny stories about their climb from exile that also conveyed the culture and philosophies they lived by, much to Sandy's delight. When introducing Sandy to groups, Dimon would often throw in a silly story about Sandy to humanize him. Dimon's storytelling and introductory remarks also served the valuable purpose of substantially reducing the amount of time a still-nervous Sandy had to spend at the podium. Invariably, Sandy's growing reliance on Dimon and their constant presence together prompted remarks about a "father-son" team, remarks that discomfited both men. Sandy told *BusinessWeek* in one profile, "I have a son, and he has a father. It's not a need that has to be filled. But there's a lot of love there."

In September 1991, Sandy relinquished his title as president of Primerica, bestowing it on Dimon, who continued to hold the post of chief financial officer. At age thirty-five, Dimon became one of the youngest presidents of any Fortune 500 company. "When somebody does something very, very well, they're going to be rewarded," Sandy explained. But he also made it clear that he was still in charge. Asked by reporters if Dimon's elevation portended a succession plan, Sandy, fifty-eight, responded that he hadn't given up any of his own responsibilities, adding pointedly, "I don't feel very old, either." Shortly afterward, Dimon and Bob Lipp were elected directors of Primerica, joining Sandy and Frank Zarb as "inside" directors.

By 1992 the turnaround of Primerica was well under way. In January the company reported record earnings for 1991 with the profit at Smith Barney tripling from the year earlier. The news propelled Primerica's share price up more than $2 to $40.75. The stock's surging price gave Sandy the valuable currency he needed to embark on a shopping spree. And it wasn't long before a target came into view. General Electric had bought Kidder, Peabody in 1986 as part of GE's growing financial-services empire. But over the years GE's much-vaunted management had not done well running the brokerage company. Plagued by an insider-trading scandal, a market downturn, and sibling rivalry with GE's powerful GE Capital unit, Kidder had become a drag on the parent company, and Jack Welch, GE's chairman, wanted to sell it. Not surprisingly, Primerica was first in line for a look at Kidder's books.

On the surface Kidder would be a very attractive addition to Primerica. Catering as it did to well-heeled individual investors, Kidder could give Smith Barney the critical mass it needed to become even more powerful and profitable among its Wall Street competitors. But even a cursory weekend examination of Kidder's books and systems revealed a high "risk profile" and a lax system of controls, anathema to a risk-averse control freak like Sandy. Still, at the right price . . . The Primerica executives agreed to return to GE's Rockefeller Center offices for three days of continued due diligence over the coming Memorial Day weekend. As the executives toiled away that long weekend, GE provided a continuous flow of food, starting with lox and bagels in the morning and ending each evening with a sumptuous buffet of Chinese food. By Memorial Day Sandy had concluded that he couldn't pay more than the $400 million book value for Kidder. He knew that GE had about $1 billion invested in the brokerage firm, much of that incurred in an expensive recapitalization to keep Kidder on a sound financial footing during its worst days. Negotiations were bound to be tough.

The time for Sandy's scheduled meeting with Welch that Monday afternoon came and went with no Welch. When Welch finally arrived at Rockefeller Center, the two strong-willed CEOs did not find much common ground. Sandy pushed hard to get a good deal. At the other extreme, Welch wanted a premium price for the ailing company. Neither was willing to budge. That evening Sandy summoned his weary executives to the GE boardroom. "Jack and I have agreed to disagree," he told them. "We're walking."

Sandy's decision to walk away from the high risk and high price of Kidder paid big dividends a year later when Kidder was rocked by a huge bond-trading scandal that ultimately led to the firm's demise. Joseph Jett, the firm's government-bond chief, allegedly generated $350 million in bogus profits over two years. In the immediate aftermath of the disclosures, Kidder's chairman, Michael Carpenter, was forced out for failing to detect the fraud and for papering over its potential for damage when it was discovered. Wall Street was surprised when Sandy snapped up the ex–Kidder chairman, giving him a strategic planning post at Primerica. "I have a much better feeling about Mike than I did about Kidder," Sandy told his colleagues.

AN ALLY NAMED ANDREW

The protracted weak economy of the early 1990s had taken a toll on other industries beyond the brokerage business. The insurance industry, which had invested heavily in real estate, was particularly hard hit by the collapse of the commercial real-estate market. Making matters worse, a price war in the commercial insurance markets ate deeply into profits. No insurance company seemed affected more by all the turmoil than Travelers Corp., based in Hartford, Connecticut.

Founded in 1864, Travelers was the result of a two-cent transaction. Hartford businessman James G. Batterson was organizing a company to introduce accident insurance to America when he ran into a local banker at the post office. "I'm on my way home for a luncheon," the banker said. "How much would you charge to insure me against an accident from here to there?"

"Two cents," Batterson promptly responded and took the banker's two pennies. When the banker walked the four blocks home without mishap, Batterson saved the "two-cent premium" as a souvenir of founding The Travelers. Other early policyholders included renowned merchant John Wanamaker and General George A. Custer, who took out a life insurance contract before meeting his end at the hands of Sioux warriors on the banks of the Little Big Horn River. After originally writing policies for horse-and-buggy insurance, the company wrote the first automobile policy in 1897 to Gilbert Loomis, who insured a car he built himself. More recently, Travelers issued "space travel" accident insurance policies to cover American astronauts during Apollo and Skylab missions.

With such a rich heritage, Travelers was much beloved in its Connecticut Yankee hometown and had played a central role in Hartford's economic and social development for generations. By 1992, however, the insurer was in dire straits, starved for capital. The 128-year-old company was reeling under the weight of more than $5 billion of problem mortgages in its portfolio. With its distressed balance sheet, Travelers was struggling to maintain its financial health ratings and assure worried policy-holders.

Ed Budd, the insurance giant's chairman, sought investors for a cash infusion but kept coming up empty-handed. Finally, he decided to call Sandy. The two had met in 1983 shortly after Sandy, then president of American Express, had taken over the ailing Fireman's Fund. Sandy had invited Budd to spend the weekend in Boca Raton, Florida, to teach Sandy about the insurance business. Budd knew that Sandy analyzed issues and problems quickly and now, as the head of Primerica, he had lots of cash, too. Still, Budd didn't forget Sandy's reputation as a ruthless and voracious acquirer of distressed companies.

Sandy was delighted to talk to Budd about Travelers. The venerable insurance company hadn't entered his mind as a way to expand Primerica, but now his curiosity was piqued. Here was a company that met his two prime criteria as a target: magnitude and misery. Travelers also had a powerful lure in its established ability to sell insurance to businesses, an approach very different from Primerica's efforts to sell insurance directly to individuals. And despite its financial problems, Travelers' corporate symbol—an open red umbrella—was one of the most recognizable icons in the financial-services industry.

From the outset Budd stressed that Travelers needed only an "investment," not a buyout. Despite his propensity to take over companies, not invest in them, Sandy agreed to take a look. He gathered his key executives and headed for Hartford, where on a Saturday morning they were greeted by a stiff and formal cadre of Travelers executives all dressed in coats and ties. Inside the company's headquarters, Travelers' paternalistic nature was evident in signs on bulletin boards offering scores of free programs for better health, outside activities, transportation discounts—precisely the kind of costly perks Sandy abhorred. Bob Lipp and Jay Fishman came across one notice on a bulletin board for a seminar on "Managing Negativity."

"We'll teach them how to manage negativity," Fishman offered. "We'll just tell them their company can't afford to offer this class."

"Yeah, manage that," Lipp quipped with a chuckle.

The New Yorkers' arrival brought a dose of business reality to the insurance executives, who seemed to believe that Travelers' great size and venerable history ensured its survival despite its current problems. Sandy's team cut through the gloss in seconds, burrowing in with probing questions. When Dimon and Irwin Ettinger, Primerica's tax and accounting manager, asked for details on financial statements, it quickly became apparent that the insurance executives didn't understand their own books. "It's like being on Mars," Ettinger whispered to Dimon.

Travelers desperately needed cash, but its executives shared Budd's wariness of Sandy Weill. They wanted to limit his investment to a small minority stake, even though the Primerica chief told them he could afford a sizable interest. Budd stood firm that the insurer would accept about $350 million for 15 percent of the company. That would be enough to bolster Travelers' long-term financial health. In exchange, Primerica would be given two seats on Travelers' board.

Sandy sought approval for the Travelers alliance from his own board. "You must be their last resort," said former PepsiCo president Andrall Pearson, a longtime director. "If you think those old WASPy guys in Hartford are anxious to get in bed with a nice Jewish boy from Brooklyn, you're crazy. They're desperate."

Before the deal could close, Sandy's desire to take a bigger stake in Travelers got an unexpected boost from an ally named Andrew. On August 24, 1992, Hurricane Andrew slammed into the southeast coast of Florida with sustained winds of 140 miles per hour and eight-foot tidal surges. The storm devastated the Miami area, killing several people, leaving 50,000 homeless, uprooting huge oak trees, and smashing thousands of buildings. Travelers scrambled in the days following the disaster to determine the amount of property and casualty claims it would have to pay. The preliminary calculations were dire: Hurricane Andrew would wipe out nearly all of the cash infusion expected from Primerica.

Sandy calmly tracked the storm and its aftermath, and awaited Budd's call. It came the Sunday night after the disaster. On the phone, Budd pleaded for more cash. Sandy was in a perfect negotiating posture: He had the cash, and he wanted more control. With his back against the wall, the Travelers chairman agreed to give Sandy 27 percent of the company and four board seats for $722 million, mostly cash. But Sandy wanted even more: For such a large stake in a struggling company, the Primerica CEO demanded a big say in the Hartford giant's operations. Sandy would become the head of a new finance committee and cochairman with Budd of an operating committee. Sandy knew he couldn't trust the inept Travelers management with his money, and he planned to take full advantage of Andrew's ruinous visit to South Florida.

There was still more. Convinced by his visit to Hartford that Travelers was carrying too much deadweight, Sandy demanded that Budd agree to eliminate at least 10 percent of Travelers' workforce. And if the little guys would be hurt, so would the big guys: Budd and other senior executives must surrender their golden parachutes. Still disgusted by his experience with Gerry Tsai's ludicrously expensive golden parachute, Sandy wanted nothing to do with any more management payoffs. The Travelers parachutes would be triggered by Primerica's 27 percent stake in the company. Budd alone would stand to collect $3 million. With few bargaining chips left, Budd reluctantly consented to Sandy's tough terms. But, still fearful of Sandy's acquisitiveness, he insisted that the agreement include a clause that forbade Primerica from increasing its stake in Travelers for five years without the consent of the board.

On September 20, 1992, Primerica announced it would invest $722 million in Travelers in return for the 27 percent stake and Sandy's direct involvement in the insurer's management. At the same time, Travelers announced it was eliminating 3,500 jobs. Analysts delving into the terms of the deal discovered—no surprise—that once again Sandy had driven a hard bargain. Primerica had paid less than half of Travelers' stated book value for its stake in the insurer. And with Sandy now standing, if not behind the Travelers helm, at least beside it, investors had renewed faith in the company's prospects. The insurance giant's shares shot up 26 percent.

The reaction in Hartford, however, was less welcoming. Budd assured employees the transaction was a "simple investment." One manager responded, "But Sandy Weill is one scary investor. His cutthroat reputation doesn't mix with our value system here." An editorial in the *Hartford Courant* said the deal "gives Hartford something to cheer about, but also something to mourn." Besides the job losses, the newspaper criticized "the possible erosion of independence for an institution whose history is entwined with Hartford's." Finally, it admonished Sandy Weill that "companies are more than profits, shares, and stock prices."

But to Sandy, that's exactly what companies were. He drove managers in the name of profits, pushed daily for greater market share, and watched his company's stock price as if it were his own heartbeat. His arrival in the sedate little city of Hartford was bound to create shock waves.

At the first management meeting to be "cochaired" by Sandy and Budd, there was no announcement at the beginning about who was in charge. But it quickly became evident. Sporting an umbrella pin on his lapel, Sandy announced that henceforth Travelers would focus on bringing "value to the shareholders."

Listening to Sandy, Charles Clarke, who headed Travelers' commercial business, thought to himself: *Who are shareholders?* The only time the word *shareholder* was ever used at Travelers was once a year when the annual report was mailed to them. *Sandy Weill cares more about shareholders than he does about us,* Clarke thought, fuming. Of course, he and hundreds of other Travelers employees would soon find that Sandy would care about them by turning them into shareholders.

The confident and brash Primerica leaders started coming to Hartford once a week. Sandy and Dimon relentlessly focused on the bottom line with a crispness and discipline never seen before at Travelers. After leaving one early meeting with the Primerica "investors," Clarke ran into a couple of his subordinates.

"Does Sandy love insurance people?" a Travelers underwriter asked.

"He loves profitable people," Clarke responded. "I don't know if he loves insurance. I think he wants our name more than he wants insurance."

"But does he love us?" an agent persisted.

"If we're profitable, Sandy will love us," Clarke said.

With three quarters of a billion dollars invested in Travelers, Sandy wanted to keep a very close eye on the company. He ordered Bob Lipp, who headed Commercial Credit, to take up residence at Travelers headquarters.

"Why's this guy here?" employees asked one another when the tall, unassuming Lipp reported every day. Schemes were hatched to get Lipp out of the way. The company told Lipp that the only available office was in a nearby building that housed the "natural disaster division," part of Travelers' "weather department."

Lipp was amazed—and disgusted—that Travelers was spending $3 million a year on a department that produced the same information that could be found on the Weather Channel. Then one day the Travelers' well-paid meteorologists went on high alert, firing off predictions of severe windstorms. To what end? Lipp wondered. "We have the insurance in force already," he said. "What are you supposed to do—go out on the beach and try to blow the wind back?"

Then at five o'clock sharp, the meteorologists left. The cleaning people were already moving into the office, pushing screeching vacuum cleaners around Lipp. Furious, he called the only executive still around, Chuck

Clarke. "This isn't a real business," Lipp bristled over the phone. "The vacuum cleaning doesn't disturb anyone, because no one's here!"

"Quit making us feel like losers," rebutted Clarke, who was fast tiring of the Primerica executives' holier-than-thou attitude. "It ain't fun being bought, unless you don't think much of yourself. We may not be perfect, but we have a lot of pride in what we do well."

Lipp, taken aback by Clarke's response, nevertheless liked his backbone. "But look at all the gross inefficiencies, the sour investments—"

"That's not who we are," Clarke continued. "It's not the essence of Travelers. We've been crippled by our investment strategy and a management that forgot it needed to make money. But those of us who are professionals are very good at how we write the insurance business and analyze those risks. Don't disturb our insurance strategy; don't tell us how to underwrite or process claims."

When Lipp hung up, he made a mental note to tell Sandy that Chuck Clarke, who had joined Travelers in 1958 as his first job, would be a "keeper." The insurance veteran understood what the Primerica team needed to change to restore Travelers to profitability, but he also knew what needed to be preserved: its insurance expertise and tradition. Clarke's heartfelt advice would be Lipp's focus as he represented Primerica's minority interest for the next year.

SHEARSON

Sandy reveled in the negotiations that gave Primerica a strong foothold in Travelers and the management challenges that followed. But never very far from his mind was Shearson. The former president of American Express watched—and waited—as the credit-card company continued to struggle with its brokerage subsidiary. American Express was a company carefully built on status and prestige, and Shearson was tarnishing its image. The brokerage unit had just reported a $116-million loss for 1992, while Sandy's Smith Barney and other Wall Street firms logged record earnings amid a rebounding stock market. American Express's stock had fallen to $20 a share from $40 a share under Robinson's regime. An exasperated American Express board had named Harvey Golub, the former McKinsey consultant whom Sandy had recruited to American Express, president in 1991, while letting Robinson remain as chairman. The selection of Golub surprised many who had assumed the American Express

1

The chubby child would grow up
to become the chubby mogul.
Sandy's mother taught him the
power of numbers. His father's
betrayal imbued him with the
value of loyalty.

2

3

The targets of patrician disdain and deep-seated anti-Semitism on Wall Street, Arthur Carter, Roger Berlind, and Sandy launched their own firm to challenge the financial establishment.

4

Disparaged by the elite of Wall Street as "Corned Beef With Lettuce," Marshall Cogan, Arthur Levitt, Roger Berlind, and Sandy abandoned the snooty financial district to set up CBWL in the new GM Building in midtown Manhattan.

5

Taking over one prestigious but troubled firm after another required massive amounts of due diligence, sometimes leading to exhaustion. Sandy dozed under the scrutiny of Jeff Lane, Peter Cohen, and Hardwick Simmons.

6

Sandy loved to mix business and family, and held frequent luxurious retreats for his top managers and their spouses at places like Kiawah Island, where he and Joan went biking on the beach.

7

The patrician Jim Robinson and the upstart Sandy Weill both wanted to
control American Express after the merger with Shearson, but Robinson
kept his challenger at bay.

8

American Express general counsel Gary Beller watched helplessly as Sandy, desperate
to demonstrate his deal-making prowess, kept raising the price American Express
would pay for IDS, an obscure money-management company.

Although life in the elegant halls of American Express was frustrating for Sandy, it did have its perks: Sandy played at the star-studded Bing Crosby golf tournament at Pebble Beach with golf pros Hal Sutton and Jack Nicklaus and former president Gerald Ford.

9

Peter Cohen, Sandy's former assistant, allied himself with Jim Robinson, and the two happily threw a party to celebrate Sandy's twenty-fifth year in the securities business just before Sandy was pushed out the door.

10

11

After languishing in corporate exile for more than a year, Sandy took over sleepy Baltimore-based Commercial Credit from Control Data. Commercial Credit's employees feted Sandy when he took their company public.

12

After Commercial Credit took over much larger Primerica to get its crown jewel, Smith Barney, Sandy began dragging top executives to mandatory monthly retreats, where he preferred "soft seating" to conference tables.

13

Ted Dimon, a veteran Shearson broker, and his wife, Themis (*far left*), became close friends with Sandy and Joan. Their son, Jamie, signed on as Sandy's deputy after graduating from Harvard Business School.

An inveterate gossip with a powerful need to know, Sandy worked the phone or prowled the halls of his company constantly, probing, listening, cajoling—and sometimes exploding.

14

15

Famed violinist Isaac Stern, president of Carnegie Hall, drew the uncultured Sandy deep into the world of classical music and New York society. Sandy and Joan became major benefactors of the concert hall, second only to its founder, Andrew Carnegie.

16

Awed by powerful symbols, Sandy bought Travelers Insurance Co. as much for its iconic red umbrella as for its troubled insurance business. He sent his deputy Bob Lipp to Hartford to shake up the moribund company.

Sandy did many mergers over the years, but by far the most important was his marriage to Joan Mosher, his partner, confidante, and lifelong love. They danced at Sandy's sixtieth birthday party at the posh Four Seasons restaurant.

Years after ousting Sandy from American Express, Jim Robinson himself was forced out. He and his second wife, Linda, made a conciliatory appearance at Sandy's sixtieth birthday party, and the two executives would later help each other out.

17

18

Jamie Dimon, Sandy's smart, charismatic deputy, eventually raised Sandy's ire by taking on more and more power. Sandy was angry that this photograph, carried in *The New York Times*, made Dimon appear more prominent.

19

20

Sandy pushed to have his daughter, Jessica Weill Bibliowicz, move rapidly through the executive ranks of Travelers. But when Jamie thwarted her advancement, she resigned and Sandy was furious.

21

Sandy angered Jamie Dimon (*right*) when, upon taking over Salomon Brothers, he put Salomon CEO Deryck Maughan (*left*) on an equal footing with Jamie. Robert Denham (*next to Maughan*) represented the interests of Warren Buffett, a major Salomon shareholder.

Usually nervous when speaking to a large audience, Sandy got caught up in the spirit of this gigantic rally for Primerica salespeople, who kept cheering him on with chants of "Stud! Stud! Stud!" as Sandy recounted his rags-to-riches success.

22

23

After publicly announcing the creation of Citigroup, John Reed (*center*) and his press officer, Jack Morris, led the way back to Citicorp headquarters, trailed by an ebullient Sandy and Joan.

24

Never averse to making unusual alliances, Sandy joined with the Reverend Jesse Jackson to promote minorities on Wall Street. Both were fans of President Bill Clinton, with whom they shared a podium.

Sandy scored a giant coup when he persuaded Robert Rubin (*right*), the former U.S. Treasury secretary, to join Citigroup. In the showdown between Sandy and John Reed, Rubin would play the role of kingmaker.

As the tension between Sandy and John Reed rose, each sought allies. Sandy went to Saudi Arabia to spend time in the desert with Prince Alwaleed, Citigroup's largest shareholder.

27

Deals may be Sandy's consuming passion, but good food and drink, and plenty of both, rank high on his list of priorities.

28

At an intimate New Year's Eve gathering at the Weills' retreat in the Adirondack Mountains, Sandy predicted to his two closest advisors, Chuck Prince (*left*) and Arthur Zankel, that 2002 would be a better year for Citigroup. It was one of his few bad calls.

Sandy and Bob Willumstad cut a celebratory cake after Sandy's surprise announcement that the unassuming but highly effective Willumstad would become the president of Citigroup.

In 2002 Sandy was named CEO of the Year, a distinction he had sought all his life. The honor came just as the wrath of investors and regulators was focusing on Citigroup.

31

Televised coverage of congressmen grilling star analyst Jack Grubman about his cozy relations with executives of client companies aired the night that Sandy was named CEO of the Year, putting a damper on the festivities.

32

New York State Attorney General Elliot Spitzer touched off a firestorm on Wall Street when he launched an aggressive effort to curb the conflicts of interest that had become endemic during the bull market of the 1990s. The investigation hit Sandy hard.

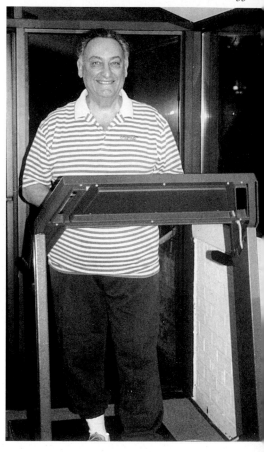

In light of the New York State attorney general's investigation, the CEO went on a "Spitzer Diet," giving up rich foods and gin martinis, and working out with a trainer. To get in fighting shape, he lost nearly thirty pounds in three months.

board would never put a Jew in such a powerful position. But the financial-services industry was undergoing a seismic shift. Where once prestige and pedigree were the gold standards by which firms—and the executives who ran them—were judged, the forces of competition and the demands of investors were setting a new standard for management. Golub, quick-witted and decisive, had impressed the American Express board ever since his days as a consultant to American Express. As president, though, Golub chafed under Robinson's conservative oversight. Finally, in February 1993, the board, led by former Mobil Corp. chairman Rawleigh Warner, gave Golub full authority to run the company, naming him chairman and demanding Robinson's resignation. That was Sandy's signal to move and to move fast.

The opening gambit was a simple offer to help ease some of American Express's financial burden. Sandy called Golub to tell him that Primerica was looking for a new headquarters. "You have these two buildings with Shearson," Sandy said. "If you want those buildings off your balance sheet, you better sign a deal with us now. Otherwise, I'm buying another building." He suggested that he and Golub meet.

"We can't risk meeting at a restaurant or office," replied Golub, who had developed a friendship with Sandy since their years together at American Express. "A rumor about a deal would start, even if we're just talking about golf."

Both executives were fully aware that the buildings were just an excuse to get them together to discuss what was really on their minds. Sandy knew Golub desperately wanted to sell Shearson, and Golub knew Sandy just as desperately wanted to buy Shearson. Because of their solid friendship, started a decade earlier when Golub hitched a ride on Sandy's American Express jet, the men didn't have to perform the typical prenegotiation "dances." Even more important, the Brooklyn-born, blunt-spoken executives trusted each other.

The fifty-three-year-old Golub invited Sandy to his American Express apartment, located near the Museum of Modern Art in midtown. The burly American Express chairman with thick glasses and a bristling moustache greeted Sandy and showed him into his study. Over coffee, the men initially chatted about their children. Sandy was godfather to Golub's youngest son, who was now in grade school.

As Golub chain-smoked, Sandy revealed that he had recently given up his trademark stogies. Despite pleas from Joan, his children, and countless

colleagues for years, it was his four-year-old grandson who finally succeeded in getting him to quit. In a deal with Jessica's first son, Tommy,
Sandy had agreed to give up smoking cigars.

"How did you stop cold turkey?" Golub questioned, as he continued
smoking.

"Chain-sucking," Sandy confided. "Lemon lollipops."

On their second cup of coffee, the men reminisced about the days in the
early 1980s when Golub was with McKinsey and Sandy was president of
American Express. After hiring Golub to evaluate IDS Financial, Sandy had
been impressed enough to tap him to run the Minneapolis-based financial-
services provider. Under Golub, IDS became one of American Express's
best performing units, propelling him to top posts at the parent company
after Sandy was gone.

With the coffeepot empty, the two got down to business. Sandy knew
more about Shearson than just about anybody, having spent two decades
rearranging and resuscitating the ailing brokerage houses that constituted
the firm. "It's not a happy environment over there—a parent company with
a broker affiliate it doesn't understand or want anymore," Sandy told Golub.
"We'll *love* Shearson, and take its problems off your hands." Sandy, always
a retail broker at heart, really wanted his first child back. "I think we can do
a deal in a week without any leaks," Sandy added. He told Golub what he
was willing to pay.

"The difference between bid and asked is close enough to justify spending more time together," Golub responded. One-on-one negotiations began on the spot. They knew it was one of the rare cases in which both of
them could come out winners. They settled on a straight asset sale of Shearson's retail-brokerage business alone. American Express would keep the
investment-banking firm Lehman Brothers, whose pedigreed and expensive bankers hadn't worked well with Shearson's brokers. American Express would eventually spin off Lehman in a public offering.

The negotiations were especially easy because Golub had no emotional
attachment to Shearson, as had his predecessor Robinson. Sandy, on the
other hand, cherished the idea of once again running the brokerage empire
he had created. Moreover, the two companies were pursuing strategies that
made the deal very attractive to both. Sandy was hell-bent on beefing up
and expanding the financial-services supermarket that Robinson had failed
to create with American Express. Golub, on the other hand, wanted to slim
down and salvage the core of his company's global credit-card franchise.

With the broad parameters of an agreement roughed out between the two of them, Sandy and Golub brought in a few other executives to work out the details in long sessions at Golub's apartment. For several days, after a full day of work at Primerica, Jamie Dimon and Chuck Prince would walk over to the apartment to meet with their American Express counterparts. Working from 6:00 P.M. until 6:00 A.M. every night, they immersed themselves in what they called the "Dracula deal," a transaction that was negotiated and drafted only at night.

On March 9, Primerica and American Express confirmed growing rumors that they were close to a deal on Shearson. Investors, convinced that Sandy could squeeze costs out of Shearson that American Express couldn't, sent Primerica stock surging 12 percent to a record $44.75 a share on unusually heavy volume. Investors cheered Golub, too, for biting the bullet and refocusing American Express on what it did best. Shareholders couldn't say enough good things about Sandy. "Investors are in love with him. There is nobody better at managing brokerage firms," said Scott Offen, a money manager at Fidelity Investments and one of Primerica's largest shareholders with 12.9 million shares. The March 10 *Wall Street Journal* said the union could be one of Sandy's "best deals ever."

By week's end the boards of both companies had given their unanimous approval, and the final deal was announced. To anyone familiar with the history of Shearson, the bargain Primerica struck was breathtaking. Sandy had sold Shearson to American Express in 1981 for stock valued at $930 million. Then American Express more than doubled its brokerage force by purchasing Lehman Brothers and EF Hutton, and spent billions of dollars more on the unit. Shearson also had built two state-of-the-art office buildings in downtown Manhattan valued at more than $600 million. Now Sandy was set to buy this much larger company and its real estate, all for about a billion dollars. For his money Sandy got nearly 8,500 Shearson brokers, an asset-management company that invested $52 billion for clients, and an agreement by American Express to assume virtually all legal liability for past Shearson problems. Combined with Smith Barney, the new firm of Smith Barney Shearson would boast 11,400 brokers and nearly 500 branches. Sandy Weill, the man who had done as much as anyone to transform the retail brokerage industry, was set to change the Wall Street landscape again. The combined firm would instantly be a juggernaut, challenging Merrill Lynch as the nation's biggest brokerage firm. Its negligible presence in investment banking gave it less clout on Wall Street, but, as Sandy pointed out, the new Smith Barney Shearson "has more money under management" than Merrill Lynch. Between them, the two mega-firms employed one of every four stockbrokers in America.

Sandy told reporters and analysts that the Shearson buy-back constituted a "quantum leap forward in achieving what would have required years to develop internally. It's a pleasure for me to be reunited with so many old friends." He named Zarb as the combined firm's chairman and CEO, and Joseph Plumeri, the managing partner of Shearson and a former colleague, as the president.

The next day's headline in *The New York Times* read BUILDING A WALL STREET EMPIRE, AGAIN. The article said: "They call it Primerica Inc., but Weill Enterprises would be more descriptive. With Wall Street's other corporations now run by a bunch of anonymous suits . . . Sandy Weill's portly profile has loomed up as the investment world's most prominent empire builder." *The Wall Street Journal*'s report elevated Sandy's status as well— calling him a "Wall Street legend" and his firm "Wall Street's New Goliath."

An ecstatic Sandy beamed throughout the day. He talked up the deal with stock analysts that morning and went to lunch with Joan. That afternoon, he headed straight for Primerica's trading room to chat with traders and watch Primerica's stock. Then Sandy immediately left on his Gulfstream jet to tour several Shearson offices around the country. It was the homecoming he dreamed of. In Dallas, Atlanta, and other key cities, the stockbrokers gave him enthusiastic standing ovations. When Sandy wasn't shedding tears in emotional reunions with old friends, he was giddy celebrating his victory. "It just doesn't get better than this," he said ebulliently.

Two days later, Sandy was feted at a lavish sixtieth birthday party at the Four Seasons. About 150 guests, including former president Gerald Ford, an honorary Primerica director, braved a record two feet of snow on this March Sunday to honor the man of the hour, "the comeback kid."

Causing more of a sensation than even the surprise snowfall was the unexpected appearance of the recently ousted American Express chairman Jim Robinson with his wife, Linda. The Weills had invited them to the birthday party long before the Shearson deal had been inked, in an effort for the onetime rivals to put aside past differences. With the guest list filled with "friends of Sandy," they all knew just how low Sandy had fallen when overpowered by Robinson in 1985 and how high he was on this night only forty-eight hours after winning back his original power base. Now Robinson was the one on the outside looking in. The dramatic change in circumstances between these two corporate titans wasn't lost on the guests assembled that snowy evening, least of all either of them.

STARSTRUCK

As the Shearson negotiations were nearing their climax, Wall Street was stunned when Morgan Stanley, the prestigious investment bank, unceremoniously dethroned Robert Greenhill as its president. Greenhill, one of Wall Street's most prominent deal makers, was the victim of a palace coup engineered by Richard Fisher, the firm's chairman, and John Mack, chief of its operating committee. While acknowledging Greenhill's ability to bring deals to Morgan Stanley, both men had lost confidence in his administrative abilities. Mack would be the new president, and Greenhill would become a "senior advisor" to Morgan Stanley's roster of blue-chip clients. Greenhill, skiing with clients in Colorado, was blindsided by the announcement and furious.

Here was yet another chance for Sandy to capitalize on a sudden turn of events. Amid all the accolades surrounding his Shearson triumph, Sandy was acutely aware that the huge firm's biggest weakness was its lack of an effective investment-banking arm. With a vast stable of brokers eager to peddle high-quality investments, Sandy decided that if he could snag Greenhill, the craggy-faced merger meister could generate a huge flow of new deals for his brokers to sell. Moreover, raiding a merger specialist like Morgan Stanley of such a prominent player would generate instant respect in the clubby world of investment banking.

"Greenie" and Sandy had become close friends over the years, especially when the busy investment banker, during the 1980s merger mania, took time every month to visit Sandy in his Park Avenue office. There he would present ideas that might get the defrocked American Express president back in the mainstream of business. Joan Weill and Gayle Greenhill were fast friends as well. In a business filled with second and third marriages to young "trophy wives," the two women had remained married to their driven and demanding husbands for more than thirty years. When Dimon expressed misgivings—he had heard the rumors about Greenhill's lack of administrative ability—Sandy dismissed his concerns. "They're just bad-mouthing him," he said.

To Sandy's astonishment, Greenhill was immediately receptive to jumping ship to Smith Barney Shearson. The avatar of the 1980s-style "merger banker" was eager to show the world that his old firm had made a terrible mistake, that he still had what it took to build a premier investment bank. With its newfound heft to challenge Merrill Lynch, Shearson could be a great platform from which to launch such an enterprise.

No one understood better than Sandy about the deep need to resurrect oneself after a downfall. Sandy believed in second chances. He knew all too well how powerful was the motivation to work harder so the second chance wasn't squandered.

But before Greenhill would commit, he pressed the Primerica chairman for assurances. For one thing, he didn't want to be just the head of investment banking at Smith Barney Shearson; he wanted to run the whole thing. Sandy was reluctant to unseat his old friend Frank Zarb, who had proven himself a talented executive. "We don't need Frank," Greenhill repeatedly told Sandy. Beyond that, he warned Sandy that getting into the investment-banking business would take Sandy and Primerica where they had never been before. "Sandy, if you take me on board, I'm going to build a world-class investment bank," the star deal maker said. "But you're going to have to go outside the U.S., and you're going to have to risk capital."

In the past Sandy would have laughed at such a preposterous notion. His entire career had been spent pursuing a more mundane retail strategy that avoided the stratospheric expenses associated with investment banking. The king of cost control, Sandy had assiduously avoided risking capital for thirty years.

But now he had stars in his eyes. This could be his big chance to show them all—the Morgan Stanleys, the J.P. Morgans, the entire snooty banking bunch—that he had arrived in their ranks. Greenhill would give him instant credibility. He made his decision: Shearson would plunge headfirst into the rarefied world of capital markets. "What blows my mind is that people thought we'd bought this big powerful retail thing and would do nothing anywhere else," Sandy said.

To prove his point, Sandy got out Primerica's checkbook. He agreed to an extravagant pay package for Greenhill: a $20-million signing bonus and 2 percent of all profits over $50 million for Smith Barney. And that would be just the start. Greenhill would recruit a team of investment bankers, but they would all come with huge price tags. It was completely out of character: Sandy Weill would be subsidizing an immense payroll for a division that would take months, at best, to start producing profits. Even more startling, he acceded to Greenhill's demand for the top job at Smith Barney Shearson.

Sandy and Greenhill sealed their deal Sunday, June 20, 1993, at a dinner celebrating the birthdays of Joan and Greenhill. "There's something special about Geminis born on June 20," Sandy said, toasting his wife of thirty-eight years and his new business partner. "They're real loyal."

On Tuesday, Greenhill showed his loyalty to his soon-to-be firm by buying Primerica stock, a move Sandy typically demanded of his executives. What was unusual was the size of the investment. Greenhill paid $35 million in cash for 750,000 Primerica shares bought directly from the company. Already rich, Greenhill, who piloted his own plane, had $125 million of Morgan Stanley stock and had earned more than $6 million the previous year.

Before announcing Greenhill's ascendancy, Sandy had to tell Zarb that he was being kicked upstairs. On Wednesday, Sandy asked Zarb to meet with him in the library. Sitting opposite Zarb on the red leather tufted sofas, Sandy told him, "Now that we're putting together Shearson and Smith Barney, we need an enormous investment bank to generate the deals."

Thoroughly familiar with Sandy's strategy of growing through acquisition, Zarb asked, "Which firm do you want to buy?"

"Another way to build this thing is bringing in a world-class team," Sandy replied, surprising Zarb, who knew that his boss didn't like to pay high-priced stars.

"We're going to bring in a new guy who's world-class," Sandy explained, adding that the new hire would assume the chairmanship of Smith Barney Shearson.

Zarb was floored. He told Sandy he was very unhappy to be replaced just as they were making strides.

"Everyone should be willing to change jobs or subordinate their jobs, if it makes sense from the company's standpoint," Sandy countered. "That's for the good of the organization." Zarb would become a "group chief executive" at the parent company. A crestfallen Zarb maintained his composure and left for home. His wife, Patricia, who had watched her husband dedicate himself to Sandy for years, was enraged.

Primerica called a press conference for Thursday, June 24, at the Drake Hotel, across the street from its corporate headquarters. Early that morning, Sandy phoned Lew Glucksman, who was Smith Barney's second in command, to tell him about the imminent announcement of Greenhill, who would be bringing his own number two. Without being told he was being shoved aside, Glucksman knew he was out of a job. As Sandy obliviously chattered away about how "business would come in buckets" under Greenhill, Glucksman, deeply hurt that Sandy didn't have the decency to give him more consideration, or at least more notice, began to clean out his desk.

Minutes later, an ebullient Sandy paraded Greenhill before the press as the new chairman and chief executive of Smith Barney Shearson. The ex–Morgan Stanley banker, a flashy dresser with a penchant for bold suspenders, called the opportunity "an exciting entrepreneurial challenge to build the firm of tomorrow." An Ivy Leaguer with degrees from Yale and Harvard, Greenhill told the press he looked forward to the change in culture from button-down Morgan Stanley to brash Smith Barney, including its in-house "hoot-'n'-holler" telecommunications link to all the branches.

Preening before the assembled media, the wavy-haired Greenhill told the packed room that he'd just invested $35 million in Primerica. "This is an expression of my confidence," he said. Sandy quickly added, "There are few people who will put their money where their mouth is. Bob Greenhill is one of those people." (Neither revealed that Greenhill would recoup a substantial part of the purchase price with the $20-million signing bonus he would receive.)

Sandy, thrilled that he had bagged such a star, uncharacteristically let his new Smith Barney chairman steal the show. The merger ace proceeded to describe his lofty ambitions for the newly combined securities firm, despite his lack of experience in a brokerage firm that catered to individual investors. He said Sandy was completely behind him.

"He trusts me, and I trust him," Greenhill blustered. "He's basically turned it over to me."

That triggered a series of meaningful glances among the Primerica executives gathered along the wall. "Is he talking about our Sandy, the one who micromanages every detail?" one whispered. As soon as the press conference ended, the executives were joking about Greenhill's "Alexander Haig act," an uncomplimentary reference to the former secretary of state's declaration that "I'm in charge here" the day President Ronald Reagan was shot.

Primerica's management team might have been skeptical, but investors certainly weren't. Primerica's stock rocketed up nearly 8 percent the day Greenhill was introduced as the new chairman of Smith Barney. Greenhill left messages of almost childish delight on Sandy's answering machine, gloating that his mere arrival could increase Primerica's market capitalization by nearly $1 billion. Part of that delight may also have been due to the fact that he had just made $3 million on his investment in Primerica stock.

That evening, Smith Barney held a cocktail party for Zarb. When Sandy tried to greet Zarb's wife with a kiss, she turned her cheek away. Eventually Greenhill made his way to her side of the room.

"Frank did a wonderful job," the new Smith Barney CEO told her. "I really hope I can do as well as your husband did."

Patricia Zarb glared at Greenhill. "And if you don't," she snapped, "Sandy will have you out of here in a heartbeat." Zarb himself didn't linger at Primerica. He eventually accepted the post of president of Alexander & Alexander, an insurance broker.

Greenhill promptly hired twenty-one bankers away from Morgan Stanley, mostly junior managers who received big promotions and raises that nearly doubled their compensation. Robert Lessin also followed Greenhill, his mentor, to become vice chairman of investment banking. When the smug deputy showed up and ordered Glucksman's assistant, Jennifer Bush, to move her boss out in three hours, she overheard him tell a colleague, "I'm not here for years. I'm here to make as much money as possible as quickly as possible."

As summer settled over New York, Smith Barney Shearson was an amalgam of three distinct firms. Smith Barney brokers clung to their sedate, old-fashioned ways of doing business with a loyal clientele. They resented the more aggressive and obnoxious Shearson brokers. And the brokers from both firms were the subject of constant ridicule and disparagement from the swaggering Morgan Stanley bankers. Day in and day out, it was "At Morgan we did it like this," or "You should see how it's done at Morgan." Greenhill even held secret morning meetings with his "team" before the usual eight o'clock firm meeting.

Yet Sandy seemed oblivious to the rocky relationships, at least in part because Greenhill got off to a quick start, bagging the role of advisor to Viacom Inc. in its megadeal to acquire Paramount Communications Inc. for $8.2 billion. With Greenhill flitting around the country to meet potential clients in their boardrooms, Primerica executives wondered aloud if Greenhill could be both a rainmaker and an effective administrator.

"Yes, he can," replied Sandy, determined his new and expensive experiment would work, "if he has good partners."

To ensure that Greenhill had the best possible partner, Sandy dispatched

Jamie Dimon to become the de facto manager of Smith Barney Shearson. Although he had no official role, Dimon began spending up to 90 percent of his working hours at the securities firm. To get better control of management, he took an office next to Greenhill's. Sandy believed that Dimon would easily compensate for Greenhill's administrative shortcomings. Certainly the Shearson and Smith Barney brokers liked the idea that Dimon's steady hand and sharp mind were guiding the business. They loved the outgoing and smart Primerica president, whose own father was a broker in their ranks. Even as they resented the newcomers, the brokers and traders knew if Dimon could hold his own with a tough SOB like Sandy Weill, he wouldn't be railroaded by Greenhill and his cronies.

Dimon was appalled at what he found. Greenhill had gone overboard in hiring new bankers, and the ones he had hired were inexperienced. "You're giving them jobs far beyond what they can do," Dimon complained. Worse still, Greenhill was paying them small fortunes. A junior banker making $400,000 a year at Morgan Stanley jumped to Smith Barney Shearson for $800,000 plus a signing bonus equal to one year's pay.

When the board's compensation committee began to be deluged with contracts spelling out such fat salary guarantees, the directors got worried. This was so unlike Sandy, a zealot about modest salaries offset by huge grants of stock options. At a compensation committee meeting, director Andrall Pearson expressed his reservations about the flood of high-paid bankers. "I've been around a long time, pal," he told Sandy. "When you start doing this, you get all kinds of jealousies. Besides, if these are people who will leave a place for more money, they'll leave you, too." Pearson became so concerned about the big signing bonuses Greenhill was promising that he asked for "evidence" of the previous salary before signing off on the disbursements.

Dimon and Greenhill, who had been friendly when Greenhill was at Morgan Stanley, soon found themselves clashing on nearly every point. "The rumors were right," Dimon concluded. "He doesn't have a clue about how to run a business."

Greenhill was frequently out of the office, flying his Cessna Citation V around the country to meet potential clients and leaving Dimon struggling to maintain order and make decisions in a firm in which no one seemed to want to work together.

Greenhill's business decisions—often made without any consultation with his colleagues at Smith Barney Shearson—revealed his lack of knowledge about how retail brokerage firms work. A month after taking over, Greenhill breezed into the offices to announce that he had committed Smith Barney Shearson to buy $500 million of junk bonds being offered by RJR Nabisco. Kohlberg Kravis Roberts & Co., who had been one of Greenhill's clients when he was at Morgan Stanley, was handling the sale for RJR, and Greenhill said he had told Henry Kravis "we could sell it through our retail network."

"Are you crazy?" asked a stunned Dimon. "You can't commit like that. There are no terms? No pricing? What are you doing?" Dimon, on his feet and in Greenhill's face, was shocked at Greenhill's hubris and lack of understanding about the kind of firm he was heading. Smith Barney Shearson dealt with conservative individual investors who had little use for anything labeled "junk." It would be impossible for the brokers to sell such a huge amount of junk bonds to their clients.

"You go back to RJR and say we can't commit to that," Dimon demanded. "You can't put the firm at risk like that."

Greenhill resisted; he didn't want to go back on a deal with the powerful Henry Kravis.

"You can't jam an offering like that down our retail guys," Dimon said with exasperation. "They can't sell junk bonds that easily."

Dimon explained carefully that Smith Barney Shearson could commit to deals only in reasonable amounts and on terms consistent with the firm's low tolerance for risk. Then the thirty-five-year-old executive, who had no official title at Smith Barney Shearson, forced the fifty-seven-year-old star banker to renege on his commitment to Kravis. Instead of $500 million, Smith Barney Shearson would take $150 million, Dimon said.

Not long after that argument, Greenhill informed Dimon that he had found someone he wanted to bring in to run the firm's fixed-income group.

"Wait a minute," Dimon sputtered. "What about Blackie and Boshart?" Dimon and others at Smith Barney Shearson considered Steve Black, the chief of capital markets, and his deputy, Jim Boshart, to be two of the smartest, most reliable executives in the firm. A new head of fixed income would report to them. "You can't just throw someone new in and risk a clash without talking it over with them."

"No, I've made a decision," Greenhill said. "And he's going to report to me."

Dimon was outraged. When Black and Boshart got wind of the change, they threatened to quit. Dimon finally persuaded them to stay, assuring them that, despite his own title as president and CFO of Primerica, he would devote ample time and energy to making certain that Greenhill wasn't allowed to run amok at Smith Barney Shearson.

Armed with such anecdotes, Dimon warned Sandy about Greenhill's erratic behavior. "He's destructive," Dimon told his boss.

Sandy had been delighted that Greenhill had hit the ground running, bringing in deals like the Viacom-Paramount merger. But it wasn't just Dimon grousing about Greenhill. Sandy might be willing to pay big bucks to get bankers like Greenhill, but he still wasn't willing to put his firm at risk. And he was worried that key managers like Black and Boshart were talking about quitting. To determine how much of the turmoil was real and how much was just testosterone talking, he sought the perspective of a woman, Heidi Miller.

Dimon had hired Miller as his assistant in 1992, luring her away from a ten-year career at Chemical Bank. The intelligent young woman had quickly assumed more responsibilities, rising to become the chief risk officer at the securities firm. A Jewish girl from Queens, New York, Miller had no academic background in business. Admitted to Princeton the second year it accepted women, Miller got a history degree and then went on to earn a Ph.D. in Latin American history from Yale. She had backed into financial services work when looking for a job with companies that did business in Latin America.

Miller was on a Caribbean vacation with her husband and two young sons when the phone rang in her hotel room. It was Sandy's secretary. "Sandy wants to have lunch with you."

"Are you sure?" she asked, knowing that she had never had, and never expected to have, lunch with Sandy Weill. Miller had met Sandy when she accompanied Dimon to meetings, but the Primerica CEO was always oddly quiet around her.

The secretary assured her that Sandy was indeed inviting her to lunch and set the date for them to meet at the Four Seasons when she returned from vacation. Before she hung up, the secretary warned, "Don't be nervous if people look at you strangely when you walk in."

"Why?" Miller asked tentatively.

"Because he doesn't have lunch with women."

Nervous and excited, Miller showed up at the famed Four Seasons in her standard dark business suit, accented by a vibrant Hermès silk scarf.

She was escorted to "Mr. Weill's table," the corner banquette along the wall of "power" tables.

With no niceties or preliminaries, Sandy got straight down to business. "What do you think about the new people? How is Steve Black handling the fixed-income people? What's your thinking about risk control in the company? What about management of the trading floor?"

Miller took the barrage of questions in stride. As they ate, she answered quickly and succinctly, all the time thinking to herself, *So much for a warm and fuzzy get-to-know-you conversation.*

Besides a discussion of credit and risk issues, she confirmed that the atmosphere at Smith Barney Shearson was becoming poisonous. "It's not a way to run a company," she told her ultimate boss. "You almost need a facilitator between Jamie and Greenhill—it's ugly. Jamie is getting angrier and angrier about having to carry the load."

Sandy liked Miller's clear thinking and her moxie. "You're a player, aren't you?" he said to her.

"Those are my observations," she said matter-of-factly, though she was thrilled that he now considered her worthy of possible promotion among the coterie of powerful executives he commanded.

The lunch convinced Sandy that he really did have to worry about the "Greenhill effect" at Smith Barney Shearson. Both Greenhill and Dimon were claiming that they had Sandy's blessing to pursue their very different visions of Smith Barney Shearson and, in a sense, they both did. Soon Sandy would have to decide: Would he wager the firm's future on hotheaded, expensive, and aloof bankers who could potentially deliver great rewards? Or would he stick with his longtime, less glamorous formula for success—his belief in the retail customer?

But for the moment those burning questions would have to wait. Despite the near civil war raging in Smith Barney Shearson, Sandy's attention was elsewhere—on a deal that could fulfill his deep desire to erase his one and only failure, American Express.

11

THE RED UMBRELLA

No question about it, the button-down executives at Travelers Corp. were terrified of Sandy Weill. They feared that this brash New Yorker would tear apart the conservative culture they had so carefully nurtured for decades. Never mind that the culture they were so eager to preserve had nearly destroyed the company.

And they were right. It didn't take the feisty Primerica chief long to begin plying his management expertise throughout Travelers. As with any other ailing company that Sandy took over, the first priority was to get expenses under control. After slashing 3,300 jobs as a condition for Primerica's $722-million investment, Sandy pushed to shed another 1,700 jobs in the coming year. Then he insisted that Travelers dump much of the depressed real estate it held in its investment portfolio. Better to get rid of a drag like that and invest in something that produces cash flow than to sit on the depressed property and await a rebound in property values that may be years away. He also ditched the executive dining room and one of Travelers' two corporate jets (he had his own Gulfstream). He did, however, relent on Travelers' helicopter. Sandy loved zooming from his home in Greenwich to Hartford in the plush Sikorsky aircraft, considered the sine qua non of corporate choppers.

Never content merely to cut costs, Sandy and Jamie Dimon went looking for increased profits, too, analyzing each of Travelers' businesses line by line. Unlike Budd, who had seldom left his palatial executive suite to wander the halls, Sandy and Dimon wanted face-to-face meetings with unit managers, not only to get facts, but also to determine if a manager was a "keeper." When Sandy reviewed the annuities division, which basically offered clients a product that combined an insurance policy with investments in mutual funds, he asked the administrator how much Travelers was being paid by the mutual fund companies whose products it sold.

"Um, um, um . . . I don't remember," the cringing manager replied. "Um, should we get paid something?"

"How can you ask *me* such a basic question about the business you're supposed to run?" Sandy raged. Not a keeper.

Sandy also insisted that Travelers' board receive monthly rather than quarterly financial reports. "I want a monthly scorecard to see how we're doing," he told his fellow board members. At board meetings Sandy was accompanied by his chosen directors—Dimon, Bob Lipp, and Frank Zarb. The smart and voluble foursome easily dominated the other twelve directors, led by Budd, who had started his career at Travelers in 1955 as an actuary. Sometimes Sandy forgot that he wasn't really the chairman of Travelers. As the board prepared for a routine vote one day, he piped up and said, "All in favor, say 'aye.'"

"That's my line," Budd remonstrated.

For all their fear and resentment, though, the Travelers executives weren't so blind that they couldn't see the results Sandy was getting. Increasingly he was setting policy at Travelers. And as he did, Travelers' profits and its stock price increased. By August 1993, Travelers stock was trading at more than $31 a share, an 80 percent increase since Sandy had bought into the company less than a year earlier and a $571-million profit on Primerica's initial $722-million investment.

The early successes at Travelers, as well as the prospect of more successes yet to come as he and his band of tireless executives applied their management expertise to the company, set Sandy to thinking. Maybe Main Street, not Wall Street, was the place to build a financial empire. Of course, Sandy had spent plenty of time on Main Street. After all, he had taken over Commercial Credit, about as Main Street as a financial firm can get. But he had always thought of Commercial Credit as a vehicle for eventually getting him back to Wall Street, where he long believed the real financial power resided. Now, as he considered the possibilities inherent in Travelers, he very much liked what he saw.

First, there was the name. Travelers had been around for more than a century and its name was known throughout America. It sure as hell was better than Primerica, a moniker he had come to loathe. Everyone mispronounced it; even his telephone operators answered "Prime America." At his last annual meeting a well-known corporate gadfly had called the company "Primreeka," like the spice paprika. Sandy had cringed.

Then there was the red umbrella. Symbolism held a special place in Sandy's psyche, one reason that he had been so enamored at the idea of becoming part of American Express, whose cards powerfully symbolized wealth and sophistication. Like the company's name, Travelers' red umbrella was well known. It didn't hurt that Travelers also was a primary sponsor of the famed Masters golf tournament, to Sandy yet another symbol of power and respectability.

At the summer meeting of his Primerica planning group in 1993, Sandy told his colleagues that he wanted the whole enchilada—he wanted to take over Travelers. "We'll be one of the largest insurers—and one of the largest financial companies—in the world," he told them. And, he added, "We can change our name to Travelers."

The proposal was greeted enthusiastically. "We all hate the name Primerica anyway," said Ettinger. "We can play golf at Augusta," another executive chimed in. "We'll have our own icon," Dimon said, chuckling. Soon they were laughing about using the red umbrella to poke Merrill Lynch's bull and push over Prudential's rock. The playful banter reassured Sandy that he was making the right decision.

Still, he wanted to be sure he would be getting what he was paying for—a respected name and symbol—if he bought Travelers. He commissioned Clive Chajet, a prominent corporate identity guru, to see how Travelers' red umbrella stacked up against the other well-known symbols of the financial-services industry, including Merrill's bull, Prudential's rock, and American Express's blue box. To his total delight, the red umbrella, first used in Travelers advertising in 1870, turned out to be "the single most trusted symbol in financial services."

"The red umbrella is Travelers' biggest asset," Chajet told him, regardless of how well or poorly the company might be doing. "It's old. This symbol has stood the test of time for one hundred twenty-five years." Chajet urged Sandy to apply the umbrella to every company in his empire. "Redefine and broaden the strength and security of the umbrella to cover all financial services. It fits with your concept of diversification and cross-selling." Then the savvy Chajet, well aware of Sandy's origins, put a personal twist on his recommendation: "Self-made people want to attach themselves to permanent and enduring symbols. If you don't have that kind of history, buy it and leverage it. The red umbrella can be that symbol for you."

That was all it took. Now Sandy *had* to have Travelers and its umbrella. Exactly one year after Primerica's initial investment in Travelers, Sandy invited Budd to his Greenwich estate to talk about a more lasting union. During that year Sandy had amply demonstrated his affection for Travelers, wearing an umbrella lapel pin to work each day and donning shirts and sweaters emblazoned with the umbrella logo around the house. On Sunday, September 19, he proposed a merger between Primerica and Travelers. Budd had already surrendered the independence so cherished by chief executives when he accepted Primerica's bailout a year earlier; his ego wouldn't stand in the way of a deal. Indeed, he remained grateful to Sandy for rescuing his company. And he agreed that a merger would be a unique opportunity for both companies. Of course, the merger would really be a takeover by Primerica of the 73 percent of Travelers stock it didn't already own.

The two executives agreed on a stock swap valued at $4.2 billion, with Travelers shareholders receiving a slight premium for their shares. In return, the insurance CEO, a staunch Hartford booster, wanted assurances that the Travelers name would survive and that the insurance company's headquarters would remain in Hartford. Done, Sandy told him, although he added that the corporate headquarters of the renamed Travelers Group would remain in New York. Sandy would be chairman and CEO of the parent company, and Dimon would be its president and chief financial officer. Sandy told Budd he could be chairman of the executive committee, carefully neglecting to mention that the executive committee never met. Finally, the Primerica chairman wanted Bob Lipp, his trusted lieutenant who had been ensconced at Travelers for the past year, to become the insurer's CEO.

Both sides had seen this day coming, and it took only two days to work out the details. Sandy presented the deal to the Primerica board on Wednesday. "It's a major acquisition," said former president Gerald Ford, pleased by Sandy's great strides since Baltimore, as well as the huge increases in the value of the Primerica stock he owned. "It's typical of your wise choices on where to take the corporation next." On Thursday the Travelers board gave its approval as well. The only remaining hurdle was Travelers' shareholders, who would have to vote on the deal.

Later that day the two companies jointly announced the deal, which would instantly double Primerica's assets to about $100 billion. "Here I've bought one of the great financial brands," Sandy gloated to reporters. "There aren't many of them left." For someone as devoted to shareholders as Sandy, he continued to personalize the victory as if it were his alone. "I'm now bigger than American Express," he crowed, revealing his lingering embarrassment over his one corporate failure. Stocks of both companies climbed on the news.

But if investors greeted the takeover with cheers, Travelers' employees certainly didn't. "We were sold down the river," charged Seymour Reitman, a Travelers retiree and stockholder attending the special shareholders' meeting to vote on the takeover. Noting that Primerica had paid only a six-cent-a-share premium over Travelers' stock price, Reitman angrily congratulated Sandy "on being a better horse trader than Ed Budd. You got yourself a real bargain and got the Travelers board to swallow it hook, line, and sinker."

Budd pointed out to the assembly that Travelers' stock had risen a stunning 118 percent since the announcement of Primerica's initial investment a year earlier. But in the minds of many older shareholders, who were on fixed incomes, the rising share price didn't make up for what they knew was coming: Primerica had disclosed in the required shareholder mailings and in filings with the Securities and Exchange Commission that the company would pay the old Primerica quarterly dividend, not the much more lucrative dividend Travelers had been paying. It amounted to a 66 percent cut in the dividend income that shareholders would receive.

Sandy's management style came under attack, too. "Working at Travelers was always very paternalistic," commented one employee. "As long as you kept your nose clean, you could work here forever. Now it's 'What is your worth? What are you producing?'"

At the end of the tumultuous meeting, the shareholders approved the merger. Amid their victory, the Primerica officials were dismayed at the bitter reaction to their hard work to save a company that had been teetering on the edge of bankruptcy.

In the Travelers helicopter on his way home, Sandy sipped a glass of gin as he soared south over the pink granite neoclassical Travelers tower, at 527 feet one of the tallest structures in New England. The takeover of Travelers certainly had redeemed his failure at American Express. But it and the other events of the past year had taken their toll, too. He had spent billions to buy back Shearson, launch the Greenhill investment-banking experiment, and acquire Travelers. For the moment his immense appetite was satisfied. But to Mary McDermott he looked tired, the bags under his eyes dark and swollen. He confirmed her assessment. "It's that feeling of fear deep down," Sandy said. "I'm running scared most of the time. But it's what keeps me going."

LIPP LAND

In the years since Sandy had lured Bob Lipp away from Chemical Bank, the former bureaucrat had become a skilled manager who doted on operations. Now that he was the CEO of the insurance operations, he would be able to move out of the remote office in the natural disasters department and into something more befitting a corporate chieftain. But Lipp's idea of a corporate chieftain's office was considerably different from the former Travelers chief's. On his first day as CEO, Lipp was escorted by the Travelers facilities manager to the suite of lavish wood-paneled rooms that took up the entire penthouse floor of the headquarters tower. Lipp's father had been in the carpet trade, and Lipp instantly recognized that the floors were covered in luxurious custom-designed, hand-tufted wool rugs by the famed Edward Fields. It was the same elite brand used in the White House, in America's largest embassies, and in countless mansions.

"What does this say to our thirty thousand employees?" Lipp barked at the hapless manager. "This entire extravagant tower symbolizes what brought this company to its knees. Let's find an office where real people do real work." The lanky chief executive with his mop of white hair strode out of the tower and across the pedestrian bridge to another Travelers building. On the way, Lipp tried to make eye contact with any employees he passed, but they kept their heads down. He began a game with himself to see how many staffers he could get to speak to him: none.

Lipp selected his new office: room 17B on the eighth floor, smack in the middle of the claims department. It was the closest thing he could find to the back office of a securities firm, the center of operations. He ordered the executive floor, with its spacious, opulent offices, converted to meeting rooms.

The new CEO's first act was the elimination of departments he despised. After his yearlong stint in "natural disasters," Lipp took particular glee in slashing the entire weather operation. He also axed the strategic planning unit. "Here are twenty-two people writing papers to each other like the House of Commons," he complained. "Strategy should be done by operations managers, not a think tank." And then he whittled the seventy-four-member government and public relations department down to one person, Keith Anderson, and warned him, "You should be hiding. This company hasn't had anything good to say for a long time." Such remarks had Travelers employees, unaccustomed to Lipp's acerbic wit, cowering.

Lipp spent days scouring every floor of the insurance giant. "This place is like Swiss cheese," he complained as he passed scores of empty offices scattered throughout the four-building complex. He demanded a list of all company phones and found that Travelers was being billed for hundreds of phones sitting in the empty offices of employees who had quit or been fired. He ordered a redesign of the offices and found, much to his pleasure, that he could squeeze everyone into two buildings and sublease the other two, saving millions of dollars.

At lunchtime on his first day as chief executive, Lipp appeared in the huge company cafeteria, touching off an excited round of whispering throughout the room. As far as most employees knew, the previous CEO had never eaten in the cafeteria. In an effort to demonstrate the new regime's dedication to shareholders and profits, Lipp wheeled a big television set into the cafeteria and tuned it to show a real-time quote of Travelers' stock price. Still unaware of how important that stock quote was to their own futures, the employees grumbled: If they were getting a TV, they wanted to watch their favorite soap operas.

When he crossed the three-story all-glass rotunda, a charming woman who appeared to be in her fifties offered to hang up Lipp's coat. *What a waste of money,* he thought. When he found that she was paid $20 an hour, he replaced her with a $10-an-hour security guard with a gun. The abrupt disappearance of the "hostess" who knew everyone's name touched a raw nerve among employees. Chuck Clarke, who early in Lipp's tenure at Travelers had warned him about undermining the culture, now scolded him again. "You're cutting the innards of the place. She was a fabulous lady, one of us, part of our culture."

Then Lipp closed down the public observation deck on the top of the tower, a move that he calculated would save thousands of dollars each year. That was too much. The employees were furious, and newspaper editorials quickly appeared condemning the "lean and mean" Weill executives for denying the local Girl Scout troops a destination for their field trips. Bowing to the fierce pressure, Lipp reopened the observation deck.

If Bob Lipp was tough on expenses, the deputy he brought with him to

Travelers, forty-year-old Jay Fishman, was an absolute terror. Fishman spent an hour each day reviewing every single invoice and expense voucher before signing checks himself. He wanted to know every instance of superfluous spending.

Presented one day with an invoice of $185 for a fancy day-planning calendar, Fishman called the manager to inquire why she had submitted it as a company expense.

"I did?" was her response.

"Now, there are a lot of things that are okay to say," Fishman instructed her. "You can say, 'Gee, I made a mistake,' or 'Gee, I didn't know the new policy,' but one thing you can't say is 'I did?' You can't take the Fifth."

Other savings included $55,000 by buying paper without a watermark and thousands more from eliminating the newspaper clipping service for managers. "There are no 'CliffsNotes' to the newspapers," Fishman decreed. He exploded one day when he spied boxes of new file folders lying in a garbage can. He pulled them out. Soon the scuttlebutt was that Sandy's "henchmen" were climbing through the garbage Dumpsters to pull out filthy files and slimy paperclips to be reused.

None of the hyperbole bothered Lipp. Indeed, he consciously sought symbols to demonstrate how serious he was about cost control. A perfect opportunity soon presented itself. The facilities manager reported that the fountain was leaking into the garage below the headquarters promenade. The repair would cost about $60,000.

"How much would a pine tree cost?" Lipp asked.

"About fifteen dollars," the nonplussed manager replied.

"Okay, drain the fountain, fill it with dirt, and put a pine tree in it," Lipp said.

Work on the fountain captured the employees' attention the next morning as they streamed in to work. When they left for home, they stopped in horror. In the place of their refreshing and fanciful fountain was a scraggly pine tree.

Again Chuck Clarke lectured Lipp. "Your exaggerations for effect are getting ridiculous," the senior Travelers veteran told his boss. "I know you're trying to teach us about changing our culture, but a tree? How painful and petty can you be?"

Lipp decided then to take a page from Sandy's playbook: When morale was low, buck 'em up with an employee meeting. A few days later he stood on a platform in the vast cafeteria before hundreds of Travelers employees.

"I'm sorry to break this to you, but this isn't the same Travelers," he be-gan. "You thought you could just sort of stay out of trouble, lay low the rest of your career. Wrong! There is no job security unless you work very hard."

The rank and file had already figured that out, but they were dismayed to hear their new leader put it so coldly. Seeing the fear sweep their faces, Lipp tried a different approach.

"We're dying," he told them. "We apologize, but we're going to tell you up front that Travelers must change."

He paused to let his remarks sink in. A hand went up; Lipp hoped the employee would offer a suggestion for improvement.

"People don't feel very good about how things are happening," the em-ployee said.

"Look, people are going to feel good when we're profitable, when we're on the upswing, not the downswing," Lipp said, trying to be under-standing.

Another hand went up. "You know, morale isn't very good among the employees," the speaker complained.

Lipp bristled. What a bunch of whiners! "We're *not* in the morale busi-ness around here," he snapped. "We're in the insurance business."

The room froze. The cavernous cafeteria fell eerily silent. Lipp stalked off the platform, but no one else moved for several seconds. So much for morale boosting.

Back in New York, Sandy reveled in Lipp's stories from Hartford. He soon adopted his own measurement for how things were going at the insur-ance company. Lipp and Fishman had discovered widespread abuse of the bus passes that Travelers had long subsidized to encourage the use of pub-lic transit. Staffers who had parking spaces in the Travelers garage would nevertheless buy as many as six passes each, then either resell them or give them to family members to use. They knew management didn't monitor the program. Some 7,000 passes were being issued each month.

"How many bus passes did we save this month?" Sandy would ask Lipp at each monthly meeting of the planning group. He let up only after the number of passes had been reduced to 3,000, a number that Lipp consid-ered legitimate.

While cost savings were a critical part of Travelers' turnaround, Sandy and Lipp had to consider much broader issues as well. Among them: the future of Travelers' health insurance business. Joseph A. Califano Jr., a Travelers director and the former secretary of Health, Education, and Welfare in the Carter administration, had warned Sandy early on: "Get the hell out of the health care business." Califano's Washington experience had taught him the inflammatory politics of health care and the increasing roles that government and managed health care would play. "There's no way it can be profitable," he said.

Then Travelers became enmeshed in dozens of lawsuits accusing the insurance company of denying benefits. It wasn't that Travelers was violating the terms of the policies it had sold. Rather, several courts had ruled that regardless of what the health insurance policies stated, Travelers and other insurance companies would be required to pay dozens of claims for experimental chemotherapy for breast-cancer victims. "It's awful to be caught between bottom-line issues, societal expectations, and life and death," Chuck Prince, Travelers' general counsel, told Sandy. "Health care insurance isn't about just analyzing risks like when will the next hundred-year storm hit."

If Sandy had any reservations about selling the health care business, they disappeared the night he was seated next to First Lady Hillary Clinton at a dinner. As the president's wife explained in detail her plans to impose more government control on the health care industry, Sandy had a sinking feeling in the pit of his stomach. If health insurance couldn't be profitable before, it certainly would be a disaster after any health care reforms were adopted. "She wants us to insure everybody whether we make money or not," Sandy told his executives the next morning as he instructed them to formulate an exit strategy. Within months Travelers had spun off the health insurance business and 10,000 employees along with it.

BURNISHING THE IMAGE

Now that he had the respected Travelers name and its familiar logo, Sandy began to feel that it was time he, too, got some more respect. When well-known British television journalist David Frost came to Sandy looking for sponsorship for a public television program called *Talking with David Frost,* Sandy leapt at the chance to associate Travelers with a quality television program. Each one-hour interview show with such luminaries as President and Mrs. George Bush, Andrew Lloyd Webber, and General Norman Schwarzkopf would end with the tag line "Brought to you by the Travelers Group of companies. . . ." As Mary McDermott worked on completing the sponsorship details, she had a brainstorm: get Frost to do an interview with Sandy for internal distribution to the Travelers troops. Grateful for Travelers' sponsorship, Frost quickly agreed, and in a few days the cameras were being set up in the library adjacent to Sandy's office. Frost and Sandy took their places facing each other in high-backed leather chairs. Frost sat with his legs crossed and his hands gripping a notepad with questions he and McDermott had prepared. Sandy clasped his hands in a thoughtful fashion that unintentionally emphasized his large girth.

Under the hot lights Frost began lobbing softball questions to Sandy that were intended to give the CEO ample opportunity to brag. But after only a few questions, Frost suddenly interrupted Sandy in mid-answer. "We need makeup," he called out. As delicately as he could, he explained that "we just need to dry off the perspiration there," pointing to Sandy's forehead and mouth.

"Am I sweating like a pig?" Sandy blurted.

The interview resumed, and Sandy began to fall into the spirit of the event, giving short but pithy answers to Frost's questions. What about succession planning at Travelers? "I don't think it would be healthy for me to retire. It's not on my mind right now." How did Sandy feel about the layoffs of thousands of employees at the companies he had taken over? "We didn't create the issues that created the layoffs. Our job is to reposition the company so that it can be in a position to grow again." What about the Weill offspring working at Travelers? Wasn't nepotism bad for a company? "We believe in nepotism. Relatives can come to work in the company. They start much more caring than somebody who doesn't know the company at all."

An hour later it was over. "Very lovely," Frost said. "That was great."

"What do you think?" Sandy asked, obviously fishing for more specific compliments.

"Very good," Frost replied.

"You're not just telling me that?" Sandy persisted.

"No," Frost said, rising to bring Sandy's grilling to an end.

Once the tape was edited, it was distributed throughout the Travelers Group empire and shown in every Commercial Credit, Smith Barney, and Travelers office. For the most part it was warmly received; the employees liked seeing their boss in the role of celebrity, being interviewed by a famous journalist. But when the video was shown in Hartford, it drew sneers of disdain, particularly Sandy's remarks about layoffs.

Another step in raising Sandy's profile was the hiring of a head of investor relations. For years Mary McDermott and Barbara Yastine had handled calls and inquiries from professional investors as part of the overall public-relations effort. When Yastine moved to another department, Sandy needed somebody else dedicated to looking out for Travelers' interests on Wall Street. McDermott and Yastine recommended a handsome, bright thirty-four-year-old named Bill Pike, who worked at a Philadelphia insurance company. After interviews at lower levels determined that Pike could indeed read a balance sheet, the final interviews were scheduled with Jamie Dimon and Sandy. Pike instantly liked Dimon, who spent much of their early-morning interview grilling him about personal things: Where did he grow up? What does he like to do? What books does he read? When the young man told Dimon he enjoyed playing with his dog, a wheaten terrier, Dimon decided to seek some personal advice: "What kind of dog should I get?" After the two spent considerable time debating the merits of various breeds, Yastine came to escort Pike to his interview with Sandy.

"Demonstrate you have an opinion," she advised Pike as they walked down the hall to the CEO's office. "Sandy wants people to be able to argue with him or disagree with him."

Faced with a plump man on an ugly leather couch, Pike sat down in a stiff-backed chair across from the sofa. "Do you like insurance?" Sandy asked, then proceeded to test Pike's working knowledge of the industry and the markets. Pike fumbled a few questions—he didn't know Travelers' price/earnings ratio—but he demonstrated to Sandy that he had a quick mind, was eager to move to New York, and would work his tail off for Travelers. He got the job.

As soon as Pike went to work at Travelers, he began taking careful notes of any conversation he had with anyone on Wall Street. To show that he was Travelers' "eyes and ears on the Street," Pike began typing weekly summaries about the callers and their comments to Sandy and the other senior executives. One afternoon Sandy strolled into Pike's office unannounced. "I really enjoy reading that thing you write every week," the CEO said. Pike was euphoric. Sandy had noticed him and been friendly with him. He ran to tell Yastine about his encounter with Sandy.

"You're not in with Sandy," she scoffed. "He hasn't yelled at you yet." Puzzled, Pike returned to his office wondering how being yelled at would show acceptance. He didn't have long to wait. Pike had prepared a slide presentation for a coming analysts' meeting that he took to Sandy for review. Immediately Sandy told him that "shareholder equity is a billion dollars higher because we just issued a billion in trust preferred."

Pike responded that the accounting department told him that this new fixed-income instrument might be counted as equity by the ratings agencies, but that "trust preferred" clearly wasn't true shareholder equity.

"No, no, no, no," Sandy said. "Put the billion in shareholder equity."

"Let me check with Irwin," offered Pike, referring to Ettinger, the company's tax expert.

"No, I'm telling you it's shareholder equity," Sandy said, his voice sharpening. "Don't ask Irwin."

Pike left Sandy's office, torn about what to do. Sandy had just given him a direct order. Yet Pike believed his job was to the protect the Travelers chief from accusations that he was inflating numbers for analysts or investors. Despite Sandy's order, the young investor-relations manager went to Ettinger's office. Just as they began talking, Sandy burst into the office.

"What are you doing here?" he screamed at Pike. "Didn't I just tell you not to ask Irwin?"

Pike had heard stories about Sandy's screaming fits but had never come face to face with someone so enraged. The startled and terrified young man didn't hear all of the cursing and yelling; in his shock he focused on Sandy's livid face and the throbbing vein that ran diagonally across his boss's forehead. *It's going to rupture,* Pike thought to himself.

Ettinger, long accustomed to these outbursts, calmed Sandy by proposing a compromise: The $1 billion of trust preferred would be included in the "shareholder equity" column but would be footnoted with a further explanation in small type.

When he finally recovered from the shock, Pike once again ran to Yastine's office to proudly announce: "He yelled at me! I'm in!"

Pike was also quick to pick up on Sandy's "manage by gossip" style. The boss would frequently stick his head in Pike's office to ask, "What's new?" Gratified by the attention, the young manager at first found himself freezing up though he longed to make some brilliant comment. Finally he began keeping a note card on his desk on which he jotted rumors about one or another institutional investor's buying or selling Travelers stock or the dates of competing companies' presentations to analysts. Pike made sure he always had three good points prepared for Sandy's surprise visits. "He's plugged in," Pike overheard Sandy telling another executive one day. Like the overly prepared student he had been in school, Pike beamed as if he had just gotten an "A" from a teacher who didn't give many top grades.

At Pike's urging, Sandy began spending more time meeting not just with analysts, but also with the big institutional investors whose massive buying or selling can make or break an individual stock. On the way to one of those early meetings, Sandy, still a nervous public speaker, offhandedly jotted down some notes on points he wanted to make. Pike, realizing that the brief scribblings summarized Sandy's entire management philosophy, later took the notes from Sandy and turned the points into a slide entitled "Keys to Success" that became part of Sandy's presentation. The six keys:

- Employee ownership
- Quality balance sheet
- Recurring and predictable earnings
- Diverse products and distribution
- Leader in every business
- Powerful brand

AN EXPERIMENT GONE AWRY

Basking in the glow of Travelers' red umbrella, Sandy didn't want to think too hard about what was looking increasingly like a failed experiment. Despite his loud bragging, Bob Greenhill simply hadn't delivered the goods that he had promised when Sandy hired him and his band of ex–Morgan Stanley cronies. Yet he and his team were collecting salaries and bonuses worthy of the Street's best investment bankers. When bonuses for 1994 were paid in early 1995, it became painfully clear not only that Greenie and his crew weren't pulling their weight, but that their attitude and pay packages were creating deep resentments throughout Travelers. Smith Barney's veteran brokers had delivered sterling results in 1994, yet many received bonuses far below what they thought they deserved, all because Greenhill's investment bankers' guaranteed payouts were siphoning off huge amounts of the bonus pool.

In the summer of 1995, with Sandy's blessing, Jamie Dimon assumed complete control of Smith Barney although Greenhill kept his title. Dimon ordered every Smith Barney department to rein in risks. When the bond department continued placing big trading bets, Dimon sent heads rolling. He forced out John F. Lyness, the bond unit's managing director, and his top aides in what became known as "the Memorial Day massacre."

It was clear to the outside world that Dimon was assuming more power within Sandy's burgeoning empire. On July 13, 1995, *The New York Times* ran an article titled: "Becoming His Own Man: At Travelers, Weill's Protégé Is on the Move." The only other executives of high stature in Sandy's organization, the *Times* noted, were Bob Lipp and Bob Greenhill, who in interviews "spoke of Mr. Dimon as if he was their superior." Trained by the master, Dimon ran Smith Barney with a tight grip and a focus on profits. He pushed the securities firm to an excellent fourth quarter, recording an amazing 30 percent return on equity.

But Dimon wasn't an investment banker, and he couldn't go out and do deals. That was Greenhill's job, and he wasn't doing it very well. Merger action was strong in 1995—eventually a record $800 billion of deals would be done globally that year—but Greenhill and his team weren't keeping pace. A year earlier Smith Barney had ranked eighth among merger advisors in the dollar volume of deals completed, a ranking largely fueled by the Viacom-Paramount deal. In 1995 the firm would fall to eleventh place, behind even J.P. Morgan, a commercial bank, and James Wolfensohn's small boutique investment bank. As 1995 drew to a close, Sandy reviewed the firm's numbers and the end-of-year bonuses that would go to his executives. With his lucrative guarantees, Greenhill would make more than Sandy, who ran the whole company! The Travelers chairman and CEO would receive $7.8 million in salary, bonus, and restricted stock. Unbelievably, Greenhill would receive his $1 million salary—and a $10.9-million cash bonus pegged to Smith Barney's profits, profits that were clearly attributable to Dimon and the Smith Barney Shearson crowd, not the expensive investment bankers.

The Travelers CEO told his secretary to track down Greenhill, who was nowhere to be found at the securities firm. Not surprisingly, she caught up with the investment banker down at the hangar where he was about to take off in his own plane.

"We have to restructure this deal with you and your people," Sandy told him on the phone.

"I don't think we should," Greenhill replied.

Sandy remained firm. "We need to, because it isn't working," he said. "It can't go on for calendar year 1996." Then the Travelers chief made official what had been unofficial for months. "And I'm making Jamie CEO of Smith Barney, but you can remain as chairman and do deals."

Greenhill would hear nothing of the sort. He would rather leave than be stripped of his title and duties. On the phone, he and Sandy worked out his resignation—at a huge cost to Travelers. Yet Sandy, sorely disappointed that his bold effort to overtake Morgan Stanley and Goldman Sachs had failed miserably, couldn't take another year like this last one. Greenhill would be gone, albeit $34 million richer.

At the beginning of 1996, Sandy named Dimon chairman and CEO of Smith Barney in addition to his continuing role as president and chief operating officer at the parent Travelers. After announcing Greenhill's abrupt resignation, Dimon knew he needed to tell the troops that he and Sandy had been wrong in forcing the tumultuous "Greenhill experiment" on them. But his words came out more quickly and succinctly than he planned. Over the firm's squawk box, Dimon said, "We made mistakes, and I'm sorry. Let's move on."

A FAMILY AFFAIR

Sandy had never made any secret of the fact that he was strongly in favor of nepotism. Travelers Group executives were encouraged to bring their sons and daughters into the company, or at least give them summer internships, and Sandy's own son, Marc, had been named a senior vice president of the company. In 1994 Sandy finally achieved his other family goal: to bring his daughter, Jessica Bibliowicz, into the company.

As ambitious as her father, Jessica had been pushing to move up at Prudential Securities, run by Hardwick Simmons, an executive in Sandy's first empire. In the two years since she had joined Pru to direct sales and marketing of its mutual funds, she had helped revitalize the business. Now she wanted to run the entire mutual-fund unit and told Simmons she wanted and deserved the job. The Prudential CEO praised her "fresh, personal, involved style" but concluded, "You need a bit more time."

Still pushing, Jessica told Simmons her father would love to hire her and had tried several times to bring her to Smith Barney, especially now that it had merged with the much larger Shearson.

"Don't work for a parent, particularly a legend like your father," Simmons warned her. "You always said one of your prime concerns in life is to be taken as a person unto yourself."

When the Prudential chief executive passed over her for the promotion, Jessica, now thirty-four years old, told her father she would consider moving to Travelers Group. Dimon, a childhood friend as the result of his parents' deep friendship with Sandy and Joan, recommended she work at the securities firm and report to him rather than at the parent company alongside Sandy. She agreed and was named an executive vice president in charge of sales and marketing for the division that managed $55 billion in mutual funds.

Nearly everyone at Smith Barney Shearson knew and liked Jessica, who possessed her mother's friendly charm and good looks and her father's common sense and verve. As teenagers, Jessica and Dimon, whose father was a broker at Shearson, had both worked summers at Shearson and often lunched together. At the time, the staff appreciated her determination not to exploit her family ties. One summer when Mary McDermott tried to pull a teenaged Jessica from her filing chores so she could attend an office party, the boss's daughter insisted on finishing her work.

But this time her appearance was greeted with curiosity and some skepticism.

"I always thought you wanted to make it on your own," a colleague told her. Jessica sighed and replied, "Wherever I am on the Street I will be Sandy's daughter, and I'll always have to fight for my credibility."

When she assumed her new job in charge of marketing for the mutual funds, attendance went up at the staff meetings. "I'm the tourist attraction," Jessica said, acknowledging and making light of her family roots.

Jessica quickly impressed her peers—and her dad—with her poise, intelligence, and marketing savvy. Unlike her father, she proved herself a lively and superb speaker, flying around the country to persuade brokers to sell Smith Barney's mutual funds, which had been losing market share. She knew how to make just enough mention of growing up as Sandy Weill's daughter to show she'd been hearing about Wall Street since she was knee high. "It's nice to have this stuff in your blood," she said. Still, Jessica referred to her father as "Sandy" rather than "Dad" inside the company.

After one of her presentations to a group of top brokers, Sandy couldn't contain his enthusiasm for his daughter's performance. Grabbing a microphone, the Travelers chief told the group how "proud" he was of her presentation, which, he noted, she gave "without the benefit of any notes." Embarrassed at such paternal exuberance, Jessica practically slid under the speakers' table.

But less than a year into the job, Jessica began pushing for more responsibility and authority. She wanted to run mutual funds, at the time the hottest business on Wall Street. The problem was that Steve Treadway, one of the firm's most respected managers, already had that job. Jessica's solution: combine the management and marketing of the funds into a single job—a job she should get. Late in 1994 Dimon, who had already facilitated Marc's promotions, moved to engineer Jessica's rise.

"Jessica should take over all of mutual funds and report to you," Dimon told Jeff Lane, the Travelers' vice chairman who oversaw asset management and mutual funds.

"Steve Treadway is doing a great job, and everyone will say Jessica is moving up because of Daddy," Lane replied. "That kind of office politics won't be good for her career in the long run."

Dimon persisted. Lane suspected the Travelers president was pushing because he was being pushed by Sandy.

"If this goes badly, it could be a fatal mistake not just for Jessica, but for you, Jamie," Lane continued. "It's a lose-lose situation. I don't want to do it."

Before the day was over, Sandy burst into Lane's office.

"Why are you standing in the way of my daughter?" Sandy growled.

"I think it's a mistake," Lane answered. "Everyone will start dumping on Jessica because she forced out a good man and she has the additional burden of being your daughter."

Sandy assured Lane he was wrong.

"It's your decision," Lane acquiesced. "But she'll be entering the lion's den."

With Jessica's promotion assured, Dimon scheduled a meeting with Treadway, who had just returned from his holiday in December.

"Would you consider heading up a new corporate-services department for all retail distribution?" Dimon asked the forty-seven-year-old Treadway. "It will be a great opportunity, and you can report directly to me as president of the entire company."

"That isn't something I really want to do," said Treadway, who could almost feel Jessica at his back, eager to take over his job. "I'd rather keep my job running mutual funds." To Treadway, the message was unmistakable: clear the path for Sandy's daughter.

On January 23, 1995, Jessica was named the head of the firm's mutual-fund operations, the ninth-largest fund group in the United States, with seventy funds and $58 billion in assets.

In the mid-1990s American investors were falling head-over-heels in love with mutual funds. The competition among financial-services compa-nies to win all the investment dollars flowing into funds became increas-ingly fierce: New funds were created, mutual-fund managers became the financial industry's equivalent of rock stars, and investors made decisions about where to invest based on funds' quarterly performance. One of the most contentious issues within the burgeoning industry was "loads," the ini-tial fees that many mutual funds charged investors. As investors became more sophisticated, many realized that loads, which helped fund companies pay broker commissions, didn't guarantee better performance. Indeed, loads often were associated with mediocre performance. As Vanguard and a few other fund companies capitalized on the performance issue by expand-ing their commitment to an increasing array of "no-load" funds, debates broke out among their competitors about how to meet the challenge.

At Smith Barney the issue injected a note of discord between Jessica and Dimon, her boss. Jessica was dead set against no-loads. She wanted to offer new funds but insisted that they all carry the high fees that had long been such a lucrative source of profits for the firm. Dimon, aware that the investing public's focus on performance put load funds at a disadvantage, wanted to supplement Smith Barney's portfolio of load funds with a vari-ety of no-load funds. Sandy, as usual poking his nose into anything he wished, became involved in the debate, voicing skepticism about no-load funds. A broker at heart, he was loath to sell any investment product with-out collecting a commission. Not surprisingly, no-load supporters won-dered to Dimon if Jessica had enlisted "Daddy" on her side. When Jessica got wind of what was being said, she marched into Dimon's office and told him, "I didn't do it, and by the way, Sandy thinks for himself."

In the end, Sandy recognized the wisdom of Dimon's analysis and in July 1996 Smith Barney began selling twenty-eight no-load fund families alongside its own proprietary funds, marking the first time a major Wall Street broker had sold no-loads.

But the no-load debate wasn't the only source of tension between Jes-sica and Dimon. The longtime friends had very different styles, and they continued to produce friction. As Sandy's daughter became the public face for Smith Barney's marketing efforts, the articulate and attractive execu-tive began appearing frequently on CNBC and CNN to talk about mutual funds and financial planning. Dimon noticed that she was stealing the limelight from other worthy Smith Barney managers.

Jessica's strength was marketing, but Dimon's was numbers, and there was no dispute from anyone who worked for Sandy Weill that numbers mattered more than anything else. At a staff meeting after a presentation by Jessica, Dimon put her through an intense questioning on the performance of the mutual-fund unit. Nearly every manager in the meeting had been grilled by the hard-driving Dimon at one time or another, but they noticed that he grew increasingly agitated at what he viewed as Jessica's inadequate grasp of the financial details.

Humiliated, Jessica took solace from Mary McDermott, another high-level woman and her first boss when she had been a summer intern.

"Jamie is making my life impossible," the thirty-five-year-old boss's daughter complained petulantly.

"No, he's not; Jamie treats everyone like that," McDermott replied, trying to calm Jessica. "I've had my moments with him, too."

"He thinks I can't do numbers and budgets," she continued. "To Jamie, if I can sell, then I can't count."

Using Sandy as an example, McDermott tried to ease Jessica's feeling of inadequacy around Dimon. "People have different strengths," the older woman counseled. "Even your father doesn't keep track of all the numbers—that's why he had Peter and now has Jamie."

In fact, however, the numbers supported Dimon. Under Jessica's administration Smith Barney's mutual funds weren't attracting new investment dollars as fast as many competing fund companies. That was due, at least in part, to the subpar performance of the funds, which were noticeably lagging behind the results of similar funds offered by competitors.

Nevertheless, Jessica continued to push to advance her own career. In the tumult of trying to integrate several companies, each of which had its own mutual funds and managers, no single person at Travelers had been named to oversee the company's entire asset-management operations. With its asset-management business growing rapidly, Sandy and Dimon knew they needed to name someone to the job. They considered Jessica for the post; Dimon didn't think she deserved it. Their colleagues held their breaths and waited to see if Sandy would force Dimon to promote his daughter.

Jeff Lane, the vice chairman who had earlier told Sandy and Dimon that Jessica shouldn't work at the firm, now had the opposite advice for Dimon. "Promote her," he warned, knowing that Sandy would brook no interference with his grand plan, not even from Dimon. "You're killing yourself if you don't."

Officially Sandy took a hands-off position. But unofficially he urged his second-in-command to give her the job she wanted. Marc already had a senior-level position, and Jessica was ready for one as well.

Dimon disagreed. "I don't want her to do it," the Smith Barney CEO told Sandy and his other executives. "She's not ready for the job. It's that simple."

Sandy clearly wanted Jessica to get the big job, but he wasn't willing to demand that Dimon promote her. Still he hoped, and probably expected, that his protégé would select Jessica for the post. Dimon did exactly what he thought was right—he picked a more senior finance veteran, Robert Druskin, to head asset management.

The boss's daughter learned that she didn't get the job from an acquaintance at another company. She didn't expect to get the post over Druskin, who had been with her father since his Shearson days. However, Jessica still resented Dimon's increasing unwillingness to recognize her contributions. After all, she oversaw two thirds of the asset-management business as head of mutual funds, and now she turned to the trusted general counsel, Chuck Prince.

Like many people in the company, Prince found himself caught between Jessica and Dimon, both of whom he regarded as good friends.

"Jamie doesn't appreciate what I'm doing," Jessica complained. "I'm frustrated that he won't let me progress."

When the general counsel asked Dimon about the boss's daughter, he replied, "She's not doing as well as she could. She's good in an outside role, a selling role, but not at running a business."

"Are you being too tough on her?" Prince asked, worried that Dimon was making Jessica feel inadequate.

"I've made a lot of people feel they don't measure up," Dimon fired back. "There's nothing personal toward Jessica."

Even key Travelers directors knew about the fracas. Arthur Zankel, a longtime pal of Sandy who had known Jessica since she was a young girl, agreed that Dimon had the right to pick someone else, though he knew the decision hurt Sandy personally. At one of the frequent social events with the Weills, he told Jessica, "You're better off the hell out of there. You don't need this bullshit, because you can do swell on your own."

But the boss's daughter still wanted to succeed at her father's firm. Although Sandy was well aware of her frustration, Jessica wanted to handle the matter herself. She went to Dimon directly to discuss her career.

"If you want to run the company someday—and I know you do—you have to go out in the field and run something," he told her. "You can't sit here at a staff job and expect to be CEO."

Jessica left Dimon's office without making any decision about a change. Dimon figured she would let him know if she wanted to move into a different position and went back to business as usual.

THE MILLIONAIRES' BALL

As his second empire neared its tenth anniversary, Sandy was on top of the world. His company was large and prosperous. More than two thirds of his 60,000 employees owned stock in the company. His son and daughter had important jobs there. His talent bank was full of up-and-coming executives like Marge Magner, Jay Fishman, and Heidi Miller. And his most important deputies were receiving their own accolades: *BusinessWeek* profiled Dimon, calling the Smith Barney chief a "whiz kid" with a "disciplined, hands-on management style" and, in another issue, named Bob Lipp, Travelers Property Casualty's chief executive, to its roster of the year's "25 Best Managers."

The Travelers chief wanted to celebrate. To begin the merriment, he had 60,000 red umbrellas delivered, one to the desk of every employee. He also set up a big celebration in Baltimore, where it all had started. The tenth anniversary party was held in the Walters Art Museum's sculpture court, a beautiful Italian marble courtyard flanked by Roman sculptures and capped by a 62-foot-high ceiling. Under a banner announcing THE BEST IS YET TO COME, Sandy and Joan presided over a cocktail party followed by a buffet dinner. Hundreds of Commercial Credit employees stood in a line that snaked out the door to shake the hand of the man who had shaken them to the core a decade earlier. Dressed in their best suits and dresses, they thanked Sandy for turning their company—and their own lives—around. Some of them told him and Joan how they could afford bigger homes or better schools for their children. Herb Seligson, who first encountered Sandy in the men's room at Commercial Credit ten years earlier, told Sandy he had used some of his accumulated wealth to buy a boat. The vessel's name: *Taking Stock.*

In December, Sandy hosted another bash, a holiday party for everyone on the two executive floors: the entire Travelers planning group and their staffs. On this chilly night, the colleagues, all of whom had worn festive attire to work that day, left together from the downtown office building that

Sandy had made Travelers headquarters. They crossed the street to meet their spouses at the ultrahip, award-winning Tribeca Grill, owned in part by the actor Robert De Niro. They were chatty and cheerful—partly because Bob Willumstad was entertaining them with his party tie containing a little music box that played "Jingle Bells" and partly because Travelers stock had risen yet again that day.

Entering the swank restaurant, the Travelers executives were greeted by a disk jockey playing dance tunes. With an ever-present drink in his hand, Sandy mostly stood on the sidelines but enjoyed hearty laughs with his executives and their spouses, all of whom he had made a point of getting to know over the years. After much drinking and revelry, some of the women managed to drag Sandy onto the dance floor, where his energetic gyrations inspired friendly laughter.

In the late hours of the night, Bob Lipp and Marge Magner took a moment to refresh their drinks and catch their breaths, enjoying the assembled throngs of merry colleagues, most of whom—like them and their boss—came from humble beginnings.

"Look at all the millionaires on that dance floor," Magner marveled.

12

CHOICES

The big truck rumbled slowly through the narrow streets of trendy Tribeca, its crimson cargo reflecting in the windows of the neat row houses. As a chilly winter dawn broke across the Hudson River, the truck pulled up in front of the Travelers Group headquarters building at 388 Greenwich Street, where Clive Chajet anxiously waited. Chajet, the corporate identity guru, had already advised Sandy Weill to slap the Travelers red umbrella logo on everything from T-shirts to business cards. Now he was here to supervise the installation of a 16-foot-high umbrella sculpture in front of the thirty-nine-story headquarters building. The sculpture had been Chajet's brainstorm, and he had overseen its design and construction. Knowing full well how powerful—or ridiculous—a symbol can become, Chajet had considered every facet of the project. The larger-than-life umbrella, made of 5,300 pounds of structural steel, would be anchored by piles sunk 30 feet into the ground. "If the symbol of security and protection toppled over, what a corporate identity crisis that would cause!" Chajet said, laughing nervously to Jeff Lane, who was observing. Welders carefully sealed each seam to ensure that no leaks would drench employees or customers. And to prevent Manhattan's innumerable pigeons from soiling Travelers' image, the umbrella's spokes were coated with a substance intended to repel birds by quivering jellylike under their feet. "The red umbrella will protect against anything," Chajet said proudly as the workmen rushed to complete the installation in time for Sandy to inspect it at 9:00 A.M.

At precisely nine, the front doors of the Travelers building swung open and out walked Sandy, arm in arm with another man. Chajet's eyes widened as he instantly recognized Sandy's companion: James Robinson! Here was the former chairman of American Express and Sandy's old archenemy chatting away with Sandy as if they were the best of friends. For a moment Chajet thought it was mere coincidence. But then he realized that this almost certainly had been planned. After the embarrassments Sandy had suffered at image-conscious American Express, he now was obviously delighted to be showing off his own powerful symbol. And Robinson was playing right along, admiring the huge umbrella and complimenting Sandy.

"I've just learned a life lesson," Chajet whispered to Lane. "Guys at that level never close a door."

Chajet was astute. Twelve years after Robinson had ousted Sandy and three years after he himself had been ousted from American Express, he and Sandy had just come from breakfast in Sandy's private dining room on the thirty-ninth floor of the headquarters building. Now sixty-one years old, the former American Express chairman was starting over. He and his son, James Robinson IV, wanted to launch a fund to back start-ups and young companies involved in information technology. Sandy agreed to provide $15 million, a paltry sum by Travelers standards. But the money was important to Robinson, both as seed capital and as a way to show the investment community that he was still in good standing despite the turmoil surrounding his last days at American Express.

And, of course, Robinson had something to offer Sandy, as well, something that money literally couldn't buy. When he took over Travelers, Sandy had gotten a peek into the rarefied world of golf at its most elite. As a sponsor of the annual Masters Tournament at the Augusta National Golf Club, Travelers received a few highly sought-after passes to the world-famous tournament. A longtime golfer and voracious social climber, Sandy was enamoured of both the manicured greens tucked among stately dogwoods and brightly colored azaleas and the idea of belonging to this exclusive club. But the rules were so rigid that one couldn't simply apply for membership or even seek a spot on a waiting list. Only by invitation could someone hope to become a member. Microsoft founder and billionaire Bill Gates, a man accustomed to getting whatever he wanted, had been snubbed by Augusta after brashly—and publicly—seeking membership.

But Sandy now had an ace in the hole. Jim Robinson might have lost a lot of clout on Wall Street and in Manhattan social circles, but in his home state of Georgia the Robinson family name still garnered respect. And not only was Robinson one of the three hundred elite members of Augusta National, he was willing to push Sandy's membership. The first step was a round of golf to introduce Sandy to the club and the club to Sandy. After landing in Augusta, Sandy and Robinson drove up Magnolia Lane to the clubhouse, where a plaque with gold lettering sternly warned GENTLEMEN ONLY. Inside, Robinson was provided with his green jacket, freshly pressed, which can be worn only on the club's grounds. As they made their way down the narrow hall to the dining room Sandy glimpsed oil paintings of Bobby Jones and Clifford Roberts, who had co-founded the club in 1931, and a bronze bust of Augusta's most celebrated member, President Dwight D. Eisenhower. That night Sandy stayed in one of the club's white Colonial-style "cabins." He arose the next morning to play the storied eighteen holes that each April challenge the luminaries of the sport playing in the Masters.

When Sandy returned to his New York office, Mary McDermott couldn't wait to hear all about it. She had made the annual trek to Augusta each spring to see the Masters with one of Travelers' passes, and she knew that Sandy would be bursting to describe the scenes inside the clubhouse. But Robinson had warned Sandy that talking about Augusta was absolutely *verboten:* Members can be kicked out for being indiscreet, and prospects can forget about ever again stepping foot on the hallowed grounds if they brag about playing there.

"Well, tell me all about it!" McDermott urged.

Sandy bit his tongue. He wanted in so badly. "Eat your heart out" is all he said.

A few weeks later the invitation to join came by mail. The Brooklyn boy who started as a runner on Wall Street was now joining one of the last old-boy networks still in power. And his long-ago rival, Jim Robinson, had opened the door for him.

GEARING UP FOR BIG GAME

Reflecting on his empire in 1997, Sandy was generally pleased. Profits at Travelers were higher than they had ever been and so was the company's stock price. He was also beginning to think about another big takeover. But something was a little out of kilter and it irritated Sandy. Given his company's profits, the stock price should have been even higher. The ratio of Travelers' stock price to its earnings per share—the P/E ratio, in financial shorthand—stood at 16, yet other financial-services companies were sporting P/Es as high as 23, indicating that investors valued those companies more highly. Particularly galling to Sandy was the P/E of 21 that investors were granting American International Group, the multinational insurance company run by Sandy's friendly competitor, Maurice Greenberg. If Sandy was going to go on a big shopping trip soon, Travelers needed a higher P/E. While there are many reasons investors give one company a higher P/E than another, chief executives automatically turn to one person to "fix" a problematic P/E: the head of investor relations.

"I'm producing the same results as some of these companies, but they're getting higher multiples," Sandy complained to Bill Pike. "Our stock isn't being valued properly."

One problem, the young investor-relations head told him, was that Sandy simply wasn't getting the word out to enough big investors. "We have to put you out there more," Pike explained. "When you're in front of an audience you can hear a pin drop when you're asked about your vision of the future."

"What's a vision?" Sandy scoffed. Not only did Sandy not think in terms of "visions"—he was more interested in the moment and taking advantage of unexpected opportunities—but he was still deeply insecure in front of audiences. He was willing to subject himself to the torture of the podium only at the most important gatherings of analysts, typically hosted by such powerful names as Goldman Sachs or Merrill Lynch.

"That's part of the problem," Pike continued. "We have to combat the perception that you're an opportunist more than anything else. You've earned the right to be a visionary."

Basking in Pike's flattery, Sandy agreed to step up his activities to promote Travelers stock by engaging in a series of "road shows" that would take him to meetings with big investors interested in picking the brains of CEOs. For his boss's first such venture Pike arranged for Sandy to travel with a leading analyst friendly to Travelers. Joan Solotar, of Donaldson, Lufkin & Jenrette, had issued recommendations that investors buy Travelers stock. Now she jumped at the chance to introduce Sandy to some of Donaldson, Lufkin's most important clients.

Their first meeting on March 14, 1997, took Sandy back to Baltimore, where he sat down with fund managers at T. Rowe Price, the big mutual-fund company. The fund managers, many of whom already owned some Travelers stock in their portfolios, peppered Sandy with detailed questions about profitability and trends in individual businesses. Full of smiles and quick comebacks, Sandy clearly loved the rapid-fire banter and demonstrated once again his deep understanding of all facets of his company.

"Most CEOs like to keep it at thirty thousand feet," Solotar happily observed to Pike. "Sandy's the opposite."

His easy manner disappeared as the managers escorted him to the dining room, where he was expected to make a brief speech. As usual, he lurched uncomfortably into his remarks but was suddenly granted a reprieve: Dow Jones & Co. had just announced that Travelers would become one of the thirty stocks that make up the famous Dow Jones Industrial Average, the best-known barometer of the stock market. "Let's check our stock price," Sandy said excitedly, ready to abandon even food—and certainly the hated podium—to watch his company's stock price go up.

After leaving T. Rowe Price, Sandy, Pike, and Solotar took the Travelers jet for the short hop to their next stop, Philadelphia. En route Sandy asked Solotar her opinion of the CEO at a rival brokerage firm.

"I don't know him very well," she replied.

"I never want you to have to give that response about me," Sandy said. "I want analysts and investors to feel they know me."

As the trio left the jet to go to their meeting with managers of the Vanguard Group of mutual funds, Sandy left instructions with the flight crew to order two pizzas with extra jalapeños for when they returned. Solotar thought Sandy had simply forgotten that the Vanguard managers would be serving dinner at the meeting. Worried that rich, heavy food might distract them from the business at hand, she had asked that fish be served. Sandy, however, made it very clear that he was disappointed with such light fare. As the jet returned them to New York, Solotar munched a slice of pizza and watched in amazement as Sandy devoured most of one pizza, washing it down with gin.

The trip paid off just as Pike predicted. The next day, Solotar released a report on Travelers reiterating her "buy" rating and noting the company's "unmatched M&A prowess," "conservative management philosophy," and "diversified business mix."

Sandy was surprised at how much he had enjoyed the trip. "It's a great way for me to get out and hear what a lot of different people are thinking," he told Pike. Encouraged, Pike began to set up regular jaunts, always being careful to warn each audience about what foods Sandy liked and what kind of gin he drank. The highlight of these dog-and-pony shows was a trip to London to meet money managers. Pike planned an easy schedule, and both Bob Lipp and Jeff Lane, now vice chairmen at the parent company, came along to keep Sandy company. As they boarded the Travelers jet to cross the Atlantic, Pike found the cabin's table covered by a buffet spread of cold lobster, sliced lamb, and other delicacies. "This is enough food for ten people," he exclaimed but soon realized that this was standard fare for Sandy on a long trip. As soon as they had buckled their seat belts, Sandy said, "Okay, let's talk deals. Do you realize our market cap is bigger than J.P. Morgan's?"

So that's the next target, Sandy's colleagues surmised. He's setting his sights on the world's most prestigious bank.

At the London airport, the Travelers team was picked up in a luxurious three-tone dark brown Bentley with a soft top and driven to the refined Lanesboro Hotel. The first full day in London included meetings with portfolio managers interspersed between meals. Pike quickly learned that when Sandy asked, "Where are we going next?" he meant to which restaurant, not to which investment firm.

Dinner that night was at the famed Le Gavroche restaurant, one of London's finest and certainly among its most expensive. Sandy had been to the restaurant many times in the past—in fact, he sent Travelers chefs to train at Le Gavroche—and tonight the owner, Albert Roux, escorted the Travelers executives to a private bar, where he served them his own special-reserve port. After drinks and small talk, they were escorted to the dining room. The three older men focused all their attention on the wine list. *This is what really wealthy, powerful men do,* Pike thought. *They talk about wine, deals, their second and third homes, their wives.* He wasn't really part of the conversation, but he didn't care; he was eating the best meal of his life and lapping up the most expensive and delicious wine he had ever tasted. When an elaborate dish of tiny birds was served, Pike was amazed: He was eating *cailles en sarcophages* (quails in coffins), the signature dish of one of his favorite films, *Babette's Feast.* The whole scene felt cinematic to him.

After dinner Sandy requested his usual Calvados apple brandy and ordered one for Pike as well. "Have you ever tried it?" he asked. Sheepishly, Pike admitted he never had. He took a sip.

"Do you like it?" Sandy asked eagerly.

"No, not really," Pike answered.

"Fine, I'll take it," Sandy said as he snatched Pike's glass and gulped it down.

Finally, Sandy stood to leave. He put his hand on Pike's shoulder. "Look at this kid," he said admiringly. "He can keep up with me."

THE SPLIT

In the year since Jamie Dimon had promoted Robert Druskin to oversee all of Travelers' asset-management businesses—and passed over Jessica Weill Bibliowicz for the post—relations between Sandy's daughter and Sandy's closest deputy had continued to worsen. Although Jessica reported to Druskin and thus didn't attend many meetings at which Dimon was also present, the few times the two were in the same room it was painfully clear to others that the rift was deepening. No one, least of all Dimon, disputed that Jessica did a wonderful job as the spokesperson for Smith Barney's mutual funds. Her charm and wit got the attention of television producers and newspaper reporters, and she was frequently quoted or interviewed. "That's free promotion for our products," Dimon told her approvingly.

But when Dimon and Jessica were involved in a meeting about operations or financial performance, Dimon frequently found fault with her presentations and her lack of knowledge. "You've got to know the details," he admonished her at one meeting. He also pushed her to boost the sale of Smith Barney's own funds, which carried much bigger profits than other mutual-fund companies' products that Smith Barney also offered. At other big brokerage firms, in-house funds accounted for half or more of all sales, but they were only about a third of Smith Barney's sales.

"You've got to sell more, do more, make more," Dimon told Jessica in his staccato style.

Jessica suggested that to get their brokers to push their in-house funds, Smith Barney should pay the brokers bigger commissions to sell them.

"I refuse to do that," Dimon countered. "It gives the wrong incentives. Customers should want to buy our funds because of performance and service, not because the broker pushes them harder so he can put more money in his own pocket. That's not in the customer's best interest."

Dimon's cocksure demeanor and his moralistic argument were typical of him, his colleagues knew. But they also sensed that it was embarrassing to Jessica to be lectured that way.

When Jessica introduced a new mutual-fund product, the Concert Series designed for corporate 401(k) programs, Dimon dismissed it to colleagues as "a lot of noise, a lot of mirrors." The funds didn't sell well. And as Jessica continued to fall short of his standards, Dimon saw to it that her job became more one of public relations than operations. Although Jessica was nominally the head of Smith Barney's mutual-funds operation, Dimon relied on the operations managers more like himself. Jessica's isolation was exacerbated because colleagues kept her out of the information flow for fear she would report to her father.

Finally, Jessica decided she should remove herself from the contentious environment at headquarters and take up Dimon's standing offer to manage one of Smith Barney's retail operations. When Dimon told his top branch-operations executives that Jessica wanted to join their division to "run retail," the executives began suggesting branches she might like to run.

"Guys, we're not talking about a single branch," Dimon said. "She wants to run a whole region of branches!"

"That's a big stretch," one Smith Barney executive responded. "I'm all for Jessica taking a branch of her own to learn the business, but a whole region?"

That's what she wants, Dimon assured them and asked for suggestions.

"If we've got to make it work, we'll make it work," replied Michael Panitch, the tough and seasoned vice chairman of Smith Barney's retail division.

Because the West Coast regional manager was retiring, Jessica sought the California-based position. There she could work without the constant stress of being the boss's daughter. Dimon and his retail-brokerage executives worried that such a large territory would typically go to an experienced branch-operations manager. They considered lopping off part of the region if Jessica took the West Coast territory.

It wasn't long before both Jessica and Sandy got wind of the efforts to give her a cut-down territory. Sandy went straight to Dimon.

"You're insulting my daughter," he charged.

"Sandy, what difference does it really make if she runs one hundred twenty branches or one hundred fifty branches?" Dimon replied. "That's no reason to refuse a perfectly good region."

But Sandy's tirade confirmed what Dimon already suspected: Far from the "hands-off" policy that Sandy publicly proclaimed regarding his daughter's career at Travelers, he was pushing to get her promoted. Still, Dimon was unrepentant. He was supremely confident that his approach was the right one, both for Smith Barney and for Jessica. He was Smith Barney's chairman, and he would do what was best for the entire company.

Then, in February 1997, Dimon named four more executives to the Smith Barney planning group, bringing it to eleven members, including its first woman, Joan Guggenheimer, the firm's senior deputy general counsel. Jessica, he told colleagues who inquired, had not even been considered.

Once again Jessica found out from others that she had been passed over for a slot that she thought should have been hers. Publicly she remained stoic, but she couldn't hide her feelings from her father. They discussed her frustrations at family gatherings, where Sandy became deeply upset. Shortly after the four new appointments to the planning group were announced, Sandy and Joan had dinner with longtime friends Joe and Ellen Wright.

"Why did Jamie do it?" Sandy asked Joe Wright, who served on the Travelers board. Wright sensed that his old friend thought Dimon was purposefully hurting Jessica.

"Jamie didn't treat her any differently," Wright responded. "Maybe he should have." For the first time since he had gotten to know Sandy and Dimon, Wright began to have doubts that this rift could be healed.

Another Travelers director close to Sandy, Arthur Zankel, was surprised at Dimon's action. "This isn't your finest hour," Zankel told Dimon. When Dimon protested that Jessica wasn't ready to be on the planning group, Zankel dismissed his reasoning.

"Come on, Jamie. It was your prerogative as Smith Barney president to pick your own asset chief last year, but you could have put Jess on the executive committee," Zankel told the unapologetic Dimon. "As businessmen, we all have to live with this stuff occasionally."

But Dimon still believed he was right. There were several longtime Smith Barney executives who ran much larger and more profitable divisions, such as global equities, fixed income, and systems, where they managed thousands of people and yet weren't members of the core group. "It would have been a joke," an exasperated Dimon told colleagues. "It would have been done only because she's Sandy's daughter."

Smith Barney executives privately backed their boss. If Dimon thought Jessica wasn't ready to move into top management, then she probably wasn't, they told one another around the coffee station and in the executive dining room. Dimon, they knew, had little time or patience for office politics, and he was driven to run a meritocracy in which only the best rose to the top. Still, as the tensions between Dimon and Jessica—and now between Dimon and Sandy—rose, the speculation began: Who would be the first to go?

In the spring of 1997 Jessica told Sandy she was on the verge of taking another job. She had been secretly negotiating a position with John A.

Levin & Co., a successful but virtually unknown money-management firm in New York, and it looked like things there would work out.

Shocked and hurt, Sandy begged his daughter to reconsider. "Stick it out with Smith Barney," he urged her.

The next day, he ripped into Dimon. "Jessica won't be around this company much longer," he said. "I'm warning you, she'll leave if you don't do something—fast."

Tired of the office politics that were making her miserable, Jessica felt deep down it was time to go. The only way she could stay at Smith Barney was to move out of New York and into the branch network. She resolved that if Dimon gave her all of the West Coast, she would stay; if he split up the region, she'd take the other job offer.

Dimon offered her the West Coast job, but gave her only half of the golden state. "California is big and it's tough," he said, explaining why she would manage the retail offices of only part of the state. Jessica was deeply disappointed. She had looked forward to moving with her architect husband and two young sons to California, where Joan's mother lived. Now she felt she had no choice, and blamed herself for thinking she could be effective in a company so dominated by her imposing father.

On Tuesday, June 10, Jessica told Sandy she was quitting to become the president and chief operating officer at Levin. She put the best possible spin on it: "We're going to be father and daughter again," she said.

When Sandy quizzed her to determine if her departure was Dimon's fault, Jessica maintained that Smith Barney wasn't working out for many reasons. For starters, she said, she never knew if colleagues were talking to her or to Sandy's daughter.

Jessica next dropped in to Chuck Prince's office and announced, "I'm leaving, and I have a great new job."

"I can't believe that," replied the general counsel, who was startled that the friction between Dimon and Jessica was enough to drive her away.

As Jessica was informing other executives of her decision, Sandy marched straight down the hall to see Dimon, who hadn't heard the news. He stormed into Dimon's office.

"She's leaving! I told you this would happen," Sandy lashed out. "You drove her out!"

"It might be the right thing for your daughter and the company," Dimon calmly replied.

"No, you're wrong!" Sandy thundered as he stomped out.

In the hall Sandy practically crashed into Irwin Ettinger, who told Sandy he was sorry Jessica was quitting.

"Jamie is the reason Jessica is leaving," the Travelers chief roared. "Jamie was unfair to her."

By the end of the week, John A. Levin & Co. announced its new high-profile executive. With her marketing savvy, Jessica made the best of her resignation as the head of the $78-billion Smith Barney mutual-fund group to run an $8-billion money-management firm. "I have an exciting new opportunity," she told reporters. "It's very entrepreneurial."

Asked if her departure upset her legendary father, the thirty-seven-year-old said she had his full support in the new venture. "He's done it a few times himself," she said. "He saw the twinkle in my eye, and he knew I was going to do it." Then she added: "When you're a child of somebody very well known, you want to make sure that you are in a position where you can be judged for what you are."

Sandy was deluged with calls from reporters asking what impact Jessica's resignation would have on Jamie Dimon, his forty-one-year-old heir apparent.

"I have never made it clear to anybody that Jamie is my successor," Sandy bristled. He was sixty-four years old now. "I have no plans to leave this company," he declared.

Instantly a chill descended over the thirty-ninth floor. Sandy was furious at Dimon for Jessica's departure. Dimon was furious at Sandy for blaming him. Their quarrels became petty and mean-spirited. When one executive casually mentioned that Dimon had approved a course of action, Sandy sputtered, "I don't care what Jamie thinks. You run it by me."

At the next off-site planning group meeting, Sandy and Dimon fought viciously over a particularly minute, complicated point. Colleagues gathered in the guest house watched the spectacle nervously. This was way beyond the usual Sandy-Jamie "debate."

Later, during cocktails, Sandy walked up to Chuck Clarke, who had been added to the planning group to represent the old Travelers insurance company.

"How come you didn't support me?" Sandy asked.

"I didn't understand what the hell you two were talking about," Clarke answered.

"I don't care," Sandy replied as he drank his wine. "In the future, you should—"

"Wait a minute," Clarke interrupted, incredulous. "The two most brilliant financial people in the world are arguing a point I don't understand, much less have an opinion on, and you want me to step in the middle of the two of you and take sides?"

"Yes. My side," Sandy said, deadly serious.

Bob Lipp, who had long been close to both Sandy and Dimon, was sufficiently concerned that he drew the two of them aside later that night.

"You're torturing each other," Lipp told them. "It can only go downhill."

Both men tensed. Lipp suggested, "Let's somehow try to get this back on the right track." Without responding, both men turned and walked in opposite directions.

A few other executives had noticed the huddle and asked Lipp what was happening.

"I only took Psych 101." Lipp shrugged. "Don't ask me."

The tension between Sandy and Dimon also became apparent to the board of directors. At its next meeting, directors noticed that Sandy, who typically praised his young protégé effusively, led the board through much of the material that Dimon usually presented. When the meeting was about to adjourn, Dimon realized no one had introduced Heidi Miller and other executives who had been added to the planning group. He stood up to make a brief welcoming speech.

That night Dimon's phone rang. "How dare you do that?" Sandy screamed at him when he answered.

Flabbergasted that Sandy would be offended by such a small gesture, Dimon said, "I thought I was doing the right thing."

Sandy slammed the phone down.

"IF YOU'RE GOING TO STAY AROUND . . ."

While the tension between Sandy and Dimon clearly was mounting, neither of the seasoned executives would let their differences stand between them and the possibility of another deal. Acquisitions were the lifeblood of the financial empire they had created. Maybe a deal would do them both—as well as Travelers—a lot of good.

Ever eager to "trade up" for a better name with more prestige, Sandy this time targeted the bluest of the blue chips: J.P. Morgan, the esteemed bank that for decades had been at the very heart of American capitalism. That he would even consider such a deal was testament to the immense changes sweeping through the financial-services industry. First, the very idea of a once-dowdy insurance company taking over the world's most prestigious bank would have been laughable. But Travelers Group, now one of the nation's largest financial empires, had a market capitalization twice that of J.P. Morgan and, more important, a higher P/E ratio. No longer would Sandy be the minnow swallowing a whale—now *he* was the whale. A few decades earlier it would have been equally preposterous for a Brooklyn-born Jew to think he could land an important job at J.P. Morgan, much less take it over. Yet Sandy was now a member of one of the world's most exclusive clubs, a club whose membership included Douglas "Sandy" Warner III, the chairman of J.P. Morgan, with whom Sandy had recently played a few rounds at Augusta National. And while it would have been unthinkable ten years earlier for J.P. Morgan to give up its cherished independence, the signals now were clear: Only the biggest and strongest financial institutions would survive the cutthroat global competition threatening them all. The precedent had already been set: Morgan Stanley, the white-shoe investment bank that resulted when John Pierpont Morgan's empire was divided by government fiat following the Depression, had agreed in February 1997 to a $10-billion merger with the decidedly downscale Dean Witter Discover & Co.

With such thoughts spinning through his head, it was coincidence that Sandy found himself attending an insurance industry conference hosted by J.P. Morgan in its stone-and-glass headquarters at 60 Wall Street. As he walked through the dark-paneled corridors adorned with oil portraits of former J.P. Morgan chairmen, the Travelers CEO decided then and there that he wanted this stately bank as part of his empire. Also by coincidence, it happened that Sandy Warner wasn't jetting to or from any of J.P. Morgan's worldwide network of offices that day. When Sandy stuck his head in Warner's door, the J.P. Morgan chairman greeted him warmly. The two had long been friendly, not least because neither viewed the other as a competitor. The 136-year-old bank had for the most part tended to the financial needs of the great commercial concerns of the world and coddled the wealthy heirs of the men who had founded them. More recently, Warner and his predecessor, Dennis Weatherstone, had been intensely focused on reinventing the institution to make it a global investment bank with dominant positions in fixed income, risk management, and mergers and acquisitions. Travelers, of course, sold insurance, loans, and stocks to the great masses.

Sitting in Warner's history-laden office, Sandy couldn't help but be impressed by the wall of leather-bound books that once belonged to J. P. Morgan himself. Over Warner's mahogany rolltop desk hung a portrait of Morgan, with his thick moustache and stern stare. The display of Morgan's storied past prompted Sandy to jump to the future.

"We should talk about merging our companies," Sandy blurted out with no preamble.

Warner wasn't entirely surprised. Everyone on Wall Street knew about Sandy's acquisitiveness. And the Morgan Stanley–Dean Witter merger had prompted many discussions between financial executives and their invest-ment bankers about how to respond to the increasing globalization of the financial-services industry.

"We could start a conversation and see if it makes any sense," the fifty-year-old Warner ventured.

Sandy was ecstatic! He hadn't been rejected outright.

"Let's start talking right now," he said.

Whoa, thought Warner. He had to slow the pace of this thing. He stood up and walked over to the hundred-year bond in a gilt frame that bore J. Pierpont Morgan's signature. Warner treasured the bond, issued in 1896, which the firm paid off at maturity in 1996. "I like this bond for the state-ment it makes," Warner lectured Sandy. "Sure, we have to change and ad-just, but J.P. Morgan is here one hundred years later because we have been true to our traditions, our good name, our culture."

Culture didn't impress Sandy. "Sounds like you're talking about yo-gurt," he said.

Still these two men, as different as their institutions, had enough cama-raderie and self-interest to continue talking. Because of banking laws that separated commercial banking from insurance underwriting, Warner sim-ply assumed that Sandy wanted to explore a combination of J.P. Morgan with Smith Barney. It didn't cross his mind that Sandy would be talking about combining J.P. Morgan with *all* of Travelers, including its insurance and blue-collar consumer-loan operations. So without confirming his as-sumption, Warner agreed that they should get their teams to the table in a few days for exploratory talks.

Thrilled at Warner's response, Sandy practically floated all the way back to Travelers headquarters to huddle with his top executives.

"How can we take over J.P. Morgan?" he demanded.

Aware from the many hints that Sandy had dropped that Travelers might next try to take over a bank, Chuck Prince had been doing his homework, researching every possible loophole in the Glass-Steagall Act and other banking legislation. On the face of it, the banking laws appeared insurmountable. Still, the general counsel explained, the laws did allow a "nonbank" financial institution like Travelers to buy a bank with the proviso that the insurance operations be spun off within two to five years to avoid the conflict that Glass-Steagall had intended to eliminate. Prince's thinking was that two to five years might be enough time to actually get the law changed. The Travelers team knew Congress had considered repealing, or at least relaxing, the restrictive laws for years, although nothing had been done. But they also believed they might have an ally in Alan Greenspan. As the chairman of the Federal Reserve, Greenspan was the single person most responsible for ensuring that the nation's financial system remained sound. There had been indications from time to time that he was willing to consider allowing the creation of broader financial conglomerates that would be better able to compete against European financial institutions, which weren't hobbled by any similar restrictions.

"I know the law cold," Prince assured his boss, even though his proposal was radical and untested. "I'm absolutely convinced we could get through the door on a merger."

"That's it!" Sandy exclaimed. "I'll call Greenspan."

"We're thinking about buying a bank," Sandy told the Fed chairman a few days later. As Prince had predicted, Greenspan indicated that he was "open to the logic" of the innovative legal argument that Travelers was proposing.

Emboldened by Greenspan's response, Sandy called Warner to let him in on this latest development. The J.P. Morgan CEO was stunned, first to find that Sandy wanted to merge all of Travelers with J.P. Morgan, then to discover that Sandy had already consulted the chairman of the Federal Reserve.

"Inconceivable! Impossible!" Warner responded. When he realized that Sandy was serious, Warner tried to apply the brakes again.

"First, our interest is only to swap Smith Barney for a piece of J.P. Morgan—" he began.

"No, I want to do the whole thing," Sandy interrupted. "I don't want to sell Smith Barney."

"Second, a merger of the two companies isn't worth talking about,"

Warner continued. "I'm sure you're not being disingenuous about your conversations with Greenspan, but I believe a full merger would be illegal at worst or pose a huge execution risk at best."

Ever the salesman, Sandy wasn't deterred. He persuaded Warner to bring his top associates to visit Travelers for more discussions. Although it was clear to Warner that he and Sandy weren't seeing eye to eye on the scope of a deal, he consented to sign the necessary confidentiality agreements and continue talking.

The due-diligence teams from each company proceeded warily. The Travelers executives quickly got the impression that the J.P. Morgan team regarded them as second-class citizens.

"They treat us like the huddled masses," Marge Magner complained after one meeting. "They're the landed gentry, the town-and-country crowd."

Dimon was particularly incensed. "We may be the ragtag team that was cobbled together, but the United States was cobbled together, too! Are we supposed to respect them just because they have a name?" Still, Dimon agreed with Sandy that J.P. Morgan represented a unique opportunity worth pursuing. Both sides spent the summer of 1997 secretly exchanging volumes of information, evaluating areas of overlap, and considering new activities that could be undertaken if some form of combination was worked out.

During that summer, Sandy and Travelers director Arthur Zankel flew to San Francisco for a benefit on behalf of Carnegie Hall, where both were directors. On the return flight Sandy confided to Zankel that he was negotiating with J.P. Morgan.

"That's one of the worst ideas I've ever heard," Zankel told him, his long friendship with Sandy allowing him to be blunt. "They'll never sell to a guy like you, up from the streets, un-Gentile. You'd be fighting the establishment all over again. You'll never live long enough to be the chief executive officer of that company."

Then Sandy brought the matter of the merger to his full board of directors, who he hoped would be more supportive than Zankel had been. He was wrong.

"The culture between Travelers and J.P. Morgan would be oil and water," said Joseph Califano, who was in a position to know. He had married Hilary Paley, daughter of the wealthy CBS patriarch William Paley. "Morgan handles the trusts for my wife's family, and the cultures would never go together."

Now Sandy was worried. He had to know directly from Sandy Warner if these discussions were bound to be futile. Warner had retreated for the month of August to his family summer house in the little hamlet of Wequetonsing, Michigan, near the shores of Lake Michigan. But that didn't stop Sandy from insisting on a face-to-face meeting. The Travelers jet could land at the small airport in Pellston, Michigan. Tucking his favorite gift into his briefcase, he asked Chuck Prince to ride along to plot strategy. This might be their only chance to convince Warner to move ahead with the merger.

Sandy and Prince brainstormed various scenarios on their way to Michigan. One concession that Sandy was more than happy to make: keeping the J.P. Morgan name. "There isn't a better name," he told Prince. As the plane settled onto the runway in Pellston, Sandy was clearly riding high. Prince, who would remain on the plane while the two titans negotiated, tried to bring his boss back down to earth: "My impression is the Morgan people basically would be happy to merge if we would all just disappear."

Warner was waiting on the tarmac, attired in casual summer clothes. He welcomed Sandy to "the country," as they climbed into his Jeep. When the pair arrived at Warner's house, a rustic, uninsulated version of a Victorian cottage, Sandy presented his gift to the J.P. Morgan chairman: two ties decorated with floating umbrellas against different-colored backgrounds.

"Let's work out a merger so you can wear these ties," Sandy said optimistically, trying to get the conversation started on a positive note.

As they sipped coffee on Warner's porch overlooking Lake Michigan, the two men, unencumbered by anxious aides or corporate trappings, cut straight to the chase: Who would run the merged company if a deal was done?

The fifty-year-old Warner clearly expected to be running his company for years to come. Yet the sixty-four-year-old Sandy had no intention of stepping down from the CEO post. The Travelers chairman offered a compromise: They would share the senior post. "We'll be equals," he said.

"No," Warner answered immediately. "Lack of clarity in leadership is very bad."

Sandy didn't like the sound of that, particularly when Warner noted that J.P. Morgan had a mandatory retirement age of sixty-five.

"Sandy, I think the world of you, but when are you going to retire?" Warner asked.

"I don't want to retire," Sandy responded. "I don't think my shareholders want me to retire."

"Well, Sandy, if you're going to stay around, this isn't going to work out," Warner said.

The Travelers chairman offered other possibilities: split duties, clearer lines of command—anything to keep the merger alive.

"Let's be sensible," the J.P. Morgan CEO countered. "When do you want to retire? We'll work back from that."

Suddenly Sandy was being asked to commit to something he had never really considered: When would he leave his business, his very life? He tried to be coy, but Warner was clearly becoming frustrated.

"A transition of twelve to eighteen months would be reasonable for you to stay," Warner insisted. "Having both of us hanging around indefinitely is unappealing to me."

Both men then turned away from the impasse and continued talking generally for an hour or so. Each hoped the other would capitulate on the leadership issue, but neither did. As Sandy walked from the Jeep to the jet's stairway, Prince could see that his boss's earlier high spirits had been dashed.

"He wants me to leave in a year," Sandy told Prince, who had become a close confidant.

"Whenever you leave, a number of other people will leave the company," Prince said.

"What?" Sandy asked. "You don't really think that, do you?"

"Of course I do," Prince responded. "This is your company, and we have relationships with you. For one, I'll leave when you do."

Tenacious as always, Sandy refused to give up. Back in New York he phoned Warner, pushing the J.P. Morgan chairman to reconsider his need for "management clarity" and to think about selling to Travelers. Sandy also wanted to get some feel for the price Warner might demand.

"No one in the world will get J.P. Morgan without paying a significant premium," Warner cautioned Sandy.

The Travelers chairman pressed Warner for a price.

"If you're determined to proceed on this basis, we'll give you a hypothetical number," Warner said, carefully leaving himself an escape hatch in case Sandy accepted the price. On August 14 Warner dispatched one of his top executives to Travelers to present Sandy with a "hypothetical" price for a merger: $30 billion.

Sandy was floored by the outrageous demand. The moment he was alone again, he called Warner. "I appreciate your hypothetical price," he told Warner, "but hypothetically, there's no way in hell we would pay this kind of price."

"I sort of knew that, Sandy," Warner replied. "Look, we're not even on the same page—not just on price, but on what to merge. Besides, you and Travelers have a very different culture and history than ours here at J.P. Morgan. You're not the same kind of institution. It won't work."

The insult was subtle, but not so subtle that Sandy missed it. After grumbling that Warner cared more about J.P. Morgan's good name and stellar past than about using that name to push into the future as a bigger, more diversified financial powerhouse, Sandy acknowledged defeat and hung up.

LOSE ONE, WIN ONE

The J.P. Morgan deal was dead and Sandy was grieving. But that same day came a telephone call that suddenly forced J.P. Morgan right out of his thoughts. It was Deryck Maughan, the chief executive officer of Salomon Brothers.

"Sandy, I just want you to know that I'm going to do something about Salomon Brothers before the end of the year," Maughan said. "I'm giving you the first call. If you don't want to talk, just tell me, because I'm serious."

Sandy knew deal talk when he heard it! Maughan had been cagey enough that he could deny it, but he had just revealed to Sandy that Salomon Brothers was for sale.

Salomon Brothers! The toughest trading firm on the street. Its boisterous offices were dominated by the bedlam of trading and bore no resemblance at all to the hushed tones and reverential demeanor in the House of Morgan.

Founded in 1910 by Arthur, Herbert, and Percy Salomon, the sons of an Orthodox Jewish immigrant from the Alsace region of France, Salomon had long since abandoned its origins as a money brokerage firm to become a gunslinging bond dealer. In its heyday during the 1980s, John Gutfreund, Salomon's gruff chairman, had driven his hotshot investment bankers to the top ranking as underwriters of corporate bonds. But the firm had also been a big risk taker, buying and selling bonds for its own account. Salomon's testosterone-fueled traders labeled themselves "Big Swinging Dicks," and the journalist Tom Wolfe, who studied Salomon's trading operations for his acutely observed novel *The Bonfire of the Vanities,* called the traders "Masters of the Universe."

But Salomon's profane, bare-knuckled atmosphere went too far in 1991, when it was discovered that the firm had manipulated U.S. Treasury auctions by submitting false bids. Nobody, but nobody, messes with the U.S. Treasury. Salomon paid nearly $300 million in fines, Gutfreund was forced out, and billionaire investor Warren Buffett, the soul of probity and already the owner, through his Berkshire Hathaway Inc., of a substantial Salomon stake, took the reins at Salomon to save it. Buffett chose Deryck Maughan, then a little-known executive in Salomon's Japanese operations—far from the scandal that nearly wrecked the firm—as the new chief executive. Maughan's British reserve and charm were rare at Salomon, previously dominated by unpolished, irreverent traders.

In 1992, a year after he took the reins at Salomon, Maughan had gotten a phone call. "Hello, this is Sandy Weill, and I'd like to get to know you," the caller boomed. "Why don't you join me on the board of Carnegie Hall?"

"I'm flattered," Maughan responded.

"Do you like music?" Sandy continued.

"Sure," Maughan replied, knowing full well that musical tastes had little to do with board membership. Once on the board, Maughan used his dry wit and political skills to ingratiate himself with Sandy. They became friends, often riding to and from board meetings together.

While Maughan had soothed angry regulators and executed Buffett's wishes in the early 1990s, he produced decidedly mixed results later in the decade. By most measures, including absolute profits, return on equity, and standings in such key categories as stock underwriting, Salomon couldn't quite regain the stature and moneymaking prowess it had enjoyed before the bid-rigging scandal. Maughan became the subject of an unflattering cover article in *New York* magazine titled "The Crash of a Wall Street Superhero."

Then earlier in 1997 came the Morgan Stanley–Dean Witter merger. The combination confirmed Sandy's strategy of building a broad-based financial empire, but it once again highlighted the lack of a significant investment-banking presence within Travelers. At the same time, it convinced Maughan of the merit in adding a retail side to Salomon's mostly corporate work. Because of his friendship with Sandy, the Salomon CEO put out his first feeler to him.

"I'm going on holiday now, but we could sit down and talk when I get back," Maughan offered.

"What are you doing tonight?" Sandy asked.

"I'm packing," Maughan replied.

"No, let's have dinner," Sandy insisted, unabashedly eager to do some deal talk.

Half expecting such a response, the Salomon CEO agreed to set up a dinner. He knew exactly where to go: the Four Seasons. "I'm bringing Sandy," he told the maître d'. "Please serve a wine that he will like." The forty-nine-year-old Maughan felt like he was getting ready for a first date: He wanted to play a little hard to get, but he also wanted the evening to go perfectly.

Few first dates go as well as that dinner. The youthful Maughan, his silvery hair carefully groomed, arrived first and ordered the roasted crispy duck for them both. He and Sandy lingered for hours as they sipped expensive red wine. As the evening wore on, Sandy was clearly smitten with Maughan, a coal miner's son who went to King's College and worked as a low-level employee of the British Treasury before joining Salomon as a bond trader. Sandy's friends had long noticed his tendency to "fall in love" with the latest person to impress him. Now Maughan was picking up signals that Sandy would be very receptive to a deal. Maughan decided to seize the moment.

"I'm not going to start with you if we're not going all the way," he told Sandy coyly.

Sandy began taking off his Hermès tie decorated with umbrellas. He handed it to Maughan as a sign of his good intentions. When they stood to leave, the rotund Travelers chairman embraced the tall, strapping Maughan in a rib-crushing bear hug right in the middle of the Four Seasons dining room.

The next morning Maughan headed straight for the office of Robert Denham, a lawyer who had long represented Warren Buffett's interests. Buffett had put Denham at the head of Salomon's parent firm to keep an eye on things. "Oh my god," Maughan said giddily, "Sandy is really interested. What are we going to do?"

"We'd better call Warren," Denham answered. He agreed with Maughan that Salomon would be hard-pressed to remain competitive without a bigger partner. But he also knew that Buffett wouldn't want to "shop" Salomon Brothers around to different buyers. That would make Salomon's clients nervous. "Be careful," Denham warned Maughan.

As planned, Maughan left for his end-of-summer vacation in Hawaii with his wife and teenaged daughter. Relaxing in Honolulu two days later, Maughan answered the phone.

"I have to meet with you," Sandy said.

"Fine, I'll be back in one and a half weeks," Maughan said. "I'll be happy to get together."

"No, come back now," Sandy persisted.

"I can't," Maughan replied. "I'm on holiday in paradise."

"Well, I want to meet you as soon as you get back," Sandy grumbled before hanging up.

Then he called Denham. "This really might go somewhere," Sandy told him. "Does Warren have any objection?" Denham had already checked: Buffett was a willing seller at the right price, but it had to be the entire company, not just part of it.

At the August meeting of the planning group, Sandy sought the counsel of his senior executives. Dimon expressed the most serious reservations. He worried that Salomon was too vulnerable to the unpredictable ups and downs of financial markets and that it took on too much risk by trading so heavily for its own account. Colleagues wondered if Dimon's reaction had more to do with his worsening relationship with Sandy than with the deal's merits. He seemed particularly irritated when Sandy praised Maughan.

"Deryck and I have known each other for five years at Carnegie Hall, where I've seen his thought process, his ethics, and his ability to be a team player," Sandy said. That struck some of the executives as a jab at Dimon for pushing to be his own man. "Deryck's created a comfort level with me to move ahead."

Early in September executives for both sides settled in to do their due diligence. To prevent any leaks, the companies took two suites at New York's stylish Four Seasons Hotel, which had no relationship with Sandy's preferred eatery. Travelers executives dubbed the effort "Project Global," signifying their keen interest in Salomon's international heft, particularly in London, Asia, and South America. But they remained leery of Salomon's proprietary trading. Each day the firm bet hundreds of millions of dollars on market moves, and most of the time the firm's traders got it right. Still, Sandy wanted to be sure he wasn't just buying a big casino. He directed Dimon and his son, Marc Weill, to apply special scrutiny to Salomon's proprietary "book," including measures of capital at risk, inventory, balance sheet, and historical profit-and-loss data.

Maughan explained to the Travelers officials that Salomon had to provide a significant market-making function to back up its extensive underwriting business. "If you're going to be a big underwriter, you have to commit capital and trade the securities," he explained, uncertain if Sandy could tolerate that kind of risk.

Dimon sat down for a lengthy tutorial with the chief of Salomon's proprietary trading unit, Shigeru "Sugar" Myojin. Myojin operated out of London, where he oversaw, or personally placed, many of Salomon's biggest bets. More important, he won a lot more of those bets than he lost. Consequently, his salary and bonus made him one of the highest-paid financial executives in the world: In 1996 he earned $31 million in cash and stock, more than twice Maughan's compensation. Dimon, whose own staccato conversation could be difficult to follow, struggled to keep up with the explanations that Myojin made in precise, rapid-fire English. By the end of the session, Dimon felt better about Salomon's risk profile. "Trade by trade, this isn't hard to grasp," he said, "although overall, it's much tougher to accept."

As the Travelers team's concerns about risk eased, the deal pieces began to fall into place. Then Sandy dropped a bombshell on Dimon.

"I want you to be co-CEO with Deryck," Sandy announced to Dimon after the two had returned to their offices from a session at the Four Seasons.

"I don't think that's right," Dimon shot back. "I don't know why we need to do that."

"We need to have overlap in leadership," Sandy said. "It will smooth the way for the two sides to work together."

Dimon, upset, stalked out of Sandy's office. A few minutes later he was back.

"I don't think it's right for the organization, and I don't think it's right for me," he told Sandy.

Sandy didn't give an inch and remained quiet as Dimon spent the next few days pacing back and forth between their offices, stopping in periodically with another argument why Maughan should not share power with him. Dimon had helped build the Travelers empire. He considered Maughan a sweet-talking ass-kisser who was far less capable than himself. Dimon had already shouldered the burden of running Bob Greenhill's feeble excuse for an investment bank, and he shouldn't have to do it again just because Sandy had fallen head-over-heels in love with Deryck Maughan.

"It's a stupid way to organize things," Dimon told Sandy. "I don't want to be co-CEO with Deryck."

Finally, as the due diligence and contract negotiations were coming to a head, Sandy ended the argument. "We're going ahead with this deal and this is the way we'll do it—you and Deryck are co-CEOs."

"Okay, if you're going to, I can't stop you," Dimon replied. "You're the boss, but I think it's wrong."

Sandy didn't immediately tell Maughan of his decision. Before he did that, he wanted to set a price. Sandy and Bob Denham met at Sandy's apartment on a sunny Saturday morning. The two narrowed their differences on the ratio of an exchange of Travelers stock for Salomon stock but couldn't quite settle on a figure. Their bids were close enough that Sandy called Maughan.

"What do you want to do?" Sandy asked him.

"You should just decide about Salomon, and the management will be up to you," Maughan replied, in a show of deference that Sandy relished, particularly after his bruising encounters with Dimon.

"Would you consider co-CEO with Jamie at Salomon Smith Barney?" Sandy asked.

"That would be great," Maughan said. "Is Jamie okay with that?"

"Yes," Sandy replied.

The deal quickly fell into place: Salomon shareholders would get 1.13 shares of Travelers stock for each share of Salomon stock. It worked out to a $9-billion purchase of Salomon. By most standards, that was cheap. Sandy had gotten a discount because everyone else who might have been interested in taking over Salomon would have been put off by the huge risks the firm took. But it was also the biggest deal Sandy had ever done. He felt reassured that Warren Buffett had agreed to vote Berkshire Hathaway's substantial Salomon stake in favor of the merger.

On Monday Sandy called the ratings agencies to set up appointments "to review my ratings." He said he would bring Dimon and "Theo Terrofore," a name the ratings executives had never heard before. When Sandy strolled in with Deryck Maughan beside him, it was instantly clear to the agency executives what was happening. "Good god, Deryck!" one rating executive exclaimed. "Oh, no, Sandy, you haven't bought Salomon, have you?" The agencies weren't thrilled with the deal: Here was Sandy Weill, the financial Rock of Gibraltar, in bed with a gunslinging trader. Nevertheless, they assured Sandy that Travelers was big enough that the acquisition of Salomon wouldn't result in a lower rating.

The deal drew a similar reaction from Travelers directors. "We have to be the banker of choice, and we aren't," Sandy told the board. "Salomon Brothers helps get us there."

"You don't have the stomach for trading losses," Arthur Zankel warned Sandy.

Sandy said Travelers could handle the increased trading risk, which would amount to less than 10 percent of the combined companies' profits. He also noted that Salomon's trading operations had been extremely profitable over the past seven years. The board unanimously approved the deal.

Just before the Salomon directors were to vote on the deal, Sandy asked Bob Denham to get a quote from Buffett to put in the news release that was being prepared. Buffett took a piece of paper and began writing by hand: "Over several decades, Sandy has demonstrated genius in creating huge value for his shareholders and skillfully implementing . . ." He stopped to scratch out "implementing" and wrote "blending" over it, then continued, "and managing acquisitions in the financial-services industry. In my view, Salomon will be no exception."

Denham took the paper back to the telephone to read the quote to Sandy. "Will you save it for me, the actual piece of paper?" Sandy implored. As soon as he got his hands on it, Sandy had the paper framed for his office.

On September 24, 1997, Travelers and Salomon Brothers announced their deal before the stock market opened. Many industry analysts and Travelers employees reacted just as did the ratings agencies, fearful that the volatility and risk inherent in Salomon's business might hurt Travelers.

"Aren't you concerned that Sandy will shut down proprietary trading?" Joan Solotar, the Donaldson, Lufkin analyst, asked Maughan. In his clipped British accent he responded, "Well, why would he buy Salomon and then shut down the crown jewel?"

Later, in a meeting with Travelers employees, one person asked Sandy how someone who deplored risk as much as he did could buy Salomon Brothers.

"I have been risk averse, but now we are so big, with the insurance and consumer-finance companies, I can deal better with risk," Sandy explained. "I can probably take a loss of fifty million dollars if I had to." Then he quickly turned to Maughan, also on the platform. "Of course, I don't want to."

Just three weeks later, though, Sandy's new appetite for risk was put to the test. Asian markets were beginning to unravel and Salomon was hit with a loss of almost $50 million. Suddenly Sandy was getting a fast education in how costly trading can be. That hit was followed a few days later by a stunning $100-million loss: Salomon's famed traders had bet wrong that British Telecommunications would acquire MCI Communications, which was snapped up instead by WorldCom.

That was it. Whatever stomach Sandy thought he had for risk was gone now. Salomon's proprietary trading unit was largely disbanded, its traders reassigned. Sugar Myojin and other senior traders saw the handwriting on the wall and left. The word went out: Salomon was to be recast into the mold of the much more conservative Smith Barney. Sandy would receive daily reports on the results in all revenue areas of Salomon Smith Barney. Gossip on Wall Street asked if Sandy's biggest deal was his worst deal. When Sandy took a group of top Salomon officials golfing at Augusta National, Eduardo Mestre, Salomon's investment chief, asked how he was feeling.

"Today I'm feeling sorry I ever met you guys," Sandy replied with no trace of humor.

Salomon's trading imbroglio prompted Sandy to begin poking his nose, Sandy style, into everything going on in the brokerage operations. Whether intended or not, his interference further enraged Dimon, who had become accustomed to calling his own shots. When Sandy asked Heidi Miller to resolve a complicated reserve issue, she sought Dimon's help. After all, he could probably explain the problem in just a minute.

"Figure it out yourself," Dimon barked at her. "I don't have a role in it."

Miller quickly retreated. She knew her friend hadn't intended to be mean. He was just chafing under Sandy's rule.

With their relationship clearly on the rocks, both Sandy and Dimon were constantly on edge. As 1997 drew to a close, Travelers Group stock had gained an astounding 78 percent, ranking far and away as the best-performing stock in the Dow Jones Industrial Average that year. But nobody seemed in the mood to celebrate. Sandy barged into a Salomon Smith Barney management meeting that Dimon was running. He began firing questions without taking any notice of Dimon's agenda or answers. As the meeting concluded, Dimon drew his boss aside.

"You're flitting around all over the place," he said, his temper barely in check. "You were disruptive. We had serious work to do."

Sandy, his face flashing scarlet, yelled so loudly the entire floor could hear.

"Goddammit, Jamie, this is *my* company!"

13

THE MOTHER OF ALL DEALS

A cold forty-mile-an-hour wind pounded the windows of Sandy's Washington, D.C., hotel room as he nervously awaited his visitor. To ensure no one would see them, Sandy had asked for the meeting to take place in his room at 9:45 P.M., Wednesday, February 25, 1998. Tonight's encounter was as secretive and high stakes as they come. Sandy hoped to persuade the man coming to see him to join him in a highly controversial venture, one that was possibly illegal and that would surely shock world markets. To break the ice with his guest, Sandy had one of his favorite robust red wines waiting on the brass and glass coffee table.

He knew he shouldn't be so anxious. He would turn sixty-five in a few weeks, and by all rights he should be secure with his place in life. Indeed, it was his position of power that enabled him to set up a clandestine meeting with someone of this stature. But tonight's meeting—though a long shot—could establish him once and for all as the ultimate deal maker, *the* power in American finance.

When he heard the knock, he hurried to throw open his hotel-room door. There stood John Shepard Reed, the world's best-known banker, the man whose vision had ushered in the era of automated teller machines and global consumer banking. Reed, chairman and chief executive officer of Citicorp, looked every bit the conservative banker in his pin-striped suit, starched white shirt, and perfectly parted, slicked-back hair. Trim and polished, the fifty-nine-year-old Reed hadn't a clue why Sandy Weill had asked to see him while they were both staying at the Park Hyatt Hotel for their Business Council meeting of the nation's top executives.

Trying to appear casual—and to calm himself—Sandy offered Reed a glass of wine. As Sandy was awkward, brazen, and instinctual, so Reed was to an equal degree refined, reserved, and cerebral. The erudite banker, who ate and drank like a bird, declined the wine.

"John, I have a very interesting idea," Sandy began, preparing to deliver the script he had gone over in his mind a hundred times. But, as in scores of earlier planned presentations, Sandy couldn't help but cut straight to the heart of the matter: "Will you merge?" he blurted.

"Gee, I didn't think this is what you wanted to talk to me about," replied a stunned Reed. He had figured that Sandy was going to press him to pony up several thousand dollars for a table at some charity event. "I haven't even thought about something like this."

Little wonder. Sandy's startling proposal was nothing short of revolutionary. Not only would it challenge laws prohibiting the consolidation of financial services, it would instantly create the world's largest financial empire: Citibank, with its international deposit base, branches in every capital in the world, and the largest credit-card portfolio in the nation, and Travelers, with its broad-based financial businesses including insurance, securities, and consumer finance.

"I know you well enough to know you're too pragmatic to just come up with some strange idea," Reed said, urging Sandy to continue. Encouraged, Sandy pulled out all the stops, becoming the consummate salesman. First, he tried to ingratiate himself with his would-be partner, telling Reed how much he respected him and the blockbuster franchise he had built at Citibank. Sandy laid it on thick, bowing to Reed's worldly experience and sophistication. "I can't spell some of the countries you've spent a lot of time in," Sandy said, chuckling. It was true. Reed was raised in South America, traveled overseas on business about half the time, and was fluent in three languages.

Next Sandy explained the business rationale with a passion that was both persuasive and sound. He laid out the details of how surprisingly well the two companies complemented each other. With little overlap either in product lines or distribution, Travelers and Citi would have a unique opportunity to "cross-sell" to each other's customers: Travelers could tap Citi's enormous credit-card customer base to sell its Smith Barney mutual funds or Travelers annuities, while Citi could offer its checking accounts and Visa cards through Sandy's vast distribution network of stockbrokers and insurance agents. Citi would be able to provide large corporations with stock and bond underwritings and merger-and-acquisition advice from Travelers' Salomon Smith Barney. Travelers would gain access to Citi's prestigious roster of blue-chip clients who did their banking and borrowing at Citi. Geographically, the combination would be truly global, Sandy told his visitor. Travelers had thousands of offices throughout the United States filled with stockbrokers, insurance agents, and financial consultants; Citi, while its U.S. branch system was concentrated in the New York area, had branches in one hundred countries and automated teller machines in such outposts as the Russian Parliament building.

"We would create the model of the financial-services company of the future," Sandy enthused. He was on a roll. He sensed such an historic opportunity appealed to John Reed. But he was saving what he considered the deal clincher to the end. For weeks, Sandy had racked his brain for the right approach to make this merger happen, and concluded he would have to sacrifice his need for supremacy to pull it off. "John, neither of us would be the boss over the other. We would share power as cochairmen and co-CEOs." Sandy knew that checking his ego—and John's—would be a gargantuan task, but he implored: "The only way this could possibly work is if we are both equal, the shareholders are equal, and the boards are equal. Citicorp and Travelers get the benefit of both."

Reed, normally cool and collected, couldn't help but be fascinated by the excitable and eager Weill. For years, Reed had tried to shake up Citicorp, which, despite all its strengths, had grown into a huge, bloated bureaucracy. Sandy's skills as a merciless cost cutter, shrewd negotiator, and results-driven manager could come in handy to whip Reed's huge bank into shape. *Citi could use some of Sandy's DNA,* Reed thought. On a personal level, Reed was running out of steam, tired of worrying about the market's reaction to Citi's latest earnings, for example. A monumental merger could be the capstone of his legendary career.

"Why not?" Reed said calmly, almost casually. "Let's take a look at it." He left Sandy's room after promising that Citicorp's vice chairman would explore the possibility right away, even though Reed would be traveling overseas for a few weeks.

With Reed gone, Sandy enjoyed his wine alone, basking in the knowledge that he, the pudgy deal maker with a reputation for buying sick and ugly companies, had finally gotten the attention of the prettiest and smartest partner one could imagine. Suddenly Sandy felt highly desirable. John Reed was interested in him and his company! He switched on the TV to catch what was happening in the Asian markets, but couldn't concentrate.

He had just made the most important proposal since he asked Joan to marry him forty-three years earlier, and John Reed had said, "Why not?" It wasn't quite "yes," but it sure as hell wasn't "no"!

"LET'S TALK DEALS"

Jamie Dimon had already read the day's newspapers and the firm's weekly financial reports when his office phone rang at 7:00 A.M. Thursday, the morning after Sandy's secret meeting with John Reed. On the other end from his Washington hotel room, Sandy was practically spitting into the phone. "You won't believe it! You won't believe it! This could be the greatest deal of all time!"

Dimon knew instantly what that meant—Citicorp! "The mother of all deals?" he exclaimed.

"Yeah, the deal to beat all deals," Sandy responded breathlessly. "John is interested! John thinks it actually could make a lot of sense. We have to really start thinking about this seriously now."

Dimon could tell from Sandy's voice that his boss was virtually in shock, amazed that he could be talking about even the chance that Travelers and Citicorp might merge. They had both agreed years ago that snagging Citicorp would, indeed, be the ultimate coup.

While Sandy and Dimon had often spoken with each other about Citicorp as a potential partner, Sandy had not raised the possibility with other Travelers executives until just five weeks before he made his offer to John Reed.

At the monthly "planning group" retreat in January 1998, the managers gathered at the brand-new executive planning center in Armonk, New York. With the company's growth, Sandy had decided to take the idea of the old Primerica "guest house" to a much higher level by building a glorified campus for executive meetings on adjoining property. He had supervised the design and construction of the three-building complex, down to selecting the stones for the large fireplaces, the fabrics for the overstuffed armchairs, and the black-and-white marbled bathrooms for each guest in the fancy executive dormitory. A lover of fine things and comfort, Sandy was proud of his creation—and the executives were happy to be out of the decrepit guest house for their overnight meetings.

When the men rose this January morning, they barely had time to check on European markets on the guest house's single television set before

Sandy began hustling them to the meeting house for breakfast. In the chilly morning air, the group followed the stone pathway, the resident golden retrievers cavorting around them. After breakfast, the Travelers CEO and his team moved upstairs and took their places in the comfortable, overstuffed armchairs of the meeting room. Sandy plopped into his favorite chair and opened the meeting with his signature line: "Let's talk deals."

That was Dimon's cue to take up a position in the front of the group and begin writing on a Dry-Erase white board column headings such as "insurance" and "securities." The other executives called out names for possible merger candidates. "How about Hartford Insurance?" said Jay Fishman. "Or CNA?" Others suggested Merrill Lynch and Goldman Sachs. Within a few minutes, Dimon had filled the entire board with names of fifteen companies.

"Well, what about Citibank?" Sandy tossed out. The executives looked at one another—as if to make sure Sandy wasn't serious—and then chortled. It's too big, too regulated, just too blue-chip for us, the managers scoffed. Dimon, black marker in hand, nevertheless shrugged and said, "Okay," and then scrawled the name diagonally down one side because he was out of space. The others didn't give it a passing thought.

Except Sandy. The next day Sandy arranged the Washington hotel meeting with John Reed, whom he had gotten to know in the 1970s when they served on the board of an ailing real-estate company. They weren't social friends; indeed, they were polar opposites. Yet the magnetic pull was unmistakable.

"THIS IS A GOOD DAY, PARTNER"

Acting on Sandy's breathless directive to "get serious" about Citicorp, Dimon summoned Chief Financial Officer Heidi Miller and head of investor relations William Pike. Without divulging why, he ordered them to obtain the financial reports and Securities and Exchange Commission filings on the nation's five largest national banks. "Get it fast," he barked.

When the Travelers helicopter delivered Sandy to downtown Manhattan later that morning, his ruddy face was beaming. Sandy swept into his thirty-ninth-floor office suite with the bounce in his step that colleagues recognized as "deal bliss." In addition to Dimon, Sandy told only a handful of his top executives whose help he would need right away. The merger of these two giants would be "a marriage made in heaven," he gushed. Of course, he expected them to ramp up for "Sandy deal speed"—due diligence at a breakneck pace. Recognizing the need for absolute secrecy, the inner circle immediately formulated code names: Travelers was named "Jupiter," and Citicorp dubbed "Saturn."

As John Reed promised, Citicorp's vice chairman Paul Collins, a long-time bank veteran, called Sandy later that day. A close advisor to Reed, Collins was accustomed to handling matters for his notoriously reclusive boss and would spearhead the exploratory talks for Citicorp. Sandy and Collins chatted easily; they saw each other regularly at board meetings of Carnegie Hall, where they both served as directors. Since Sandy had taken over as chairman of the Carnegie Hall board in the mid-1980s it had become *the* charitable board on which other executives wanted to serve.

Collins told Sandy they could begin preliminary talks, but he had a much more basic question: Are you sure this merger is legal? Before calling Sandy, Collins had briefed Citicorp's general counsel, Jack Roche, about the late-night meeting between Reed and Sandy. "I don't see how this can be done. It's not legal," Roche responded matter-of-factly, citing Glass-Steagall and other laws preventing banks from entering the securities and insurance businesses. First, a Depression-era law prevented banks from doing business on Wall Street, and vice versa. In 1933, after scores of bank failures and crumbling confidence in the nation's financial system, Congress passed the Glass-Steagall Act, which separated commercial and investment banking and forced banks to choose which side of the business they wanted to pursue. For example, J.P. Morgan spun off its investment-banking arm in 1934, creating Morgan Stanley. Second, the Bank Holding Company Act, passed in 1956, barred banks from most forms of insurance underwriting. These laws still prevailed in 1998, even though financial institutions had been lobbying Congress for their repeal or modification for two decades, arguing that financial deregulation would level the playing field against foreign competitors that don't labor under the same restrictions, Roche told Collins.

Sandy assured Collins that his lawyers had figured out a bold though untested strategy to get the merger through, albeit perhaps only temporarily. He promised that his lawyers would show Citicorp's lawyers how the companies could operate as a combined entity for two years under bank holding-company regulations and apply for extensions for three years after that. By then, Sandy predicted this deal—if nothing else—would set the stage for Congress to remove the legislative shackles and free U.S. financial firms to compete globally. The worst-case scenario? We might have to divest some businesses in five years, Sandy explained.

Collins and his general counsel were floored by the audacity of Sandy's proposal. Roche, a colorless, technical lawyer, was taken aback by the tricky legal hurdles facing any Citicorp-Travelers merger. Apart from the legal concerns, which were significant, Collins told Sandy real progress couldn't occur until Reed, who was on his way to Asia, had time to evaluate the proposition more thoughtfully. Because Reed likes to put his thoughts down on paper—testing the logic of propositions to see if they develop holes in theory—Collins explained, Sandy should expect a letter from the Citicorp CEO soon.

Waiting for the letter drove the anxious Travelers chief to distraction. Suddenly Sandy, who rarely read memos, was standing over the fax machine repeatedly, watching as dozens of faxes poured in daily. Nothing from John Reed. Finally, after several days, the machine spat out a six-page handwritten letter from Reed's Singapore hotel. Sandy's secretary, who discreetly brought in his messages and Travelers' stock price every hour, raced into his office ahead of schedule. Sandy saw all the pages, but went to the last page first. Without reading another word, he barged into Dimon's office next door. "He likes it! John likes it! John says this deal could work! He faxed me a long letter—look!" Sandy ranted, calling out key phrases written in John Reed's own hand. "Strategic rationale could make tremendous sense!" "Complementary on the consumer, corporate, and international businesses!" "Structure the deal so that ownership is fifty-fifty share for share!" In his head, Dimon quickly calculated that would give Citicorp a small premium, but who cared, if Travelers could pull off "the mother of all deals"?

Reed's missive, soon to be referred to as the "Memo from Singapore," showed that the two men agreed on the broad concepts almost entirely and focused on the notion that this wouldn't be a takeover by one or the other, but rather a "merger of equals." Only the throwaway lines in the conclusion would turn out to be explosive many months later. Reed concluded that he and Sandy must form a partnership that works together and then leaves together. Sandy wholeheartedly endorsed the partnership notion; he was silent about any exit strategy.

On March 19, Sandy invited John Reed and their two confidants, Dimon and Paul Collins, to the Travelers conference center in Armonk, where they met for several hours, including dinner. The next day, Charles

Long, Citicorp's corporate secretary, joined them, as did Travelers general counsel Chuck Prince. After a sausage-and-eggs breakfast buffet, the six executives hashed out the deal's structure during an eleven-hour marathon. They got so far along in negotiations, they even agreed on a new corporate name—Citigroup. Sandy successfully pushed for the beloved red umbrella he acquired along with Travelers, which he always wore on some part of his clothing, to topple Citi's weird "Sputnik" symbol as the new logo. But Citi would contribute its "shades of blue" background behind the new name and logo.

Still Reed, known as off-putting and remote, had another important item to discuss with Sandy. Regarding publicity, "I'd be happy to cooperate in the beginning," he told his Travelers counterpart, "but I don't want to suddenly become a great public figure." It was a position Sandy didn't understand. Sandy Weill loved being in the spotlight. Acting as if he understood Reed's aversion to publicity, Sandy assured him that was no problem.

That evening, Sandy walked Reed to his car in the Travelers parking lot. "This is a good day, partner," Reed told him. Sandy was on top of the world. He was entranced with Reed—and the idea of sitting atop the world's largest financial empire.

"WE'RE DOING ANOTHER DEAL—A BIG DEAL."

Even as the Citicorp negotiations progressed at "Sandy deal speed," most of Sandy's top executives remained in the dark. In fact, some of them were negotiating for Travelers to buy a different financial giant, Beneficial Corp., for as much as $7 billion, which would have been one of Sandy's largest acquisitions ever. Beneficial, with assets of $17 billion and more than 1,100 offices nationwide, put itself up for sale in mid-February amid pressure from big institutional investors over lower earnings. Because Travelers' Commercial Credit unit catered to the same working-class consumers, Bob Willumstad, Commercial Credit's president, thought Beneficial would be a sensible acquisition with immediate cost-cutting opportunities from combining loan offices. Willumstad, who had cleared the effort to start due diligence on Beneficial with Sandy prior to the Travelers chief's hotel meeting with Reed, ran into his boss in mid-March at a black-tie gala honoring one of their colleagues at the Waldorf-Astoria Hotel.

"Sandy, Beneficial is the best deal we could ever do," the normally taciturn Willumstad asserted.

To his surprise, Sandy cut him off. "We're doing another deal—a big deal."

Willumstad was confused; $7 billion for Beneficial was a big deal. "How big?" he asked.

Sandy looked up at his tall Nordic colleague and told him mysteriously, "But keep doing due diligence on Beneficial."

"Why?"

"Because I don't want this transaction to leak out—I want all speculation on what I'm doing on Beneficial."

Willumstad was dumbfounded. *There aren't too many deals bigger than Beneficial,* he thought. Unless Sandy was looking at a bank.

Reed and Sandy, speaking again on Sunday, March 22, discussed how Travelers, as the acquiring company, would prepare the application to the Federal Reserve as a bank holding company under the unique legal strategy designed by the Travelers lawyers. That was because the technicalities of banking regulation made it impossible for a bank to buy Travelers with its significant insurance business. The deal makers were betting that the Fed would give them as much time as possible before requiring the new company to divest operations in accordance with the old banking laws— while Sandy and Reed pushed to change the statutes in the interim.

Sandy agreed to set up a meeting for the next week with Federal Reserve chairman Alan Greenspan, with whom he had spoken the year before about Travelers' interest in taking over J.P. Morgan or some other bank-related concern. "You remember that thing I talked to you about last summer?" Sandy asked the Fed chairman. "Well, I've made a deal to merge with a bank, and I'd like to bring the other guy down to talk to you." Greenspan inquired who the banker was. "It's John Reed," Sandy replied. Greenspan said he and the Fed's lawyers would take that meeting.

Because journalists frequently stake out the Fed offices and bankers are often there for meetings with their chief regulator, the Citicorp and Travelers teams arrived separately and used back doors, arranged in advance. Only the two corporate chiefs met privately with Greenspan, while their general counsels waited in a public lobby. Travelers' chief lawyer Chuck Prince glanced down at his briefcase and cringed when he spied his own name tag flashing the Travelers name and logo. Would he blow the whole thing? If any competitor or reporter saw a Travelers executive at the Fed, the rumors would fly that the big insurance and securities company was after a bank. Such speculation would certainly unleash a raft of controversy. Prince, Sandy's most devoted loyalist, tried to remove the tag without catching anyone's attention. When Reed and Sandy emerged an hour later, they took different cars to their respective corporate jets. Mission accomplished: Greenspan was open-minded, possibly receptive, to the mega-merger. The Fed chairman had been pushing for a breakdown of the historic barriers between banking, insurance, and securities. This deal, fortunately with two of the country's strongest companies and chief executives, would break new regulatory and possibly legislative ground.

In addition to the Fed, the two giant companies wanted to clear the transaction with two other important players for publicly traded companies. Sandy knew the importance of securing the blessing for the deal by the ratings agencies, which had upgraded ratings in the AA range for both Travelers and Citicorp in recent years. To make certain that the merger wouldn't jeopardize these important ratings, adversely affecting the new entity's costs, Sandy arranged for highly confidential meetings with the agencies. When he started the meeting, he warned, "You better sit down," and then obtained a positive reading to go forward.

Next, he wanted to alert the Securities and Exchange Commission about what would be the biggest combination in U.S. history, mostly as a courtesy call, before the impending public filings. Sandy relished making this call himself; the powerful head of the SEC was none other than Arthur Levitt, his former partner of years ago. Levitt had long harbored resentment at what he perceived as Sandy's taking the lion's share of credit for their early success when the firm was sold to American Express in 1981. Sandy, he felt, had never acknowledged that it was Arthur Levitt who saved a shy and scared young Weill in an early power struggle at their tiny brokerage firm thirty years ago. But with this phone conversation, the longtime friction dissipated. The friendly rivals seemed at peace with each other, understanding that each had his own power base now, and excited at their increasing statures in the financial world.

While Sandy and John Reed were getting to know each other as partners, the long-simmering feud between Sandy and Dimon boiled over. As the two were going over details of the merger at the Weills' Manhattan apartment one night in mid-March, Sandy suddenly turned to him and said flatly, "Jamie, you're not going to be on the new board." Dimon knew that the combined board would have an equal number of Citicorp and Travelers directors, but assumed that he, as the Travelers president and a current director, would be on the new Citigroup board of directors.

"I completely disagree with that," Dimon shot back. "That's wrong."

Sandy responded, "But if we put you on the board, we'll have to put someone else from Citi."

"Fine, put Paul Collins on," Dimon said, referring to Reed's right-hand man. "I don't know why I shouldn't be on the board. I've been on the board of Travelers for seven years. You and John have talked about my being president of the new company—I would be the only president of a company not on his own board, for god's sake."

"I would have to put Deryck on the board if you're on," Sandy replied, bringing up the very sore subject of Dimon's new co-CEO. The reference to Maughan sent Dimon into a rage.

"I helped build this company for fifteen years! This is a disgrace," Dimon answered, seething, perched on the edge of his chair. His angry voice brought Joan into the room, but they both ignored her and she left.

"What about Bob Lipp?" Sandy asked. Lipp had also been with Sandy since the company's start in 1986.

"Bob may deserve it, too, but he wouldn't be upset if it's me, not him." Blood rushing to his face, Dimon was enraged, fighting for the position of respect and stature he thought he had earned. "Put him on the phone. Ask Bob who should be on the board. He'll say me."

As the two men continued fighting, Dimon's thoughts flashed back to 1981. Right before Sandy merged Shearson Loeb Rhoades with American Express, he had coldly informed his president and chief lieutenant, Peter Cohen, that he wasn't putting him on the new board. Dimon's mind was racing—that effort to deprive Cohen, as important to Sandy then as Dimon was now, of a board seat signaled the end of that relationship. Dimon tried to shake such thoughts. "It's wrong, Sandy, just wrong, to keep me off the board," Dimon repeated over and over.

Finally, Sandy had had enough. "That's what we're going to do," he concluded, as if he and John were resolute. "We've decided."

Dimon knew the conversation was over. "I'm pissed off," he said, storming out.

On March 27, in the boardroom of Travelers' Lower Manhattan headquarters, Sandy for the first time briefed the Travelers directors on the audacious bid to merge with Citicorp. The directors were stunned that the Travelers Group could even consider merging with the illustrious Citicorp.

Founded in 1812 as City Bank of New York by a group of merchants and having long ties to the Rockefeller family, Citicorp, with offices in the capitals of one hundred countries, symbolized the American domination of global finance. Looking at the list of directors on the Citicorp side, Travelers director Arthur Zankel, who often joked about being a "guppy" in the corporate sea of sharks, feigned a snobbish air and pronounced the Citicorp board as "very august." He and his fellow directors immediately concluded that the plan was brilliant. With one exception: co-CEOs.

"We're nervous as hell about the power-sharing thing," Zankel told Sandy in the board meeting. "Power-sharing is full of pitfalls—especially for you."

"Nobody likes to share power," Sandy acknowledged. "No company likes it. It hasn't worked well in practice. But John and I have known each other for thirty years. We get along very well." Sandy continued to sell his board on the extraordinary fit between the two companies. "The combination will bring such power in the marketplace and enhance our growth prospects," Sandy told them. "The reward would be gigantic."

"The question then is whether these benefits are worth the risk that you and John Reed will have trouble," continued Zankel, a fellow Carnegie Hall director. "Are you sure you're willing to put your career on the line to make this merger happen?"

Zankel, one of Sandy's closest friends since the 1960s, reminded him of what had happened when Sandy merged with American Express: "You did this with Jimmy Robinson and lost."

Then former president Gerald R. Ford weighed in on Sandy's behalf, predicting that the two senior executives would make their proposed duopoly work. A career politician who never had much money, Ford had been a director of Sandy's growing empire for years and felt a great loyalty to Sandy for making him rich with stock for his board service. That was enough to convince the other directors that Sandy was willing to take his chances personally to catapult Travelers into new frontiers. They granted Sandy the approval to proceed to a merger agreement.

Still only a handful of Travelers and Citicorp executives knew about the merger that would change their companies—and their lives. History's biggest merger was being assembled by a remarkably tiny team of players. One reason was that Sandy and Reed, two of America's top financiers, knew what they were doing and didn't need much advice. Second, they were determined to prevent a leak, working with only their most trusted two or three lieutenants and even eschewing the standard engagement of investment bankers to certify the transaction's fairness. But this approach, coupled with the unprecedented rush to complete the agreement, meant that a lot of important, and potentially thorny, details—from how to structure the various business groups to who would hold which senior positions—were left undecided.

"WE SHOULD CALL CLINTON!"

On Thursday, April 2, 1998, Sandy called a special board meeting to present the final agreement to the board. Travelers directors had grown accustomed to Sandy's springing takeover proposals on them at the last minute for quick approval. Even though this merger was many times bigger than any before and had been negotiated in a record four weeks by only six people, the directors gave it their blessing. Rather than scrutinizing the final negotiations, Sandy's board cheered him on. "It's such an exciting possibility," Travelers director Judith Arron, Carnegie Hall's director, told the group. "If anyone can do this, Sandy can."

Now it was up to Reed to get his much stodgier and more elite board's approval. The Citicorp CEO prepared handouts for the board presentation. One showed the numbers he had run to justify the merger. The institutions were almost equal in terms of equity capital, size of businesses, and credit ratings. Reed had obtained from William Campbell, his marketing guru and head of retail banking, a sales document to show directors the "compelling business logic" of the deal. Campbell, a twenty-six-year veteran at cigarette maker Philip Morris who oversaw the "Marlboro Man" campaign, had constructed a "matrix" showing the uncanny fit between the companies' products (deposits, loans, investments, insurance) and their distribution channels (branches, telephone/mail solicitation, stockbrokers, insurance agents). Even Campbell, who had no banking experience prior to joining Citicorp in 1996, was amazed at how these giant companies could mesh.

Yet while explaining the matrix to Reed prior to the board meeting, Campbell noted that his boss seemed more persuaded by Travelers' management expertise than by its business offerings. Turning philosophical for a moment, Reed told Campbell, "Citi is too cerebral—not action oriented like Travelers. I haven't been able to modify our culture that's too big and too comfortable." The Citibank chief, a corporate experimenter prone to focus on process over people, had moved managers in and out of the executive suite in an attempt to bring about change. In addition to Campbell, Reed had recruited executives from other big consumer franchises, including Federal Express, Viacom, General Electric, and Heinz, hardly a typical bank roster but all part of Reed's shaky efforts to wake up Citi. In an admission that his odd mix of managers who had little or no experience in financial services wasn't producing desperately needed reforms, Reed was actually looking forward to having Sandy's team do the heavy lifting. He and Campbell laughed about how much Sandy and his merry band would relish slicing and dicing through the massive and excessive costs within Citibank.

Underlying the jokes, however, Campbell heard in his boss's voice frustration—almost defeat—about changing Citibank's swollen bureaucracy. Believing Sandy Weill to be a brazen suitor who measured his worth by the size of his next deal, Campbell had assumed that Reed was succumbing to the arduous advances from the Travelers chief. Yet, in this moment of candor with the Citi CEO, Campbell suddenly realized: John Reed wants, needs, and is pursuing this merger as much as Sandy Weill.

On Friday, April 3, the Citicorp board took up the historic merger proposal. Unlike Travelers Group, which had grown by leaps and bounds through acquisitions, Citibank had grown organically since its last significant merger in 1955, between National City Bank and First National Bank. Now the bank's chieftain, who assumed its leadership at the tender age of forty-five in 1984 from the legendary Walter Wriston, stood before his stellar board to seek approval for what would be the biggest merger ever in the United States. In earlier years, the directors had stuck with Reed as he lost tons of money getting into credit cards and automatic teller machines, both of which ultimately proved visionary in making Citicorp a world-class consumer bank. Now he was asking them to support him for something equally radical and ahead of its time.

The agreement before you, Reed told his heavyweight directors, would create the world's largest financial-services company. With his typical certitude and aloofness, Reed described the proposal as a "transforming merger" that would trigger a restructuring of the financial industry "directionally" to meet the increasingly complex and international world of financial services. Other positives from Travelers: its "proven selling and cross-marketing competence" and "management competence in delivering performance."

After Reed's presentation, nearly every director's first question and the one that kept coming up over and over in a meeting that stretched for more than seven hours: Can you really share power with Sandy Weill? Richard Parsons, president of Time Warner, told "horror stories" about the time when Steven Ross, a flashy, friendly Brooklyn boy (not unlike Sandy) and Nicholas J. Nicholas, a cold and impersonal analytical type (not unlike Reed), failed miserably as co-CEOs. Just two years after Time Inc. and Warner Communications Inc. merged and the two were named co–chief executives in 1989, Nicholas, thought to be a shrewd corporate politician, was out after losing a power struggle with the more popular Ross. The question, though not bluntly articulated, hung in the air: Could Reed suffer the same fate after tangling with the wily Weill? An inside director, Vice Chairman Onno Ruding, countered that co-CEOs could work, as they had at Unilever, another board on which he sat.

Reed, regarded as the Boy Wonder of banking when he assumed the helm at Citibank, realized this deal wouldn't get board approval unless he convinced them that he and Sandy could work together. "We have both run companies for a long time," he told the directors. "We've had successful and difficult times." Just as Sandy was forced into a corporate exile of sorts after leaving the presidency at American Express in the mid-1980s, Reed nearly lost everything in the early 1990s when Citicorp almost collapsed from bad real-estate and Latin American loans. Yet each man launched an impressive turnaround that vaulted him to the pinnacle of the financial-services industry. As if to assure the directors that they would "play nice," Reed noted that he and Sandy were approaching the ends of their careers, implying they had nothing else left to prove by fighting each other. "We are big boys," he assured his skeptical board. As the day wore on, Citi's seasoned directors—men like Reuben Mark, chief executive of Colgate-Palmolive; Alain Belda, president of Alcoa; Chevron CEO Kenneth Derr; former Central Intelligence Agency director John Deutch; and Franklin Thomas, ex-head of the Ford Foundation—continued to question the logic and wisdom of the move. In the end the board agreed to the deal on the proviso that it was clear that Reed and Sandy—and by extension Citicorp and Travelers—would be on equal footing.

That same Friday, Sandy gave an Oscar-worthy performance playing the part of an acquirer eager to buy Beneficial Corporation. Under orders to act as if Travelers were still interested in Beneficial, Bob Willumstad arranged for Sandy to have a breakfast meeting at a midtown club with

Beneficial chairman Finn Caspersen, who still believed Travelers was interested in bidding for his company. Upbeat and enthusiastic, Sandy laid out compelling reasons why Travelers and Beneficial would make a good fit. Willumstad, who had been greatly disappointed when Sandy told him a couple weeks before that he was interested in a "bigger deal," found himself even more convinced by Sandy's arguments on the merits of acquiring Beneficial. *Maybe he'll still do this deal,* Willumstad thought hopefully.

Sandy's persuasive performance brought the desired result. When word began leaking out that week about Travelers' special board meeting and Sandy's meeting with Caspersen, all speculation focused on Beneficial. Later that morning, Sandy revealed to Willumstad the identity of the real target that was being protected by their breakfast deception—Citicorp. Willumstad, who had joined Sandy at Commercial Credit from Chemical Bank, was floored. He had gotten out of dull, dumb banking to go with the exciting, entrepreneurial style of Sandy. Still, he instantly recognized the value of joining Citi's consumer franchise with the brands under the umbrella: Salomon Smith Barney, Travelers, and Commercial Credit. Willumstad asked for permission to tell Marge Magner. As the chief operating officer of Commercial Credit, she had been heading up the due diligence with Willumstad for Beneficial, a deal Magner wanted so badly she was dreaming about it.

Magner's cell phone rang just as she was about to dash into Bloomingdale's to grab a new pair of stockings to replace the pair that had developed a run. It was Willumstad. "We're not doing Beneficial. We're doing Citi!" Standing in front of the store's revolving doors as honking taxis barreled down Lexington Avenue, Magner was floored. *"No! No! No!* Nothing could be worse. We hate Citibank. Bob, it's the bad guy." Willumstad knew why the news hit her so hard. Working in the retail system at Chemical Bank, as they both had for many years, meant they were engaged in a constant war against Citibank. Typically, the two rival New York banks had branches across the street from each other. Magner, a feisty competitor, had toiled daily to get more checking accounts, more deposits, more customers than her arch competitor, Citibank. Now she would be working with the enemy she was trained to defeat. Even worse, it trumped the Beneficial deal. "I'm brokenhearted about Beneficial," Magner told Willumstad. "I know. Me too," he said softly, because he also believed it would be a great acquisition. "Sandy says if we're trying to pull off two huge deals—Citibank and Beneficial—it will confuse the regulators who have to approve the Citi transaction, which is tricky to begin with."

On Saturday, April 4, both Travelers' and Citicorp's boards approved the final merger agreement by phone. Now the two companies needed to rush to announce their deal to the public; public-relations and investor-relations managers were called to a special meeting at Travelers' conference center for the day. A graphic designer was summoned (under threat of death if he talked) to create the new logo with Travelers' red umbrella on Citi's sky-blue façade, as well as a new typeface for the new name: Citigroup. Travelers' public-relations pro Mary McDermott and Citi spokesman Jack Morris drafted an announcement, while public-relations guru Gershon Kekst sent out invitations to analysts and the press for a nonspecific announcement on Monday morning, April 6. Over lunch, the executives ironed out the details for the big announcement.

The Citi executives, who were visiting the Armonk facility for the first time, were instantly struck by Sandy's dominance of the situation. Accustomed to running not only takeovers but also his own conference center, the Travelers CEO was the center of attention, the grand pooh-bah. Everyone was jumping to please Sandy, as officials from both companies sat in the meeting room's upholstered armchairs. The Travelers team casually slouched in their seats, while the Citi executives sat stiffly and uncomfortably, fighting the plush goose-down fill to maintain an erect posture and not knowing that most future meetings would be conducted per Sandy's "soft-seating" mandate.

As more people learned of the impending merger, the risk of a leak, or even an educated guess, grew. Reporters routinely called Citicorp's spokesman Jack Morris to be certain that nothing was happening they might need to cover. If they sensed something was up, journalists would start snooping around, calling directors or management, to piece together any new development. To prevent any such clues, when Morris left home Saturday morning, he instructed his wife, "If anyone calls, I'm sailing."

The next day, agreements were delivered to each CEO's home for signing. When presented with the merger documents, Sandy turned to Joan. "Can you believe what we're doing?!" They both knew this was the ultimate coup. Every previous deal had meant more prominence and more money for Sandy; this one meant fame and respect, something he had long craved. He called Dimon, who was still smarting from being excluded from the board. But Sandy was so gleeful, it rubbed off on Dimon. Sandy was practically chirping: "Can you believe it? Can you believe where we've gotten?"

Dimon, as the co-CEO of Salomon Smith Barney, invited his management team to his Manhattan apartment on Park Avenue that Sunday afternoon. He handed out the newly drafted press release announcing the $70-billion merger between Travelers and Citicorp. "This is a joke," said one executive, laughing. "Be at Citicorp's auditorium tomorrow at nine o'clock and see for yourselves," responded Dimon, hoping for a special moment with his managers. To most of them, the deal was a complete surprise—and not a pleasant one. Like Marge Magner and other Travelers officials on the consumer side, these executives on the corporate side of the house were equally distressed about the union. "Jesus Christ, what a nightmare," blurted out Eduardo Mestre, investment-banking chief. "We're still struggling to put together Salomon Brothers and Smith Barney—now this!" Investment bankers considered themselves the apex predators of the financial world and disdained commercial bankers as mere bottom feeders who spent their days filling out loan documents. Stars in the rarefied world of investment banking, Mestre and his cohorts were horrified, and their grumbling showed it. The deal meant they would be working alongside people who couldn't cut it in the big leagues.

Later that Sunday evening, Sandy and John Reed spoke one last time before the next morning's big announcement to Wall Street analysts and the press. Sandy suddenly suggested, "We should call Clinton!"

"Who?" Reed asked.

"The president!" Sandy replied. "Let's tell him about our merger."

Reed was still puzzled. "Why?"

Undeterred by his new partner's lack of political savvy, Sandy told an assistant to place a conference call to the White House. The Travelers chief was a big fan of the president ever since traveling with him and Jesse Jackson at events promoting minorities on Wall Street. In minutes, the president was on the line. Sandy couldn't contain his excitement—he could call the president of the United States on a Sunday night and get him! Reed dutifully joined in on the call. After Sandy briefed him about the merger to be announced the next morning, President Clinton told them about his recent trip to Africa, the young people he had met there, and the countries' prospects for economic growth. Reed assured the president that Citibank, which had a long presence in Africa, intended to increase investments in that region. After their ten-minute chat, Sandy hung up, crowing, "We just made the president of the United States an insider."

In his office at 10:00 that evening, Travelers' general counsel Chuck Prince, a particularly compulsive and hardworking lawyer who personally reviewed practically everything for Sandy, was rereading the announcement and proxy statement to be filed the next morning. One sentence stopped him cold. In essence, it stated that once the merger was successfully implemented, the cochairmen would retire. Knowing his sixty-five-year-old boss adamantly refused to talk about retiring, Chuck called his Citi counterpart Jack Roche.

"Jack, this isn't true."

"John says it is true," Roche countered, speaking on behalf of Reed.

"For something to be true about two people, both of them have to say it's true," Prince argued. "It is not true, so, Jack, this line has to come out."

Roche was reluctant to delete a line given to him by Reed, but Prince was adamant.

"This is *not* the deal," Prince asserted. "John's model may have them walking off into the sunset together, but that isn't part of the merger agreement."

Roche removed the offending sentence, deciding it wasn't legally necessary for the proxy. And it saved a possible dispute from arising at 10:00 the night before the media and Wall Street would descend on Citi. The proxy was ready to file.

"I'M USED TO BEING TOLD WHAT TO DO"

On Monday morning, Sandy, looking like a kid who was going to burst with excitement, practically sailed into the Citicorp executive offices on Lexington Avenue in midtown. Joan was by his side, partly in recognition of her crucial role in his career trajectory and partly out of superstition. When Sandy, Joan, and their bodyguard, Gus Chappory, came out of the elevator on the floor where the merger operations were being secretly conducted, the Citi staff closely eyed their new boss, or co-boss, or whatever he might be. Accustomed to a cold and detached John Reed, they were taken aback by his backslapping "call me Sandy" friendliness. Walking down the hall, the exuberant Travelers CEO handed out his beloved ties with the red umbrella logo. "Here, I want you to wear this," he said to one surprised young manager. "I want you to have this tie," he told another startled vice president. Jack Roche, the Citi legal advisor who first questioned the merger's legality, was walking by when Sandy stopped him to shake his hand. Suddenly Sandy's bodyguard was handing Roche an umbrella tie and umbrella pin.

Reed stayed in his office until minutes before he and his new partner were scheduled to speak to analysts and reporters. When he emerged, he was sporting the Hermès silk tie adorned with umbrellas and the red umbrella lapel pin that Sandy, who wore them almost every business day, had suggested they both wear as a sign of unity. Reed's bright red tie, covered with its even brighter umbrellas colored yellow, blue, green, and orange, looked incongruous on the well-groomed banker with his conservative navy pin-stripe suit and button-down white shirt. Sandy, with wiry hair and a splotchy face, wore a navy tie with colorful umbrellas and a pink shirt with white cuffs and collar.

Citicorp spokesman Jack Morris told them it was time to address the waiting press corps, which had been notified of the merger through a release put out over PR Newswire at 7:27 A.M. Already CNNfn, calling this "the deal of the century," was standing by to go live with the press conference. The Travelers-Citicorp combination would be twice as large as last fall's merger between MCI and WorldCom, at that time America's biggest corporate merger ever. Financial reporters breathlessly called the creation of the new money colossus "the best-kept secret on Wall Street," evidence that "bigger is better on Wall Street" and stunning in "size, scope, and strategy." Heading to the Waldorf-Astoria five blocks away on Park Avenue, Reed and Morris walked side by side, followed by Sandy and Joan Weill next, and Chappory, Sandy's armed bodyguard, trailing the group.

Practically hugging with their arms around each other's backs, Reed and Sandy entered the packed ballroom where dozens of TV news cameras and newspaper photographers crowded the stage. With cameras flashing, photographers yelled out: "Sandy, look over here!" "John—turn to this side!" The eruption of the press when the pair entered the room thrilled Sandy and startled Reed. Seeing Reed's "deer-in-the-headlights" response, his spokesman yelled to the jostling media, "Behave yourselves, or I'll throw you out!" The raging bull market of the 1990s and the extensive coverage that corporate leaders received on CNBC and other financial news programs had created the "cult of the CEO," and Sandy Weill felt at that moment its leader.

The new cochairmen took their seats at a table set up with glasses and bottled water. Sandy, his name tag twisted sideways, immediately took a swig from his Poland Spring plastic bottle; Reed, with his name tag properly secured on his lapel, poured his water into a glass. Their talking points in manila folders were set before them at their places. Sandy's paper had extremely large type because he didn't want to put on reading glasses in front of cameras. Reed quickly placed his reading glasses on the end of his nose, assuming a professorial air.

CNBC's Allan Chernoff asked the same first question of Reed and Sandy that their boards had posed. "Do you see any potential conflict in actually sharing the top position of this new company?" The pair's responses set the tone for how differently they would conduct themselves in this news conference. Reed, once described as having the personality of cold oatmeal, was blandly grave. "Let's be straight here. Two people sharing a job is inherently difficult." He rambled on, "So, I would start out by saying that I'm going to learn a lot from Sandy and I am going to have to change because of that. My suspicion is he is going to find he will have to change a little bit, too." Despite the tangible electricity in the air, Reed somehow managed to drone on, launching into didactic principles of management and integration of business models, throwing in terms like *heretofore* and *human dimension*. Sandy kept his responses light and often amusing. "I've been married to my wife for forty-three years, so I'm used to being told what to do," he said, grinning in response to the question about power sharing. When another reporter asked if this historic merger would mark the end of the pair's illustrious careers, Sandy quickly shot back, "God, I hope not." More laughs. The final scorecard for generating laughs: Sandy, 9; Reed, 0.

After the questioning was cut off, Sandy and Reed stood shaking hands and mugging for the cameras. It took them several minutes to push their way through the mass of reporters and photographers pressing against them. When the powerful duo emerged on Park Avenue, another set of photographers was waiting to capture more candid shots. As Reed hurried down the sidewalk, Sandy gave a thumbs-up, then began smiling from ear to ear and waving to everyone walking down the street. Passersby must have wondered, Who is that stocky, giddy man surrounded by paparazzi? He didn't look like a movie star, but he certainly seemed famous.

Once back at Citicorp headquarters, Sandy wanted to see the stock market's reaction and TV coverage of the press conference. He scurried around the executive floor. "Does anybody have a TV?" pleaded Sandy, who kept his office set tuned to CNBC all the time. "Hi Sandy, my name is Ed Horo-witz, and I have a TV," said Citi's technology guru to his new co-CEO. With-out saying anything, Sandy swooped into Horowitz's chair and watched as if in a trance. Wall Street loved the deal! Prices of both Travelers and Citicorp shares were soaring. Sandy relished the run-up in his company's value and the marketplace's broad validation of his idea. "I'm about to pass out," Sandy whooped when Travelers spiked to $73 a share. "If it hits seventy-five, my chauffeur will be a millionaire, and I'll have to drive him!"

Reed had to pry his publicity-hungry partner from the TV set to join him for a luncheon he arranged for just the two of them in his private fourteenth-floor dining room. Desperate to escape the hoopla, Reed wanted some "downtime" before the slew of one-on-one interviews with national media—arranged by Sandy's people—that afternoon. During those inter-views with *The Wall Street Journal, The New York Times, Fortune,* and oth-ers in the library next to Reed's office, Sandy kept tabs on both companies' escalating stock prices. At day's end, with Travelers closing up 18 percent at $73 and Citicorp vaulting 27 percent to $180, another $14 billion was added to the value of the transaction, making it worth $83 billion. The deal—and the run-up in other financial stocks on the speculation that they would follow suit—propelled the Dow to record territory, closing for the first time above 9000.

In the Manhattan apartment where the Weills usually spent the week, Sandy woke up the next morning to find himself—and artists' renditions of him—all over the newspapers. Leading with the headline BOSOM BUDDIES ON TOP, the tabloid *New York Post* ran a caricature of Sandy and Reed em-bracing. Even the staid *New York Times* used a large graphic with the heads of Sandy and Reed on gorilla bodies sitting astride the Citicorp and Trav-elers headquarters buildings. The caption read: "Throwing their weight around. The merger . . . brings together two larger-than-life executives who are used to being in charge." Even as the press acknowledged the "love fest" between the newly "married" co-CEOs, the next day's reports were already predicting the corporate union would end in its leaders' di-vorce. Sandy instead focused on the reports such as "Wall Street's takeover king joins the prince of American banking," "Money Titans . . . cast gigan-tic shadow over Wall Street," and "Two trailblazers make merger history."

Joan and Sandy invited Reed and his wife to join them for a celebratory dinner that evening, but not before the new co-CEOs had to take care of more publicity—an appearance with financial TV's leading personality,

Lou Dobbs, on CNN's *Moneyline.* Joan and Cindy Reed accompanied their husbands to the CNN television studio near Penn Station in Manhattan. While the couples were waiting for *Moneyline* to start, Reed turned to Citicorp spokesman Jack Morris to ask about the night's dinner plans. "Sandy is taking us to dinner at this place, Le Cirque. What's it like?" That Reed had never been to—indeed, didn't seem to have ever heard of—one of Manhattan's poshest, celebrity-filled dining venues spoke volumes about the differences between Reed and Sandy Weill. As the two couples dined on osso buco with burgundy, seated at one of the most prominent tables in the famous eatery, Le Cirque's owner and well-heeled diners stopped by to congratulate Sandy. Many appeared not to even recognize that his polite, fresh-scrubbed dining partner was the other half of the mega-deal, John Reed.

Despite the adulation, Sandy still had several more obstacles to confront. What could go wrong? What if the regulators, Congress, or the stock market frowned on the deal? What if he couldn't make all the businesses work together as he envisioned? He knew he was facing the biggest challenge of his career.

14

THE HYDRA-HEADED MONSTER

The sleek corporate jet carrying Sandy Weill streaked eastward high over the Atlantic, bound for the lush island nation of Bermuda. Sandy was heading for another of his beloved corporate retreats. But this wasn't a routine meeting of his long-standing planning group. This time he would rendezvous on Bermuda with John Reed. The two trailblazing executives would sit down with their highest-ranking deputies to secretly lay the groundwork for the astounding merger of Travelers Group with Citicorp, a deal they had announced only days earlier, on April 6, 1998. The task before them was critical: They had to decide who among the many ambitious and talented executives at each company would run the various units of the merged company, the world's largest financial conglomerate. Although the two companies had little overlap in their markets, the merger inevitably would mean the loss of positions and prominence for many high-ranking executives. Indeed, Sandy and Reed had taken extraordinary steps to keep this meeting secret, lest the politicking and lobbying for rank and power overwhelm them. As the jet swept low over Bermuda's spectacularly pink beaches and turquoise waters, Sandy knew he would see little of the island's charms. This was going to be a heavy-duty working session.

At the luxurious Fairmont Princess Resort, Sandy met Reed. The two CEOs were joined by their chosen subordinates. Jamie Dimon and Bob Lipp represented Travelers. Reed had chosen Paul Collins, Citicorp's vice chairman, and Bill Campbell, head of the retail bank, to join him. When the absence of all six men was noted that weekend, the four subordinates were quickly dubbed "the Untouchables," on the assumption that their attendance at the session guaranteed them some of the highest posts in the merged company. Without ever asking Sandy, the Citicorp officials assumed that the bright and seasoned Dimon would emerge in the highest post under the co-CEOs. While Reed admired Sandy's business acumen and his relentless drive, he was much more drawn to the young, thoughtful Dimon, with whom he felt intellectually simpatico. Certainly Reed envisioned Dimon as the successor to the CEO title in the not-too-distant future. Beyond that, the slate was clean, a consequence of the haste in which Sandy and Reed had reached their agreement.

Hunkered down in one of the Princess's penthouse suites, the six men labored for a day and a half, subsisting on room service food and breaking only once for naps and to return important phone calls. Filling up white boards and paper charts with diagrams and names, the six men found their work going amazingly smoothly. At the highest levels, Jamie Dimon would be the chief executive officer of Citigroup's global corporate unit, including Salomon Smith Barney's investment-banking and securities operations, as well as Citibank's corporate-banking business. Reporting to Dimon would be Citibank's Victor Menezes, who would oversee the commercial-banking side of the business, and Deryck Maughan, who would be responsible for Salomon Smith Barney. Bob Lipp and Bill Campbell would become co-CEOs of all consumer operations: Citibank, Commercial Credit, Primerica Financial Services, and Citi credit cards. The pair got along very well and agreed that Lipp would actually run domestic operations while Campbell would head international, which consisted almost entirely of Citibank branches abroad. Nearing retirement, Paul Collins wanted to help Sandy and Reed without taking direct line responsibility and eventually would spend more time in England. Below those levels more than two dozen executives were selected to head key components of each operation, while another two dozen were passed over for the top spots, to be offered less prestigious and powerful posts. While there would be a management committee, consisting of some thirty executives, that met quarterly, Sandy also insisted on forming his favorite management tool—a "planning group"—that would meet monthly.

Pleased with the decisions they had made, the senior executives returned to New York and began informing the most senior executives about their futures. When Sandy told Deryck Maughan he would soon be working *for* Jamie Dimon rather than *with* him, Maughan voiced no objection.

The next day, when the Bermuda team gathered to review the internal reactions they were getting as word of the pending changes spread, Sandy told the group that Maughan shouldn't be placed below Dimon in the corporate hierarchy.

"Why not?" asked Reed, who had never considered people more important than process in running a company.

"I don't want to upset Deryck," Sandy explained. "I don't want to lose him."

"You have to make the right decision for the company," Reed countered. "If it's the right thing to do to have him report to Jamie, let's do it. So what if Deryck leaves?"

The Citicorp executives couldn't understand Sandy's allegiance to Maughan, who had joined Travelers only a few months earlier when it acquired Salomon. Since then, Salomon had caused Travelers nothing but trouble. As far as Reed was concerned, Salomon was the least attractive part of the merger.

But Sandy wouldn't be deterred. "We have to find a different solution," he insisted. Clearly, Sandy enjoyed being around Maughan. In contrast to Dimon, who had no compunction about criticizing his boss openly, Maughan went to great lengths to praise and flatter Sandy. In addition, Maughan's worldly background and debonair manner were qualities Sandy admired but did not possess.

Suddenly all that hard work in Bermuda became virtually worthless. A new plan had to be devised, and fast. Executives at both companies, as well as the analysts and the press, were clamoring to know how the combined company would be run. Pushing for Maughan, Sandy proposed that the ex–Salomon chief and Dimon keep their co-CEO status as heads of the global corporate and investment-banking division. In other words, their relationship wouldn't change, but their joint responsibilities would increase.

"Get the machine guns ready," Dimon shot back. "Co-CEOs will set up an obsession with who's winning, and factions will discredit each other and destroy careers."

Sandy pointed out that he and Reed were willing to be co-CEOs.

"Honestly, it's okay for you two to be co-CEOs because you want to be a true partnership," Dimon responded. "But for line jobs over operations, co-CEOs are absolutely unworkable."

When the Travelers chairman tried to move on to a review of proposed positions for other executives, Dimon kept harping on the job sharing with Maughan. Reed finally felt compelled to weigh in on Sandy's side, mostly to support his new "partner." But Dimon persisted in challenging their decision. The Citibank executives were shocked at the intensity of the fighting between Sandy and Dimon.

Despite Reed's vote in favor of Sandy's solution, the other Citibank executives were troubled. Sandy's proposal put two Travelers executives in the highest positions over the corporate- and investment-banking operations. Citibank executives would naturally feel left out. So a new proposal was offered: tri-CEOs. Victor Menezes, who under the Bermuda plan would have served on equal footing with Maughan while reporting to Dimon, would now be named as a third CEO over corporate and investment banking.

Dimon was flabbergasted. "We'll never get anything done if we have three heads," he retorted. But before he could launch into a tirade against such an unwieldy management structure, Sandy returned Reed's favor. "Three co-CEOs it is," he said. When he spied Dimon about to lash out, he glared directly at him and ordered: "Shut up."

Despite the brief clash, Reed was still very impressed with Dimon and wanted to distinguish the young executive from the rest of the pack. He proposed that Dimon be named Citigroup president, a position that implied Dimon had more authority than anyone else under Sandy and Reed, and that would set him up, at least nominally, as the heir apparent to Sandy and Reed. Sandy agreed but pointedly didn't offer the additional title of chief operating officer. Just as Sandy had been deprived of the chief operating officer title he so desperately sought at American Express, he was depriving Dimon of it. And Sandy went further to ensure that the president's title was little more than just a title: Only the company's chief financial officer—Heidi Miller had been selected for that post—would report to Dimon. All the other top managers would report directly to Sandy and Reed.

The outcome hit Dimon hard. He sensed that deep down Sandy was very, very angry with him. He had noticed, too, that Joan Weill seemed colder toward him since Jessica had left the company. Still, Dimon was confident that his relationships with the two Weills would soon improve. After all, he and Sandy had worked together hand in hand for fifteen years to reach this point in their careers, and the Weills remained the best of friends with Dimon's parents. Any relationship has its ups and downs, Dimon reasoned, and they would work it out for the common goal of taking over Citicorp.

Reed, on the other hand, was eager to nurture a relationship with Dimon. He and his wife invited Jamie and Judy Dimon to dinner in their

Greenwich Village apartment, where Reed cooked. Reed also invited the new Citigroup president to travel abroad with him on his next business trip. It would be an opportunity for them to get to know each other better and to discuss a wide range of issues involved in such a mammoth merger. Dimon was flattered and knew he would enjoy a closer relationship with the cerebral Reed. Yet Dimon also remembered Sandy's deep anger when Peter Cohen had cultivated a special relationship with Jim Robinson at American Express. Dimon didn't want to make the same mistake. *If I go on the trip with Reed, Sandy will be paranoid, he'll think I'm a turncoat,* Dimon thought. Reluctantly, he turned down Reed's offer.

Before announcing the new management slate, Sandy and Reed wanted to be sure the managers knew one another. At the end of April, about one hundred top executives from the two companies gathered for dinner at Travelers' Armonk conference center. Small slips of paper, each bearing one of their names, were put in a pot and drawn to determine who would sit with whom at dinner. The random drawing forced Travelers and Citibank executives to mingle.

Marge Magner, the chief operating officer of Commercial Credit, laughed at what she dubbed the "mating game" that forced the executives to get to know one another. But she got more serious after spending several hours sitting at a table with top Citibank officials Brian Ruder and Norman Selby. She was shocked at their lack of financial-services experience. In Reed's effort to bring in unorthodox talent to shake up Citibank, he had recruited Ruder from a top retailing post at H. J. Heinz, the ketchup-and-pickle company, to head Citi's global marketing effort, and lured Selby from the consulting firm of McKenzie & Co. to become chief auditor. "They know nothing about the business," she whispered to her colleague Bob Willumstad later in the evening. Magner and Willumstad had thirty-five years of combined experience at financial institutions; between them, Ruder and Selby had two.

Yet Citibank did have some veterans who knew banking intimately and were proud of their company's heritage. Charles Long, Citicorp's longtime corporate secretary, buttonholed his Travelers counterpart, Chuck Prince, and pressed on him a copy of a book entitled *The First Billion: The Stillmans and the National City Bank,* a history of the forerunner of Citibank written during the Depression. "I'm going to make you read this old book on Citibank," he told Prince.

THE ARK

On May 16, 1998, Sandy and Reed announced the new management structure that would go into place as soon as regulators approved the proposed merger. At the top were Sandy and Reed as co-CEOs. Below them would be two co-CEOs running the consumer bank and three co-CEOs running the corporate business. The top-heavy structure was instantly dubbed "the Noah's Ark School of Management." Noah and pairs of all the animals were on the ark for a limited time to survive the flood. Most managers regarded the various pairs and trios of CEOs as a transitional tool to get the merged company off to a fast start. It would also provide some continuity while both sides struggled with the inevitable "social issues" involved in any merger.

Sandy's next task was particularly onerous for the gregarious CEO: He had to pare the Travelers board down to nine from fifteen members, the result of early negotiations in which he and Reed agreed that each of the two companies would have equal representation on the combined board. For the most part Travelers board members were people Sandy liked and admired. Firing them would be difficult, but Sandy figured out a way to avoid the worst aspects of it: make Arthur Zankel and Ken Bialkin, his oldest friends and longest-serving directors, do the job. Their solution was to have the board vote on which nine members would be invited to join the new Citigroup board. Ballots would be secret so that no single director would know who had voted for whom. Zankel and Bialkin took the results to their old friend to be sure he approved. Among those with the fewest votes were Linda Wachner, the controversial head of Warnaco Group, a giant clothing manufacturer; Joe Califano, the former Carter administration official; and Joe Wright, the former Reagan administration official and one of Sandy's longtime friends. The decision to remove Wachner was easy: She was routinely late to board meetings, contributed little to the discussions, showed up at one emergency meeting in an aerobic exercise getup, and was constantly enmeshed in trying to save her ailing company. Dropping the other two, however, would be more difficult. Both had made valuable contributions to the company and were social friends of the Weills.

"I have to tell you," Sandy said in a call to Califano, "you aren't one of the guys who's going to survive."

"That's fine. I enjoyed my years on the board," Califano graciously responded. "I still have all my stock. Sandy, you're my retirement."

Joe Wright's removal didn't go as smoothly. Joe and Ellen Wright had been friends with Sandy and Joan since the late 1970s, long before Sandy had achieved power or, indeed, even basic social graces. At dinner one night early in their relationship, Sandy had paused next to the piano in the Wrights' living room to grab a handful of what he thought an appetizer in a dish on top of the piano. Instantly he gagged and began spitting out the concoction. "What the hell is this stuff?" he demanded. "It tastes horrible."

"Well, Sandy, you're not supposed to eat the potpourri," Joan informed him amid the Wrights' delighted laughter.

But there was no laughter this time. Joe Wright had known Sandy long enough to surmise that he was hiding behind the "vote" to pare the board. Long ago Wright had worked at Citicorp and hadn't gotten along well with Reed. But even if Sandy had good reason to dump Wright to stay in good stead with his new partner, Wright thought he shouldn't have had his cronies handle the chore, and he told Sandy as much in a phone call. "You're the CEO," Wright said. "The board serves at your pleasure." Uncomfortable at being lectured, Sandy hastily ended the call.

Joan Weill, attempting to smooth over the situation, soon phoned Ellen Wright, with whom she had long shared confidences about their children and their lives. Ellen Wright, convinced that no move would be taken without Sandy's approval, didn't buy the official explanation of her husband's removal from the board. She let Joan know the move seriously damaged their friendship.

Certainly Sandy could be ruthless, even to his old friends, but his relationship with his new partner was as generous and solicitous as it could possibly be, and Reed responded in kind. At one early meeting with the new planning group, both the Travelers and Citicorp executives were surprised at how deferential the two men were to each other. Chuck Prince deemed the meeting a "love fest."

"John, what do you think?" Sandy asked at one point in the meeting. "You're so good at strategy."

Later Reed returned the compliment. "Sandy, what do you think? You're so good at operations."

The astonishing rapport between the volatile Sandy and the coldly calculating Reed set the tone for the first few weeks as the executives on each side of the merger squared off to assess their counterparts. The lesson for these power-hungry and aggressive men and women was clear: Play nice!

Yet it was also clear that there were going to be problems. After all, any big corporate merger is a difficult adjustment process for all involved, and this was one of the biggest, with 200,000 employees around the world. Further, each company had a distinctive operating style: Travelers managers were lean and mean and willing to get their hands dirty; Citicorp management preferred a think-tank atmosphere free of constant bottom-line pressures.

Confident that the Federal Reserve would approve their merger, Sandy and Reed moved quickly to create an aura of togetherness. Sandy happily abandoned his downtown office in Tribeca to move into the landmark Citicorp tower that occupied a block of Lexington Avenue and East Fifty-third Street in midtown Manhattan. The dramatic silvery skyscraper, with its distinctive angled roof, would be the corporate headquarters. Construction began immediately for a working fireplace as the centerpiece of a sitting room that divided Sandy's office from Reed's. The Travelers CEO was convinced that meeting with other clients, fellow executives, and employees in such comfortable surroundings defused tensions and made for more relaxed discussions.

But the finished product didn't turn out quite as Sandy had hoped. The cozy, comfortable library that Sandy had envisioned was nothing like the almost sterile room that resulted. In keeping with the rest of the executive floor, the cream-and-beige décor was modern to the point of being cold. Even the bookshelves and tabletops were bare. Unlike Sandy, who had filled his previous libraries with scrapbooks, photos, awards, and trinkets, Reed disdained knickknacks and memorabilia. Moreover, Reed preferred to work in isolation in his office, while Sandy delighted in talking with others while propping his feet up on a coffee table. Sandy had used his libraries as convivial watering holes for after-hours cocktails with his top executives; Reed neither drank nor mingled.

Eager to better understand how to work with Sandy, Citi executives asked their Travelers counterparts to brief them on Travelers' "policies and procedures." "We don't have any" was the typical response. If the Citicorp executives wanted to know more or to get a decision on some issue, they were repeatedly told to "ask Sandy." And Sandy thrived on making nearly all the important—and many of the not-so-important—decisions. He promptly named himself and Chuck Prince to the charitable board of what would be the new Citigroup Foundation, joining Reed and Citi's philanthropy professional, Paul Ostergaard. Before the merger was proposed, Ostergaard had the authority to make grants of up to $250,000, involving

Reed only in decisions on larger sums. Sandy drastically lowered the threshold, setting $25,000 as the limit before a grant had to receive his approval.

The Citi managers, accustomed to Reed's hands-off management style, quickly dubbed Sandy's top deputies the "Sandy Sez" guys. They were amazed at the adoration and deference even the most senior Travelers executives had for their boss, who seemed to rule more as an emperor than a CEO. The whole place reflected Sandy's mood and thinking, changing almost daily. No wonder Sandy's office sported a flashing sign that signaled either THE CHAIRMAN IS HAPPY or THE CHAIRMAN IS NOT HAPPY, they observed.

Reed clearly noted the difference in style and remarked on it in an interview with *Fortune* magazine. "Travelers is a company that was built by an individual. The role Sandy plays is perceptible. People work for Sandy. I don't think it's the same thing at Citibank. I happen now to be chairman, but Wriston was before, and somebody else will be afterward. So I don't think it's quite as personalized a company."

Chuck Prince put it more succinctly to a Citi executive seeking guidance on how to work with Sandy: "What you have to learn about Sandy is that he wants to be the captain of the ship, ring the bell, blow the whistle, and navigate by the seat of his pants."

Under their captain, the Travelers executives—most of whom had been together since the beginning of Sandy's comeback, if not from his first triumphs—knew one another intimately and had worked together in planning-group sessions or cross-selling efforts. But many of the senior Citicorp executives had little history with their company and didn't know one another or even Reed very well. Jack Morris, who handled press relations for Reed, saw more of Sandy in the first few months of planning the merger than he had seen of Reed in ten years. "Jack, do we need to talk?" Sandy would call out to Morris if he saw him down the hall. In contrast, Citi officials had trouble getting appointments to see Reed.

The frustrations began to set in toward the end of June. The Federal Reserve still hadn't approved the merger. Under Travelers' novel strategy, the financial giant was converting to a bank holding company in order to purchase Citicorp. The Fed, which would regulate the new entity, didn't want to take any chances. It wanted to examine all aspects of the transaction and expose and analyze all the risks that might affect the combined company. In essence, the Fed was performing its own due diligence with an eye toward protecting the public's interest. To that end it demanded reams and reams of paperwork from both Travelers and Citicorp. Chuck Prince and Heidi Miller worked overtime providing the Fed with detailed explanations and information to reassure the regulators that the new company would be governable and easily monitored after the deal was approved.

Sandy, of course, had never before acquired a highly regulated company, and the delay was irritating him. That irritation was evident in more than the usual screaming. When Travelers tax executive Irwin Ettinger sought guidance from the Securities and Exchange Commission on a complicated accounting issue, Sandy went through the roof.

"If you hadn't raised the question, maybe it would have been ignored!" he yelled at Ettinger. "You better not derail this deal!"

The Fed's hearing in June on the proposed deal attracted protesters waving red umbrellas. They urged the regulators to reject the deal on the grounds that neither company had done enough business in minority and low-income communities. "By definition, the proposed entity is too big to address local community needs," declared Sarah Ludwig, attorney with the New York City Community Reinvestment Task Force.

Prince, representing Travelers at the hearing, tried to make light of the protesters and their red umbrellas. "That shows we have a powerful brand," the attorney quipped. "Even our opponents are using it."

Sandy wasn't amused. By August, he was livid at the lack of progress. He pestered Miller to set up meetings with regulatory officials to nudge them along. "We can't," she responded. "It's August, and no one is in Washington. They're on vacation."

"What do you mean, they're on vacation?" Sandy growled.

"No one's around," Miller said, "and the point person on our application is in Alaska for the month."

That touched off another rant. "Why is this guy in Alaska when we have a deal to do?" Sandy screamed.

CULTURE CLASH

Even as the Fed was considering whether to allow the merger, Travelers and Citicorp executives were pushing ahead on the assumption it would be okayed. One day Citi's retail banking chief Bill Campbell phoned Bob Willumstad, who was visiting his daughter in California. Campbell told the Commercial Credit head that a giant state-owned bank in Poland was being put up for sale.

"What the hell do you want me for?" Willumstad asked.

"Well, it's a bank with a lot of branches," Campbell replied, "and we don't have anybody in Citicorp who has any experience with large branch systems."

Willumstad was floored. For years at Chemical Bank he had fought Citicorp to establish the biggest and best branch banking system in the country. Now here was the head of retail banking at his former competitor confessing that they didn't know what they were doing.

"If that's the case, then maybe we shouldn't do this merger," Willumstad said.

Campbell ignored the remark. "Don't worry, I'm sending the G-4 to pick you up," he said.

When Willumstad met the corporate jet at the airport, he knew Sandy hadn't approved this particular trip. The expensive jet had flown to California "deadhead," with no passengers aboard. Sandy would never have approved such an extravagance. *Come to think of it,* Willumstad said to himself, *Sandy would have told me to fly back coach class.* In New York the jet stopped long enough to pick up two Citicorp executives and then flew on to Warsaw. The trio met with the Polish finance minister, then spent three days studying the state-owned Pekao Group, which had 700 branch offices.

Back in New York, Willumstad met with Bob Lipp, John Reed, and Bill Campbell.

"This bank is a great opportunity," Willumstad told them. "We just need to install strong management and strong technology to run it."

"That's a problem," Campbell replied.

"Why?" asked Willumstad.

"We have lousy systems, and nobody at Citi has run anything that big," Campbell explained.

Again Willumstad was shocked to find that the mega-bank known as a technology pioneer couldn't easily absorb the much smaller Polish bank. "Then why the hell are we merging with you?" he shot back.

As Willumstad and Marge Magner, working under their old boss Bob Lipp, delved into Citibank's retail operation, they realized that Campbell wasn't exaggerating the problem. The two Chemical Bank veterans found they knew far more about running a branch bank system than their Citi counterparts. Moreover, behind Citi's renowned international branch was a network of mini-fiefdoms that didn't have uniform standards, technology, or accountability. "Citibank doesn't run as a whole, but as parts that don't work together," Willumstad informed Magner and Lipp.

That didn't daunt the trio. They had long ago whipped Commercial Credit's branch system of loan offices into shape, and they could do it again at Citibank. They quickly began setting up systems to apply the same discipline and training around the globe and began merging the bank's consumer operations into Travelers'. Willumstad would manage all consumer lending and Citibank credit cards, while Magner ran not only Commercial Credit, but also risk management for the entire consumer group. Just as she had years earlier in Baltimore, Magner set up data-driven processes to monitor credit risk and performance. The two kept Lipp and Campbell, their co-CEOs, apprised of their progress and were gratified that Campbell, a former tobacco executive, didn't interfere but instead concentrated on his own strong suits, marketing and branding.

But other aspects of the merger revealed the strong cultural differences that marked the two companies. Joseph Plumeri, a veteran brokerage executive who had been with Sandy since the early days, had finally turned around Primerica's insurance operations in the wake of Art Williams's ouster. He had been successful in no small part because he used many of Williams's methods, including huge revival-style stadium gatherings where he made inspirational speeches. At one meeting he spoke for five hours straight, pausing only long enough midway through to change his sweat-soaked shirt. Now appointed head of North American branch banking for the combined companies, he immediately brought to his new post the same zeal and inspirational tactics. He invited Citibank branch managers to a raucous cheerleading event in Madison Square Garden, where he promised to "transform" Citibank branches and employees. He ordered everyone in the branches to become licensed to sell insurance and securities. Tellers were renamed "financial associates," and if they successfully completed the licensing requirements they would become "client financial analysts." Branches would be called "financial centers." Bill Campbell attended the meeting and was amazed at Plumeri's evangelistic style, especially when he urged his audience to reply loudly and repeatedly to his exhortations.

"Crazy Lord Jesus, this is one of the most incredible things my eyes have ever seen," Campbell muttered to himself—and he didn't mean that as a compliment. Many of the branch managers in attendance found Plumeri's display offensive and demeaning.

Soon afterward Plumeri pushed the branch managers to improve sales. His relentless pressure began to annoy, then antagonize the managers, many of whom at first complained about his tactics, pointing out that theirs was a customer-relations job, not a sales job. Brokers and insurance salesmen were paid lucrative commissions, they argued, but bank managers received nothing but their customers' ire if they tried to push too many products and services down their throats. Then they began resigning. Reed badly wanted to see improved sales and profits from his branches, but he couldn't stomach this sort of radical shift in how business was done. He took his branch managers' complaints to Sandy, who eventually agreed that Plumeri's tactics weren't working.

At the same time Plumeri was trying to impose his high-pressure salesmanship on Citibank branch managers, Citicorp executives were trying to convince their Travelers colleagues to become more analytical and thoughtful. Their favorite tool was Six Sigma, a system for improving the quality of processes and products to achieve extraordinary customer satisfaction. Named for a statistical concept, the system measures every process in a business with an aim toward reducing errors to the smallest possible number. John Reed, along with such notable executives as Jack Welch at General Electric and Larry Bossidy at AlliedSignal, was a strong advocate of Six Sigma. After much cajoling, James Bailey, a Citi veteran who was the corporate Six Sigma quality director, persuaded Sandy to visit AlliedSignal in New Jersey to learn more about the system's perfect-performance objectives. After listening to the AlliedSignal executives explain the process and the benefits of Six Sigma, the group sat down for lunch. Sandy began probing to discover the direct benefits of Six Sigma.

"How does it increase revenue?" he asked.

Well, it improves performance, which will eventually result in improved revenue.

"Does it help cut expenses, in technology or people?" he asked.

Bailey ventured that Six Sigma could produce an estimated $500 million in savings.

"I don't see it anywhere," Sandy retorted.

"This guy is making this stuff up," added Lipp, who knew a thing or two about cost cutting.

Sandy made one last attempt to find a benefit in Six Sigma: "Does it help the stock price?"

When Sandy didn't get a definite answer on that, Bailey knew Sandy would never become a dedicated follower of Six Sigma. Soon thereafter Bailey went to Reed and asked to be reassigned. "I can see Sandy's not going to buy into Six Sigma," Bailey told Reed. "Sandy has to have immediate impact."

Other tensions between Citi's and Travelers' consumer operations arose over the credit-card business. Citicorp, the nation's top issuer of credit cards, had purchased AT&T's Universal Card portfolio for $3.5 billion in cash earlier in 1998. Just as the Citibank branches operated in independent territories, Citicorp's pervasive credit-card business comprised twenty-four different systems. With the addition of the AT&T card portfolio, Citicorp's card business was far and away the largest, 50 percent larger than its closest rival, MBNA. As Willumstad reviewed the new portfolio, he realized that no one at Citicorp had taken steps to integrate the Universal Card into the existing credit-card business, a step that would produce immense cost savings. Angry and baffled, he started asking questions. He found that the credit-card managers and the technology staffs refused to work together. Keeping their separate territories was costing about $150 million annually, Willumstad figured.

"This is real money being thrown away," Willumstad told Bill Campbell in a meeting at Citicorp Center. "We've been screwed by this transaction."

Campbell, normally an easygoing executive, blew up at the Travelers executive. "You guys keep criticizing us. You weren't here. You don't know what we've dealt with," Campbell yelled, then stormed out of the meeting. He apologized for the outburst the next day.

CORPORATE CHAOS

If occasional tensions marred the integration of the various consumer operations, they still looked idyllic compared to the problems arising as Travelers and Citicorp executives tried to mesh the corporate operations. Travelers had acquired Salomon Brothers only months before the merger with Citicorp was negotiated. Travelers had been struggling to meld the risk-hungry traders and investment bankers from Salomon with the more staid Smith Barney brokers. Now a new source of potential friction— Citicorp's global corporate bankers—was being thrown into the volatile mix. Dimon and Maughan had been openly warring before the merger, and now they had to deal with yet a third "co-CEO," Citi's Victor Menezes.

The mission was straighforward enough: create a corporate banking colossus that could do any financial transaction anywhere in the world for any company. In theory, the combination had much promise. Each side could bring to the party not only new products and services unfamiliar to the other side, but also a new list of clients to whom both sides could sell their various products and services. Citibank prided itself on its Global Relationship Bank, which provided loans, cash management, and other financial services to 1,700 of the world's largest companies. Salomon viewed itself as having a leading global franchise in bond underwriting, specializing in companies with less-than-stellar credit records that paid high rates for bonds and loans.

In practice, the combination simply wasn't working. The Citi bankers wanted to preserve their reputation as globe-trotting bankers to the world's elite corporations, customers that demanded the highest levels of service from conservative financial experts. They wanted a work environment heavy on staff and bureaucracy to ensure that their customers never wanted for anything and that Citicorp's name was as recognizable around the world as that of Coca-Cola or Gillette. Salomon Smith Barney's culture was more entrepreneurial, focused on taking advantage of developing situations. It was an environment in which any executive would jump in to clinch a deal, and they resented Citicorp's obsession with its brand name. "I used to be an investment banker, now I'm a brand manager," Maughan joked to his Salomon colleagues.

Turf battles erupted over who would get the first shot at a new client and over who would manage the relationships with existing clients. One of the most serious rifts developed abroad, where Citibank had a strong presence in corporate banking but was weak in securities underwriting. Salomon was exactly the opposite: strong in securities underwriting but without an extensive foreign presence. What on paper seemed a good fit that made sense for both clients and the new company in practice dissolved in a heated battle over who would serve which clients.

The three co-CEOs tried to resolve some of the problems in "integration meetings." But too often the meetings became mired in Citibank's quantitative, chart-laden presentations, after which Salomon executives would joke that they had been "Citibanked." The commercial bankers came away worried that the investment bankers weren't taking the problems seriously enough and were looking for ways to evade their responsibilities to the overall organization.

Then in late summer disaster struck. Russia repudiated much of its international debt, sending financial markets into a tailspin. The resulting meltdown in world credit markets in turn triggered the collapse of a big hedge fund called Long-Term Capital Management. Citicorp suffered enormous losses in the credit markets. Salomon, too, was hit hard by the credit markets' plunge, but it took a big hit as well from its dealings with Long-Term Capital.

Amid the financial carnage the three heads of the corporate-banking operations became even more protective of their individual turf. Dimon, especially, seemed to make it his mission to save Salomon Smith Barney at the expense of everything else. He became so entrenched in fighting for his "baby" that he rarely made appearances in his president's office at Citicorp Center headquarters. That made it easier to avoid Sandy, too.

At the same time, Dimon became openly derisive of Maughan's management capabilities and his obvious talent for "sucking up" to both Reed and Sandy. Dimon's behavior became disruptive enough that Bob Lipp, his longtime friend, warned him to tone it down. Arthur Zankel, a Travelers director, told Dimon, "I have the greatest regard for your abilities, but you're treating Deryck, an enormous asset, like an enormous liability." Many Citi insiders had high regard for Maughan's skills; he was a great "customer's man" with the polish and stature to impress clients. With his extensive experience in Japan and in Europe, the dapper Brit had excellent international contacts and credentials.

Maughan also was far from happy with the corporate bank's ruling triumvirate. Citi's Menezes, a native of India, was Citibank's chief financial officer and hadn't run a commercial-banking operation in years. He was struggling to catch up with Dimon and Maughan, which only increased Maughan's frustration with the power-sharing arrangement. He began openly making wisecracks about the "hydra." "We have so many heads around here, it just spins," he started saying to anyone who would listen.

Lacking clear lines of authority, the corporate bank was in disarray. The three-headed executive team couldn't reach agreements, their troops were squabbling, and the integration of the two companies was effectively stalled. By September, Dimon, Maughan, and Menezes agreed on one thing: The triumvirate wasn't working. In a rare display of unity, the trio wrote a two-page memo asking Sandy and Reed to kill the hydra. They set up a meeting with the two co-CEOs at which they planned to plead that one person be named for the job while the other two were reassigned.

"Deryck, you make the pitch," Dimon said. "You're excellent at making presentations."

At the meeting, Maughan acted as the hydra's spokesman. "We're doing the best we can, but it's not optimal for us individually and certainly not for the people who work for us," he began. "This is a very tough, hugely competitive business against very capable firms. The hydra is slowing us down and is confusing. It's unreasonable to force this on the three of us."

"We want the three of you to work it out," Reed responded.

Having the problem thrown back at them wasn't what Maughan, Dimon, and Menezes expected. They looked at one another helplessly. *What are they hoping we'll do?* Maughan thought to himself. *Do they expect one of us to withdraw?* he wondered as he prepared to answer.

"We're saying we can't work it out. That's why you're paid gazillions," Maughan said. "Go ahead, we offer ourselves for you to choose."

"Well, I guess we need to do something," Sandy said.

"Okay," Reed added.

Then dead silence. If Sandy's office sign had been in the meeting, it would have been flashing THE CHAIRMAN IS NOT HAPPY. The mounting losses and the internal chaos were driving down the stock of both Travelers and Citicorp, erasing billions of dollars of market value. Even worse, the Federal Reserve still hadn't approved the merger, punishing the stock prices. The meeting adjourned with no further comment.

Finally, on October 8, 1998, the Federal Reserve Board approved Travelers' application to merge with Citicorp. Citigroup was born. But the Fed cautioned that without legislation overturning longtime banking laws, Citigroup would be required in a few years to divest itself of certain operations.

BALLROOM BRAWL

At the first meeting of the new company's board of directors, Sandy and Reed appeared confident that their plan would work, despite the pall of the sagging stock price hanging over the new company. The board consisted of eighteen directors, nine from each of the two companies; for the most part, they were older executives. For the first time in years, the youthful Jamie Dimon wasn't a director. When, early in the meeting, Sandy cracked,

"It's nice to have adult supervision," some directors took the comment as a jab at Dimon. As the meeting progressed, Sandy seemed poised to place the blame for the merger's troubles on the president. Andrall Pearson, one of the directors, tried to cut off that line of reasoning before it could be extended. "Sandy, you can't blame Jamie or any other one guy when you have hydra-headed monsters running everything," the former Harvard Business School professor said. "Three guys are reporting to two CEOs— for Christ's sake, that's an organization design that won't work."

When the new company's management group assembled at Armonk for its next meeting, Jamie Dimon seemed angry and isolated, as did the executives dubbed "Team Jamie" for their loyalty to him. They talked to one another but to hardly anyone else in the group. When Dimon reviewed the corporate group's problems, he acted as if questions from anyone, even Sandy or Reed, were inappropriate or ill formed. At a break in the meeting, Citi's Bill Campbell, who liked Dimon, warned the younger man, "You don't talk down to Sandy Weill or John Reed."

Nevertheless, Dimon didn't change his condescending, almost belligerent, behavior when the meeting resumed. Some Citi executives found his attitude disrespectful. *Everyone in this room is a type A personality,* Citi's technology expert Ed Horowitz thought. *But Dimon isn't adapting to the new environment.* On the other side of the room, Chuck Prince, who had probably spent more time with Sandy and Dimon than his own family since 1986, also watched Dimon's strident behavior and concluded that Dimon wanted to run his own show. *Dodge City isn't big enough for both Sandy and Jamie anymore,* Prince thought to himself.

Sandy and Reed, who were trying hard to work together, shared their thoughts about Dimon after the management meeting. As much as Reed liked Dimon and respected his enormous talents, he found the personal dynamics between the mentor and his protégé unacceptable and strange. For Sandy, bringing Reed into Travelers was like bringing a new spouse to meet one's family. All of a sudden, Sandy saw his increasingly difficult relationship with a family member from an outsider's perspective, and it looked terribly dysfunctional.

To celebrate the unprecedented merger, Citigroup planned a lavish weekend getaway for the top one hundred forty executives and their spouses at the grand Greenbrier Resort in the West Virginia mountains. It was classic Sandy—bringing managers into the "family" in a relaxed social setting, mixing business with pleasure. Citi had never invited spouses to a corporate retreat.

At the business session during the day, Sandy and Reed asked their top executives to make presentations to the group on the merger's progress. When it was Dimon's turn, he gave an obligatory summation without seeking input or discussion. He clearly viewed the presentations as inconsequential.

Then Michael Carpenter, who ran Travelers Life & Annuity, stood up and shocked the room when he bluntly said, "There's too much infighting." The managers broke into small groups to devise recommendations for smoothing the merger process. Various solutions were suggested, but every group had a similar plea: "Fix the management of the corporate business."

That evening, on October 24, 1998, Citigroup threw a black-tie dinner and dance. After the tense meetings earlier, the executives enjoyed drinking and dancing. Dimon, his wife, Judy, and his closest Smith Barney colleagues, Steve Black and Charlie Scharf, with their wives, sat by themselves at a table off to the side. The tuxedo ties were off, their shirts open, the alcohol flowing.

Around midnight, many of the couples were trading dancing partners as the band played rock-and-roll tunes from the 1970s—when many of the forty-something executives had come of age. Black, who had never gotten along with Maughan, told his wife, Deborah, they should switch partners with the Maughans, dancing nearby.

"Why?" she asked, knowing that Maughan had been dismissive of her husband since coming in as co-CEO with Dimon.

"Come on, it's not a slow dance," Black said playfully. "It's the right thing to do."

Black then offered to dance with Maughan's wife, Va, as a peace overture. Maughan didn't return the gesture. He looked down at Black's wife, then turned and walked away. Deborah was left stranded on the dance floor. Black immediately dropped Va Maughan and went to rescue his humiliated wife. He escorted her off the floor, then stormed over to Maughan.

Unleashing a torrent of expletives, Black seized Maughan's arm, squeezing it hard. "It's bad enough how you treat me," Black yelled, as the music stopped. "But you're not going to treat my wife like that!" Maughan said nothing. But Va came charging across the ballroom floor to confront Black herself. Poking her finger in his chest, she yelled, "Don't you ever talk to my husband like that again! He's the CEO of this company!"

The melee caught Dimon's attention. He rushed over and pulled Black aside to see what was happening. "I'm going to kill him," Black fumed to his close friend.

Shocked at Maughan's rude behavior, Dimon confronted him as Maughan was about to leave the ballroom. He grabbed the taller Maughan and yelled, "I want to ask you a simple question. Either you intended to snub Blackie's wife or you didn't. Which is it?"

Maughan didn't answer and pulled back to turn away. Dimon spun him around, popping a button off Maughan's shirt, and shouted, "Don't you ever turn your back on me when I'm talking!"

Va Maughan started screaming, "This man is attacking my husband!" When the two men separated, Maughan's wife fled to the Weills' suite, interrupting their late-night drinks with the Lipps.

The next morning all the gossip was about the confrontation. Eduardo Mestre, Citi's investment banking head, and his wife had left the dance before midnight. They were eating breakfast when Jim Boshart, another Salomon Smith Barney official, ran up to their table. "You're not going to believe what happened last night! Jamie and Deryck had a fight!"

"What?" Mestre gasped. As Boshart described the attempted blows, Mestre kept repeating, "Oh my god."

Minutes later, two vans pulled in front of the Greenbrier to take two groups of executives to the Citigroup jets. The group returning in Dimon's plane stood on one side; the other group included Maughan. No one said a word as Dimon approached Maughan.

"Sorry," Dimon said. "I shouldn't have done that."

Maughan harrumphed, saying nothing. As it had on the dance floor the night before, Maughan's silence came off as pompous and condescending. But shrewd corporate politician that he was, he had carefully weighed the risks and refused to be drawn into the fray.

Reed and Sandy talked later on Sunday about the fracas.

"Jamie's the problem," Sandy told Reed.

Reed acknowledged that Dimon hadn't done his part to smooth the difficult management transition. "Maybe you're right," he told Sandy. The Citibank chief, a decorous executive with a strict moral code, found Dimon's confrontation with Maughan totally unacceptable.

"Jamie's got to go," Sandy said.

"We're co-CEOs, so if that's your opinion, I'll support you," Reed replied.

On Monday morning, the Citigroup chieftains called Chuck Prince into their library and asked him to conduct an investigation of the incident and report to them at the end of the week.

Arthur Zankel stopped by on Wednesday to see Sandy. As a director and friend, he knew that Sandy was weighing whether to dump his once-beloved protégé.

"You tried A, you tried B, you tried C," Zankel said. "Everybody is calling for something to happen. This is impeding the progress of the company. It is enough. You tried."

"We haven't been getting along for a long time," Sandy offered. "But something like this is so final." He also wondered aloud what firing Dimon would do to his and Joan's longtime friendship with Ted and Themis Dimon. But he added, "John is ready to fire Jamie."

"Well, you know how John is about firing people," Zankel replied. "It's as easy as belching to him."

Indeed, in the last decade Reed had forced out several possible successors: Former president Richard Braddock left in 1992; Christopher Steffen came from Kodak in 1992 and left in 1995; and Pei-yuan Chia, who had spent twenty-two years at the bank and had risen to lead Citibank's consumer businesses, suddenly retired in 1996.

When Prince reported to Sandy and Reed on Friday, he found them in shirtsleeves and acting very much like a team. The general counsel recounted the recollections from fifteen individuals who witnessed the event, described by some as a "ballroom brawl" or "a heated round of pushing and shoving." At the suggestion of physical contact, Reed flinched as if there had been violence. Sandy, the street fighter, took it in stride; Dimon was a virile, dominant man who had a tendency to get excited.

"You have to do it for the good of the organization," said Reed, looking pained. "I always thought Jamie would succeed the two of us. I thought it would be great, but Jamie's behavior was totally inappropriate, especially for someone who's going to be the next CEO."

The co-CEOs also discussed Maughan's involvement and decided he shouldn't escape unscathed.

"Let's sleep on it," Sandy said, dismissing Prince.

"NO HUGS, PLEASE"

On Saturday, Sandy called Prince at home. "We have to ask Jamie to leave the company. Get everything ready for tomorrow." The general counsel knew this Saturday would not be one for relaxing. As he sped toward Citigroup's Manhattan headquarters from his home in Weston, Connecticut, Prince mentally reviewed what he had to do in the next twenty-four hours: Firing Dimon would be a material event that would require board approval, legal documentation, and press releases. Citigroup's global corporate unit had already planned a meeting for Sunday at 4:00 P.M. to discuss the managers' pleas for change at the top. They wanted change, they were going to get change.

On Sunday, November 1, 1998, Dimon relaxed in a Smith Barney sweatshirt at his large Park Avenue apartment. He believed that the afternoon meeting at Armonk would finally answer his and his colleagues' request to change the corporate group's leadership. For a while he had assumed he would be selected as the sole survivor to run the operation. But something didn't feel right. Normally he would have been consulted during the week about his opinion of possible changes. *Well, maybe Sandy and John just want me to move to headquarters and work full-time as president,* he mused.

Dimon didn't have time to worry about it; he was hosting a brunch for about one hundred investment bankers and recruits, and the doorbell was starting to ring. As guests chatted in his living room and on the terrace, Dimon was summoned to take a phone call from Sandy.

"Can you come up to Armonk a little bit earlier?" Sandy asked. "Around one or two?"

"I have people here," Dimon answered. "I'll come up early, but I can't leave so soon."

Sandy, Reed, and Prince were in Armonk by early afternoon. They had briefed the board about recent events justifying Dimon's removal as president. As the director most knowledgeable about recent events, Zankel explained, "Greenbrier isn't the deciding factor. It only serves to make the hot griddle hotter. You can't sit around with this thing anymore." With Reed and Weill in agreement, the board approved, even though many of the Travelers directors did so with a heavy heart. They had watched the young and talented Dimon blossom into a powerful leader they would have supported to lead Citigroup one day.

When Sandy and Reed placed a confidential call to Bob Lipp to inform him of the action they were about to take, he was aghast. "You guys are crazy," he said. "Don't do that."

Next, Prince presented Sandy and Reed with two press releases he had prepared. One announced, in effect, Jamie Dimon Resigns as Citigroup President; the other, Jamie Dimon Is Fired as Citigroup President. If Dimon wouldn't resign when asked, they were prepared to fire him.

Dimon arrived at the Armonk planning center after two o'clock that afternoon. He casually followed Sandy and Reed into one of the small meeting rooms, and they sat down in comfortable armchairs. On the drive up, Dimon had figured the co-CEOs would ask him to work more closely with them. He was excited to have the tri-heads out of the way, so the corporate group could get down to working out the merger. Even though he sensed that Sandy was fed up with him, Dimon believed he would be a vital force in Citigroup's future.

"We've made our decisions, which we want to share with you," Sandy began. "Deryck is going to leave the corporate group and become vice chairman of strategy and Japan. We've decided Victor Menezes and Mike Carpenter will be co-heads of the corporate bank."

Dimon was puzzled. *Great, let's move out Maughan, but Carpenter? What a shocker,* he thought. *His tenure at Kidder Peabody had been criticized and he hasn't been involved in the securities business since then.* But Dimon's mind stopped racing when he heard Sandy's next words.

"And we want you to resign."

Dimon froze. "Okay," he gulped, in a complete state of shock. Never in a million years did he expect this. He expected heads to roll, but definitely not his.

"The board understands this is happening and believes it's in the best interest of Citigroup," Sandy continued.

"If that's what you want," Dimon said calmly, stoically, still in utter disbelief.

"Is that all you have to say?" Reed spoke up. "Boy, you're sure taking this well."

"What do you expect me to do?" Dimon asked, sensing that Reed anticipated he would come out swinging. "John, you've obviously thought this through, and there's nothing I can do about it."

"Would you like to see the press release?" Reed asked.

"Yes," said Dimon. *They've got this whole thing orchestrated,* he realized, *a fait accompli.*

"Would you like to talk to the press with us in a conference call?" Reed continued.

"Yes, I would be happy to do that. But first I'll want to tell my wife and family," Dimon replied. "I'll do the call from home."

"Would you like to speak to the management committee when they arrive?" Reed queried. Dimon nodded.

"Do you want us to explain our decision?" Reed inquired.

"You don't have to explain it," said the newly unemployed forty-two-year-old, as Reed and Sandy walked out.

That was Prince's cue to enter. He shut the door and sat down. "Well, here we are," the general counsel said. For the first time since he had known Dimon for twelve years, the talkative Dimon was speechless. He looked as if he'd just been run over by a truck, completely blindsided. "Jamie, I'm sorry," Prince offered.

"Chuck, I understand," Dimon finally said. "It's not your fault."

Prince then reviewed with the former company president the press release about his resignation. "It's absolutely fine," Dimon said without requesting a single change.

Then Reed came back into the small room to wish Dimon "the best." He added, "Don't worry about severance. We'll be generous."

Dimon hadn't even thought about money. He felt as if his own family had just thrown him out. It was his company, too, and he still wanted to build a great business.

By now, it was only three o'clock, so Dimon had to wait a long, painful hour until the management team arrived. Alone in the meeting room, he called his wife.

"Judy, I'm going to tell you something and please, please, don't tell me I'm making a joke," Dimon said. The agonized tone of his voice made it clear he wasn't joking. "They asked me to resign, and I resigned." Before she had a chance to respond, Dimon promised to be home in a couple of hours after meeting some senior executives.

Bob Lipp and Mike Carpenter, who knew what had just happened, came in to see Dimon privately. Lipp simply hugged his good friend and colleague. "Mike, whatever you need, I'm at your service," Dimon told Carpenter. When Dimon left his meeting room, he crossed paths with Maughan, who was also leaving an adjoining room. Maughan had just been informed of his demotion—being kicked upstairs and taken out of operational authority. Dimon's and Maughan's failure to get along had cost both men their jobs, but Maughan was still with the company.

"Best of luck to you," Dimon said.

"And to you," Maughan replied.

As the twenty top corporate banking executives began arriving, they immediately knew something serious was about to happen. The public-relations managers were standing by, and the two most animated and funny executives among them—Dimon and Maughan—were eerily silent, almost beaten. The managers took their seats in the down-filled armchairs, anxious to find out what was happening. After several minutes of uncomfortable chatter, Reed announced, "Jamie is resigning."

Before anyone could gasp, Dimon stood up. "Look, I've been with this company for fifteen years. I put my heart and soul into it. I want to tell you it's a fabulous place. Keep on making yourself proud."

Dimon caught his breath; every executive in the room was motionless. Then in his typical rapid-fire manner, Dimon continued: "I am sorry it didn't work out. I know that I have some blame for it. If I can help anybody, that's what I'm here to do. I still love this company. It has an incredibly fantastic future. You are all friends of mine, and I wish you the best."

The executives, many of whom had been at Dimon's house hours before, jumped up to give him a standing ovation. Dimon walked out; Sandy followed.

"You've been very gracious and very nice," the onetime mentor said. "I still respect you and love you."

Dimon tensed at the sudden show of affection. "Look, Sandy, I don't know what to say."

"I'm sorry it had to come to this," Sandy said, moving to embrace Dimon.

Dimon recoiled. "No hugs, please."

With Armonk an hour north of Manhattan, Dimon had time during the drive home to think about what to tell his three daughters: Julia, thirteen; Laura, eleven; and Kara, nine. They were young, but they were certain to hear about his firing. They attended a prestigious private girls' school where many parents worked on Wall Street. Besides, starting tomorrow, they would see their father home and not working. Dimon arrived at his apartment around 5:30 P.M. The conference call with the press was scheduled for thirty minutes later.

With tears in her eyes, Judy met her husband at the door. She gave him a hug and a kiss, clearly stunned. "What did you do that was so bad?" she asked in bewilderment. Like Joan Weill, Judy Dimon—a smart, attractive woman—had worked tirelessly to get to know the families of Dimon's colleagues, especially at Smith Barney.

"Judy, get the girls," Dimon said, knowing he had to tell them before the press call came. They gathered at the kitchen table.

"Girls, I was the president of Citigroup and Travelers before that. I resigned today," Dimon said, looking into their blue eyes like his. "What that means is that I've given up my positions and titles. I was asked to resign, but . . ." He hesitated, but he wanted them to hear it from him. "I was fired."

"You were fired, Dad?" Julia blurted out.

"Yes," Dimon said.

"Who did that? Who fired you?" the other two continued.

"Sandy and John," their father said.

"But isn't Sandy your partner, your friend?" another asked.

"Sometimes things go bad and you don't see eye to eye. Some of your friends' parents have gotten divorced. It doesn't make either side bad."

Dimon then turned to the conference call. Sandy, Reed, and Dimon spoke amiably of one another and of their optimism about Citigroup's prospects. The co-CEOs explained that Dimon had trouble integrating the corporate businesses of Salomon Smith Barney and Citicorp, and that employees voiced concerns at a retreat at the Greenbrier Resort. No mention was made of any brawl. The chieftains decided it was time to institute a clearer chain of command, they explained, with a new hierarchy that would have given Dimon less authority than he wanted. That decision ultimately led to his departure, they told the press. Dimon confirmed that the decision was "mutual."

A reporter on the call asked Sandy if his daughter Jessica's departure was a factor. "Absolutely not," Sandy said. "That happened a long time ago."

After the press call ended, Sandy called the top executives who weren't part of the corporate group meeting that afternoon, such as consumer banking head Willumstad and CFO Miller. As one of the few high-ranking women on Wall Street, Miller had gotten a lot of favorable attention, even being named *Fortune*'s number-two most important woman in business. She originally had joined Travelers as Dimon's assistant.

"John let Jamie go," Sandy told her.

Miller thought for a minute. She had seen Sandy distance himself from her close friend Dimon, but Sandy seemed to be pinning the decision on Reed.

"I understand," Miller said matter-of-factly. "Then we will go forward." She hung up and began frantically trying to reach Dimon. His line was busy past midnight, when she finally gave up.

The firing of Citigroup's heir apparent stunned Wall Street Monday morning. Worried about the loss of a leading industry star and likely successor, important analysts rushed to downgrade Citigroup stock, as they raised questions about the viability of the financial-services mega-merger. The stock, which had already declined 36 percent from its high reached not long after the merger's announcement in April, tumbled nearly 5 percent on the news of Dimon's abrupt departure.

A heartsick Dimon went to his downtown office at Salomon Smith Barney to say his good-byes. After he bid farewell to the hundreds of employees on the huge trading floor, he turned to leave. First there was one clap, then another, then ten, then twenty until the floor erupted in applause. Dimon felt like he was in a movie. He blew a kiss and left.

As he walked out the front door under the metal umbrella sculpture, a tearful executive assistant, Jennifer Bush, hugged him. "I'm so sorry you're leaving. It will never be the same without your leadership." Dimon spread his arms toward the office tower. "Look what we've all built together. It still goes on, and I'm proud of that."

That night, at a nearby Italian restaurant, about one hundred senior managers stopped by to join Jamie for drinks. After the rounds of toasting, Dimon groaned, "Guys, I feel like I'm laid out at my own wake."

After the stock market's pummeling, Citigroup management called an employee meeting that was broadcast throughout the company. Instead of a rousing pep rally that played down the loss of Dimon and played up Citigroup's exciting future as the biggest financial empire in the world, the downbeat executives issued a sober call to arms to turn around the troubled company. Over the public-address system, Carpenter, their new boss, urged the corporate group to put "the tribes to one side," a reference to the many different firms that Sandy had cobbled together in the past decade to create this huge new company. "The Shearson tribe, the EF Hutton tribe, the Citi tribe, the Salomon tribe, the Smith Barney tribe—I don't belong to any one of those tribes," he proclaimed. "I belong to the tribe of share-holders. I would hope we could all put aside these individual tribal issues and form a new tribe."

When someone asked if Dimon's ejection was similar to Sandy's own ouster from American Express, the Citigroup co-CEO tried to make light of the comparison: "Jamie is going to end up getting a heck of a lot more calls than I did."

Those colleagues closest to Dimon were in a quandary about whether to stay at the firm. Steve Black, a Salomon Smith Barney vice chairman, was particularly angry—not only at Dimon's treatment, but also at the eleva-tion of Carpenter and Menezes, who had much less experience in the secu-rities industry than he did.

Sandy didn't want to hear it. "I'll be damned if you're going to benefit from the changes," he told Black, a handsome man with a moustache. "I blame you, too, for what happened." Then Sandy gave him a choice: "You must get behind the new heads, or—"

But before Sandy could finish, Black interrupted. "You just blew Jamie's brains out for all the wrong reasons—I can't condone that."

"Then it's time for you to go," Sandy said briskly. "I need everybody on the same team."

"Fine, I'm out. I'm done," Black responded angrily. After leaving Sal-omon Smith Barney, he accompanied his wife, Deborah, and three chil-dren on a safari in Zimbabwe and took race-car driving lessons in Italy. When he returned, he joined Citigroup's rival, Chase Bank, as its head of global equities.

In the following weeks, Citigroup and Dimon worked out a severance package worth $30 million in cash and stock. A key point: The forty-two-year-old was barred from poaching ex-colleagues for three years.

Dimon, until then the prototypical Wall Street Mr. Big, didn't have a clue what to do, except that he wanted to get back into fighting shape. He began taking boxing lessons. After missing family dinners for fifteen years, he insisted the family eat together every night. He also saw more of his parents, who no longer would have anything to do with their old friends Sandy and Joan.

For the first time in his life, Dimon had to decide what he wanted to be when he grew up. He took out the proverbial white pad and wrote: in-vestor, teacher, author, stay-at-home dad. He decided his "craft" was fi-nancial services. Until the right opportunity came along, he set up an office in the Seagram Building, the same place to which Sandy had retreated with Dimon during his own corporate exile. Like the old days, Dimon occasionally lunched downstairs at the "company cafeteria," the elegant Four Seasons.

Within days of moving into his new office, Dimon was noshing with an old friend when Sandy strode into the Four Seasons. Nearly everyone in the restaurant's celebrity-filled Grill Room, many of whom had watched Dimon grow up at Sandy's side, knew what had happened between the two men only a few weeks earlier. Dimon sat directly in his former boss's path. Neither man made a move toward the other. Sandy, his gaze straight ahead, walked to his regular power table. Dimon, jaw clenched, looked down at his table as a chill settled over the room.

15

STALEMATE

The year 1998 had been one of courtship, engagement, and marriage for Sandy Weill and John Reed. But as 1999 opened, the honeymoon clearly was over. The real work of living together on a daily basis began in earnest. These two powerful personalities would be thrust together in the immense task of running the world's largest financial empire. There were branches to consolidate, operations to downsize, billion-dollar budgets to approve, and thousands of employees to lay off. Their original agreement to merge dictated that the two of them would make all decisions jointly and each would have an equal say. Their senior staff quickly discovered how difficult it would be to abide by such lofty rules.

The problems started with simple things. Scheduling a meeting, for instance. Reed, who thrived on international travel, was out of the country almost as often as he was in. Finding a time when Reed was in that was also convenient for Sandy—not to mention any other executives who might be involved—was nearly impossible. Once the two co-CEOs were corralled in a room, they confounded their subordinates by taking two entirely different approaches to problems. When the advertising department presented a campaign to introduce the world to the new Citigroup, Reed wanted to think conceptually about how to make the financial behemoth a globally recognized brand. Sandy wanted to zero in on the bottom line.

"We're in the personal-care business, like Gillette, who gets people to make an emotional decision to pay for their triple blades," Reed mused. "Finances are very personal to an individual much the same way—"

"As a shave?" Sandy asked playfully. He wanted to cut to the chase: How much would this ad campaign cost? How would it help profits?

Reed didn't take the hint. "The model I have is of a global consumer company that really helps the middle class with something they haven't been served well by historically," he continued, adding that Citigroup should become the Coca-Cola of finance, a brand name known around the world. "That's my vision. That's my dream."

"My goal is increasing shareholder value," Sandy interjected, glancing frequently at a nearby computer monitor displaying Citigroup's changing stock price. "I don't want to spend money without seeing results."

The advertising executives were bewildered. Which CEO's concerns should they address first? Moreover, they wondered how two people who seemed so out of touch with each other had ever worked out the complex details that brought their two companies together. When the meeting stretched past three hours, Sandy had enough of visions and conceptualizing, brands and images. The meeting was adjourned, leaving the advertising executives wondering what to do next.

Then a decision had to be made about benefits for Citigroup's 170,000 employees around the globe. By most measures Travelers benefits were stingy, consistent with Sandy's long-standing practice of slashing costs by reducing benefits and replacing them with stock options. Citicorp, like other big global banks, provided generous benefits.

Sandy wanted to immediately scale back Citicorp's lavish benefits. It would be a quick way to achieve cost savings and show the world how much more efficient the merged company could be. But Reed refused to be rushed. Citing a "moral obligation" to employees, Reed took the question under advisement and began one of his excruciatingly thorough analyses of the situation. Four months later, after what he told colleagues were "zillions of hours" of labor, Reed finally agreed to a plan that relied more heavily on stock options and less on direct expenditures from Citigroup's coffers. But he insisted that it wouldn't take effect until the year 2000.

That decision prompted a debate about the value of stock options. As usual, Sandy was an enthusiastic proponent of options for everyone. He wanted to encourage all employees to become part-owners of the company so that they would "think like shareholders."At his behest, 33,000 Citigroup employees were awarded "founders' stock options," increasing dramatically the number of Citi workers who owned stock.

But Reed didn't share Sandy's zeal for options. He feared they would become an end in themselves, prompting managers to quit caring about the company and its long-term future and to worry instead about their own personal net worth and how to get the stock price higher faster.

When Sandy insisted that top executives follow Travelers' policy of retaining all their stock options until they left the company, Reed and his Citibankers balked. "All or nothing is hard," said Reed, who had a number of older executives looking to sell stock for retirement and estate-planning purposes. The two men went back and forth for weeks before settling on a compromise: The top seventy executives must retain 75 percent of their stock holdings while part of Citigroup. Travelers executives were secretly delighted with the decision: At last they could sell some of their valuable holdings to diversify their portfolios.

As Sandy and Reed grappled with decisions, the differences in their individual styles were painfully obvious. Sandy preferred talking over problems with his executives while lounging on his couch or in one of the cushy chairs in the "library." Reed insisted on receiving detailed memos, to which he responded in like fashion. Sandy didn't like to read any memo longer than three pages, and usually read only the last paragraph or two of those. At planning meetings at Armonk, Sandy delighted in eating, drinking, and bonding with his management team. Reed, trim and remote, preferred to take a solitary stroll around the wooded property. Citi executives soon realized to their dismay that they were expected to spend the night at Armonk, and their Travelers colleagues took delight in warning them that Sandy or his bodyguard might make a bed check to be sure that no one had slipped away to spend the night at home. Reed was highly uncomfortable with so much intimacy, and he often distanced himself from the group, mentally if not physically. He confided to a colleague, "I get very quiet. I create space by not getting overly engaged." Sandy was all instinct and intuition; Reed, with his reading glasses frequently perched on the end of his nose, had the aura of a thoughtful college professor rather than a take-charge chief executive.

Selecting key executives for important jobs was a continual task in an organization as large as Citigroup. Reed almost always deferred to Citibank's large and experienced human-resources department, which had a staff, a budget, and power unheard of among most large companies. Sandy considered human resources a colossal waste of money. He relied on his line managers who ran businesses for advice about whom to promote or demote or fire. Reed took innumerable factors into account in making personnel decisions. "Sandy wants performance and loyalty, and not a hell of a lot else," Bill Campbell, the Citibank retail executive, explained to Reed.

For Sandy, business was his life. He wanted to talk about business all day and well into the night. Reed had outside interests. The MIT graduate liked to escape the world of finance by reading science books; he occasionally made references to the metaphysical poet John Donne. Sandy couldn't stand to be far from a stock-market tape. Citibankers swore that Sandy's head jerked to the up and down ticks of Citi's stock. Reed had little use for the minute-to-minute or even day-to-day fluctuations in his company's stock. He checked the stock price about once a month.

These disparate styles and methods of approaching decisions led executives to complain to one another that meetings with Sandy and Reed were much akin to watching a Ping-Pong game. Others suggested a more apt analogy would be two ships passing in the night, their lights only faintly visible to each other.

The co-CEOs posed a particular challenge to Bob Lipp, who had run Commercial Credit and then Travelers' insurance operations for Sandy and was now in charge of Citigroup's retail operations. The gregarious Lipp, a disciple of Sandy's cost-cutting, bottom-line management school, openly scoffed at Citi's formal, bloated structure. "We're getting back into the bureaucracy we all ran away from," he grumbled to his friend and colleague Bob Willumstad. "This isn't fun anymore."

Reed, who more than anyone else was responsible for ushering in the modern era of consumer banking, wanted to be intimately involved in that side of the business, much to Lipp's chagrin. Reed and Lipp collided often. Reed would devise plans, and Lipp would find ways to avoid implementing them. Eventually Lipp delegated Bob Willumstad to tend to Reed and make sure that his meddling didn't get out of hand.

"I really wish that my job were to run only the consumer side of the business, because I think it's a fantastic business," Reed candidly told a group of consumer bankers. "But I have been destined—you know, God punishes us all—to be constantly surrounded by the other part of the business, which inevitably gets us into trouble."

When Sandy got wind of those remarks, he was furious. And when a reporter for *Fortune* magazine called to inquire about Reed's preference for the consumer half of Citigroup, Sandy took it upon himself to speak for his co-CEO. "John now loves the corporate side of the business, and he's never going to say anything like that, ever again."

The tensions and pressures of being part of a new organization took a toll on former Travelers executives. Jeff Lane and Mary McDermott both chose to call it quits rather than endure the travails of the merger. "I've been through more mergers than any human being should ever be asked to," McDermott told Sandy when she retired.

Others stuck it out but desperately sought ways to cope with their dysfunctional bosses. Heidi Miller, Citigroup's chief financial officer, needed to meet frequently with the co-CEOs. At first she prepared her presentations to suit Sandy, her longtime boss. But as she learned Reed's priorities and idiosyncrasies, she tried to incorporate them into her reports, along with the myriad items required by bank regulators.

That drew Sandy's ire. He criticized Miller for spending too much time calibrating risk. He wanted to focus on actual returns. He understood risk in his gut and didn't need a bunch of figures that supposedly quantified it. "Every bank, per the Fed, must perform a risk-adjusted return analysis," Miller calmly explained. Reed much preferred the extreme analytical equations; he trusted numbers, not his gut.

After one particularly challenging session with Sandy and Reed early in 1999, Miller's head was spinning. "Reporting to John and Sandy in the same room at the same time requires doing a split-brain," she complained to Bill Pike, the investor-relations executive. "Even if both of them agree, I have to convince Sandy with one argument and John with a different argument. It's impossible to deal with them together."

Pike confessed that he, too, was completely frustrated. "We're being put in a horrible position trying to please two CEOs constantly wanting opposite things," he said. "What we do to please Sandy doesn't suit John. It's so nerve-racking because we have no clue how this co-stuff will pan out. John could win . . ."

Then Miller had an idea. Rather than give what amounted to two different presentations simultaneously, why not suggest that she would brief Sandy and Reed separately? It might be in violation of the merger agreement, but it would be much easier for her to make a logical, organized presentation to each of the two co-CEOs. She could spend her time with each one addressing his concerns and not wasting the other's time. Nervously, she took her idea to the two bosses. They agreed so hastily and enthusiastically that it dawned on Miller: They really don't like being in the same room together.

Still, the Citigroup chieftains professed that their partnership was thriving. Perceived conflicts were just part of the adjustment process for two men accustomed to running their own shows. When *BusinessWeek* asked how they were faring, Sandy replied, "I have no problem being a partner with John." Reed added, "We do have differences of temperament, but they work out pretty easily."

But then, just six months after the merger was approved, their simmering irritation boiled over for the first time. The inaugural quarterly earnings report for the new Citigroup was released on April 19, 1999, and it showed an astounding $3.36 billion in net income, the most of any American company, including giant General Electric. With merger efficiencies kicking in and global markets improving, the earnings topped Wall Street's most optimistic estimates. At the same time, Citigroup stock was soaring and now stood at $73, more than double the share price when the merger was completed in October 1998.

The customary conference call with Wall Street analysts presented a perfect opportunity for Sandy and Reed to show that their new business model was succeeding. The investor-relations executives set up the conference call from a "neutral zone"—a conference room on the executive floor—rather than from either CEO's office. As they ushered Sandy and Reed into the small, windowless room, they sensed trouble. Both men seemed uncomfortable rather than celebratory. Certainly Sandy wasn't happy with the setting. He traditionally conducted conference calls from the comfort of his tufted leather couch, where he could relax and banter and take full advantage of his skill in answering questions spontaneously. Reed clearly didn't want to even do the call.

Nevertheless, Sandy prepared for the call by poring over the numbers and firing questions at managers. He wanted to be fully conversant with the results. "Wall Street should love these earnings," he enthused, trying to pump up his partner.

"I just don't care about quarterly earnings," Reed said. "My concern is what the company is making five years from now—increasing market share, building the franchise."

Bill Pike winced. Quarterly earnings and minute-by-minute stock quotes were what Sandy lived for. *Well,* he thought to himself, *the actual call will go better than this.*

Once the analysts were all connected, Sandy diplomatically urged Reed to speak first. The longtime banker briefly described revenue growth, the effect of expense controls, and the company's return on equity. But then he added a kicker: "It won't get any better than that."

Sandy, acutely attuned to Wall Street's perceptions, moved quickly to counter Reed's pessimistic outlook. "We made more money than any company this quarter," he crowed, "and we're just getting started!"

As the conference call continued, Sandy and Reed went back and forth, almost as if they were arguing with each other. When Sandy touted the benefits of globalization, Reed interjected, "Yes, but the markets in Asia and Russia . . ." and went on to point out every negative associated with having a global presence. Sandy's face grew redder with each question and answer. The co-CEOs were tripping all over each other. Neither said anything inaccurate, but each man's "spin" on each issue was diametrically opposed to the other's. To the analysts, they sounded disjointed and inconsistent, unable to articulate a comprehensive strategy or even a shared opinion.

When the call ended, Reed and Sandy, trailed by their subordinates, strode swiftly to their individual offices. Reed closed his door to be alone. Sandy angrily plopped onto his office couch while Bill Pike and Heidi Miller braced for the explosion they knew was coming.

"I never want to be on another conference call with John Reed!" Sandy said, fuming. "That kind of mixed message will confuse the Street! Don't ever let that happen again!"

Miller and Pike were stunned. They knew Sandy was angry at the way the conference call had gone, but they expected him to lay the blame on them for not preparing better. But here he was bad-mouthing his new partner! They had been so in love. What happened?

Miller was the first to gather her wits. "Sandy, you're going to have to talk to him," she said. "We can't go to John and say, 'You can't be on a conference call.' "

PLAY NICE

The next morning, April 20, 1999, a hard, cold rain fell as Citigroup held its first annual meeting at Carnegie Hall. The executives, directors, and shareholders had to walk through demonstrators protesting Sandy's $167-million compensation package in 1998, which made him the third highest-paid executive in the country. Groups calling themselves United for a Fair Economy and Responsible Wealth handed out fortune cookies with messages that highlighted the growing disparity between the CEO's compensation and that of an average Citigroup employee. One cookie read:

"Sandy Weill makes more in 22 minutes than the typical bank teller makes all year." Another fortune asked: "Economic boom for whom?"

But if Sandy was disturbed by the protesters or angry with his co-CEO, it didn't show. "John and I have delivered incredible results for shareholders," he boomed from the concert hall's stage, with Reed at his side.

When a shareholder criticized Sandy's pay, another yelled out, "He earned every penny of it." Both Reed and Sandy had received $9.5 million in salary and bonuses for 1998, but the Travelers CEO had exercised the right to buy $157 million in stock from options granted in his 1986 takeover of Commercial Credit.

Anyone who hadn't heard the previous day's conference call would have been startled to be told that friction was growing between the two co-CEOs. Sandy and Reed were the picture of unity, backed on the stage by their all-star board of directors. The annual report distributed to shareholders featured on its cover a photo of the rear of a car with a sign emblazoned "Just Married."

Yet the friction continued to grow. Sandy was particularly irked by Reed's constant refrain about the pair retiring in the not-too-distant future. In meeting after meeting, Reed remarked privately and publicly that the merger "is a nice way to cap our careers." Each time he heard that, Sandy would mutter to one of his lieutenants, "I'm not ready to crown my career." Reed's remarks reminded Chuck Prince, the general counsel, of the last-minute change to the proxy that removed Reed's language about the two CEOs retiring together. Citicorp's mandatory retirement age of sixty-five had been scrapped during the merger negotiations, since it would have forced Sandy, sixty-five, to retire immediately after the merger was complete. *The two of them still disagree about when to leave,* Prince thought to himself.

During the spring, a CNBC reporter snagged an impromptu interview with Reed and asked, on the air, about succession planning at Citigroup. Reed took the bait, something Sandy would never have done, and confirmed that he expected to leave with Sandy when the merger was well in place.

Sandy happened to be watching CNBC at that moment. Angry at this public commitment that seemed designed to force him out before he was ready to go, he summoned Citibank's longtime public-relations executive Jack Morris.

"Tell John to quit talking about retiring," Sandy ordered. "He doesn't need to do that, and he shouldn't speak for me."

Despite the cracks beginning to mar the façade of cooperation between Sandy and Reed, the troops remained under strict orders to work together harmoniously. They certainly didn't need much encouragement. Everyone was well aware that Jamie Dimon was still unemployed months after his dissension led to his ouster. But being cooperative didn't necessarily win any brownie points with the co-CEOs.

Bill Pike was in charge of preparing Sandy and Reed for their first formal meeting with securities analysts who covered Citigroup. On the Friday before the Monday meeting, Pike routinely prepared a set of discussion points that reviewed the latest financial results and how well the company was executing its strategy. It was intended not so much to set an agenda for the meeting, but to make sure Sandy and Reed covered all the salient points that Pike thought the analysts needed to know about. As part of the "play nice" mandate, Pike shared the document Friday afternoon with Reed's investor-relations executive. He considered it a courtesy and prepared to put the document in the overnight package that would be delivered to Sandy's weekend retreat in the Adirondacks of upstate New York. But before he could do that, Reed's aide returned his copy to Pike with a new cover sheet outlining an agenda for the meeting. It read:

> Heidi Miller: Review results
> John Reed: Review strategy
> Sandy Weill: Review recent trip

Pike frowned. This isn't how Sandy would usually want to handle things. He would want to talk about both results and strategy, and his recent trip to Japan to close a minor deal wasn't particularly interesting. But if Reed wanted an agenda, Pike figured he'd best go along. The overnight package went out.

Late Saturday afternoon Pike was lounging in his weekend beach house in Bay Head, New Jersey, when the phone rang.

"Who sent this package?" Sandy bellowed, his voice seething with anger.

"I did," Pike said.

"What's this outline thing?" Sandy demanded.

"Well, we put together the normal stuff for the conference, and Reed's guy suggested this for how we approach the meeting," Pike answered.

Sandy let loose a vicious tirade. "John Reed reviews strategy?! His fucking strategy?! Who had the idea to create Citigroup?! Who am I?! A goddamned travel agent?! I'm going to review a recent trip! He's the one always running around the globe while I run this place!"

The tantrum went on virtually uninterrupted for ten minutes. Pike had seen his boss angry before, but nothing like this combination of rage and bitterness. Sandy repeatedly pressed Pike: "Whose idea was this?" as if to see if Reed himself were behind Sandy's diminished role.

Pike tried halfheartedly to defend his Citi counterpart, but now he knew he should have heeded his instinct and fought the agenda.

After Sandy wound down, he asked a final question, his voice tinged with resentment and sadness: "How could you do this to me?" Then he slammed down the phone.

Pike burst into tears. The thirty-seven-year-old executive sobbed uncontrollably for twenty minutes. He felt as if he had just betrayed his own father. When his sobbing subsided, Pike understood that Sandy's vituperative reaction had less to do with him and more to do with his anger at John Reed. Sandy's frustration was coming through loud and clear. *It's worse than I thought,* Pike concluded as he washed his tear-stained face.

By early summer 1999, other Citigroup executives were reaching the same conclusion. Gone were the days when Sandy and Reed were joined at the hip. They no longer tried to maintain the appearance of solidarity, even before shareholders and Wall Street. When Citigroup stock opened for trading on the New York Stock Exchange under the new symbol "C"— Chrysler had given up the symbol when it was acquired by Daimler-Benz—only Sandy turned up at the exchange to ring the opening bell. Sandy reveled in such stunts; Reed hated them.

Executives attending high-level meetings noticed that the banter and jokes between Sandy and Reed had stopped. Indeed, they barely spoke to each other. And when they did speak, there was an undertone of hostility. At one meeting Sandy, ever conscious of costs and profits, asked Reed for the financial implications of one of his proposals. When Reed launched into a lengthy discourse, Sandy rolled his eyes. When Sandy resumed talking, Reed picked up a newspaper and began reading.

By June, the relationship between the two financial titans had deteriorated enough that people inside and outside the company were talking about it. News of the soured relationship reached Saudi Prince Alwaleed bin Talal, whose nearly 5 percent stake in Citigroup made him its largest single shareholder. The forty-two-year-old nephew of King Fahd had helped Reed rescue Citicorp in 1991 with a $590-million investment, his first outside Saudi Arabia. That stake was now worth nearly $7 billion. Worried that his investment might be in jeopardy, he flew to New York early in July to check out the power-sharing situation in person. His arrival and the reason for it were chronicled in the *New York Post,* with the headline: THIS UMBRELLA AIN'T BIG ENOUGH FER BOTH OF 'EM. The article stated that "one of the world's richest men flew in to meet with the most overpaid man on Wall Street . . . to discuss how he's getting along" with Reed.

Sandy was nervous about the visit. Reed was traveling and Sandy would be meeting with the prince, who had a long-standing relationship with Reed, by himself. He called in William McNamee, Citigroup's head of corporate events. "The sheik is coming to Citigroup," Sandy said. "I've got to give him a gift."

McNamee, who knew how much his boss loved the corporate logo, returned with a stack of Citigroup ties and scarves adorned with umbrellas.

"We don't need to give him that much," Sandy remonstrated. "Let's give him stuff worth just fifty dollars, not four hundred dollars."

Prince Alwaleed arrived the next day. After Sandy handed him an umbrella tie, the Saudi prince presented the Citigroup co-CEO with an ornately engraved sterling silver tea set. Clearly, Sandy had miscalculated the protocol of exchanging gifts with princes, but he made a good impression nevertheless.

"You are very cost conscious," the prince said. "I'm impressed."

Alwaleed didn't ask Sandy directly about his relationship with Reed. He simply expressed his concern that just the "perception" of tensions between the two co-CEOs would have a negative effect on the company and its stock price.

Then Sandy turned on the charm. Compared to the stiff and introverted Reed, Sandy exuded warmth and confidence. He reassured the prince that the merger was proceeding well and the combined company was producing strong results. Before leaving, Alwaleed and Sandy agreed that they would meet again at the prince's compound in Riyadh. Alwaleed acknowledged that "two high-geared, high-powered chairmen" would have differences, and he encouraged Sandy to continue his relentless focus on the business. Separately, the prince met with Reed's closest confidant, Vice Chairman Paul Collins, to discuss the tensions between Sandy and Reed, and urged the company to correct the perceptions of friction between them.

SEPARATE. BUT EQUAL?

Citigroup's senior executives knew, however, that the friction wasn't just a perception, it was very real. "When is this place going to blow up?" Bill Campbell asked Bob Lipp. Campbell and Lipp, co-CEOs of the consumer-banking side of Citigroup, had been getting along very well, mostly because they stayed out of each other's way. Campbell, as a former Philip Morris head, didn't interfere with banking operations, focusing only on marketing and image. Lipp, who didn't like to spend money on advertising, left Campbell free to pursue his interests. "Maybe they should divide up responsibilities like we do," Lipp speculated.

Spurred by Prince Alwaleed's warning, that was exactly what Sandy was thinking. He proposed to Reed that he and his fellow co-CEO follow the example set by Lipp and Campbell: separate but equal responsibilities. Under his plan Sandy would manage all financial and business operations—the profit centers that made money. Reed would oversee the technology, legal, and personnel departments—the areas that cost money. The proposal clearly played to each man's strengths and interests.

The co-CEOs brought their idea to Citigroup's board at its mid-July meeting. They told the directors that the behemoth they were charged with running was simply too big and complicated for them to be making every decision jointly. The process was cumbersome and inefficient. Everything would run more smoothly if they divided power.

"The space we will give each other will be good for both of us," Sandy said.

The directors weren't surprised that the joint decision making foreseen in the merger agreement wasn't working. None of them had expected it to be efficient or to last very long. But they were shocked at the way the two co-CEOs were proposing to divide their powers. It was certainly separate, but it was far from equal.

The original Citicorp directors couldn't believe that Reed was voluntarily ceding so much authority to the ex–Travelers chief. Frank Thomas, a Citi board member who had been the president of the Ford Foundation, asked Reed pointedly: "John, are you sure you want to do this?" His question was echoed by one of Reed's most devoted backers, Edgar Woolard: "Are you sure you will be happy with this?"

"I'm happy with the arrangement Sandy and I have made," Reed assured them.

Arthur Zankel, Sandy's old friend, was incredulous. *Reed, reputed to be a coldhearted corporate killer willing to fire anybody at any moment, was rolling over and playing dead himself,* Zankel thought. He wanted to be sure Reed understood the implications of what he was agreeing to. "Do you realize how much authority you're placing in Sandy's hands?" he asked. Reed nodded.

With Reed's assurances that the power-sharing arrangement was what he wanted, the directors warily gave their blessing. While Citigroup had just reported another record profit for the second quarter, the directors knew that if the old system of power sharing continued, it would eventually hurt the company.

On July 28, 1999, Sandy and Reed co-signed an internal memorandum to senior managers outlining the division of duties.

"We no longer feel the need to attend every meeting together or read all the same memos," they wrote. "Instead, we can better divide the job of leading this great company and simplify the decision-making process."

The memo continued: "After several months working side by side, we feel we know each other well, know the company well, and instinctively rely on each other's judgment."

Widespread skepticism greeted the memo. The senior executives could easily read between the lines: Sandy was now running the world's largest financial empire while John Reed was thinking about it. Still, if this is what it took to keep the company on course, then that was fine.

But the truce didn't last long. The next clash between Sandy and Reed came over what role the Internet would play in Citigroup's strategy. It was a debate about the future not only of Citigroup, but also of their own careers.

John Reed, the undisputed visionary of banking technology, had made ATMs a household word by putting them on every corner despite the huge capital outlays required. Now he wanted to make the same dramatic push into online territory with Internet-based financial services. A few years earlier, Reed had hired Edward Horowitz, a media executive at Viacom, to set up an Internet incubator at Citicorp, called "e-Citi." Horowitz was to create the systems and products to reach one billion customers around the world via the Net. Reed, a true believer in the power of technology, was willing to devote whatever resources necessary to continue his track record of technological innovation.

But Sandy wasn't buying into the Internet or the technology-stock boom. He didn't know how to turn on his computer, much less send an e-mail or execute a stock trade electronically. And value-conscious investor that he was, he was acutely suspicious of the skyrocketing values of technology stocks, particularly the start-ups with no product, no track record, and no profits. "The Internet boom is being built by free working capital," he warned Horowitz. "People can just go public and get capital without paying for it. Obviously, that can't last."

When Sandy looked at e-Citi, he didn't see the future. All he saw was red—a deep hole that already had consumed $300 million and had little to show for it. He was particularly irritated that Reed had designated e-Citi a "think tank" that effectively isolated it from the business units that would require it to produce fast and profitable results. E-Citi became the focal point of disagreement between Sandy and Reed about how the entire empire should be run.

Sandy complained to old friends on the Citigroup board that Reed wasn't abiding by the new power-sharing arrangement. "John still shows up at meetings and slows down decisions," he said. Still, with the majority of top-level jobs held by Sandy's loyalists, he continued to try to run the company his way.

Reed mounted his own attack on Sandy, but he did so indirectly. After asking Andrall Pearson, one of Citigroup's directors, for a meeting, ostensibly to discuss "Citigroup's future," Reed journeyed to Greenwich, Connecticut, to meet Pearson in his office. Although he had originally been a member of Travelers' board, Pearson had never been particularly friendly with Sandy. He could be openly skeptical of Sandy's ideas, and he frequently asked stern questions at board meetings. Also, Pearson remained friendly with Jamie Dimon. If Reed was going to sway a Travelers director against Sandy, Pearson would be the logical choice.

When Pearson greeted him, Reed said, "I want to get to know the directors from the Travelers side." But as soon as they were seated in Pearson's corner office, the get-acquainted meeting turned into a get-Sandy session.

"He doesn't know anything about the Internet," Reed complained. "He doesn't know anything about banking. And, really, he doesn't know anything about running a global business."

"Well, that's not good," Pearson said, startled at the sudden attack on Sandy. "What's he good at?"

"Sandy's a detail guy," Reed answered. "He knows all the numbers but can't articulate a strategy."

As a director of Sandy's burgeoning empire for thirteen years, Pearson agreed with that assessment. "He can't consciously tell you what the hell he's doing," he told Reed. "Still, you follow Sandy because he tells you it's going to be good and it's good."

Pearson was impressed with Reed's dissection of Sandy's faults. He wanted to know more about the growing conflict between the two co-CEOs over technology, a hot topic among executives all over the country.

"The banking business could easily be branchless," Reed said. "We're behind. Sandy won't invest in the future because he's so worried about this quarter's earnings."

When Reed left, Pearson pondered what had just happened. *John just tried to kill Sandy with me,* he realized. *The conflict at the top is worse than any of us thought.*

Within days Pearson began getting phone calls from Reed loyalists on the Citigroup board. "Sandy isn't up to the job," one director told Pearson. "He'll be a disaster if we let him have control of the company," said another.

By the time of the fall board meeting, every director—as well as Sandy and Reed—knew that the infighting and backbiting had become intense. They had all known from the beginning that the two co-CEOs were polar opposites in so many respects. But Sandy and Reed had worked hard in the early stages of the merger to keep those differences hidden, or at least under control. Now just how strongly each man felt about his approach to running the company was out in the open.

The directors assembled for their customary board dinner the night before the meeting in a private dining room at Le Cirque, one of Sandy's favorite restaurants. No one said a word about all the lobbying and attacks of the recent weeks. But when Pearson left the room to go to the bathroom, Edgar Woolard, an original Citicorp director and former chairman and CEO of DuPont, hurried after him. The word was obviously out that Pearson could be the swing vote in any showdown between the two co-CEOs. "You have to do something about this," Woolard said. "It's getting out of hand."

"I agree," said Pearson and continued on his way.

The next morning, the directors gathered in the Citigroup boardroom. Despite the reorganization of their duties, Reed and Sandy acknowledged their partnership wasn't working. The co-CEOs diplomatically asked the directors for their ideas on what to do. Each board member offered suggestions: Maybe they should change the organization again, or perhaps reduce the number of "two-headed monsters" under Sandy and Reed. Maybe more one-on-one meetings between Sandy and Reed would smooth things out.

When it was Pearson's turn to speak, he thought for a moment about what hadn't already been said and decided to plow ahead.

"This is all bullshit," he told his fellow directors. Their various ideas, he said, "would work under normal circumstances, but this is an extraordinary situation." He had everyone's rapt attention.

He looked at the co-CEOs. "Sandy and John, we can reorganize this business until hell freezes over and it won't fix it. The main problem is that the two of you guys don't agree on one single thing about how to run this company.

"Holy Christ! One of you likes salary, the other stock. One of you is formal, the other does nothing formal. One is into process, the other guy hates process. Unless the two of you can just sit down with the six or eight fundamental notions of how to run this business and say, 'I can buy this point of view,' you'll never be able to get along."

No one said a word as Pearson's comments sank in. Then another director suggested a break. As they rose, John Deutch, a longtime Citicorp director and former chief of the Central Intelligence Agency, told Pearson, "It's what needed to be said. No one would be frank."

After most of the directors had left the room, Reed came up to Pearson. "That really was a remarkable, perceptive conclusion. That's exactly the problem we have."

Yet despite Pearson's forceful comments, the board meeting concluded without reaching a solution. Neither of the co-CEOs volunteered to bend in the other's direction. Sandy and Reed were at a complete impasse.

THE THIRD PARTY

Suddenly, though, it looked as if it wouldn't matter who was running Citigroup. Since its creation a year earlier, Citigroup had been operating under a temporary exemption from federal banking laws requiring the separation of banks, brokerages, and insurance companies. The two-year waiver would expire in 2000. Thus, it was crucial that Congress soon pass new laws lifting the legal barriers to consolidation within the financial-services industry. Otherwise, Citigroup would have to undo much that it had done.

Citigroup wasn't alone in seeking repeal of the Depression-era Glass-Steagall Act and other laws designed to prevent a concentration of financial power. Other banks, securities firms, and insurance companies had long been lobbying for such changes in order to become more competitive in the international marketplace. But the merger lent renewed impetus to those efforts, and by the fall of 1999 the two houses of Congress had passed their own versions of bills and were struggling to work out a compromise satisfactory to both and the Clinton White House. In October, though, the legislation became bogged down. The issue was bank lending in low-income neighborhoods. Years earlier, in response to obvious discrimination in the way banks made loans, Congress had passed the Community Reinvestment Act, which required banks to increase the amount of lending in poor neighborhoods and to document those efforts. Senator Phil Gramm, the Texas Republican who headed the Senate Banking Committee, opposed any restrictions on the way banks did business and was determined to use the new legislation to undercut the Community Reinvestment Act. But the Clinton administration and many consumer-advocacy groups were equally determined to prevent banks from practicing discrimination. The impasse threatened to kill the legislation that was vital to Citigroup's survival as the first American "universal bank" in seventy years.

Sandy took the lead in lobbying for the legislation. He called on Treasury officials and congressional leaders, often accompanied by other financial executives. And he played his most important trump card. Years earlier, with no fanfare, Sandy had founded a charity aimed at training inner-city high-school students for jobs in the financial industry. The gesture, a nod to the difficulties Sandy had experienced breaking into the deeply discriminatory finance business, attracted the attention of Jesse Jackson, the outspoken civil rights leader, who recruited Sandy as the first cochairman of his own fledgling Wall Street Project, an effort to create more diversity within the big banks and brokerages. During the past six years the white Jewish mogul and the African-American Christian activist had become friends and mutual allies in various projects, including the Alvin Ailey American Dance Theater, the acclaimed modern-dance troupe consisting of mostly black performers for which Joan Weill served as chairwoman. Now Jackson came to the defense of his old friend. He met with Gramm privately to tell the committee chairman that he would support a watered-down version of the community-reinvestment provisions, a move that would signal to other consumer groups that they should back off and let the legislation proceed.

The only remaining hurdles were President Clinton and the Democratic members of the committee following his lead. On October 21, 1999, during a marathon negotiating session with the Democrats, Gramm couldn't persuade them to give sufficient ground. Furious, he stormed out of the committee meeting room and strode angrily over to Roger Levy, Citigroup's senior lobbyist.

"You get Sandy Weill on the phone right now," barked the senator, jabbing a finger into Levy's chest. "Tell him to call the White House and get them moving, or I'll kill the bill. You have one hour!"

Sandy placed a call to Clinton late that night to tell him that the bill coveted by Wall Street was on the verge of collapse and needed him to compromise. At the same time, Gramm was sending his own message to the president about Hillary Clinton's bid for political office. "If my wife were running for Senate in New York, I would not veto this bill."

At almost three o'clock in the morning, the congressmen emerged to announce that a deal had been struck. President Clinton soon signed into law the Financial Services Modernization Act of 1999. Critics predicted a wave of mega-mergers, but the biggest one was now secure. The legislation was soon tagged the "Citigroup Authorization Act."

In a rare public act of unity, Reed and Sandy issued a joint statement praising Washington for "liberating our financial companies from an antiquated regulatory structure . . . to unleash the creativity of our industry and ensure global competitiveness."

Privately, though, the two co-CEOs were working together to achieve another goal. They agreed that a third person, someone of unquestioned ability and integrity, might provide them with a buffer that could allow them each to do their individual jobs without running afoul of each other.

And they knew exactly who they wanted: the newly departed and highly regarded Treasury secretary, Robert Rubin.

Heralded for guiding one of the greatest economic expansions in history, Rubin had left the Clinton administration in July and was taking his time deciding what to do next. In September, Rubin's wife hosted a welcome-home party for her husband at the Metropolitan Museum of Art and invited many Wall Street players who had known her husband when he was the co-CEO of Goldman Sachs. Sandy took the opportunity to buttonhole Rubin: "If you want to go back into financial services, you have to come and talk to me."

The next day, Rubin called on Sandy at Citigroup. The ex–Treasury secretary politely told Sandy he was on the verge of deciding to join another company. As long as he hadn't signed anything, Sandy said, why not talk a little more to us? If Bob Rubin was "in play," the deal maker in Sandy wasn't about to let a competitor snag one of the world's most coveted financiers. Rubin, sixty-one, was known for his deeply analytical thinking, his sober judgment, and, not unimportant to Sandy, a willingness to let his boss take lots of credit.

Sandy soon steered Rubin to a sit-down with Reed, who knew Rubin well, since Citicorp had been Goldman Sachs's bank when Rubin was a co-CEO at the securities firm. Every day for the next month Sandy called or met with Rubin. He tried to appeal to Rubin's interest in international affairs and complex finance, pointing out Citigroup's global reach and the unprecedented range of financial services it offered. For his part, Rubin, who was being courted by some of the world's best financial institutions, remained noncommittal. Still, he couldn't deny that he was attracted by Citi's scope and size.

"It's a fascinating place," Rubin would tell his wife after each meeting with Sandy. "I'm not going to do it, but it's really fascinating."

Finally, Judy Rubin said, "Every time you go there you seem so excited. Why don't you just do it?"

When Sandy called the next day, Rubin was ready to talk. He had two conditions. First, he didn't want any line responsibility, meaning that no business would report directly to him. Rather, he wanted to advise on "strategic and management operational issues" to help Citigroup realize its lofty ambition of becoming the leading financial firm in every part of the globe. He certainly had unprecedented access to people around the world who could help make that happen. Second, he wanted contractual recognition that he would have his own independent involvement in public policy, free to pursue his own interests in politics. Bluntly put, he didn't want to work full-time. That was fine with Sandy. Rubin's mere presence gave Citigroup added credibility and stature, regardless of how many hours a week he worked.

Sandy and Rubin worked out the details. Rubin would become a Citigroup director, chairman of the executive committee, and a member of the newly created "office of the chairman." Rubin, already a wealthy man as a result of his career at Goldman Sachs, would go from the $150,000 he earned as Treasury secretary to a combined package of salary, bonus, and stock options worth at least $33 million a year. In their negotiations Sandy and Reed quickly found Rubin to be low-key and self-effacing. During his Washington tenure, Rubin had earned a reputation as a conciliator who helped find common ground between warring camps. They hoped he could do the same for Citi.

The last day of negotiations with Rubin kept Sandy away from his beloved planning group meeting at Armonk. But as soon as the three shook hands on the final details, Sandy called the Armonk facility and told the operator to put him on the speakerphone.

"Bob Rubin is joining Citigroup!" he exclaimed.

"Congratulations," Heidi Miller responded. "It's another acquisition."

Jay Fishman, who now ran Travelers and was much more deferential than Miller, punched her on the arm for being sarcastic. "Fabulous, Sandy," Fishman said. "Brilliant move."

The next morning, on October 25, 1999, Citigroup called a press conference for a major announcement. Rubin, with his mane of thick, silvery hair and dark eyes set in an angular face, was already in the library that separated the two co-CEOs' offices. With a bounce in his step, Sandy walked in and proudly presented his new hire with the famous burnt-orange gift box from the Parisian retailer Hermès. Sandy could barely contain his excitement as Rubin untied its signature brown ribbon and opened the ultimate status box to find a handmade silk tie covered with umbrellas.

"Are you going to put it on?" Sandy asked eagerly, as he sported his own Hermès umbrella tie.

"No, I'm not going to put that on," Rubin said dismissively, handing the box to an aide.

Sandy was crestfallen. It took several minutes for him to recover his high spirits and prepare for the excitement of the press conference, set to begin in ten minutes.

In the twelfth-floor auditorium at Citicorp Center, TV camera operators, reporters, Wall Street analysts, and Citi managers packed in to see what announcement was about to be made. Speculation was rampant that the co-CEOs would announce another blockbuster acquisition, now that financial deregulation had passed. When Sandy and Reed walked onto the stage with Rubin, the room erupted in applause.

"Wow! What a coup!" yelled one bank analyst.

Rubin told the enthusiastic gathering, "I was very attracted to Sandy and John's vision of the future," adding quickly, "I didn't want to be a CEO."

That prompted the obvious question: If not Rubin, then what about a successor to Reed and Sandy? Sandy quickly snatched the microphone before Reed could offer an answer. "John and I are enjoying what we're doing. We think at an appropriate time we will have a successor, but it's not an issue that we are currently worried about, and we have not discussed it with the board."

When the press conference was over, the three men stood on the stage for the photographers. Sandy inserted himself in the middle and put his arm around Rubin, but not around Reed. After posing in a three-way handshake, Sandy and Rubin continued taking questions. Reed played with his pen for a few minutes, then left the stage.

Sandy immediately set to work to make Rubin his ally, bringing him into the fold, turning on his "we're a family" charm. And Rubin just as quickly settled in. Padding down the halls in his stocking feet, Rubin would bring a clean yellow pad to Sandy's office. "What are the issues?" he asked Sandy. "How do you think I can be helpful?" Sandy even began walking around in his socks occasionally.

From the start, the former Treasury secretary found much confusion about who made decisions, even though Sandy and Reed had split duties. He also discovered that senior managers were confused by mixed messages from the top. He suggested that the co-CEOs go beyond the monthly planning meeting and create a weekly business-heads meeting. Sandy agreed to start Monday mornings with a meeting of the top ten executives, as long as they sat in a room with the "soft seating" he preferred. The meetings were an immediate success, helping coordinate strategy and the week's events for the massive company.

Rubin also recommended that he, Sandy, and Reed have their own weekly meeting as the "office of the chairman." The chieftains wanly agreed. But after just two tense and unproductive meetings of the trio, the co-CEOs couldn't find time in their schedules for further powwows.

Even as Rubin tried to ease the tensions between the two men, they showed little willingness to meet each other halfway. Just as Reed had launched his own quiet campaign to get to know the Travelers directors, Sandy soon worked to make inroads with Reed allies.

He planned his own globe-trotting adventure in November. To build a relationship with Citigroup's largest individual shareholder, Sandy accepted Prince Alwaleed's invitation to visit him in Saudi Arabia. Knowing that his elaborate $130-million palace wouldn't make a big impression on a billionaire like Sandy, the prince suggested that Sandy and Joan would get a better feel for his country if they went somewhere special. When Sandy and Joan Weill arrived in Riyadh on November 2, 1999, Saudi guards drove them in one of the prince's sumptuous recreational vehicles to a vast stretch of desert in central Saudi Arabia where he maintained his weekend camp. Dressed in traditional Arab garb, the forty-four-year-old prince warmly welcomed the Weills and led them into one of the camp's open-air living rooms, strewn with huge, elaborate rugs and pillows. That afternoon, the prince and Sandy rode and milked camels and went target shooting. When they returned to camp, the men, both of whom were serious business-news junkies, checked the prince's wall TVs, two of which were tuned to Bloomberg and CNBC via the prince's $700,000 custom Chevy Suburban communications truck with its satellite downlinks.

That chilly evening, Prince Alwaleed, his entourage, the Weills, and a few Citigroup associates gathered around a huge fire in a pit, as Bedouin nomads lined up to kiss the prince's shoulder, recite poems of adulation, and ask for money. Sandy, now clad in Arab dress, too, quickly grabbed one of Alwaleed's aides to translate for him. When the wind and sand whipped up, the party moved to the prince's huge fiberglass tent, nearly the size of a football field, for a lavish feast of Arabic, Lebanese, and Saudi dishes, which they ate with their hands while seated on the floor.

"Frankly, I never bought the idea of cochairmen and co-CEOs," the prince confided as the night went on. "But if this process, for better or worse, is the price to make Citigroup, it's worth it." Still, Alwaleed expressed no favoritism for either man and told Sandy he wanted "to build a relationship" with him, as he had with Reed. By the time Sandy left the prince's desert camp very late that night, he took comfort in knowing that he and Citi's largest shareholder had become friends.

Sandy also toured India, where Victor Menezes, an Indian native and co-CEO of the corporate and investment bank, met him to show off the full range of Citi's business relations in the world's second most populous nation. He also wanted Sandy to see some of the extraordinary sights of the country. At the Taj Mahal, Sandy and Joan were inspired to have a traditional Indian wedding ceremony as a renewal of their long-ago marriage vows. Sandy, in full traditional regalia, including a turban, rode a camel to meet his bride with Menezes at his side. The co-CEO had asked the long-time Citibank executive, a devoted Reed loyalist, to be his best man.

Sandy took other steps to shore up his position in any showdown with John Reed. Acutely conscious that his lack of social standing had hurt him badly at American Express, he resolved that he wouldn't be so naïve as to think that Citigroup's remarkable profits would be enough to ensure victory. He and Joan pledged $100 million of their fortune to his alma mater, Cornell University, for its medical school and hospital, a contribution that Cornell acknowledged by naming its medical center—situated near the prestigious Memorial Sloan-Kettering Cancer Center and Rockefeller University—the New York Weill Cornell Medical Center.

He and Joan also became much more visible among New York society, attending a black-tie gala or business dinner nearly every night. The society pages of the newspapers, which years earlier had mostly ignored Sandy and Joan, now scrambled to get shots of the powerful couple. Sandy was delighted at the number of times he and his elegantly clad wife appeared in *The New York Times*'s Sunday "Evening Hours" column. Such attention was gratifying enough to Sandy's insatiable ego, but it represented a form of power, too. And power would be what determined the outcome of the showdown.

RAPPROCHEMENT

A year had passed since that shocking day in Armonk when Sandy and Reed had fired him, and still Jamie Dimon was pondering what to do next. With a net worth of $125 million, he clearly didn't need to return to work. He had fended off feelers from Amazon.com, Starwood Hotels & Resorts, and the British Barclays bank. He had spent a lot of time, too, coming to terms with his behavior toward Sandy, the blunt criticisms and challenges that had gotten him ousted. Invited as a guest lecturer at a Columbia Business School seminar on what Shakespeare might offer MBA candidates, Dimon pointed out how the Earl of Kent, who publicly disputed King Lear's judgment and was exiled, could have been more diplomatic, yet still honest and candid in criticizing the king.

More than ever, Dimon was convinced that his future lay in finance. But in what role? Sandy and Reed were the aging lions of that industry and they had fired him. In early December, Dimon visited with Andrall Pearson, who as chairman of Tricon Global Restaurants, the parent company of several restaurant chains, had named him a director. Pearson decided Dimon needed a heart-to-heart talk.

"Jamie, if you ever have any aspiration to be the head of a financial company, you don't need Sandy as a practicing enemy," the Citigroup director said. "You have to run up the flag. Sandy will never forgive and forget or accept responsibility."

Dimon, brainy and confident, took momentary offense at the notion he might need to "make up" with Sandy to get a job. "If I do it, it will be for personal, not professional, reasons," he responded. If nothing else, Dimon didn't want any more chilly scenes at the Four Seasons. The two men had been dining simultaneously several times and had never spoken.

"It's time, Jamie," Pearson continued. "You're both going to be characters in this industry. Move on."

A few days later, Dimon called Sandy's office and left a message. Within minutes, Sandy was on the line.

"In the spirit of Christmas, let's sit down and break bread and try to reestablish a relationship," Dimon offered.

"Great, I would love to," Sandy answered.

"Wherever you want," Dimon said.

"The Four Seasons," Sandy replied.

At lunch on December 16, 1999, Sandy and Dimon sat at the Citigroup chief's usual power spot, a booth in the corner. Unaccustomed to discussing delicate personal situations, Sandy was nervous and fidgeting.

Dimon quickly broke the ice. "Sandy, we're going to have a fine lunch. I want to talk about the past for a few minutes . . ." Seeing Sandy flinch, Dimon added, "And it won't bother you.

"Sandy, I never would have done what you did," Dimon began. "But I want you to know I share a lot of the blame. It doesn't make sense to apportion the share sixty-forty or forty-sixty. I'm not sure it matters."

Sandy shifted in his seat. He hadn't really come for a heart-to-heart, but Dimon had to get this off his chest.

"I understand that you didn't want me in the room anymore, because I disagreed with you too much and we were fighting too much," Dimon continued, sensing that he better wrap up this part of the lunch. "I made a series of mistakes, and I'm sorry."

"Thank you very much for saying that," Sandy said stiffly.

Dimon didn't hear and didn't expect an apology from Sandy, mostly because he didn't believe Sandy was sorry to have him gone. But then Sandy added what would be as close as he would ever come to an apology: "It takes two to mess up a relationship like we did."

It was done. With the sensitive conversation out of the way, the men talked about business and a little about their families. Of course, family was still a delicate topic. Judy Dimon and Joan Weill had not seen each other again, and Dimon's parents, Ted and Themis Dimon, still refused to socialize with the Weills.

The next day, the *Financial Times* carried news of great moment on its front page: the record U.S. trade deficit, civil war in Russia, and SEASON OF GOOD WEILL AS FEUD WITH DIMON ENDS. The article reported: "It must be Christmas. One of Wall Street's best-known feuds . . . is over. The two have made up at Wall Street's favorite power restaurant, the Four Seasons, a place where bankers go as much to be seen as for the food."

16

SHOWDOWN

As a new century began, Citigroup was a highly successful but very miserable place. Jamie Dimon was only the most visible casualty of the merger. Hundreds of other smart, talented, and experienced executives had left in the past year. Nearly 80 percent of Citicorp's most senior executives were gone, and 60 percent of the Travelers management had departed. The turnover was dramatically higher than normal attrition after a merger, and it signaled how difficult and costly in human terms the transaction had been.

The remaining executives were tired, troubled, and tempted to leave as well. The unusual and unhappy alliance between Sandy and Reed was hurting not only the two at the top but also those many layers beneath them. Even Sandy's most loyal lieutenant, Bob Lipp, told him in January that he would leave later that year.

At the annual management conference in February, the mood was gloomy, even as business was booming along with the economy and stock market. Citigroup's top sixteen executives flew to The Boulders, a luxury resort complete with lush golf courses and spas north of Scottsdale, Arizona. Wrapped around giant twelve-million-year-old boulders, the resort was touted as a "legendary hideaway in the high Sonoran Desert foothills" where guests would experience "the healing serenity of the desert."

Wrong!

After the first day of the usual agenda of strategy and analysis of operations, the executives gathered on the second day to find the meeting would be devoted to "management issues." Sandy, Reed, and now Rubin individually had heard for months all the griping through separate channels. This meeting was designed to get everything on the table in front of their leaders.

"Let's go around the room," Sandy began, reminding his older executives of their collegial Baltimore dinners.

At first, the executives were tentative, pointing out only the most obvious symptom: Decision making had slowed down. But then it came to Bob Willumstad, the ultimate straight shooter. He looked directly at his two co-CEOs. "Your inability to get along affects how we run the business. It's no longer just a distraction. You two guys are actually hurting this organization."

Rubin, who was taking his new role as mediator very seriously, seized the opportunity: "Give me an example."

Willumstad described how Reed was pushing him to install thousands of ATM machines across the country at a staggering price of $40 million. Reed already had the machines sitting in a warehouse and had begun a costly experiment to install them in Blockbuster video rental stores. "And Sandy's telling me he expects x-amount of earnings from the branches, to go back and figure out where I need to cut expenses."

Jay Fishman agreed. "Just tell us which hill, and we'll take it," the Travelers CEO said. "But we can't go up two different hills at the same time."

Victor Menezes was next. A savvy corporate politician, he rarely took a stand, which made his comment all the more startling: "A compass can have only one north pole. We don't know which way you're pointing."

A newcomer to the management group, Sir Winfried Bischoff, the head of Britain's Schroders banking division, which Citigroup had just bought as part of its European expansion, found the meeting depressing and surprising. Sandy told him he didn't have to contribute, since he had just joined the company.

"For god's sake, I just want to say something," Bischoff interjected. "You are in fact shortchanging yourself. What you have achieved in the last eighteen months is absolutely staggering. Looking from the outside, you're being far too despondent about your difficulties." He looked around the room, with gloom looking back at him. "It's natural to have culture clashes," he added, "but don't get yourselves down."

Reed took copious notes; both he and Sandy were mostly quiet. After everyone had spoken, one executive told the co-CEOs: "We have been real plain with you, and you owe us an answer about how you intend to address this. It's in your court."

"Okay, we've heard you," Sandy said. Reed added, "We are taking it on as our assignment to think about this—and respond."

The meeting ended and the executives moved on to the day's next agenda item: free time and the order to "have fun." *Right,* Miller thought to herself as she entered the spa. *We've just had a brutal meeting—now let's relax.* The outspoken CFO had been particularly muted that day. She had already made up her mind to leave Citigroup, though she had told no one of her decision.

Willumstad considered the emotional session a "watershed event" for the new company as he headed to the golf course. He was put in a group with Reed and Fishman.

"John, are you sure you want to play?" Willumstad asked Reed, who clearly looked beaten.

"I'm fine," Reed said coldly, showing no emotion. "I just have to be back by five o'clock."

The trio played terribly, especially Reed.

When the executives returned to New York, the Citi directors got an earful. Board members from both sides of the merger transaction traded phone calls with one another about the "mess." There was a lot of debating, maneuvering, and thrashing around for a solution.

Arthur Zankel wanted to do his own investigation. He invited Menezes, originally from Citicorp, to lunch at the exclusive Sky Club high above Manhattan. Zankel had a delightful wit; if he was in a room and people were laughing, Zankel was certain to be in the middle of it. But he struck out with Menezes. After the meeting, Zankel phoned a fellow director and grumbled, "All I got was name, rank, and serial number. Zippo."

Then, in the middle of February, Heidi Miller sprang her surprise. At forty-six years old, she had decided to take on a new challenge—and to flee Citigroup. A year earlier, she had been named the number-two most powerful woman in business after Carly Fiorina, CEO of Hewlett-Packard. But life at the top at Citi brought the mother of two more pain than pleasure. She knew she couldn't go home many more nights feeling this miserable. It wasn't fair to her family or to herself. She had developed high blood pressure from the constant stress. After being seated at a dinner next to the chairman of Priceline.com, the high-flying Internet retailer, Miller began discussions and quickly agreed to become its CFO and strategic-planning head.

Now she needed to tell Sandy, who was traveling. Miller, who was slated to travel to India and Africa as well, had his secretary connect them by phone.

"Look, Sandy, I'm leaving," Miller said.

"Goddammit, is this because of John?" Sandy screamed into the phone. "I'll drive a stake through his heart!"

Miller was so shocked by his violent reaction that she wrote the words down on the paper in front of her but didn't answer the question.

"I don't want to leave abruptly," Miller said. "I'll stay for a transition if you want."

Sandy didn't answer her directly either. His mind was on John Reed. "Don't tell John," Sandy ordered.

"But I have to tell John. I report to both of you," Miller said.

"Are you sure you don't want to stay?" asked Sandy, who had no logical candidate to replace the talented CFO.

"I can reinvent myself" at Priceline, Miller told him, expressing eagerness to go to the startup retailer known for its name-your-own-price system of selling airline tickets and other services.

Sandy quickly changed gears. If Miller was leaving, maybe he could use her resignation to his advantage. "Would you mind taking a few phone calls this weekend? I'll have a couple directors call you," he said. "Be honest and open and tell them how you feel." Then he added, "But don't tell John about the calls."

As Miller hung up, she knew Sandy wanted her to point the finger at Reed. The John-and-Sandy show had been a nightmare, she thought, but she was leaving as much because of Sandy as Reed, although Sandy would never know that. She headed to Reed's office to give him the news.

"What a wonderful opportunity," enthused Reed, who was equally enamored of the prospect of Internet business. "And I know this isn't a particularly fun place to be right now."

Miller attempted to obliquely warn Reed that her resignation might become a political issue. "Now, John, I just want you to know I'm not leaving because of you—no matter what people will be saying," said Miller, who liked Reed quite a bit. "You might be surprised that people will use this—"

"No, Heidi," Reed said. "It's fabulous for you."

Miller walked out with one thought: *John Reed is like a lamb. It's so obvious that he's going to be sacrificed, and he doesn't even realize it.*

That weekend, Miller took calls from board members. Reuben Mark, chairman and CEO of Colgate-Palmolive Co., asked, "What's your attitude about Sandy and John? How much is that contributing to your decision to leave?" Miller acknowledged the turmoil had affected her negatively.

"Under what situation could both of them stay?" continued Mark, who was originally a Citicorp director.

"Probably none," Miller replied.

When she returned to the office on Monday, Bob Rubin took time out from one of his trips to phone her. He pointedly asked which co-CEO had given her the most trouble.

"Sandy's really difficult to work for," Miller said, thinking back to all the times he undercut her authority.

"Who has more skills to manage this place?" Rubin queried.

"That's not clear to me," Miller replied. "Each of them has failings. Bottom line: This is a dysfunctional company."

Rubin was about to end the call when Miller, always opinionated, tossed out another idea. "You have an obligation as a board member with insight to do what's right. You should temporarily assume the helm and put a management team in place. Now is the time to do it."

Rubin hung up. He was surprised at Miller's strident tone and directness about the problems at Citi. Worried that she would go to the press, he called Chuck Prince, the general counsel.

"That's not Heidi," Prince said, but he immediately went to her to make certain.

"I was honest with Rubin, but I'm not going to talk to the press," Miller assured him, sensing that the former Treasury secretary was concerned with his and Citi's public image.

On February 23, 2000, Miller shocked Wall Street with her announcement that she would leave her high-profile post at the world's largest financial institution for an Internet gamble that hadn't turned a profit. Priceline's stock jumped 9 percent on the news. All the coverage posed the same question: Is it impossible to work for both Sandy Weill and John Reed?

Bob Rubin began his own internal poll of the executive ranks. He dropped in on several, including Bob Willumstad, a strong leader of the consumer bank, and asked, "For this time in the company, if you had to pick one CEO, whom does this company need more?"

That week, Sandy asked Marge Magner to lunch for only the second time in their fourteen-year association, just as he had sought out the only other high-ranking woman, Heidi Miller, a few years earlier when the company experienced inner turmoil. At the Four Seasons, Sandy offered no chitchat but wanted Magner's opinion of what was becoming a management crisis.

"I've always been straight with you," Magner said. "It's difficult, but I can only speak for myself." She told him working in upper management at Citi felt like "having two parents who completely disagree about how to raise the children."

Sandy returned to the office. He asked Reed: "Is it time we consider a single CEO?"

Reed agreed. Each man knew the impact of that decision: One or both of them might not survive. Yet each CEO seemed confident that the board would pick him as the sole leader.

THE VERDICT

They called an emergency board meeting. Chuck Prince, as the corporate secretary, told each director, "We have to have a board meeting about management issues this Sunday in our office at Citicorp Center. Please keep it as quiet as possible."

Andrall Pearson was in China on business for Tricon, opening Pizza Hut and Kentucky Fried Chicken restaurants overseas. He refused to return to New York. Prince told Sandy, who called Pearson.

"I'm halfway around the world. I'm CEO of this company, and I can't just cancel these meetings," explained Pearson.

"The Citicorp guys insist you be there," Sandy explained, knowing that many of them felt Pearson was the most objective Travelers director. "I want you there, too."

"Well, we have a dilemma," Pearson said.

"How about we charter a plane to fly you to our office in Singapore and put you on videophone?" Sandy suggested. "Then fly you back to your meetings."

"Okay," Pearson replied.

On Sunday, February 27, 2000, Citigroup directors gathered in the large boardroom around the contemporary light wood oval table. Orchids decorated the side tables. The largest art prominently hung on one wall was an ornately detailed ink drawing of a sturdy, overarching tree with scores of branches and limbs. The trunk was labeled "Citigroup" and the branches bore the names of the dozens of companies Citicorp and Travelers had brought together to build this mighty company. One of the sturdiest branches was the National City Bank; one of the smallest limbs was labeled "Carter, Berlind & Weill," Sandy's very first company begun in 1960. The art, commissioned shortly after Sandy and Reed had created Citigroup, represented their new "family tree." After this day, one of the family patriarchs would be gone.

At ten o'clock in the morning, the emergency meeting of the Citigroup board was about to begin. As they took their seats, sixty-eight-year-old Arthur Zankel, Sandy's friend since the 1960s, overheard a comment that gave him the distinct impression that the original Citicorp executives had already met to map out a plan. *Hell,* he thought, *we haven't coordinated anything among the original Travelers gang.*

Zankel started to complain—this is a "put-up job"—and then it hit him: Sandy's supporters have one less vote! Even though the original configuration had an even number of Citi and Travelers directors, one of Sandy's directors, Judith Arron of Carnegie Hall, had died of cancer several months earlier. Sandy had never replaced her.

The Citigroup co-CEOs sat together, seeming almost collegial. The outside directors and Rubin, as the third inside director besides Sandy and Reed, sat down just as Pearson's face appeared on the video screen from Singapore. Chuck Prince sat on the side as corporate secretary.

The co-CEOs were cordial and diplomatic. "This isn't working," Sandy said succinctly. "We need the board to decide what happens from here."

"For Sandy and me to cohabitate any longer would be a mistake," Reed agreed. "Our views as to what the company should do and how to run it are so divergent that it's impossible for people in the company." As usual, Reed's presentation was much lengthier than Sandy's. Ironically, the co-CEOs were now asking their board to do for them what Dimon, Maughan, and Menezes had requested the pair do for them more than a year before.

"Our people are scared; if they go to Sandy, I might get mad, or if they go to me, Sandy would get mad," Reed continued.

The directors did not hide their anger and disgust.

"You put together the biggest financial company in the world. You got longtime banking laws knocked down," one director snapped. "But you can't get along? You can't solve this yourselves?"

After sufficiently scolding the two most important financial CEOs in the world, the board sent them out of the room, along with Rubin and Prince. Then the directors called them back individually.

Reed, the architect of the modern consumer bank, was summoned to the boardroom first.

"The events in this business have reached a point where the two of us ought to leave together," Reed proposed. "The board should take on the responsibility of going outside and picking a new chief executive."

Reed's solution to the management crisis wasn't entirely unexpected. Early in the negotiations that formed Citigroup, he had understood that he and Sandy would retire together. He added that he had long told "my board" that he wanted to retire at sixty years old. He had just turned sixty-one earlier that month.

A board member wanted to know if there were not some executive in the huge and profitable company who could take over.

Reed said there was no one. "If I knew then what I know now, I wouldn't have aided and abetted Sandy in getting rid of Jamie. He would be the logical successor," Reed said. "If I had known Jamie better at the time all this happened, I think I could have saved him."

The directors looked at one another. Nearly all of them had liked and admired Dimon but followed the will of the co-CEOs. Now one of them was saying it was a mistake. But Pearson, watching silently on the videophone, didn't think Reed should be so quick to wash his hands of Dimon's dismissal. *It doesn't take long with Dimon to realize how talented he is,* Pearson thought to himself.

Reed, however, proposed that a completely new CEO might be better anyway. "I feel strongly we should bring in a successor from the outside who would be neither of Citi or Travelers—who could put the company together without any historic record or loyalty," he said. He tossed out the names of Philip Purcell, the chief executive officer, and John Mack, the chief operating officer, both of Morgan Stanley Dean Witter & Co., as possible candidates. He suggested the board form a special committee to get a successor in place and operating within a year.

Then Reed took his shots at Sandy, albeit in the course of explaining what an ideal chief executive would possess.

"I believe the objective of a manager is evolutionary success—not maximizing shareholder value or pricing your stock or profits or market share," Reed said. "Do you plant the seeds for the future of the company, or do you just exploit your current opportunity and you're exhausted at the finish line?"

Finally, Reed left the board with a thought about his and Sandy's original agreement to merge. "We agreed, after a period of time, we would leave for the good of the combined company. The time has come."

The very point that had become an issue on the night before the deal was announced—whether the two co-CEOs would walk off into the sunset together—was still firmly in Reed's mind. And he hoped the board would also remember how Sandy led them to believe he would leave with his co-chief.

Then Sandy was ushered in to the boardroom. His proposal was straightforward: make him the sole chief executive.

"What I think needs to be done is for one person to take over," Sandy said. "I think it might well be me."

Sandy was being diplomatic. Every director in the room knew Sandy desperately wanted the job. As one director had joked, "He needs to run Citigroup like you and I need to breathe." Still, Sandy laid out his case for a single leader cogently and concisely. Even though he had been criticized in the past for his limited vocabulary, on this day his direct and statesman-like approach helped his cause.

"There's still too much to do," Sandy concluded. "I'm ready to do it; I'm not ready to retire." There was his counterpunch at Reed.

The directors then wanted to speak with Rubin, who had been asked to leave because he was an "inside" director. Every board member respected the former Treasury secretary, even though he had made no effort whatsoever to be more than an advisor at Citigroup. Naturally, the directors asked if he would take the top job.

"I will not be CEO," Rubin said definitively.

"What would you do in our shoes?" one director followed up.

"If they could work it out, that's the best solution," said Rubin. "They complement each other with such different skill sets." He noted that he and Stephen Friedman successfully split the highest job at Goldman Sachs between 1990 and 1992.

"The worst solution is for both of them to leave," Rubin said, calling that scenario "nonsensical."

The directors then posed to Rubin the same question he had been asking Citi executives in recent weeks: If he had to choose one man, who would it be?

"The most sensible solution is Sandy," Rubin answered. "The group that reports to Sandy is the best management team I've seen in my business career." That impressed several directors, because Rubin had seen some very able and experienced managers in his years on Wall Street.

Then Rubin was gone, and the directors were left to make their decision: Sandy, Reed, or someone entirely new. Without their cochairmen, they chose Franklin Thomas to lead the discussion. A lawyer and star Ivy League basketball player, the sixty-six-year-old was the retired president of the Ford Foundation, the first black to head a major philanthropic institution. As the directors began their deliberations, Sandy, Reed, Rubin, and Prince settled in for what they expected would be a few hours of waiting. In the four oversized armchairs outside the boardroom, the men began reading the Sunday newspapers. When noon passed, club sandwiches were brought in. Every so often a director would walk past the foursome in the waiting area and simply nod on the way to the bathroom.

Inside the boardroom, the directors took turns expressing their reactions to the unwelcome ultimatum given them by their co-CEOs. The opinions quickly divided between the original Citicorp directors and the original Travelers directors. It became clear that each side was sticking with his favored CEO's proposal. If a vote were taken, Reed would win: eight to seven.

Zankel, fully aware of the likely outcome of a vote, urged that Rubin be asked to rejoin the deliberations. *At least the vote would be tied*, Zankel thought.

But Edgar Woolard, the ex–chairman and CEO of DuPont, steadfastly refused. Woolard was no stranger to boardroom hot seats—he had been on the IBM board when it replaced John Akers with Louis Gerstner.

"Rubin is a director," Zankel fought back. "He should have a vote." Woolard disagreed, because Rubin, as a company employee, was an "inside" director.

At this juncture, it became obvious to Pearson, sitting in front of a television camera in Singapore, that the Citi directors were prepared to support Reed's proposal that the co-CEOs leave together. He leaned into his microphone and got the board's attention.

"If we take a vote, it looks pretty clear, it's going to be eight to seven for both to leave. I think that will be a disaster for the company," the Tricon chairman said. "Two years ago, either man would have made anybody's all-star list. To get rid of the two of them and hope for somebody better is crazy."

Even the Citicorp directors listened carefully to Pearson, whom they regarded as shrewd and elite—much like themselves.

"So here's what I think," Pearson began. "Number one, we can't go on the way we are. Number two, we need to pick one of these two guys. And number three, I think it ought to be Sandy."

Then Pearson fired off three reasons for making Sandy the sole CEO. "He wants the job, all but one of the executives reporting to him is a Sandy person, and he brings more to the party in terms of leadership skills."

But a Citicorp director quickly disagreed about handing over the reins to Sandy. "If we leave Sandy as the sole CEO, it would look like Travelers bought Citicorp. Then people would say Sandy ended up with the business."

"Who gives a damn?" Zankel blurted out.

"The reputations of both John and Sandy will be preserved if they both leave together," another Reed loyalist added. "The more gracious solution is for them to retire at the same time."

"That's outrageous!" Zankel sputtered. "You're putting the interests of these two men before the interests of the shareholders. Throwing out both guys is not in the interest of millions of shareholders." At this point, Zankel, one of Sandy's closest friends, knew he was fighting for Sandy's corporate life, but that wasn't what really mattered. He was really fighting for the shareholders, the people for whom Sandy had spent his own life fighting.

"It's risky enough to have an incomplete merger, but bringing in a new man is a risk that doesn't need to be taken," Zankel continued. "We have a competent leader before us. He has a real record."

The hours dragged by as the debate continued behind closed doors. Sandy, Reed, Rubin, and Prince were getting antsy. They located two television sets in the vicinity. In one conference room, Sandy and Reed tuned in a big-screen TV to watch Tiger Woods battling for the lead of the Accenture Match Play Championship in Carlsbad, California. Rubin, who disdained golf, found a small TV in an office and turned on the New York Knicks basketball game at Madison Square Garden.

"Did you see that last shot?" Sandy asked his co-CEO.

"Unbelievable," Reed answered.

Prince, returning from a visit to his own office, saw the two men, clearly in the final moments of the most momentous battle of their immensely successful careers, calmly discussing a golf game as if they were the best of friends. *This is the most astonishing thing I've ever seen,* Prince thought to himself.

During a commercial, the co-CEOs wandered over to the office where Rubin was watching the Knicks at a critical moment in the game. "Can you believe Patrick Ewing missed that layup?" Reed marveled to Sandy.

The co-executives might have been the model of calm, but behind the closed doors of the boardroom, tensions were growing hotter. Neither side was budging. Finally, as the meeting had stretched past seven hours, Franklin Thomas, who, like Sandy, grew up in Brooklyn, made a powerful point.

"We can't have an eight-to-seven decision," Thomas said. "That is impractical going forward. There would be a non-board."

Yet Sandy and Reed had drawn a line in the sand about working as co-CEOs. Obviously, one of them had to go.

"But John wants to retire," one Travelers director noted.

"But he'll stay if he has to," a Reed supporter countered.

"That's a hard case to make for John to be the sole CEO," Zankel argued. "He's already given it up. The split duties, the management is all Sandy . . ."

A compromise was offered: Reed would become chairman, and Sandy would be named chief executive officer. No one liked it, but it passed unanimously.

Frank Thomas left the boardroom to tell Reed and Sandy. "We're electing Sandy CEO and John chairman, a non-executive chairman."

Both men were stunned. Each one had felt confident he would prevail.

"No," Reed said. "I won't do that."

Sandy said nothing.

Thomas returned to a boardroom filled with angry, tired directors. "John said no," he told them amid a chorus of groans. That left the board with Sandy as the only choice. But the Citicorp directors still worried about saving face for Reed and resolving his demand that a successor be found.

"We have to find some compromise that satisfies people who want to be sure Sandy doesn't stay until he's ninety years old," Pearson offered over the video connection. "At the same time, we need to give Sandy a chance to function effectively until the company is welded together."

Pearson's solution: fudge the succession issue. Sandy would be named chairman and CEO, Reed would retire as per his wishes, and a "plan of succession is formulated within two years."

A motion for that scenario was quickly made and ratified unanimously.

The directors asked Pearson and Thomas to head a new board "succession committee" to put pressure on Sandy to groom a successor.

Eight rancorous hours after they began, Frank Thomas emerged and found Reed, Sandy, and Prince in one of the offices near the boardroom. The director looked at Reed, who was propped on one hip on the desk. "We decided we're going to go with Sandy."

Sandy and Prince left the room immediately. Thomas closed the door and stayed in the room with Reed for five minutes. The new Citigroup CEO and his general counsel saw the open door of the boardroom and walked in. No one congratulated Sandy. The directors shuffled papers, stood up, and put on their jackets, all the while saying nothing.

Thomas returned to the boardroom and brought up the need to issue a press release. Suddenly Reed stuck his head in the door.

"I'm leaving now," he said, waiting a beat. When no one moved, he turned to leave. Two Citicorp directors—Woolard and ex–CIA director Deutch—grabbed their papers and rushed after him but failed to catch Reed before he got on the elevator.

Reed rode the elevator down to the subway station under the Citicorp Tower. He boarded a subway car and rode underground alone for hours.

SOLOING

Upstairs, Sandy was physically and emotionally drained. His tie was askew, his shirt was drenched in sweat. No one noticed. The directors practically vanished; they wanted to leave as soon as the deed was done.

On Monday, February 28, 2000, Citigroup announced that John Reed would retire at the April annual meeting, ending his thirty-five-year career with the bank. The press release stated that Sandy would become the chairman and CEO and had "advised the board of directors that, in light of his own plans for retirement, intends to work with a committee of the board on a plan of succession with the objective of coming up with a successor within two years."

The implications of the press release were clear: In a boardroom showdown Sandy Weill had emerged victorious over John Reed. Savvy insiders and analysts also found a lot of wiggle room in Sandy's commitment on succession—sure, he had to come up with a plan, but he didn't have to execute it. Citigroup stock rose 3 percent. Morgan Stanley upgraded Citigroup to a "strong buy" with Sandy in charge.

On a telephone news conference that afternoon, Reed said they talked about "various configurations, but it was pretty clear that I was the person who most wanted to retire."

Sandy joked that with Reed's 4.7 million shares of Citi stock, "John is going to be one of the biggest shareholders. We want to keep him happy so he doesn't complain."

He didn't have to worry. Reed immediately began selling his Citigroup shares and laid plans with his second wife to buy a house on an island off the coast of France.

The next month, Sandy created a new Internet operating group, putting control of the technology unit under business groups. He slashed Reed's beloved e-Citi from 1,600 to 150 people. By dismantling Reed's organization, he obliterated his former partner's fanciful dream. The new CEO put Bob Druskin, a savvy operations executive from his Shearson days who knew little about the Internet, in charge of the new group. "I will approach technology as a business issue," Druskin told the group. "It's a bad thing to have technology because you're in love with it."

On March 16, 2000, Sandy turned sixty-seven. In an annual ritual carried out by Prince, a "surprise" birthday party was held in his honor. As usual, Sandy pretended to be surprised. "Oh my god, a party!" he exclaimed. Prince dressed Sandy as Moses who delivered his people to the "promised land."

A week later, Chicago-based Bank One, the nation's fifth-largest bank, named Jamie Dimon as its new chairman and CEO. Bank One's stock surged 12 percent. Taking a page from Sandy's playbook, Dimon spent $58 million of his own money to buy two million Bank One shares. He moved his wife and three daughters to the Windy City, and the native New Yorker bought his first car. The youthful-looking Dimon wasted no time in shaking up the institution. He replaced managers throughout the ranks, demanded bottom-line accountability, slashed expenses, and wrote off bad loans by the billions of dollars. Asked who would be his model in turning around Bank One, he instantly answered: Sandy Weill.

In April, Citigroup held a retirement party to honor Reed, the banking wunderkind who had become Citicorp's chief executive in 1984 when he was just forty-five years old. Sandy was out of town.

The Citigroup annual shareholders meeting was held the following week, where Sandy presided alone over the session at Carnegie Hall. A microphone descended from the decorative ceiling, ready for Sandy's solo performance, one that he had been practicing for his whole life. After a lifetime of doing bigger and bigger deals, he alone was now running the world's largest financial conglomerate, a company that was earning more each quarter than any other company. Sandy had envisioned and created the world's first global financial firm of the twenty-first century.

Alone on the stage, Sandy praised Reed as "a great partner to me and a very good friend." He noted that Reed was out of the country, to which a shareholder in the audience yelled out, "He didn't know if he could get a seat."

After the annual meeting, Arthur Zankel put his arm around his old friend. He knew how important this day was to Sandy, who had barely survived the boardroom showdown. "You told me on the beach forty years ago that you wanted to build a great company," Zankel said. "Now you have."

But the showdown had been bloody. Citibankers left in droves, including vice chairman Paul Collins and technology head Edward Horowitz.

That spring, about 170 of the remaining top Citigroup executives met in a hotel in Bal Harbour near Miami. At a breakfast meeting to get feedback on their feelings about the company, the message was clear: Travelers managers dominated most of the important jobs, and it was clear that now things would be one way—Sandy's way. And that way meant an executive corps with unquestioned loyalty to Sandy, streamlined operations with lower costs, and a constant push to get better results—now, not later.

John Reed quickly became a nonentity. He was given an office in Citicorp Center, but Sandy moved the headquarters to the next block to be located on the more prestigious Park Avenue. Reed took away a $30-million retirement package plus $5 million a year for life, and lectured occasionally at the Massachusetts Institute of Technology, his alma mater, and at Princeton University, where he had a home. Clearly, he felt betrayed that Sandy had refused to honor what Reed thought was a commitment to retire together. Not long after his ouster, Reed was presented with the Lifetime Achievement Award by the *American Banker* newspaper. When asked about his crowning glory, Citigroup, the normally reserved Reed offered his take on the negotiations that had led to the merger and its aftermath.

"You should avoid lying during the courtship, if you can," Reed said, "because the trouble is, you have to then live through the breakdown of the lies."

17

SEEDS OF DESTRUCTION

Life was grand for Sandy Weill. With John Reed vanquished, Sandy, at sixty-seven years old, was everything he had ever yearned to be: sole head of the world's largest financial empire, an industry innovator, sage, and diplomat. "Elder statesman" would have been an appropriate term, but it implied he might soon be put out to pasture. And Sandy Weill had no intention of going anywhere now that he was reaping the rewards and respect he had spent his life seeking.

When Louis Rukeyser hosted a live broadcast of the thirtieth anniversary of his PBS show *Wall Street Week,* he hailed Sandy, who broke out in a terrible sweat on air, as the "most important figure in modern finance." When world-renowned chef Alain Ducasse opened his new, hugely expensive Manhattan gourmet restaurant, he emerged from the kitchen to personally welcome Sandy and his guests. And when President George W. Bush wanted to consult with the nation's corporate leaders, Sandy was invited to the White House.

Sandy's employees treated him as something of a deity, and their boss indulged them. The Primerica unit commissioned a nearly life-sized oil painting of Sandy and Joan, an expense Sandy never would have permitted back in the lean days when cost cutting was his paramount mission. When it was unveiled at a black-tie gathering of Primerica executives and agents, the flattered chairman was awestruck. "I never had a picture before," he marveled, gazing blissfully at the artwork.

"Portrait," Joan corrected him.

"Every time I became chairman of a company, we stopped doing portraits," Sandy quipped.

His exalted position atop Citicorp attracted other honors, especially from the city's nonprofit institutions that were eager to tap his fame and his company's deep pockets. At the annual fund-raiser for New York's public-radio station WNYC in November 2000, Sandy was honored along with Sarah Jessica Parker, the sultry star of the HBO hit television series *Sex and the City.* Sandy had never heard of the young star or the sizzling show, but that didn't matter. He arrived so early that only the waiters and a few guests were milling around. Citigroup had bought two tables at $25,000 each, and the Salomon Smith Barney unit bought a third.

As more guests arrived, Sandy and Joan took their places to receive homage. "Good evening, your lordship," said New York schools chancellor Harold Levy, a former Citibank executive, to Sandy's obvious pleasure.

For some socialites unfamiliar with the corporate world, the event offered a first glimpse of the now-legendary chief executive. "He's short and fat," one impeccably dressed, ultrathin society matron intoned. "That's the banking tycoon?"

Sandy indulged himself, as well. One day Heidi Miller, who had left Citigroup when it was mired in the conflict between Reed and Sandy, attended an insurance meeting at Citigroup's conference center in Armonk, where she had spent many a planning group session as an executive at Travelers and then Citigroup. She was surprised to find a new, much larger building near the three original structures. When she walked in the massive front door, she burst out laughing. There stood a huge, three-story stone fireplace. She could have walked into the cavernous firebox. *That's got to be Sandy,* she thought, chuckling. "What a phallic symbol," she whispered to the only other woman at the business meeting. "Size counts!"

Sandy also moved swiftly to improve Citigroup's cuisine. Reed, who didn't eat or drink much, had paid little attention to the food served in the executive dining rooms, but that wasn't Sandy's style. Indeed, many Citibankers joked that the best part of Sandy's reign was that the food in the dining rooms went from dreadful to delicious. The unappetizing blobs of cottage cheese on lettuce leaf disappeared, replaced by elegant salads of arugula, aged cheese, toasted walnuts, and radicchio.

Sandy supervised the renovation of nearly half an entire floor at Citigroup's Park Avenue offices to create a suite of about a dozen private dining rooms, a new boardroom, a gourmet kitchen, and a host station where reservations were maintained and visitors escorted to their meetings with Citigroup executives. A new menu was prepared for each meal, offering at least six choices. In the elegant modern wood-paneled dining rooms, tables were set with expensive china, linen place mats, and vases filled with fresh roses. Sandy's private dining room—the grandest one, in the corner—had a separate seating area, bar, and private staff entrance. The only other executive with access to it was Bob Rubin—and then only if Sandy was traveling.

At times it seemed almost too good to be true. "I wake up every morning and pinch my ear to make sure I'm not dreaming," Sandy unabashedly told a group of business colleagues.

Still, not everything was perfect. In July 2000, Sandy abruptly told the Citigroup board that his son, Marc, chief of the firm's $113-billion investment portfolio, was leaving the company. Sandy told the board that his forty-four-year-old son would be replaced, and then he moved on to the next topic on the agenda with no further explanation. Rumors had swirled for months about Marc, who had been acting erratically, especially in business situations, and dozing through meetings. Sandy generally turned away any inquiries about Marc, even from close friends. Months later, *The Wall Street Journal* reported that Marc Weill had left his $2-million-a-year job amid a battle with cocaine dependency, and the *New York Post* gossip column chronicled Marc's active nightlife under the headline CITI HONCHO'S SON AND PORN QUEEN.

For all his successes, though, Sandy remained awed by how far he'd come, displaying an endearing wonderment along with his oversized ego. His corner office reflected his need to show off both his increased prominence and his humble start. As the awards, honorary doctorates, and magazine covers proliferated going into 2001, Sandy carefully arranged the trophies, framed certificates, and covers on the shelves along the two walls of windows overlooking Park Avenue and Fifty-third Street. Gag gifts, such as the "Weill-opoly" board—"for advanced players only" with every square representing a deal—were relegated to the walls of his private bathroom.

At the same time, the large framed photograph of his modest Brooklyn boyhood home, shared with his grandparents and another family, occupied a prominent wall in his seating area. He liked reminding himself—and others—of how far he had climbed. Early family photos, still in the original cheap plastic frames, shared space with the tattered fake-leather scrapbooks of his early career, many missing their labels. His favorite perch, his leather tufted sofa, was peeling and cracked in numerous spots.

Even Citigroup's competitors were paying him tribute, albeit not directly. J.P. Morgan, which had rejected Sandy's overtures to merge three years earlier, and Chase Manhattan Bank—until Citigroup's formation, the largest bank in the nation—were both fiercely independent. Yet in the fall of 2001, they merged in a tacit admission that neither could survive long term against the financial-services juggernaut that Sandy had created.

BUYING TROUBLE

Merging Citicorp with Travelers may have been the "mother of all deals," but it certainly wasn't the end of all deals. Firmly ensconced as Citigroup's CEO, Sandy once again began indulging his passion for acquisitions. Deryck Maughan, who had been kicked upstairs and put in charge of acquisitions as a result of his ballroom brawl with Jamie Dimon, quickly discovered just how important his new post was. Together, he and Sandy oversaw dozens of acquisitions in 2000 and 2001, ranging from the minor purchase of a $100-million credit-card portfolio auctioned off by a small bank, to the $31-billion acquisition of Associates First Capital, the biggest consumer-finance company in the United States and a deal that, for Sandy, was second in size only to Citicorp.

Ever since Sandy had jump-started his stalled career by buying dowdy little Commercial Credit Corp., he had nurtured a fondness for the reliable if unglamorous business of lending at high rates to customers most banks wouldn't let in the door. Associates, which had been founded in 1918 as part of Ford Motor Co. to help people finance the purchase of Model Ts, had long been a vexing challenge to Sandy and his Commercial Credit team. Every time they wanted to buy a smaller lender, they found themselves bidding against Associates. When Ford spun off Associates in 1998, Sandy put it on a target list of possible acquisition candidates. In late August 2000, after a dinner with Associates chairman Keith Hughes, Sandy had the makings of a deal. A really big deal.

Sandy quickly tracked down Bob Willumstad at his weekend house in Vermont and told him to start due diligence on Associates. Willumstad, who had planned to spend the Labor Day weekend in Vermont, told Sandy he would get right on it when he returned to the office on Tuesday, the day after Labor Day.

"No! No! No!" Sandy screamed. "I want to take it to the board on Tuesday. Start Friday and work through the weekend."

On his way back to New York for a weekend of wading through financial documents, Willumstad mused that even though Sandy was now the king of the financial empire, he was still obsessed with deals and with doing them at "Sandy deal speed." The Citigroup CEO called Willumstad several times each day, as if the deal were a patient in intensive care, Willumstad thought. The patient pulled through. Citigroup announced the all-stock acquisition of Associates the next week.

But Willumstad's due diligence had turned up a problem. The largest player in the business of making loans to people with poor credit histories, Associates had long been under attack from consumer advocates and state regulators angered by what they considered the company's high-pressure and misleading tactics. Sandy and Willumstad figured that Citigroup's reputation for fair business practices would earn Associates a reprieve from such attacks. But they figured wrong. Suddenly, the vocal critics who had labored to bring an obscure outfit called Associates to heel found themselves with a much, much bigger target, a target with a name everyone knew: Citigroup. Suddenly Citigroup was being accused often and loudly of predatory lending.

Taken by surprise, Willumstad and Marge Magner scrambled to fix the problem. They suspended business relations with 3,600 independent brokers of subprime mortgage loans—about 60 percent of Associates' contractors—for having inadequate licenses, using questionable tactics, or failing to sign a code of conduct. But that wasn't enough.

The critics shifted the focus of their criticism to one of Associates' most lucrative products: single-premium credit insurance for home owners. Basically a mortgage-insurance product for home owners who might lose their jobs, Associates was minting money off single-premium credit insurance policies. Not only did it charge far more than the product was worth, but it also convinced new home buyers to amortize the cost of the premium over the life of the loan, a huge cost to the borrowers and one that often put the new home owners in default within a few years of their purchase. Even politicians maligned the product and scheduled a Capitol Hill hearing to investigate and publicize the problem. Now fully aware that Citigroup's big name and deep pockets made it an extremely attractive target, Willumstad and general counsel Prince flew to Washington. They told lawmakers that Citigroup would drop single-premium insurance. The decisive action headed off the hearing, but soon the Federal Trade Commission began an investigation into the product. Certainly the problems that Citigroup had blithely assumed would disappear once it took over Associates had made the acquisition much more costly than originally intended. But it had removed the biggest competitor in the consumer-finance arena and in that sense was well worth the price.

As acquisitive as ever, Sandy still wasn't going to pursue anything and everything. When American General Corp., a Houston-based life insurer, was put on the block, Deryck Maughan thought it attractive enough to present to an Armonk meeting of senior executives as a possible target. The Citigroup executives knew that American International Group, the insurance giant, was also sniffing around American General. AIG's strong-willed chairman and CEO, Maurice Greenberg, had been a friendly rival of Sandy's for years. After a lengthy discussion of the merits of American General, Sandy went around the table one last time to decide whether to offer the $20 billion or more it would take to win the bidding against AIG.

"We can make it work," said one executive. "It would be interesting," said another.

"It can't just be a good idea," Sandy warned. "Good execution is just as important." He looked at the gathered executives and sensed that none of them really wanted to run American General. Maughan knew that Sandy backed people, as well as ideas, and clearly no one wanted to "take ownership" of the project hook, line, and sinker.

"We'll pass," Sandy concluded. Within weeks, AIG announced that it would pay $23 billion for American General.

GOING GLOBAL

Citigroup didn't have to seek out deals. In many cases, the deals were brought to the company. As the first financial firm to hit $1 trillion in assets, Citigroup was the eight-hundred-pound gorilla of global finance. Any financial company anywhere in the world that wanted to sell knew it was a deal-making machine.

When the Polish government called Citigroup to solicit a bid for its Bank Handlowy, which was being privatized and had been targeted as an acquisition by another foreign bank, Sandy traveled to the country from which his parents had emigrated many years earlier. The country's president, Aleksander Kwasniewski, welcomed the global financier almost as a native son. Sandy's Eastern European heritage might have been a huge hurdle to his early career on Wall Street, but here it made negotiating a deal easy. Citigroup bought Bank Handlowy for $1.2 billion.

Acknowledging to his joking executives that the biggest move he had ever made was from Brooklyn to Manhattan, Sandy clearly relished the idea of "going global" in a big way. For his sixty-eighth birthday in 2001, his lieutenants gave him a handheld computer that, with the push of a button, could spit out sentences in different languages. It was already programmed in every available language: "Hi, I'm Sandy Weill, and I want to buy your company."

Citigroup eagerly snapped up foreign targets, including credit-card portfolios in Britain and Canada and a stake in Fubon Group, a Taiwanese financial firm. But what really attracted Sandy were the emerging markets of the world, countries that in Citigroup parlance were "underbanked" and thus ripe for growth. Sandy and his management brainstormed to select five or so key target nations in which to build market share. Mexico emerged at the top of the list, not only because of the North American Free Trade Agreement, but also because of the rapidly growing Hispanic population in the United States.

Almost coincidentally with the decision to focus on Mexico, Bob Rubin one day strolled down the short hall to Sandy's office and laconically mentioned that "I just got a kind of interesting call." The former Treasury secretary, who had spearheaded a $40-billion bailout of a crisis-racked Mexico six years earlier, had just had a call from his old firm, Goldman Sachs. Roberto Hernandez, Mexico's most prominent banker, wanted to know if Citigroup was interested in talking about a merger with his bank, Grupo Financiero Banamex, represented by Goldman.

"That sounds terrific," Sandy said, almost salivating at the thought of teaming up with a bank that had a whopping quarter share of Mexico's market.

"I'll call Hernandez and see if he wants to meet us," Rubin said.

"Tell him we can be in Mexico City tomorrow night," Sandy pushed.

The Mexican bankers didn't like that idea at all. They felt that Rubin, who had such a high profile in the country's crisis in the mid-1990s, would be recognized and sink the deal before it could be formalized. The talks had to be highly secretive; any hint of selling a national bank to "gringos" would be politically explosive in Mexico. Hernandez, Banamex's billionaire chief executive, suggested they meet the next evening deep in the Yucatán jungle at Hacienda San Jose, his family's elegantly restored small hotel.

Sandy and Rubin left without telling anyone else at Citigroup where they were going. In Mexico, they boarded a helicopter for Mérida, a scenic colonial city in the north of the Yucatán peninsula. Under the cover of darkness, the pair landed on ground that had been quickly cleared of the thick jungle brush. Emerging under the chopper's beating blades, the Citigroup executives were surrounded by guards armed with machine guns. Once inside the hacienda, Sandy and Rubin spent the evening with Hernandez and Manuel Medina-Mora, the chief executive of Banamex's holding company.

By the time the Citigroup executives left the next morning, the men had found they had a lot in common and began serious negotiations. After quick due diligence, Sandy closeted the Mexican bankers at Armonk to agree on terms.

"Look, Roberto, rather than sit here and go back and forth, let me just tell you what works," Sandy said after meeting only for an hour or so. The Citigroup CEO preferred getting to the bottom line quickly rather than posturing. "We think this is fair and this is the right number. Hopefully you will find that acceptable."

Hernandez phoned his partners in Mexico. After minor tinkering, they agreed that Citigroup would buy Mexico's second-largest bank for $12.5 billion and give Hernandez and another Banamex official seats on the conglomerate's board. "This speaks to how important that business is," Sandy said. As a concession to the Mexicans, Sandy agreed that he would not sell Banamex's palace headquarters or its historic trove of Mexican art—something he normally would have put on the block in a heartbeat.

The acquisition was hailed in the United States as a brilliant move into America's most important emerging market, making Citigroup the largest bank in a country that remained severely lacking in financial services for the average citizen. But Sandy showed just how shrewd the move was. "This isn't just about growth of the Mexican market but the fast growth of the Hispanic population in the U.S.," he told reporters at the deal's announcement in May.

But the reception wasn't so warm in Mexico. Critics complained that their country's banks were becoming branch offices for foreign firms. The Banamex acquisition represented the biggest foreign investment ever in Mexico. Within a week after Banamex's sale to Citigroup, bombs exploded in branches in protest.

MELLOWING MOGUL

Sandy was in fine form when he presided at Citigroup's annual meeting that spring. A fanatic about punctuality, he appeared on stage at Carnegie Hall several minutes early, when the first two rows of seats—reserved for Citigroup's directors—were empty. As the throngs of shareholders took their seats, Sandy quipped to the crowd, "As soon as we find our board, we'll start. Anyone seen them?" His hands clasped across his ample stomach, he was able to shed some of his anxiety over public speaking by tossing off one-liners. When the high-profile directors filed in, Sandy joked, "I was beginning to think you mutinied."

After his glowing state-of-the-corporation speech, Sandy opened the floor to shareholder questions. After routine inquiries from various shareholders, Dr. Clinton Weiman, the former medical director of the predecessor Citibank, stood. He wanted to know the state of the sixty-eight-year-old CEO's succession plans and his health. Avoiding the issue of succession, Sandy went straight to his health.

"I'm in good shape," he said, then quickly added, in acknowledgment of his obvious girth, "though it doesn't look like it." Then he began reeling off his vital signs: "My blood pressure is 128 over 80. That's good. My cholesterol is 183, and my good cholesterol is 68."

"That's good," agreed the startled physician shareholder.

"I have no lung problems," Sandy continued, alluding to past indulgence of cigars. Then he formed a thumb-and-finger circle and boldly announced his prostate specific antigen reading: "And my prostate number is close to zero."

"I didn't ask that question," Weiman observed amid the giggling shareholders. Still the doctor persisted about Sandy's successor.

Suddenly Sandy's genial expansiveness disappeared. "We have a dialogue between myself and the board of directors about succession," he said, adding only that Citigroup had a cadre of good leaders. In a dig at GE chairman Jack Welch, Sandy said he had no plans to set up a beauty contest among his senior executives, the sort of contest that at GE had resulted in the loss of several excellent executives when they were passed over for the top spot. "Our goal is not to create battles between people. We intend to do this in a quiet, appropriate way."

Suddenly an older lady resplendent in a red hat made her way to the microphone. "Thank you for being the best possible CEO, and please don't be in any hurry to look for someone to take your place." Grinning, Sandy blew her a kiss and happily called the meeting to an end.

Behind the scenes, however, the two directors charged with pursuing succession, Franklin Thomas and Andrall Pearson, were pushing Sandy to expand the responsibilities of executives he thought showed promise. With his longtime lieutenants Bob Lipp and Jamie Dimon gone, the Citigroup CEO reached into the next layer of senior management.

Using his prestigious membership at the famed Augusta National, Sandy invited Lipp, Bob Willumstad, and Jay Fishman to join him for a weekend of golf. After playing two rounds on Saturday, the men returned to the cabin to change for dinner and have drinks. As Sandy sipped his martini and the others drank wine, Sandy told them that Lipp's retirement meant he needed more help. Turning to the fifty-three-year-old Willumstad, he said, "Basically you'll take over Bob's responsibilities on consumer banking." Upon the forty-eight-year-old Fishman, who was running Travelers, he bestowed new responsibilities at the parent company, naming him chief operating officer. General counsel Chuck Prince would also be elevated as another COO. Without saying anything about succession, Sandy ushered them to the clubhouse for dinner.

A beaming Sandy was given his kelly-green member jacket when they entered. He immediately ordered a bottle of fine wine, and then another—this time a much larger magnum—which the four finished off with their rare steaks. Back at their cottage, Sandy and his colleagues shed their coats, ties, and shoes and stayed up past midnight drinking and talking about how to run the vast empire of Citigroup.

But just as Sandy was promoting some longtime aides, others were leaving to join Jamie Dimon, whose non-compete agreement was expiring. Even before Sandy and Dimon had "made up" at Christmas, the new Bank One CEO had hired several high-level Citigroup executives. Dimon had been forbidden under his severance agreement from soliciting Citigroup executives, but he couldn't stop them from coming to him to offer their services. Very soon after Dimon's appointment as CEO of Bank One, Michael Cavanagh, Charles Scharf, and Jim Boshart—Dimon's closest friends at Salomon Smith Barney—moved to Chicago for prominent positions. Even an original Citicorp executive, retail-banking chief Bill Campbell, joined Bank One as a consultant.

Although Sandy and Dimon had renewed their friendship, Jamie's parents, Ted and Themis Dimon, remained steadfastly aloof from the Weills, still resentful over Sandy's treatment of their talented son. Since Sandy's and Dimon's make-up lunch at the Four Seasons, the two had gotten together a few times more for drinks when Dimon was in New York. At one of those occasions, Sandy made what was for him an uncharacteristic first move to mend the hard feelings with the Dimons. He told his onetime deputy how much Joan missed Dimon's mother.

The next night, Dimon, still in Manhattan, had dinner with his parents. His mother confided to him, "I miss Joan."

"So, Mom, start seeing her again," Dimon responded, knowing that Joan would be receptive. He had never told his parents to break off their long friendship with the Weills. Now Dimon decided to help the healing process and phoned Joan the following day.

"I want you to know that my mother misses you," Dimon began. "If Sandy and I can make up, it's probably just as easy for anyone else to make up."

Soon Joan and Themis Dimon exchanged letters and had lunch as they sought to become the friends they once had been to each other. By mid-2001, the women persuaded their husbands to have dinner with them.

As the freeze between the Weills and Dimons thawed, Sandy also began to accept that some of his executives would want to join Dimon at Bank One. When the first round of executives followed Dimon to the nation's fifth-largest banking holding company, Sandy had blown up and let his competitor know it. Telling an intermediary because the pair weren't speaking at the time, Sandy had warned: "CEOs don't behave like that." By the summer of 2001, when Dimon took the initiative of dipping into the Citigroup talent pool, Sandy held his fire, even as the talent drain prompted observers to dub Bank One "Citi West."

9/11

The first huge jetliner slammed into the north tower of the World Trade Center at 8:45 A.M. The second smashed into the south tower at 9:03 A.M. Within minutes of that second strike, Citigroup officials were ordering the mass evacuation of some 16,000 employees from a dozen sites in Lower Manhattan. By 10:30 A.M. both World Trade Center towers were nothing more than smoldering ruins. Nearly 3,000 people were dead. All of the Citigroup employees evacuated from neighboring buildings escaped safely; six Citigroup employees making calls at the World Trade Center that morning died. Later that day the now-evacuated 7 World Trade Center, a building in which Citigroup occupied 39 of 47 floors, collapsed, the result of damage from the fall of the Trade Center towers.

The horrific attacks struck hard at the nation's financial markets. Vital communications systems were severed, forcing the stock, bond, and commodities markets to shut down. In a flurry of phone calls that morning, Citigroup and J.P. Morgan Chase, the nation's two largest banks, offered chilling field reports to the New York Federal Reserve and the Securities and Exchange Commission. The bank executives described a phenomenon they had never seen before: cash hoarding. Dozens of big companies were trying to draw down their credit lines at banks. At the same time, terrified individuals were lining up to pull cash from ATMs around the country. By 11:30 A.M., the two banks were under siege.

J.P. Morgan, its Lower Manhattan offices undamaged but evacuated, had to tell clients it simply couldn't execute their requests for drawdowns of cash from their credit lines. Frantic finance executives accused the bank of stonewalling to avoid the unknown risks to the nation's financial infrastructure in the aftermath of the terrorist attacks. While Citigroup's downtown offices were empty, too, it was able to quickly shift authority for funding decisions to its offices in midtown New York and in New Jersey and provided the necessary short-term liquidity to its corporate clients who couldn't use the securities markets or other banks.

Early the next morning American Airlines, whose planes had been used as weapons in the terrorist attacks, wanted to draw down on its $860-million revolving credit facility. J.P. Morgan could not immediately fund its $100-million portion, and other, smaller banks indicated they were in the same predicament. Citigroup, the lead lender on the American Airlines syndicate, funded the entire loan on behalf of the bank group without any assurance of timely reimbursement from the other banks.

Almost immediately after the attacks, Citigroup shifted the responsibility for global consumer services to its offices in London, Chicago, and San Francisco to prevent an interruption of service. On September 12, Travelers Insurance catastrophe-response vans arrived just a few blocks from Ground Zero, processing claims and approving overdraft limits for people hit hard by the attack.

Sandy Weill personally intervened to aid competitors. Like many financial firms, Lehman Brothers Holding Inc. was displaced from its Wall Street–area headquarters and sought office space in midtown, including

Citigroup's Park Avenue building. Because Citigroup had been hurt by the attack, too, its real-estate planners told Lehman CEO Richard Fuld that Citi had to use its extra space to relocate its own professionals.

Fuld decided to pay their boss a visit. "Sandy, this is what I need: five hundred thousand square feet," Fuld implored the Citi CEO. "Your guys say they don't have it to spare."

"We don't," Sandy replied, adding that he would nevertheless do anything he could to find the space. Within hours, Sandy gave Fuld 450,000 square feet on seven floors on Park Avenue by reconfiguring Citigroup's own real-estate plan.

Fuld phoned Sandy with a simple message: "Sandy, I owe you."

In the terrible days following the attacks, Sandy took steps to help victims and the U.S. government. He announced a $15-million gift from Citigroup to pay for the education of children whose parents, whether workers in the towers or rescuers, died in the attacks. His officials, including former Treasury Secretary Rubin, offered advice to the Treasury Department and FBI on how money flowed around the world, as well as what additional steps could be taken to prevent the financing of terrorism.

A few weeks after the tragedy, Sandy, along with other business leaders, met with President George W. Bush to discuss the economy, which had already been in a slump before September 11. Citigroup had one fifth of the U.S. market for credit-card transactions, and Sandy could provide detailed data on sales volumes, delinquency rates, and other indicators of how the public was reacting. After the meeting, Citigroup continued to supply updates on credit-card data to Treasury Secretary Paul O'Neill.

Amid the overwhelming sorrow of the losses from the September 11 attacks, Sandy had to endure the loss as well of a close personal friend. On September 22, Isaac Stern, the president of Carnegie Hall and the man who had introduced Sandy to the grandeur of classical music, died at eighty-one years of age of complications from heart surgery. Years earlier Stern had reassured a demoralized Sandy, who had just been forced out of American Express, that Carnegie Hall still needed his advice and energy. Now Sandy stood before a packed Carnegie Hall audience to eulogize his friend.

"Welcome to Isaac Stern's favorite room," he began. "Isaac loved to say what made Carnegie Hall so special was the spirit of Tchaikovsky, Horowitz, Toscanini, and countless others in these walls. Now Isaac joins those spirits within Carnegie Hall." Sandy's were the only words from the stage. The remainder of the tribute came from the instruments of Itzhak Perlman, Emanuel Ax, Yo-Yo Ma, Midori, and other famous musicians who let their performances speak for them.

October didn't get any better for Sandy. On the Tuesday after Columbus Day, Jay Fishman, whom Sandy had made a co-chief operating officer months earlier to recognize emerging talent at Citigroup, asked to see his boss after the weekly management meeting.

"This is a difficult conversation for me, and I'm certain this is going to surprise you," Fishman said. "I've been offered the job of chairman and CEO of St. Paul Companies, and it's a remarkable opportunity for me."

"I'm shocked," Sandy said. "I'm shocked."

"I want to go and run my own place—just like you did," Fishman said, explaining why he would leave his huge job at Citi for a much smaller insurance company based in St. Paul, Minnesota.

"I'm shocked," Sandy repeated. "I'm shocked."

Then Fishman, an ambitious executive widely considered to covet Sandy's job, told his boss that St. Paul wanted to announce his hiring in a couple of days. Sandy's shock turned to anger. It wasn't right to give Citigroup so little notice! Fishman pleaded with Sandy to understand: "This isn't about loyalty but about opportunity."

After Fishman left his office, Sandy called Bob Willumstad to tell him of Fishman's plan. "I feel like a stranger by what he has done," Sandy told Willumstad. Sandy's only solace came a few days later when press releases from Citigroup and St. Paul announced Fishman's switch: St. Paul's stock jumped 9 percent. It was the "Weill premium"—anyone who had risen through the ranks under Sandy Weill had to know how to run a company.

As the end of the year drew near, more problems arose. The nation's economy sank into recession. The stock market continued to decline as chastened investors surveyed the wreckage of the great bull market of the 1990s and the bursting of the high-tech "bubble" in 2000. Companies, too, that had ridden the stock market mania to huge valuations in the late 1990s were now struggling to survive. And the economic malaise was spreading abroad. Argentina, where Citigroup had a huge presence, was in particularly grave straits.

On December 21, 2001, Argentine president Fernando de la Rúa resigned amid mounting economic turmoil. That caught Sandy's attention. He began asking his executives—in meetings and in the halls—questions: "Is everything okay? How is Argentina?"

"Argentina will get through this," he was told.

But when bread riots and antigovernment melees toppled five presidents in December alone, Sandy realized that Citigroup had a real mess on its hands. "I want to know how much I can lose," the CEO roared in one intense meeting. His emerging-markets executives, led by Victor Menezes, acknowledged that the company would have significant securities losses, unrecoverable loans, and deficits from the peso's decline against the U.S. dollar after Argentina devalued its currency. Their prediction: $300 million. Executives who had been with Sandy for more years than Menezes, who came from Citibank, knew that the number had better be right. Sandy had a steel-trap mind for numbers; if you promised a number, you sure as hell better deliver.

Closer to home another huge problem suddenly loomed. Enron Corp., the Houston energy firm once touted as the nation's most innovative company and the world's biggest buyer and seller of energy, suddenly stood on the brink of collapse, the result of massive fraud and mismanagement. Citigroup had lent Enron large amounts of money and had insured numerous aspects of the company. Worried, Sandy began phoning Chuck Prince each morning with long lists of questions about Enron's prospects and Citigroup's exposure. As Enron spun out of control, Bob Rubin, speaking as a banker and ex–Treasury chief concerned about the risks an Enron collapse might pose to markets, called the Treasury Department to see if the Bush administration could help save Enron. No, was the answer. And the fact that he had even asked for government intervention on behalf of a Citigroup client drew widespread criticism of Rubin and the company.

In December, Enron filed for bankruptcy protection, then the largest ever in U.S. history. With thousands of workers laid off, the Enron stock in their retirement portfolios virtually worthless, and company officers acknowledging that the company had overstated its profits for years, the firestorm began. The anger and legal maneuvers were focused on Enron's executives, under criminal investigation, and Arthur Andersen, the accounting firm that failed to detect the frauds or warn investors or regulators.

Even though Argentina and Enron were huge failures in their own right, Sandy nevertheless was in a position as the year ended to tell analysts and ratings agencies that his model of a global financial supermarket was working. Certainly Citigroup had been hurt by September 11 and by the problems engulfing Argentina and Enron. Nevertheless, Citigroup's reach and diversity, in geography, clients, and products, had allowed the company to weather the setbacks with little financial damage. In the last quarter, profit rose 36 percent as lending to consumers surged, even after writing off nearly $700 million for Enron's collapse and Argentina's default. Convinced by Sandy's leadership, the depth of management talent at Citigroup, and the company's business model, Standard & Poor's and Moody's upgraded Citigroup's ratings to one notch below triple-A.

On New Year's Eve, Sandy and Joan traditionally invited a few couples who were their closest friends to spend the evening with them at their retreat in the Adirondack Mountains of upstate New York. On December 31, 2001, Citigroup directors Arthur Zankel and Ken Bialkin and their wives were there, as usual. A new addition to the group was Chuck Prince, who had become Sandy's closest confidant inside Citigroup. After Jamie Dimon's firing, Sandy looked to Prince, whom he had discovered at Commercial Credit, as a sounding board and advisor. Indeed Prince, recently separated from his wife, had intensified his devotion to Sandy and Citigroup. Humorous and intelligent, Prince was so protective of his boss that he would even put his arm around Sandy when they crossed a street.

"I'm glad 2001 is over," Sandy told the close-knit group as they went around the table reminiscing about the difficult year. "Next year should be a much better year," the Citigroup CEO cheerfully predicted as he toasted 2002.

18

BLINDSIDED

In January 2002, Eduardo Duhalde became Argentina's newest president. His was supposed to be a caretaker government until elections could be held in March. But Duhalde was no mere caretaker. Determined to end the financial crisis besetting his country, Duhalde took severe measures: He broke Argentina's decade-old link between the peso and the dollar and froze all deposits to halt a run on the nation's banks. These were moves that Citigroup's emerging-markets specialists had never anticipated. As the news went from bad to worse, Sandy named Chuck Prince, a lawyer by training, to be the new chief operating officer of Citigroup's emerging-markets unit. He needed someone he trusted to find out how much Citigroup might lose. Within a few months, the shocking answer came back: Huge loan and currency losses would slash Citigroup's profits by $2.3 billion, two billion more than Citigroup executives had first predicted.

Sandy was livid. The vast losses were bad enough. But to have been caught by surprise was unforgivable. Menezes suddenly found himself kicked upstairs, a vice chairman with no further operational authority. Deryck Maughan, who had quietly bided his time overseeing acquisitions and Internet strategy, was put in charge of all international business, including emerging markets. Sandy told Maughan to overhaul international operations. No more think tanks! From now on, executives were accountable for any losses in their business units. To outsiders, it suddenly seemed that Maughan, who had recently been knighted Sir Deryck by Queen Elizabeth, was back in the race to succeed Sandy.

But Sandy wasn't saying a word about succession. If anything, he continued to make changes that clouded the issue.

Early in 2002, Sandy told Bob Willumstad, who ran all consumer operations since Lipp's retirement, that he wanted to see him the next morning to talk about bonuses for Willumstad's top lieutenants. *Damn*, thought Willumstad, *we aren't supposed to do that for two weeks*. He spent the rest of the day scurrying to put together the facts and figures he would use to argue for big bonuses to reward the consumer group's outstanding performance in 2001. At 8:30 A.M. the following day, Willumstad went to Sandy's office. He purposely sat in the chair next to Sandy's stock-quotation terminal. That way Sandy would be looking at least in his general direction for most of the time they talked. Willumstad began reciting his group's terrific year and the unbelievable results consumer banking had achieved.

"Yes, yes, yes," Sandy responded, clearly not paying much attention.

Willumstad paused to see if something was bothering his boss. He was surprised when Sandy got up and shut his office door, something he seldom bothered to do no matter how sensitive the matter under discussion. Then Sandy plopped onto his couch and hoisted his legs sideways across the sofa.

"Now let me tell you what I really want to talk about," Sandy began. "I've been thinking about making some changes. There's a lot going on around here." Indeed there was. Some analysts had begun to question how one man could possibly manage the financial behemoth that was Citigroup. Then Sandy blurted out his plan: "I would like to make you president but this has nothing to do with succession."

"I'm surprised," Willumstad replied, noting to himself that Sandy's sentence contained no punctuation separating the offer from the matter of succession. The succession issue clearly was *not* under discussion.

"Really, why?" Sandy asked.

"I didn't think you were prepared to do this, with me or anybody else," the tall, unassuming executive said. Since Dimon's ouster, Sandy hadn't named anyone to the position of president. They talked a few minutes about the additional duties Willumstad would assume, as he carefully weighed the post.

"Do you accept?" Sandy pushed.

"Well, I guess so," Willumstad answered tentatively.

Willumstad spent the weekend pondering the role he was being asked to take at Citigroup. Perhaps it was a bigger job than he was ready to take on. And why was Sandy doing this now? A year earlier, when Bob Lipp began talking about retirement, he was clearly hinting that he wanted to be named president, but Sandy had let him retire without even broaching the question. *And Lipp and Sandy were a lot closer than Sandy and I are,* Willumstad thought. *It just seems weird that Sandy would name me president when he wouldn't give Lipp the title.*

On Monday, Willumstad called Sandy to say he needed to talk some more about the job.

"What's the matter?" Sandy asked.

"Let's talk about what this means," Willumstad replied.

Sandy quickly rearranged his schedule to have lunch with Willumstad that day in his private dining room at Citigroup headquarters. The fifty-six-year-old banker, who had left Chemical Bank to join Sandy at Commercial Credit years earlier, was a standout in Sandy's management ranks. Consumer banking had put in an impressive performance in a bad economy. Sandy respected Willumstad's fervor and finesse at cutting costs, as well as his masterly ability to integrate new operations, from Citi Cards to Associates branches.

"I would really like to know the context in which you made this decision," Willumstad began at lunch. "I know you said this has nothing to do with succession, but do you have a time frame in your mind as to how much longer you're going to be around?"

There it was again, the hated question.

"Well, some days I think I won't be here much longer," Sandy said evasively. "Other times I have no intention of retiring."

"I'm not asking to be the successor," Willumstad clarified. "But clearly becoming president has some meaning to the outside world and the rest of the organization. And I don't know whether I ever would want your job."

"That's no problem." Sandy grinned. "I'm not offering it to you."

"But at some point in time, you'll leave. . . ." Willumstad tried again to pin Sandy down. He was still grappling with why Sandy wanted him to be president and why now. Maughan was no longer in the doghouse, and Mike Carpenter was running Salomon Smith Barney at a profit. Outsiders considered them to be much more likely to inherit Sandy's mantle, and Willumstad knew it.

"I don't know what I would do if I retired," Sandy said, revealing his unwillingness to give up his corporate identity. "What am I going to do? I can't play golf every day."

"But if you had some point in time, in the next year or two, you intended to leave and you thought I might be a candidate for your job, you probably should not give me this title," Willumstad said.

"I'm not going to be out of here that soon," Sandy said, still evasive but clearly pleased that his choice for president wasn't breathing down his neck to take his place. "I just want some help running this place. It's a big company, and we could do better."

"Does this make sense for the organization?" Willumstad asked. "Are you sure I'm the right person? There are just so many different pieces in the business."

"Don't worry about it," Sandy assured him. "In six months, you'll feel differently."

Finally, Willumstad, who had never finished college but had methodically propelled consumer banking to account for more than half of the Citigroup's profits, agreed to become president. "This is a big deal," he told Sandy.

"Yes, it is," Sandy agreed. "I remember when I was told I would be president of American Express, I couldn't wait to go home and tell Joan."

The Citigroup board approved Willumstad as president, although some conceded that while he was an excellent executive, he didn't cut a very high profile. "One day we woke up and Willumstad was running half the business and the most profitable half," one director noted as they discussed Willumstad's qualifications. Other directors wondered if Willumstad's promotion fulfilled the letter, if certainly not the intent, of Sandy's promise to the board two years earlier to come up with a succession plan. Director Andrall Pearson had been pushing Sandy to give greater responsibility to his executives to see if they could grow to become "successor material."

When Willumstad's appointment was announced, however, Sandy made it crystal clear that he wasn't anointing anyone. "If I were naming an heir apparent, I would have said that," he chided reporters. *The New York Times* headline called the new president "a quiet banker in a big shadow." Insiders at Citi generally welcomed Willumstad's new role, because his personality was so different from Sandy's—he never lost his temper, he loved giving others credit, and he didn't play favorites. And Willumstad could be fun; for his fifty-fifth birthday, the avid snowboarder and Elvis Presley fan donned an Elvis wig and flashy jumpsuit for the party.

One of Willumstad's first big assignments as president came as a surprise—he was to help Sandy, the Grand Acquisitor, *sell* one of Citigroup's core companies. Even when Citigroup had been doing well amid a healthy economy, Sandy hadn't been happy with the company's price-to-earnings multiple. And he knew the source of the problem: Travelers Property Casualty insurance company. Certainly Travelers was profitable. Sandy had made sure of that when he took it over back in 1993. But within Citigroup, Travelers wasn't as profitable as the other financial-services units, and thus it became a drag on Citigroup's profits and on its stock price. It would have to go. Sandy had devised a plan to cut the insurance company loose in a spin-off, leaving Citigroup with the faster-growing financial businesses.

Underlying Sandy's move was the realization that the property and casualty insurance business—even Travelers', the jewel in the industry—wasn't a good "cross-sell" with banking and other financial services. Citigroup would, however, keep the smallest part of Travelers, its life and annuity business, because the bankers and brokers had been successfully selling its insurance and investment products to their clients.

Sandy had chosen the right time to sell Travelers. While it was true that insurers had been hammered by the disastrous losses—estimated at more than $50 billion—associated with the attack on the Twin Towers, it was also true that they had taken those onetime losses as an opportunity to hike their rates sharply, and those hikes likely would remain in effect for years to come. The prospect of a prolonged period of higher revenue had persuaded investors that insurance was a good bet, and stock prices of insurance companies had reached dizzying heights amid an otherwise sickly stock market.

Sandy's plan called for an initial public offering of 20 percent of Travelers to investors; the rest was to be spun off to Citigroup shareholders to do with as they pleased. And Sandy had just the guy to run the new company. Bob Lipp had already confessed that he was "flunking" retirement and was itching to be back in charge of something. Lipp had been the driving force behind Travelers' turnaround after Sandy acquired the insurer in the mid-1990s. He was delighted when Sandy asked him to return to the helm. But the delight faded fast. During his years with Sandy, Lipp had always been negotiating alongside Sandy or with his backing. Now, suddenly, he was on the other side of the table, and it wasn't a pleasant place. Sandy was unmerciful in trying to structure the transaction for Citigroup's maximum advantage at the expense of the new, independent Travelers. Lipp knew how critical it was to get the new company off to a sound start and balked at Sandy's demands. Tensions quickly rose between the two former colleagues. Sandy infuriated Lipp by implying that since Lipp had never run a public company, he should defer to Sandy's wishes. They feuded over real-estate valuations and the size of Citigroup's reserves for Travelers' asbestos liability. Willumstad, caught between his close friend Lipp and the boss who had just made him president, often reluctantly stepped in to mediate.

Eventually the financial issues were settled. But then came the biggest question: Who would get the red umbrella? Each man wanted the beloved logo for his company.

"It will always be known as the Travelers umbrella," Lipp argued. After all, the red umbrella had been part of Travelers' advertising since the insurance company's beginnings in the 1800s. "Even twenty years from now, it will be the Travelers umbrella!"

Sandy, who had been enamored of the umbrella since taking over Travelers in 1993, vehemently disagreed. "Now it means Citigroup," Sandy retorted. Citigroup had slapped the red umbrella on every single entity from Salomon Smith Barney to Citibank and spent millions of dollars on advertising, signage, and stationery, he added. Besides, "I've probably invested in more umbrella clothes than all the people up there put together," Sandy said, referring to the Travelers employees in Hartford. That may have been true, especially when counting Sandy's dozens of expensive Hermès silk ties. Ultimately, Lipp accepted the loss of the red umbrella as the price for Travelers' independence. Sandy simply was not going to give up the cherished icon that he had so tightly woven into Citigroup's identity—and his own.

Emerging victorious from the Travelers sale, Sandy began to think that 2002 really would be a better year for him and Citigroup. Then the first suggestions that it might not emanated from an unlikely venue: tiny Augusta, Georgia. The National Council of Women's Organizations was orchestrating a push to force Sandy's cherished Augusta National Golf Club to admit female members. Other golf clubs—indeed, all sorts of clubs—excluded women from membership. But Augusta, site of the Masters golf tournament each April, was a high-profile target, assuring the women's group that its efforts would get plenty of publicity. Sandy had taken special delight over the years in being a member of the club and having Citigroup among the major sponsors of the Masters. Now he was horrified to find the club—and himself—the focus of news stories about the controversy. Many of the stories posed exactly the question that the women's council was using as an economic lever to pry open the club's membership rolls: How can the chief executive officers of publicly traded companies that supposedly value women employees and women clients belong to a discriminatory old-boys' club or use their companies' money to support its tournament?

At first, Sandy tried to abide by the club's policy that members were forbidden to talk about the club. The club itself, in an expensive effort to squirm out of the issue, simply dropped all television sponsors for the tournament. Given the immense wealth of its members, it could afford to ignore the kind of economic pressure the women's coalition was trying to apply.

But economic pressure was only one weapon in the arsenal of the National Council of Women's Organizations. It wasn't nearly as effective as another—bad publicity. Suddenly Sandy found his picture flashing on network newscasts that identified him as one of the members of the all-male bastion and corporate sponsor of its tournament. Sandy was trapped: certainly Citigroup valued women, whether as employees or customers. As if to prove it, around that time *Fortune* magazine unveiled its list of the most powerful women in business in 2002. Marge Magner, now chief operating officer of Citigroup's entire consumer bank—which the magazine called the company's "crown jewel"—was ranked as the twenty-second most influential, up from her spot as thirty-third a year earlier. Her Citigroup colleagues surprised her with a cake and champagne party the afternoon the issue came out. When Sandy dropped in, he gave Magner a big hug and a kiss on the cheek.

"Congratulations—you're moving up," the boss told the fifty-three-year-old Magner before the group gathered in the executive lounge. "I'm so proud of you. You're number one to us!"

Then Sandy looked plaintively at his highest-ranking female executive and asked her, "What am I going to do?" He didn't have to tell her he was talking about the difficult situation in which he found himself with Augusta.

"If you're a member of a club that's restricted, you have to evaluate how important that membership is to you," Magner responded.

Damn! Sandy didn't want to hear that. He loved being a member of the most exclusive club in the world.

But Magner wasn't backing down. "You know what I think—you shouldn't belong to a club that discriminates against women."

A few days later, Magner, flying to Japan on Citigroup business, picked up a newspaper. As she was about to toss out the sports section, Sandy's mug caught her eye. Sandy in the sports section? Then she read that the Citigroup chairman had sent a letter to the National Council of Women's Organizations promising that he would work within the club to support the admittance of women into Augusta National. He was the first CEO to come out publicly in favor of female members. He hadn't resigned from the club, but he had taken a groundbreaking stand for women. *Good for him.* Magner smiled.

But even that bold step wasn't enough. After Augusta National chairman William "Hootie" Johnson reiterated that the all-male club wouldn't change its admission policies to add women in the near future, *The New York Times* weighed in with an editorial suggesting that Tiger Woods should skip the Masters as a gesture against sexism. It also called for the chief executive officer of Citigroup to "lead the way" for other prominent executives by resigning his membership. Despite his vow to work internally for change, Augusta National continued to haunt Sandy.

TARGET

By the spring of 2002, millions of individual investors had gotten past the shock and denial of seeing the value of their stock portfolios collapse and were now in the anger phase of the lingering bear market. That anger was fueled by disclosures of corporate misdeeds and the astounding greed of some executives. Activists and politicians, always keenly attuned to shifts in public attitudes, sensed that they had a huge opportunity to capitalize on the public's anger. In many cases—including Citigroup—corporate leaders were shocked at the vehemence of the attacks against them.

When Sandy took the podium to conduct Citigroup's annual meeting in April 2002, he was ill prepared for the barrage of angry questions and criticisms aimed at him and his beloved company. Some issues had almost nothing to do with the heart of Citigroup's business. The Rainforest Action Committee accused Citigroup of "destructive lending" to finance pipelines and other projects that they said ravaged old-growth forests and contributed to global warming.

When Sandy nominated George David, chairman and CEO of United Technologies Corp., as a Citigroup director, a shareholder questioned the move, noting that Sandy already served on the United Technologies board.

It was noted that Sandy had the same cozy relationship with Mike Armstrong, AT&T's chief: Each man sat on the other's board of directors.

"We look for the best possible people," Sandy replied curtly. "I can't imagine a conflict."

Then other shareholders spoke up to lambaste Armstrong—and Sandy, as a director—for the drastic decline in AT&T under Armstrong's leadership. As the rants continued, Sandy impatiently shifted his weight behind the podium on the Carnegie Hall stage. He tried to defend the AT&T chief executive. "I think Mike Armstrong is one of our best directors," he said. The attacks were taking a toll on Sandy. More than usual, he looked down at Joan sitting in the second row. Their eyes locked many times during the morning as Sandy's ethics, more than his business acumen, were called into question. It was as if the Citigroup chairman was looking to his wife for advice: Do I cut this guy off or let him keep criticizing me? Finally he called a halt to the AT&T attacks.

"Mr. Armstrong is not available for comment now," Sandy said tersely. "This is a meeting of Citigroup."

Another sign of the declining awe in which shareholders held Sandy and other rich executives was the deafening silence that accompanied the Weills' gift of another $100 million to Cornell University's medical center. Sandy and Joan's initial contribution had resulted in the medical center's naming its building for them, and reams of publicity. This time the immense gift received barely any mention in the media, except in the *New York Times* society column and in coverage of the new mayor of New York City. Self-made billionaire mayor Michael Bloomberg showed up for Cornell's announcement of the Weills' second gift despite his packed schedule. Sandy's invitation to appear "wasn't a question, it was an order," Mayor Bloomberg quipped, knowing how to stroke the ego of one of the city's biggest employers and a fellow business mogul.

Certainly in the midst of a bear market, executives in the financial-services industry—including Sandy—could expect to take a little heat. "This, too, shall pass" seemed to be the prevailing philosophy. After all, the Bush administration was clearly pro-business, and while Congress often postured about taking action against Wall Street, too much money flowed to incumbents' campaigns from the financial-services industry for anyone to take those threats too seriously. But on April 8 the industry was blindsided by an attack from an unexpected direction: Eliot Spitzer, New York State's ambitious but little-known attorney general, unleashed a masterful campaign against corruption in the financial world. Stunning Wall Street, Spitzer accused Merrill Lynch & Co. of misleading investors by issuing overly bullish and biased stock research. He backed up his charges by releasing dozens of damning internal Merrill Lynch e-mails in which research analysts privately derided stocks that they were publicly touting as good investments. Spitzer charged that the company had given clients investment advice that was dishonest, tainted by the firm's hope of persuading the companies that were subjects of the glowing reports to hire Merrill as their investment banker. His crusade had remarkable similarities to the last time the nation had dealt with out-of-control greed and deception on Wall Street in the 1980s. The then U.S. Attorney Rudolph Giuliani helped put Ivan Boesky and Michael Milken in jail.

But Spitzer, scion of a family real-estate fortune and a graduate of Harvard Law School, didn't seem so much interested in putting miscreants behind bars as he did in revamping the way Wall Street did business.

Some Citigroup executives took pleasure in archenemy Merrill's woes. But Sandy was worried. At a management meeting the week after Spitzer leveled his charges at Merrill, Sandy told his executives that "this criticism of research on the Street is bad for the industry, not just Merrill."

Then he pointedly turned to Mike Carpenter, the head of the corporate and investment bank. "I don't like the looks of this," Sandy said. "What are we going to do?"

Every man at the meeting on this Monday morning in April knew full well how research was conducted during the raging bull market of the 1990s. Research analysts worked hand in glove with investment bankers to garner the huge banking fees from which they all drew their spectacular annual bonuses. Few firms routinely disclosed in their supposedly unbiased analytical reports that the company under discussion was an investment-banking client. Under the prevailing system on Wall Street, the majority of stocks covered by analysts were rated a "buy." Only under extraordinary circumstances would an analyst brand a stock "sell."

"The whole research issue could turn into a question of public trust," Sandy said. He knew that during the bull market it had become industry practice for firms to do what they could to win and keep investment-banking business and the lucrative fees that came with it. He had done his share of pushing and prodding his subordinates and corporate prospects to propel Salomon Smith Barney to the top of the all-important "league tables," the standings showing which brokerage firms are doing the most business. "Mike, check with your people down there [at the Tribeca building] to see if this could be a big thing," he ordered Carpenter.

In May, the venerable Merrill Lynch agreed to pay a $100-million settlement and to implement a set of measures to reform its stock-research process. Dubbed the "Spitzer principles," the reforms would wall off bankers' influence over how analysts were paid and limit the practice of analysts' attending meetings with bankers to pitch for securities-underwriting and merger business. At Sandy's behest, Citigroup's Salomon Smith Barney quickly and voluntarily adopted the reform measures, hoping such fast and decisive action would address Spitzer's concern.

It didn't. In fact, the heat on Sandy and Citigroup intensified as Spitzer, fresh from nailing Merrill, set his sights on other securities firms. The New York attorney general began seeking from the industry what had been his best source of ammunition against Merrill—internal e-mails.

On the night of May 6, 2002, Sandy was set to pick up another honor, the Distinguished Leadership in Business award from Columbia Business School. All afternoon, Citi officials had been debating what e-mails to turn over to the regulators. They haggled over whether e-mails counted in the "books and records rules" requiring retention under federal securities laws.

Leaving his deputies to hash out the dilemma, Sandy hurried along the three blocks from his headquarters on Park Avenue to the Waldorf-Astoria Hotel for the black-tie gala. Before entering the private reception to honor him, Sandy angrily noticed that he had forgotten to put his red umbrella pin on his tuxedo lapel. He never went anywhere without that umbrella pin; he was distracted by the e-mail issue when he fled his office.

Later that evening, his aides, now clad in formal attire, entered as the cocktail party was concluding, just in time for the dinner presentation honoring their boss. But their minds weren't on honors. The e-mail controversy was still at the center of their attention. During dinner, their fingers worked furiously over their handheld BlackBerries rather than their silverware. In the darkened ballroom, as Sandy was recognized for his stellar leadership, his subordinates anxiously e-mailed one another and lawyers back at the office about what position Citigroup would take on the preservation of e-mail communications. In addition to the attorney general, the press also was pushing for answers.

The next morning, *The New York Times* reported the regulators' efforts to secure the e-mail correspondence from Wall Street firms. Salomon

Smith Barney was quoted as saying it had taken a "reasonable approach" on e-mail retention without providing specific parameters.

Within weeks, the general scrutiny of Wall Street's biggest firms narrowed to become a spotlight on the biggest: Citigroup and its securities company. And the pressure was coming not just from one front but from several. Spitzer might have led the charge, but right behind him came an army of lawyers representing aggrieved investors and a phalanx of harrumphing lawmakers eager to curry favor with their angry constituents.

If biased stock research wasn't enough of a problem for Wall Street, Enron's debacle provided critics and investigators with a new window on the Street's sordid inner workings. Enron's senior executives and its accounting firm certainly bore a huge amount of the blame for the company's stunning collapse. But investigators probing the mess found that J.P. Morgan Chase had provided Enron with complex financing that helped hide debt and mask the company's growing difficulties. That scared Sandy. Citigroup had also been a lender and advisor to Enron, and he didn't want to be caught in the same crosshairs as J.P. Morgan.

"Do we have anything like this?" he demanded of his Salomon Smith Barney executives.

"Don't worry," they reassured him. "Our deals are different."

But in a matter of days congressional investigators had turned up information showing that both Citigroup and Merrill Lynch had also provided financing to Enron that might have been used to deceive investors. In congressional hearings, J.P. Morgan, Citigroup, and Merrill Lynch were all grilled about how and why they agreed to provide Enron with $8.5 billion in loans, which Enron disguised as commodity trades conducted through offshore shell companies. Citigroup's deal with Enron, called "Yosemite," involved contracts for the future delivery of oil that helped Enron raise money. Enron didn't book that money as debt but as cash flow from operations, a distinction investigators said hoodwinked ratings agencies and investors.

As the investigation of Citigroup continued in Washington, Sandy sought Chuck Prince's counsel. Both felt misled about Salomon Smith Barney's work for Enron. "When we asked questions if we could get in trouble, we weren't told 'no,' but we weren't told 'yes' either," Prince said. "Now we know that should have set off alarm bells." They resolved to monitor Salomon Smith Barney more carefully, even as its head, Mike Carpenter, told them he was managing the turmoil.

As the political pressure to unravel Enron continued, investigators raised questions about Citigroup's multiple roles in lending, advising, and underwriting securities for the energy company, an arrangement that earned it tens of millions of dollars. This line of inquiry called into question the very basis of Citigroup as a global financial-services supermarket offering an entire suite of products and services. Sure, during the boom times Citigroup enjoyed the best of both worlds—lucrative investment-banking relationships as well as commercial loans. But now, in the middle of a bust, Citigroup was suffering under a double burden: bad loans and bad deals. Sandy fumed as he reported to his board that Enron would cost Citigroup $1 billion, not to mention whatever hit there would be to the company's—and, by inference, Sandy's—reputation.

On June 25, 2002, Chuck Prince, deeply enmeshed in handling the securities probes, came in from a rare evening out with his girlfriend, attorney Margaret Wolff, and checked his BlackBerry. A headline flashed across the screen: WORLDCOM ENGAGED IN MASSIVE FRAUD. He turned to Wolff and told her simply: "This is going to be ugly. This is really going to be ugly."

WorldCom, based in tiny Clinton, Mississippi, had been one of the fairy-tale growth stocks of the bull market, when the telecommunications industry attracted billions of investor dollars with promises of fiber optics, fast Internet connections, and other fabulous advances. WorldCom, a long-distance provider, had grown by leaps and bounds, taking over dozens of other companies including the much larger MCI. And it had been one of Salomon Smith Barney's premier clients, a virtual money machine churning out vast investment-banking fees. The headline Prince had just seen was enough: If serious allegations of fraud were made against WorldCom, Citigroup, as WorldCom's lead advisor and underwriter, would be swept into the maelstrom.

Jack Grubman, Salomon Smith Barney's rock-star telecom analyst, had been the point man in the firm's dealings with WorldCom. Grubman had a knack for using colorful language rather than the dry verbiage of most stock analysis, and he had insinuated himself deep within WorldCom during the heyday of the telecom boom, forming a tight relationship with WorldCom founder Bernie Ebbers. Grubman was featured on magazine covers and was constantly being interviewed by the business press, both print and television. Goldman Sachs had tried to lure Grubman away from Salomon Smith Barney, but his fawning bosses persuaded Grubman to stay with the promise of $20 million a year, the kind of compensation usually reserved for only the most productive investment bankers and certainly far beyond the amounts most analysts earned. And for that kind of money, what kind of advice did Salomon Smith Barney's investor clients get? As the telecom boom turned to bust and prices of telecom stocks headed for the cellar, Grubman continued to recommend that investors snap them up. He kept a "buy" rating on WorldCom stock as it skidded from $64.50 to $4. Only a week before the company ousted Ebbers as chairman did Grubman finally downgrade it.

The news of nearly $4 billion of financial fraud at WorldCom shook a stock market already reeling from a loss of investor confidence. Looking for culprits, the politicians and the press discovered Grubman's cozy relationship with Ebbers and his steadfast hyping of the critically injured stock. Overnight the brash, fast-talking Grubman was dubbed a villain. A CNBC reporter even ambushed him on a New York sidewalk in late June, trailing behind him with questions about what he knew about WorldCom—and when. Grubman spun around and screamed on camera, "Why are you harassing me?"

Though Sandy and other Citigroup officials cringed at the harsh spotlight, they publicly voiced support for the forty-nine-year-old Grubman, who was quickly summoned to testify before the House Committee on Financial Services. Chuck Prince went to Washington the weekend before the hearing to help prepare the controversial analyst. Grubman also hired his own counsel, Lee Richards, a respected corporate-defense lawyer, who sat behind him at the hearing. Prince didn't stay in Washington for the hearing. He was needed back in New York to help Sandy prepare the remarks he would give when honored as the CEO of the Year, the prestigious annual award given by *Chief Executive* magazine.

Unknown to Citigroup, a high-profile plaintiff's lawyer, William Lerach of the law firm Milberg Weiss, was preparing a shareholder class action against WorldCom. As told by *The New Yorker* magazine, Lerach, having developed a mutually beneficial relationship with congressional investigators probing executive misconduct, passed along information that during the heyday of the technology boom Salomon had given WorldCom executives special access to hot initial public offerings. Salomon would dole out shares of companies about to become publicly traded, and the WorldCom executives could "flip" them once trading began, often at huge profits. The practice amounted to giving the WorldCom executives huge amounts of free money.

At the hearing on July 8, 2002, Representative Paul Kanjorski, a Pennsylvania Democrat, asked Grubman if he or his firm had given IPO shares to WorldCom executives. The analyst was visibly rattled by the question and stuttered an inconclusive and evasive answer. The exchange, which cast a huge cloud over Sandy's night of glory in Manhattan, fanned the controversy over Salomon Smith Barney's conflicts of interest. Did the lucrative IPO allocations come with the quid pro quo that WorldCom would return the favor by giving Salomon Smith Barney the company's investment-banking business? Grubman acknowledged that he had sat in on several board meetings of WorldCom and other large investment-banking clients, a disclosure that raised more questions about the independence of his analysis. He had been giving advice to the very companies he was supposedly analyzing on behalf of Salomon Smith Barney's investors, the same investors who suffered immense losses following Grubman's recommendations.

On July 21, barely a month after the disclosure of deceptive accounting and fraud, WorldCom filed for bankruptcy, supplanting Enron for the dubious honor of the largest bankruptcy in U.S. history. The next day Citigroup's stock price plunged 10 percent. Clearly investors were assuming that Citibank—the most profitable bank in the world—would be held at least partly responsible for WorldCom's collapse in the lawsuits and investigations that would result from its demise.

Citigroup's tumbling stock price was painful for Sandy in many ways. Sure, he had personally lost $300 million in Citigroup stock, a hefty hit to his nearly $2-billion net worth. But having built a company on the basis of stock rewards, he knew that his employees were watching their own wealth decline, too. He fired off a letter to Citigroup's 270,000 employees: "I feel badly and I truly regret the pain that has been caused."

The damage hit not only his pocketbook but also his reputation. *The New York Times* ran a headline on July 27: IN TWO DAYS, CITIGROUP CHIEF TRADED HALO FOR HEADACHES. News stories and analysts started asking: Is Citigroup out of control? Will its problems ever end? Is it a bottomless pit of conflicts of interest?

Sandy was looking tired and stressed, but, to the surprise of his longtime colleagues, he wasn't screaming as he did in his earlier days. He determined quickly that he needed veterans from earlier crises to help with the latest one. He turned to Bob Druskin, a trusted lieutenant who had been

with him since his first empire back in the 1970s. Druskin was chief operations and technology officer at Citigroup, an important post with immense responsibilities. But it was more important that Sandy get someone
into 388 Greenwich Street, Salomon Smith Barney's headquarters in
Tribeca, who could objectively assess the situation and report back to him.
In the early days, Sandy had been able to micromanage the securities business or else rely on Dimon to run the business as he would himself. But
Mike Carpenter hadn't been trained by Sandy, and since he had taken over
Salomon Smith Barney it had become a "closed shop," in which information going to Citigroup headquarters came from Carpenter. It was a sharp
contrast to the way Bob Willumstad ran the consumer-banking operation.
Willumstad freely permitted other executives or directors to work with any
of his management team directly. After maintaining for months that he
could run Salomon Smith Barney by himself, Carpenter suddenly agreed
with Sandy that he needed help.

The Citigroup CEO called on another longtime confidant, the highly respected lawyer Marty Lipton. "I want a fresh pair of eyes," Sandy told the
seventy-one-year-old Lipton. "I want you to go into Salomon Smith Barney for me to find out how we are running our business." He told Lipton to
review all e-mails, documents, anything he needed for an objective assessment of the overall corporate model, the firm's processes and business activities. "I want advice, not a defense of what we've done," Sandy told the
lawyer. The two men's relationship went way back. Sandy had called Lipton the weekend he was being pushed out of American Express. The
lawyer had stayed up all night to work out Sandy's severance agreement in
1985. Now Sandy needed him at a critical juncture again.

Seeking relief from the steady drumbeat of bad news, Sandy and Joan
left for a long weekend cruise around the Mediterranean island of Capri on
their custom-built 87-foot luxury motor yacht. Knowing that Chuck Prince
had borne much of the burden of handling the successive waves of scandal,
Sandy invited him and Wolff, now his fiancée, to join them. This would be
Sandy's last cruise on the yacht, staffed with a crew of three, before he sold
it to take delivery of a 156-foot luxury yacht, boasting five bedrooms
and requiring a nine-person crew, that was under construction. He hoped
Prince would savor the island getaway with Wolff.

Prince and Wolff eagerly agreed to join the cruise. But it didn't take
Prince long to discover that even a luxurious yacht can become a virtual

torture chamber. There was nowhere he could go to escape Sandy's incessant questioning and probing. The cruise was more like an interrogation under hot lights, Prince thought, as his boss asked about every line of business, conflict of interest, and legal exposure.

On the flight home in Sandy's Gulfstream, Prince, exhausted from the ordeal of the "pleasure" cruise, fell fast asleep. Joan confided in Wolff her worries about the toll the enveloping crisis was taking on her husband. The stress, along with Sandy's love of food and drink, was evident in his expanding waistline. He ate and drank even more when he was nervous. Joan asked how Prince, who had been heavy, was slimming down since he and Wolff got together. Not only was Prince eating less, Wolff told her, he was also exercising several days a week by walking around the neighborhood. Prince suddenly awakened when he heard his name, just in time to hear Wolff volunteer that he could pick up Sandy, whose apartment was near theirs on the Upper East Side, on his walk. Back in Manhattan, Prince and Sandy began taking brisk morning walks together.

When Sandy returned to his office, he called in Mike Carpenter to discuss whether Salomon Smith Barney should ask Grubman to resign. The notorious analyst, whose reputation had plummeted along with the share prices of the companies he once covered, was no longer effective, the men agreed. Even worse, Grubman was being tagged as the current era's Michael Milken, the Wall Street felon and onetime junk-bond king, even though the telecom analyst hadn't been charged with a crime. Denying that he had done anything wrong other than failing to predict the telecom meltdown, Grubman resigned in early August, walking away with a $32-million severance package. "Right or wrong, I always called them as I saw them," the high-profile star analyst said in a statement.

But the Grubman controversy didn't walk away with him. Later that month, Attorney General Spitzer raised questions about whether Sandy, a director of AT&T, had pressured Grubman to change his negative rating on AT&T in order to win a role in a $10.6-billion offering tracking its wireless business. Underlying the charge was the question of whether the Citigroup CEO had played a role in producing allegedly false or inaccurate research. AT&T chairman Armstrong, on the Citigroup board, had questioned Sandy about Grubman's negative rating on AT&T. Sandy had asked Grubman to take a "fresh look" at the company. But the Citigroup chairman staunchly denied that he ever told an analyst what to write.

The realization that Spitzer's scrutiny could threaten even the shrewd and successful Sandy Weill, now a Wall Street legend, elevated Spitzer's reputation and power. Suddenly the once-obscure state attorney general was the most feared man on the Street. In September, the earnest and tireless Spitzer appeared on the cover of *Fortune* magazine with the cover line "The Enforcer: He nailed Merrill. He's after Citi. Eliot Spitzer is just getting started." Soon a consensus began to develop in the securities business that some kind of "global" settlement should be reached to prevent "the enforcer" from taking on a new target. If Sandy Weill—who had more lives than anyone in the business—could go down, anyone could, some executives worried.

19

TAKING COMMAND

August 2002 had been something of a respite for Sandy. He and Joan had taken their grandchildren to Venice for a vacation. Freed from the minute-by-minute decisions he was constantly making in his office, Sandy used the vacation to think more clearly about the precarious situation facing him and his company.

Competitors and analysts, who months earlier were awed by Sandy's groundbreaking business model for weathering the storms breaking over corporate America, turned vehemently critical. They raised disturbing questions: Had the Wall Street legend finally gone too far? Was his integrated powerhouse a hotbed for internal conflicts, fostering duplicity between his analysts and investment bankers? Was his conglomerate vulnerable because he had removed the longstanding barriers to financial businesses being housed under one roof? And most troubling of all, should Sandy be forced to dismantle the financial empire he spent his lifetime building?

Deep down, Sandy knew this attack was more serious than scores of others in his long career. In past business downturns, he had exploited bigger firms' troubles to his advantage; now the tables were turned. Finally, he stood atop the largest citadel of all, and the barricades were being stormed. A billionaire, the Citigroup CEO no longer needed to fight for his fortune. This fight was for respect—for himself and his corporate creation. It demanded that he do much more than lead the most profitable company in the world, once thought to be the ultimate accomplishment. With a proverbial gun to his head, Sandy needed to execute a radical—and pragmatic—change in how Wall Street worked, just as he had done decades earlier.

Returning from Venice, Sandy prepared to face his critics. He and Joan retreated to their weekend home in the Adirondacks for the Labor Day weekend.

As he opened an accumulated stack of mail on Sunday, September 1, Sandy came across an envelope containing a recent photograph of him with the first President Bush. In other circumstances, Sandy would have been delighted with the photograph, eager to show it to Joan and frame it for his office. But this time the sixty-nine-year-old chairman didn't like what he saw. He looked huge! His profile was virtually round. He knew, of course, that he had been gaining weight. His overindulgence in rich foods and alcoholic beverages had carried his weight to nearly 250 pounds, an all-time high. But his appearance frightened him. *No wonder I don't feel good,* he thought. He wasn't in any condition to fight the battle of his life. On the spot, he made a decision: He would begin a strict regimen to lose weight. *Something good has to come out of all this stuff,* he thought.

"I'm going to get back in shape," Sandy announced to Joan. He would do severe penance: no gin, no bread, no dessert. He also told Joan that he intended to work out six days a week, either with a personal trainer in their Manhattan apartment or in the state-of-the-art gym she had installed in their Greenwich mansion a year earlier. "I'm going to do this until all these issues are resolved—hopefully by the end of the year," Sandy said, warning her, "If I don't have a martini during the holidays, I'm going to be cranky."

After committing to this drastic shift in his personal behavior, Sandy was ready to make an equally dramatic change in his corporate leadership. He called Chuck Prince, who was in Nantucket with Wolff for the Labor Day weekend. "I've done a lot of thinking," Sandy said. "I want to meet with you tomorrow."

"Great," Prince said, as he thought to himself that surely this could wait until Tuesday. He and his fiancée had planned to take three-day weekends in Nantucket over the summer but had managed only two Fridays off. Now he had to tell her they would return early on Labor Day.

Prince went in to see Sandy the next day and expected the CEO to ask for a full briefing on what had happened while he was in Europe.

"I want a better Wall Street, not just a more profitable company, to be the capstone of my career," Sandy said.

Prince was stunned. "What were you drinking on vacation?" he said, laughing nervously. He knew Sandy's ambition to deliver record profits was unparalleled.

Sandy didn't laugh. He was solemn, even thoughtful. "If I have only a few years left on this earth, I want to spend it leading Wall Street to a new place," the Citigroup CEO answered.

Prince was completely taken aback. In his sixteen-year association with Sandy, he had never seen his boss this worried or morbid. Sandy had been through every kind of market cycle in his long career, and had survived them all. For the first time, the powerful CEO was acknowledging he wouldn't be around forever and that he felt a responsibility to the business he had grown up in. Then Sandy gave Prince another shock.

"I think we need to make a change," Sandy said. "I think you ought to be the person to go down and run the business."

"Why do you think that?" the fifty-two-year-old Prince asked in disbelief. Had Sandy just said he should go downtown to manage Salomon Smith Barney?

"We have all these difficulties. We have to turn a corner. We have to show new leadership, a new face, a new approach," explained the somber Citigroup chief, who desperately wanted to get the whole research and investment-banking mess behind him.

Prince wanted to know why someone already there, even Carpenter, couldn't offer a new approach that included reforms sought by Spitzer.

"It's hard for anybody to defend what they've done in the past and put in changes at the same time," Sandy said, suggesting that Carpenter was more interested in proving he and his team had done nothing wrong. "I believe it is much more serious for the future of our industry than others think."

The Citigroup CEO was determined to make a strong preemptive move, to take the lead in reforming the abuses that had developed during the long bull market. Sandy's past statements, like those of every other Wall Street executive, had maintained that his company had done nothing illegal. But such proclamations of innocence weren't moving the industry forward. He told Prince that he had watched William B. Harrison Jr., the chairman of J.P. Morgan Chase, trying to defend his institution's actions in an interview on CNBC. "It was dumb," Sandy said. He also criticized an op-ed piece that Harrison had written for *The Wall Street Journal* as simply failing to grasp the magnitude of the industry's problems, not just with regulators, but also with the public.

The Citigroup boss made another surprising change: He told Prince he would agree to "expense" stock options on the company's income statement, regardless of the adverse impact on earnings. Despite Sandy's devotion to options, he—like many prominent CEOs—succumbed to the pressure on all corporate America to show the true cost of the options that made their executives so rich.

The events of the next day convinced Sandy even more that drastic action was necessary. Prudential Securities told investors to sell Citigroup stock. It cut its rating on Citigroup from "hold" to "sell," something rarely done to one of Sandy's companies. Moreover, Prudential's bearish financial-industry analyst, Mike Mayo, predicted that lawsuits and investigations could cost Citigroup as much as $10 billion in settlements and damages. He criticized the management for "just-in-time corporate governance." Sandy was floored that anyone could come up with such an off-the-wall number. And he was stunned at the stock market's reaction. Citigroup shares tumbled 10 percent that day. Sandy phoned Arthur Zankel, his long-time friend who held 500,000 Citigroup shares.

"Punishing our stock by this outlandish prediction shows the fragility of the market," Zankel, a money manager and investor, told Sandy. "Good news is discounted and bad news is amplified."

With this day's losses added to Citigroup's price decline since the controversies began, the financial empire had lost an astounding $100 billion in market value.

Bob Druskin, now the chief operating officer of Salomon Smith Barney, returned that afternoon to the Park Avenue headquarters for a meeting. Like every other Citigroup executive whose main source of compensation was stock, Druskin had been mentally calculating at the end of each day how much money he was losing with the stock's decline. He ran into Sandy in the hall.

"How do you feel?" he asked his boss.

"I feel like crap," Sandy said. "This is really very difficult."

Druskin, who had seen Sandy under pressure many times in their long association since the Shearson days, had never seen his boss act so personally pained. Sandy behaved as if the attack on Wall Street was an attack on him personally, Druskin thought.

"I just can't defend things that I don't feel good about," Sandy explained, in an uncharacteristic acknowledgment of past mistakes.

On Wednesday, Jamie Dimon came to New York from Chicago on Bank One business. He already had several former Citigroup executives working with him at Bank One, including Heidi Miller as his chief financial officer and John Reed as an occasional advisor to the Bank One board. He had just hired another one, Jay Mandelbaum, from Salomon Smith Barney. He called to tell Sandy himself. His former mentor invited him to lunch in his private dining room at Citigroup, rather than the Four Seasons, where the pair had met since mending their relationship.

Dimon could tell instantly that Sandy was deeply troubled, and suddenly he felt bad for taking one of his managers.

"About Jay, I don't want it to look like I'm making your life more difficult," Dimon said, though he knew Sandy was aware of his past camaraderie with Mandelbaum.

"I appreciate it," Sandy said. "I actually feel better that Jay is joining you rather than somebody else." Then the Citigroup CEO even agreed that Dimon's forceful opposition to co-heads of business had proved right. "I'm more understanding of your point of view now," Sandy said.

They talked about the pressures on Wall Street. Though Dimon hadn't yet significantly expanded Bank One into the stock-brokerage business, he was widely expected to make a Wall Street play soon. Rumors abounded that Dimon would try to take over Citicorp's biggest competitor, J.P. Morgan Chase, whose merger had been much maligned. Acknowledging that his one-time protégé could challenge him from a corner office just across the street, Sandy told Dimon, "It would be interesting." More generally, Sandy conceded that industry practices that had seemed acceptable at the top of the bull market—principally the erosion of the "Chinese wall" that was supposed to separate stock analysis from investment banking—looked terrible in hindsight.

"I'm going to gut this out until we get it right," Sandy said confidingly.

"Sandy, I've always believed you're better when times are tough than when they are good," Dimon said.

When the men finished lunch, Sandy took Dimon up one floor to his office to show off his latest photographs, including the picture of the new custom-built luxury yacht to be ready next year. Citigroup executives who spotted their longtime colleague eagerly came up to shake his hand, assuming that it was okay if Sandy was with him. A few years earlier, Citigroup managers who kept a friendship with Dimon would have gone to extraordinary lengths to hide it from Sandy. Several secretaries hugged and kissed the forty-six-year-old Dimon, who was as dashing as ever despite the gray tinges in his hair.

That evening the Citigroup board's succession committee was scheduled to have a secret dinner. Held in a private suite at the Lowell, a small luxury hotel on Manhattan's Upper East Side, it was intended to be the first in a series that would give the committee members a chance to get to know and talk informally with a possible candidate for Sandy's job. The meeting tonight would bring three of the committee members—Andrall Pearson, Franklin Thomas, and Arthur Zankel—together with Sandy and Bob Willumstad, who certainly was considered a leading contender for the chairmanship. Richard Parsons, the chief executive officer of AOL Time Warner, wouldn't be able to attend; his own company's problems were multiplying daily. The directors agreed with Sandy to meet early to have a chance to talk about the storms buffeting the company before dining with Willumstad.

As they took their seats in the hotel suite, the three directors launched straight into their concerns. They believed that Citigroup's problems were no longer just about the rules and regulations of the securities business. The multiple controversies had become a real threat to Citigroup's entire business and to the company's reputation.

Particularly disturbing were the barbs aimed at Sandy personally. "Sandy is now appearing in the articles about the guys from Enron, Tyco, Adelphia—the fucking crooks!" Zankel complained. "That's when it's apparent to me and to everybody else that we're facing a franchise risk. We're getting pounded and pounded and lumped in with the crooks."

The Citigroup CEO readily agreed, and decided to test with them his theory that Carpenter had to be removed as head of the corporate business. The directors acknowledged that someone new must be named, even as they expressed reluctance that Carpenter be made to appear the "scapegoat." After dinner with Willumstad, the directors, with their jackets and shoes off, talked more about strategies to resolve the crisis. The conclusion: Sandy should make a preemptive move to get ahead of the regulators.

That was all the encouragement Sandy needed to come out swinging. On Friday morning, September 6, 2002, he seized an opportunity to defend his company and to present himself and Citigroup as reformers, not perpetrators.

"We should be held to the highest standard," Sandy told analysts and investors at a scheduled Merrill Lynch conference in New York. "Citi intends to be a leader in corporate governance and a leader in creating value for our shareholders." Still, he couldn't resist a little jibe at his audience: "I used to think all you cared about were earnings."

He told the conference he was forming an oversight group for all business lines to ensure that the conglomerate was "doing all the right things" from a "moral" and "ethical" point of view. "As we look back, certain actions that we did during the bull market look inappropriate, but nothing has come to anyone's attention that we did anything illegal," Sandy said. He also told the audience that Citigroup would pay the Federal Trade Commission $200 million to settle the charges brought against consumer lender Associates First Capital, bought by Citi in 2000.

Clearly feeling better about being on the offensive rather than the defensive, Sandy told the audience that he would not be able to take questions because he had an appointment to attend a historic joint session of Congress, an invitation that had come from Senate Majority Leader Tom Daschle. "With all my newfound friends and their interest, I thought I should show up," Sandy joked, referring to the intense interest Congress was taking in how Wall Street worked.

The joint session was no joking matter. Congress was meeting on Wall Street, near the site of Ground Zero, to pay tribute to the victims and heroes of the September 11 terrorist attacks. The lawmakers and their invited guests met in the rotunda of Federal Hall, the site at which Congress first convened in 1789 and where George Washington was inaugurated as the first president. Mayor Bloomberg hosted a lunch after the special session.

Suddenly, amid the milling members of Congress and their guests, Sandy came face to face with Eliot Spitzer, the man who almost single-handedly was forcing Wall Street to mend its ways. After an awkward moment, the Citigroup CEO seized the opportunity. He told Spitzer that he urgently wanted to resolve the investigation and would "take a leadership role to clean up Wall Street." The exchange was brief, only a minute or so, but Sandy wanted to leave an indelible impression on the ambitious and aggressive Spitzer: In effect, I'm one of the good guys and we're on the same side. Spitzer was noncommittal.

Sandy called for an emergency meeting of the board of directors to be held Sunday in Armonk. That weekend, Sandy asked Prince to come by his office. His deputy knew that Sandy had been talking to directors all week long, testing the idea of putting him at the helm of the corporate business. Now Prince would find out what his next assignment would be. The Citigroup CEO knew deep down that he could trust his career and reputation with Chuck Prince. Ever since taking over Commercial Credit, where Prince was serving as general counsel, Sandy watched the lawyer put his company's best interests before his own time after time. As they were negotiating to buy Salomon Brothers in 1997, Prince had just been diagnosed with cancer in one kidney. Yet he had delayed the operation necessary to save his life until the transaction was completed.

"You can do this," Sandy told his loyal colleague and friend, indicating he intended to make it official that he was naming Prince the chief executive officer of Salomon Smith Barney. At that moment, Prince suddenly wanted Sandy to tell him everything he needed to know to run a business, something he had never done. But the Citigroup chief told Prince that he had been at his side in every deal and every crisis for the last sixteen years. "You've done this before," he reassured Prince.

For years Prince had been happy to be the trusted aide, laboring almost anonymously to help Sandy build an empire. Now he was about to take on one of the most high-profile, high-risk jobs on Wall Street. He felt as though this conversation with Sandy was one of those monumental "birds and the bees" talks with a dad who was telling his son what it meant to be a man.

"This is the only way to get people to understand they're working in a new environment," Sandy explained, noting that Prince's legal background was perfect. "We have to lead the industry to a new place."

Sandy next told his president, Bob Willumstad, that Carpenter was out and Prince was in at Salomon Smith Barney. "When you're in the eye of the storm, you can't see much," Sandy observed. He said his planned shake-up would be aimed at answering a critical question: "Are we trying to lead the industry to a new place or are we trying to defend the past?"

Finally, Sandy summoned Carpenter. The veteran securities executive was shocked and angry that he was being forced out and tried to talk Sandy out of his decision. He maintained that he had done a good job and he didn't want to leave.

But Sandy was adamant. It was critical, he said, for Citigroup to have a "clean slate" to give credence to the changes it was making.

On Sunday morning, September 8, 2002, the Citigroup directors solemnly gathered at 10:30 in the big meeting room at Armonk. Sandy was casually decked out in a golf shirt. Some of the directors, aware of Sandy's penchant for keeping rooms cool, had brought sweaters. Arthur Zankel glanced around, noted that no one else was wearing a tie, and took his off. As usual, the plush armchairs were arranged in a U-shape and the buffet table was groaning under the weight of a brunch spread. But no one seemed comfortable or hungry this morning. The directors were horrified at the turn events had taken over the past few months. Yet none of them was prepared to question Sandy's leadership. Indeed, most of them felt that Citigroup needed Sandy's wisdom and experience now more than ever.

Sandy wasn't his usual self. There were no jokes, he wasn't heaping his plate at the buffet table, and he wasn't slouching in his chair. Usually Sandy would begin a board meeting by simply talking from his seat. But this morning he did something unusual: He stood up to address his directors as if he were giving a speech.

"I've been doing a lot of thinking," the Citigroup CEO began. "We all seem depressed. We have to take this crisis very seriously, and we have serious choices to make.

"As the leading financial-services institution, I think we need to set the standard for the industry," he continued. "That's what I'm determined to do."

He then told them that Marty Lipton and his lawyers had been examining Salomon Smith Barney's actions and practices, and turned the meeting over to him. Lipton, the legendary Wall Street lawyer, began reviewing the particular transactions and management actions his law firm had investigated. Some directors interrupted to ask for specific details, especially about Jack Grubman and his dealings with Sandy and others at the firm. After twenty minutes, Zankel was getting restless with the drawn-out blow-by-blow recitation of Grubman's actions.

"I know Sandy didn't tell Grubman anything to write, because that would be fucking stupid," Sandy's old friend interjected. "Marty, why don't you tell us where we're going and then we'll circle back if we need all this information?"

Lipton got to the point. "The business isn't out of control, the house isn't on fire," he assured the directors. "But it's clear in the harsh light of hindsight that there have been industry excesses in which the firm participated. "

"So there's no feeling or finding that there are a lot of sleazy crooks here?" Andrall Pearson asked. "You're saying Salomon Smith Barney did what the securities industry had been doing for years—that the problems are the product of an industrywide disease?"

Lipton nodded. "But to rein in the excesses and correct the problems, you must be prepared to take convincing action," the lawyer advised. "Small changes around the margins won't be sufficient."

Reuben Mark, the chairman and chief executive officer of Colgate-

Palmolive Co., asked what specific steps Sandy planned to take to improve the business culture and his oversight of the securities business. Something of a self-appointed conscience of corporate governance, Mark could be a stickler for demanding details.

At Mark's prompting, Sandy said he wanted to recommend that Chuck Prince replace Mike Carpenter as head of Citigroup's corporate and investment bank. In the past, he would have simply told the board that he was going to make the change and would expect their acquiescence. But chastened as he was by the firestorm surrounding him, he politely asked for the board's advice. "That's what I'm thinking, but there are other alternatives." Prince, who was attending the meeting as the corporate secretary, made a swift exit.

"Let's discuss if this is a good thing to do," said Andrall Pearson. "It's unusual for a guy with no management experience in the business to take on a job like this."

Several directors quickly echoed that their main concern about Prince was his lack of an operations track record. At the same time, they agreed that Carpenter should be replaced with someone from the inside, someone who knew Citigroup thoroughly, who was well respected and could work effectively to overcome the regulatory and legal hurdles confronting the company. The only other executive at Citigroup that the board believed had those qualities was Bob Willumstad, its president and consumer-group head.

"But should we take him out of the consumer business, which is the best performer right now?" one director asked.

No, Pearson said adamantly. "You have to focus on the business while you're cleaning all this stuff up. If the business goes down the tubes, then it doesn't matter too goddamned much what else you're doing." As directors debated the notion of moving Willumstad, Pearson tried again to convince them that the overall business needed Willumstad right where he was: "You have to clean up the stable, but the horse race is what it's all about," he said.

The mood in the room had shifted from depressed to determined. The directors liked the bold steps Sandy was prepared to take. Still some, led by Mark, wanted him to go further to improve Citigroup's corporate governance. The Colgate-Palmolive CEO, who had a tendency toward bombast once he had climbed on his corporate governance soapbox, pushed hard for a new "business practices committee" to provide vigorous scrutiny of operations and to ensure that Citigroup embraced the industry's highest standards. The directors agreed.

Mark also proposed a separate nominations and governance committee inside the board. The directors agreed and selected six of their members to serve on it, three from the original Citicorp and three from the original Travelers. Despite the fact that Citigroup had been a single entity for four years, the directors weren't forgetting their origins. The new committee determined that it would persuade Jack Roche, Citicorp's longtime general counsel, to come out of retirement and act as counsel to the committee.

Next they agreed with Sandy's proposal to move Carpenter out of Salomon Smith Barney "to make a clean break" from past management practices. Carpenter was given the low-profile job of heading Citigroup's investment unit, which managed the bank's more than $100 billion in assets.

After four hours, the board meeting broke up. Directors passed Prince, who was waiting in a sitting room, as they left. "Good man for the job," one told him with a handshake. Sandy was the last one out of the room.

"Well, I guess you're it," the CEO said, turning over to Prince the job of saving his company and his legacy.

Sandy asked the senior executives of Salomon Smith Barney to come to Armonk at 4:00 that afternoon. When Druskin got the call, he remembered only one other time when they had been summoned to the conference center on a Sunday afternoon—the firing of Dimon. He guessed that Carpenter was about to be next.

Once the eight top securities executives arrived, they began speculating about who their next boss would be. Most of the bets were on Deryck Maughan, the former head of Salomon Brothers before it was purchased by Travelers.

Then Sandy, Bob Rubin, Chuck Prince, and Mike Carpenter walked in. Carpenter looked ashen, almost gray. Surveying the foursome, the managers tried to figure out what was going on. Rubin wouldn't return to the securities business, they thought, even though he had headed Goldman Sachs before going into the government. And Prince, he was Sandy's right hand, firmly planted at the Park Avenue headquarters. What was going on?

When Sandy announced Prince's appointment as chief executive of Salomon Smith Barney, the men didn't know how to respond. Druskin, the only executive who knew Prince well from his time at the parent company, jumped in to fill the silence. "Chuck is a great guy with great judgment," the new chief operating officer of Salomon Smith Barney told his colleagues. "Whenever anyone at 399 Park has a thorny problem, they gravitate to Chuck's office. You'll see that."

Rubin assured the executives that he stood ready to help Prince and them. He supported Prince as the right man for the job, someone who could start fresh in the industry where "standards of behavior are changing."

In an unusual move, Citigroup issued a press release announcing the management shake-up that Sunday night at 6:00. Prince's appointment as CEO of Salomon Smith Barney was a big surprise. But observers inside and outside of the company recognized it for what it was: a strong signal that Sandy Weill meant business. Prince was dubbed "the Fireman." He was expected to put out the fires that were threatening Citigroup and to reach speedy resolutions to the numerous probes into the company's securities business. After all, if Citigroup didn't solve its reputation and regulatory problems, there wouldn't be much of a business to run, some analysts said, noting dryly that in this economy there wouldn't be much activity anyway.

One phrase in the company's press release was especially surprising to Citigroup insiders. In the statement, Sandy said: "Although we have found nothing illegal, looking back, we can see that certain of our activities do not reflect the way we believe business should be done. That should never be the case, and I am sorry for that." Sandy Weill apologizing?! His colleagues knew Sandy had a deep-seated aversion to apologies. Whenever he blasted one of them, rightly or wrongly, he never apologized later. Instead, he just acted a little nicer for a while, or at least acted as if nothing had happened. Others worried that the apology was premature.

When Sandy came to the office on Monday, an executive asked him point-blank: "How can you write 'I'm sorry'? Doesn't it sound like we're conceding guilt?"

"Of course I'm sorry," Sandy said, trying to make light of it. "Look at the stock price. I'm really sorry!" Joking aside, he knew that the regulators and investigators were looking for remorse, something they hadn't seen a lot of lately among financial executives.

Later that morning, a meeting was called at Salomon Smith Barney's twenty-seventh-floor auditorium at 388 Greenwich Street. Sandy spoke first.

"This was an uncomfortable weekend for a lot of people," he said, fully aware that Carpenter was well liked by the securities troops. "This change is made in the best interest of the firm. Mike has been terrific. He's not a scapegoat."

Carpenter looked even worse than he had the day before at Armonk. His appearance was pasty, like "death warmed over," one banker whispered to a colleague.

Prince told his new subordinates that Sandy and Bob Rubin would be available to help out with clients.

"Not so fast with my time," Rubin quipped.

When it was Carpenter's turn to speak, he noted that most of the problems had been inherited through mergers, which some took to be an attempt to deny responsibility for them. Then he tried to put on a good face and told his colleagues, "You're a winning team."

At noon, Carpenter appeared at the private dining room for executives, where he rarely ate lunch. Colleagues knew he was putting up a brave front. That night, all of Carpenter's personal belongings and furniture were moved out and Prince's were moved in. On Tuesday morning, September 10, 2002, Chuck Prince was in place in the CEO's downtown office and already scheduling meetings with officials representing Spitzer and the SEC to move a settlement along.

Soon a flurry of other changes were implemented at Salomon Smith Barney, but only after Sandy reviewed every single document and release. The current heads of research were retired or reassigned. A new policy on IPO allocations was established. Structured financing transactions—the type of complicated deals that Citigroup had done for Enron—that were in the works were canceled. Some executives who had been with Sandy since Commercial Credit were reminded of how Sandy could roll up his sleeves and wade right in, getting involved in every detail and nuance of the business, acting as if the very fate of the company depended on his ability to motivate and guide the troops.

This time, however, more than half of the company was producing record profits. Citigroup's consumer business was the star of the conglomerate, carrying the load for the rest of the firm, just as Sandy had predicted when he pushed for repeal of Glass-Steagall. The consumer bankers decided they'd better be certain that the corporate side's "headline" issues weren't harming their half. Magner ordered up a market-research poll of American consumers, done by phone over a three-week period in September. The results were encouraging. For Citibank, CitiFinancial, and Citi Cards, the impact of Citigroup's corporate scandals was minimal, at most.

Few consumers were following the latest news on Jack Grubman and IPO spinning. The client base was remarkably stable: They weren't cutting up their credit cards or closing their accounts. To its customers, the most important concern was solvency of their bank. And with more than one trillion dollars in assets, that wasn't a problem.

The changes in Citigroup's management had been sudden and bewildering to the company's thousands of employees, including many senior executives. Each September Sandy and Joan invited a few hundred upper-level executives and their spouses and children to pick apples in the Weills' Greenwich orchard. Coveted invitations to the stylish affair, which featured a lavish smorgasbord, entertainment for the children, and even Porta Potties adorned with fresh flowers and running water, guaranteed important "face time" for executives with their top bosses. On a warm fall Saturday in 2002, many Citigroup executives used the opportunity to chat with or just observe Bob Willumstad and Chuck Prince, the two once-obscure quiet and affable men each of whom now, more than anyone else at the huge company, seemed positioned to be Sandy's successor. Since last year's apple-picking party, the two men had gained immense power, unsought and unanticipated. Now Prince, the new head of Salomon Smith Barney, was being joshed for taking the worst job on Wall Street. Willumstad, the conglomerate's president, happily chased his one-year-old granddaughter Samantha all over the Weills' rambling estate.

Other executives huddled under the buffet tent to speculate about the penalties that Citigroup would surely face to settle all the securities investigations, apart from investors' class-action lawsuits. A "global settlement" was being negotiated between Wall Street and government regulators. It looked as though Citigroup's Salomon Smith Barney would pay the biggest fine, perhaps as much as $500 million. But some of the senior executives knew enough to put such a huge fine in its proper perspective. Granted, Citigroup's stock-price declines as a result of the scandals had resulted in the loss of up to $100 billion in market value. But that could easily be regained when investors once again became confident about the company's future. And if this year was any indication, what a future it would be—Citigroup in 2002 was poised to earn an amazing $16 billion in profit, itself a record, making Sandy's empire the most profitable in the world. Even though a $500-million fine might look bad, it would bring Sandy's most difficult crisis to a close, and the cost would amount to a measly two weeks of profit for the world's largest financial superpower.

Yet few questioned that Sandy Weill would still be their boss come apple-picking time next year. The harsh turn of events this year had seemed to weigh on him heavily at first. But, true to form, he had rallied under pressure, and lately he seemed energized, ready for any challenge. They knew he would never leave in the midst of difficulties. There was a reason insiders at Citigroup referred to it as "Sandygroup." He might be talking occasionally about his last years in the business, but everyone noticed that it was "years," not "year."

THE LAST HONEST ANALYST

During the third week of September the annual "chairman's council," a gathering of Salomon Smith Barney's top-producing brokers, met at an Arizona resort for three days. Previous council meetings had given Sandy a chance to relax and enjoy himself, schmoozing and drinking with the brokers. After all, he had gotten his start as a broker. And they had always worshiped him.

But this time the brokers were far from happy, despite the setting for their meeting, the luxurious Phoenician hotel in Scottsdale. Of course, mired in a bear market, their business was dreadful. But they were also being besieged by complaints from their customers: Salomon Smith Barney's research was bogus, the hot IPOs had gone to the fat cats, not the individual investors, and on and on. And who the hell was this guy Chuck Prince who was running the company now?

Sandy knew he needed to diffuse the tension and hostility. "We gave you advice on stocks to sell to your customers, and then they lost a ton of money. You're mad, and your customers are very mad," he told the brokers and their spouses. "I'm not happy either.

"I love brokers. The last thing in the world I want is for you to lose confidence in me. If anyone can relate to brokers and the individuals they represent, it's me," Sandy said imploringly. "Look, we screwed up, but we'll fix it."

The brokers gave him a standing ovation.

At the traditional cocktail party, several executives noticed that Sandy wasn't having his usual gin martini with onions.

"I'm not drinking gin until all this stuff is resolved," the Citigroup CEO said, shocking his colleagues. "No gin, no dessert, no bread—none of the stuff I love until we get this behind us." Then Sandy turned toward Prince, who had just walked up, and added, "So Chuck, we have to hurry up!"

As Sandy mingled with his best brokers, his antennae were up and in the receive mode. What do you need us to do? he asked time after time. The brokers consistently asked for independent and valuable research, not the overly optimistic crap that had been churned out in the past to garner investment-banking business. To restore investor confidence in our company, we need to provide high-quality service including research, they told their boss. Aware of Sandy's habit of buying companies to fill organizational holes, a few of them suggested Citigroup buy Sanford C. Bernstein & Co., an independent research firm that was unfettered by ties to any investment bankers. Bernstein was known for careful, thoughtful, and— most important—*unbiased* stock research.

That gave Sandy an idea. As soon as he returned to New York, he called Bernstein's chairman and CEO, Sallie Krawcheck, and invited her to breakfast. He had gotten to know the highly regarded analyst when she covered the securities industry. A plainspoken stock researcher, she had irked Sandy by making bearish comments on Travelers' acquisition of Salomon Inc. in 1997. But, at about the same time, she had also sponsored a session in London for Bernstein's clients that prominently featured Sandy. Ambitious and attractive, Krawcheck had hitched a ride with Sandy on the transatlantic flight, taking advantage of the Gulfstream's cramped quarters to grill Sandy even as she ingratiated herself with him. When Sandy and Reed announced the giant merger of Citicorp and Travelers, Krawcheck had asked the co-CEOs to sign a photograph of her with them at the announcement. Sandy had signed it to "Sally," misspelling her name.

Since then, Krawcheck had risen to become Bernstein's CEO. Acknowledging the objective nature of Bernstein's research, *Fortune* magazine had put her on the cover of an issue with the headline IN SEARCH OF THE LAST HONEST ANALYST. This was a credential Sandy could use right about now.

Sandy and Krawcheck hit it off well. The Citigroup CEO offered the thirty-seven-year-old Krawcheck the job of running the global-research and brokerage units of Citigroup, which he would separate from the investment-banking unit. The private-client division reporting to her, with 12,500 brokers, would be called Smith Barney, dropping the name of Salomon, which was too closely tied to corporate deal making. She accepted.

The announcement a few weeks later that Krawcheck would take over as head of the research and brokerage units was another strong signal from Sandy that he was moving decisively to reduce Citigroup's regulatory woes. At the same time, Sandy also brought in Michael Masin, a Citigroup director, to be the new chief operating officer at the parent. Masin, a lawyer by training, was the president of Verizon Communications and had gotten to know Sandy on the board of Carnegie Hall before joining Citigroup's board. Masin, who would resign as a Citi director, also would head the new business-practices committee and assume many of the administrative responsibilities previously handled by Prince.

TO SEE IT THROUGH

Despite his protestations at Citigroup's last annual meeting that his interlocking directorships posed no conflicts of interest, Sandy decided to resign his seats on the AT&T and United Technologies boards in the fall of 2002. In a statement announcing his departure from the boards, he said his action was "part of our continuing effort to assure that our corporate governance reflects best practices."

Sandy was trying hard to make all the right moves, ahead of any reforms forced on the industry. Now he needed Chuck Prince to bring a close to the various probes by negotiating a broad settlement that encompassed them all. Yet the Citigroup chairman also wanted the other Wall Street firms to make similar changes in business practices. It just wouldn't be right for Citigroup to make changes that tilted the playing field against the company.

Then *The Wall Street Journal* reported that Jack Grubman, no longer an employee of Citigroup, was cooperating with Spitzer's office. The story indicated that Grubman was suggesting that he had been pressured to make calls he didn't agree with. If investigators could show that Sandy had pressured Grubman to change his reports, the Citigroup CEO might face personal culpability. The article reported that Spitzer had informed Citigroup that the interests of the firm and Sandy "may have diverged in the investigation," a signal that Sandy could be a target.

Sandy was furious. He fired off a rebuttal to the *Journal* article at one o'clock in the morning, long before most *Journal* readers had seen the paper. He volunteered to meet with Spitzer personally to get this behind him. Deluged with calls seeking clarification and comment, the New York Attorney General's office hastily prepared a statement saying that Sandy personally was not a target of its investigation, but added ominously that it would "follow the evidence where it leads us."

A large part of the evidence that Spitzer, other regulators, and investigators had to work with consisted of Citigroup internal e-mails and memos. The company's outside lawyers had been combing through millions of documents. Anything pertinent was boxed up and sent to Spitzer, the National Association of Securities Dealers, the Securities and Exchange Commission, and congressional committees, all of which were investigating. The massive culling turned up two apparently damning documents, both authored by none other than Jack Grubman.

One, an e-mail sent to Carol Cutler, an analyst for the Singapore Government Investment Fund, a money-management firm, boasted of Grubman's value to Sandy: "Everyone believes I upgraded T [AT&T] to get lead [manager role for Citigroup] for AWE [AT&T's wireless spin-off]. Nope. I used Sandy to get my kids in 92nd St. Y pre-school (which is harder than Harvard) and Sandy needed Armstrong's vote on our board to nuke Reed in showdown. Once coast was clear for both of us (i.e. Sandy clear victor and my kids confirmed) I went back to my normal negative self on T. Armstrong never knew that we both (Sandy and I) played him like a fiddle."

Seemingly more damning still was a memorandum dated November 5, 1999, from Grubman to Sandy. Under the not-so-subtle heading "AT&T and 92nd Street Y," the telecom analyst told Sandy about his continuing re-evaluation of Ma Bell's investment potential, then launched directly into an appeal to Sandy to use his influence to help get the Grubman twins admitted to the highly selective preschool.

"Given that it's statistically easier to get into the Harvard freshman class than it is to get into preschool at the 92nd Street Y (by the way, this is a correct statement), it comes down to 'who you know,'" Grubman wrote.

The sensational nature of both documents guaranteed that one privy investigator or another would leak them to the media. Suddenly coverage of Sandy and Citigroup was spreading far beyond the business press. Headlines and stories splashed across the front pages of New York's major newspapers explained, even to readers uninterested in business, that a highly paid analyst had hyped a stock's ratings to help Sandy Weill beat his archrival; in return, the powerful bank chairman pressured a prestigious nursery school to admit the analyst's kids. Another revelation: Citigroup had made a pledge of $1 million to support the tony 92nd Street Y. And yes, the Grubman kids had been admitted into what, in a certain Manhattan mind-set, is an important first step toward an eventual Ivy League education. CNN promptly dubbed the scandal "nursery-schoolgate," and radio talk show host Don Imus urged that Sandy be "hung up by his toes."

As the cascade of news stories broke around them, Sandy and Chuck Prince went on their usual morning walks. Neither Sandy nor Prince knew who had leaked the evidence, but they were both certain that the leaks were intended to squeeze Citigroup even harder by humiliating its CEO. "It's a smear effort," Prince told Sandy. Together they agreed that while it was usually better to remain silent and take whatever lumps came their way, this was too much. Citigroup and Sandy had to respond.

In a press release, Sandy dismissed the Grubman e-mails as "pure fantasy." He stated that any suggestion that Jack Grubman had upgraded AT&T as part of an effort to win Armstrong's support against John Reed "is nonsense." Sandy acknowledged trying to help Grubman with the 92nd Street Y, simply because an "important employee" had asked for his assistance. There was no quid pro quo, Sandy said.

While most of the country laughed at how ridiculous it was for a $20-million-a-year employee to ask his boss's help in getting his kids into a nursery school, New Yorkers took the disclosures with deadly seriousness. It was too true! How were they ever going to get their precious toddlers into the right school when people like Jack Grubman could summon the power and pocketbook of Citigroup to ease the way?

But suddenly Sandy had a new defender: Jack Grubman. With the scandal continuing to pare billions of dollars off Citigroup's market value, Grubman made an amazing confession via a press release: "I have said a number of inappropriate, even silly, things in a few private e-mails," Grubman said, adding that his e-mails were "personally embarrassing and completely baseless. Regrettably, I invented a story in an effort to inflate my professional importance."

Nevertheless, Spitzer announced an investigation into Citigroup's donation to the 92nd Street Y. "Nursery-schoolgate" was taking on a life of its own, focusing a harsh spotlight on Sandy's actions. After Grubman had sought his boss's influence in getting his twins into the preschool, Sandy had approached Joan Tisch, a Y director and the wife of Loews Corp. chairman Robert Tisch. The Weills and the Tisches, who were major benefactors at the 92nd Street Y, had been good friends for more than two decades. When Sandy was in corporate exile in 1985 and 1986, the Tisches would give the Weills free passes to see movies at Loews Theaters, an effort to cheer Sandy as he grappled with unemployment after leaving American Express.

In his contacts on behalf of the Grubman children, Sandy had indicated that he would be willing to arrange for a $1 million donation in five equal annual payments to the 92nd Street Y. To certain members of the Citigroup board, the donation was perceived as effectively amounting to additional compensation to Grubman, who already was paid $20 million a year. Once Grubman's daughter and son were admitted, the 92nd Street Y followed up with the analyst to make sure that the pledge was forthcoming.

Leaks to the media of Grubman's e-mails fueled new rounds of headlines aimed at Sandy and Citigroup. "This little piggy went to preschool," a *Fortune* magazine headline teased. The article argued that the one-million-dollar gift was "in effect a bribe." *Fortune* questioned how Citigroup's board of directors could look the other way, noting that the board had granted Sandy annual compensation estimated at $150 million in 2000 even as he continued to duck board requests that he formulate a succession plan. "It is outrageous," the article concluded.

Spitzer began to turn up the heat. His office notified several Citigroup directors that they would be called for questioning. Joan Tisch was interviewed about Sandy's contact with her and the subsequent admission of Grubman's twins to the 92nd Street Y, whose tax-exempt status was regulated by Spitzer.

In an effort to relieve some of the mounting pressure, Sandy, accompanied by criminal defense lawyers, secretly met in early November with Spitzer's investigators at the attorney general's office. Sandy faced a roomful of lawyers hurling questions at him for much of the day. "I have nothing to hide," he maintained, indicating that he was as eager to meet with the investigators as they were to meet with him.

Several questions focused on Grubman's memo to Sandy that linked AT&T and the 92nd Street Y. He told them he had never seen the memo until his lawyers discovered it in their internal investigation of Salomon Smith Barney. Certainly it could have been sent to him, but that wouldn't have mattered. "I don't read memos," he told them, a fact that virtually anyone who dealt with Sandy regularly was well aware of. Sandy Weill simply didn't deal in the written word. Therefore, he explained, no matter what Grubman thought in his own self-important mind, Sandy had called the 92nd Street Y after Grubman mentioned it in conversation. Indeed, Grubman's memo stated that he was following up on a recent conversation. Sandy told the investigators he didn't need Grubman's help with AT&T's CEO Armstrong, and would never try to improperly influence a director's vote in any case. And when he prodded Grubman to take a "fresh look" at AT&T, Sandy added, "I always believed that Mr. Grubman would conduct his own research and reach independent conclusions that were entirely his own."

The legal grilling behind him, Sandy hastily called a meeting of Citigroup's directors for the next morning. As the directors assembled, they discussed among themselves the Grubman memorandum and e-mails. The directors didn't need any reassurances from Sandy about the falsity of Grubman's claim that the analyst had helped Sandy "nuke" John Reed; they knew Michael Armstrong would have supported Sandy no matter what an analyst was saying about AT&T. But the 92nd Street Y was another matter. It was shaping up as a public-relations disaster, although none of the directors thought Sandy had acted unethically, and certainly not illegally.

"This is nothing to cheer about," conceded Arthur Zankel. "In essence, Grubman got a $1 million bonus, but the Y got some great programming with the gift." Other directors acknowledged that they had made calls at the behest of valuable employees and even directed gifts to favored charities. That's the way New York works, they said, privately fuming that Spitzer was stoking his political ambitions at Sandy's expense.

Sandy told the directors about his meeting at Spitzer's office the day before. He characterized it as a "polite" interrogation. Then he warned them that Citigroup would have to persevere in the face of continuing negative media coverage. "This is not something we will win in the press. We will win it with the facts," he told them. "This is horrendous, but there will be a time when the outcome will go our way."

Then lawyers from the firm of Wilmer, Cutler & Pickering, led by veteran securities attorney Robert McCaw, distributed papers marked "highly confidential." Each package contained excerpts from Grubman's e-mail exchanges with the analyst Carol Cutler.

"This is lewd!" one director exclaimed with disgust. The board members expressed shock as they read the electronic exchanges, which contained sexual content that hadn't been previously disclosed—including references to performing oral sex. This went far beyond typical banter.

One Citigroup executive labeled the messages "pornographic" and "mistress e-mails."

Suddenly the directors saw Grubman's e-mail braggadocio—and his recent statement disavowing it—in a new light. "So Grubman has been preening for a woman," one board member concluded.

It became painfully apparent that Citigroup's star analyst had pursued a personal agenda at work, whether to impress a woman or to get his toddlers into a Manhattan elite nursery school. Further, the e-mail exchanges confirmed that Grubman's "buy" rating for AT&T may well have been influenced by his personal agenda.

Sandy told his board—as he had with Spitzer's investigators the day before—that he had no idea that Grubman's AT&T rating didn't truly reflect the analyst's opinion at the time. "We were all misled by Jack Grubman," he concluded.

The lawyers warned the directors that the material was so controversial that they would have to leave the memos facedown at their seats when the meeting adjourned. As the meeting drew to a close, it was obvious to all that the board remained solidly behind Sandy. They recalled among themselves how Sandy had often stepped in to assist employees in getting the right doctor, through his contacts at the New York Weill Cornell Medical Center, or to help colleagues in other ways through his vast network of powerful friends. Even straight-as-an-arrow Chuck Prince had asked Sandy to put in a good word at Cornell for his college-bound son, who wound up going to Georgetown instead. That's the way New York worked, they acknowledged.

Angry and hurt, Sandy knew he couldn't get distracted by the personal attacks. "We will make sure the business works," Sandy told his directors and senior management. "What has distinguished us from other financial-services companies—whether Morgan Chase or European conglomerates—our company has continued to perform" despite recession, terrorism, and investigation. Sandy continued to monitor zealously the daily reports flooding in from around the world, from CitiFinancial's daily loan origination to the value of publicly traded stocks in Citi's private-equity business.

Yet the turmoil and the continuing negotiations over a global settlement that would bring his torment to an end had their chastening effects on Sandy. For one thing, the man who relished doling out his company's charitable dollars would do it no more. Even though he had placed himself on Citigroup's foundation and wanted to sign off on even the smallest donation, the 92nd Street Y debacle brought some of the worst publicity he and his company had ever received. In a board meeting near the end of 2002, a subdued Sandy told his directors, "I'm removing myself from all those de-cisions." Instead, a new corporate committee of up to six high-ranking ex-ecutives would decide how to disburse Citi's vast charity.

In another telling decision, Sandy ordered Salomon Smith Barney to withdraw from the bidding to take public the company run by his daughter. In the summer of 2002 Sandy had pressed Jessica Bibliowicz to hire Sal-omon to handle the public offering of National Financial Partners. But in November, Sandy and his daughter agreed that she should use other in-vestment bankers for the $150-million offering, rather than expose them both to questions about family ties influencing a business transaction.

By Thanksgiving, Sandy was beginning to hope it was all behind him. There had been no more damaging leaks, no more lurid e-mails discov-ered, and the industry's talks with Spitzer and the SEC were moving for-ward. On the last Saturday in November, Arthur Zankel stopped by the Weills' Greenwich mansion in the afternoon to check on his old friend. Even though the temperature was near freezing, Sandy, seemingly always hot, was wearing a golf shirt. He and Zankel retreated to Sandy's den and sat in front of a roaring fire, where, true to his pledge forswearing gin, Sandy had a glass of wine with his fellow Citigroup director.

"Where do you think things stand?" Sandy asked Zankel, who had his own circle of friends among the other Citigroup directors and executives.

"They seem to be winding down," Zankel told him. "I haven't been called by Spitzer's office after I was told I would be. I hope that's a good sign that a settlement is near."

Sandy mentioned that he was heartened by a recent phone call from Colgate-Palmolive chairman Reuben Mark, the Citigroup director who had been most vocal about the need for reform. In his call, Mark assured Sandy that the CEO still had his support.

How wonderful it would be to have all this behind him, Sandy reflected. If the rules of business were changing, no one in the financial industry was more adept at change than Sandy. He had torn down one wall after an-other—barriers based on religion, class, even the law—to get where he was.

"I'm looking forward to New Year's Eve," he confided to Zankel, who, with his wife, would be among the select couples invited to the Weills' Adirondacks retreat for the festivities. At least Sandy hoped there would be festivities. "I really want to raise my gin martini at midnight," he said with a chuckle. Having a gin martini would be delightful in and of itself. But it would really be a sign that Sandy had his old life back, free from controversy and criticism.

When it came time for Sandy to meet with the two hundred top Citigroup executives from around the world at their annual retreat, Sandy braced himself. How would all these managers feel about the crises sweeping their company and taking a terrible toll on their net worth? He was pleasantly surprised when their first reaction was to comment on his slimmer profile. He had pared away nearly thirty pounds in three months, and he confided to them that he hadn't felt this good in years. He even boasted that he was once again able to wear his custom-tailored suits from 1995.

Then it was time for business. Speaking to the executives and their spouses in the first morning session, Sandy stood behind an umbrella podium, which traveled with him for official appearances.

"I am one hundred percent committed to seeing this thing through," the CEO vowed. "We did some things that were inappropriate, but we're going to be the company that leads our industry to change—just as we did with consumer finance and predatory lending."

The conference, called "Raising the Bar," was filled with meetings to discuss how Citigroup's business standards would be improved in the future. But just in case anyone thought Sandy was getting lax with his long-standing goal of improving profits, he cautioned them, "Don't think for one minute that this relieves you of your obligation to bring in your numbers. I'm still just as focused on the business as ever."

On Saturday night, before dinner and dancing, Sandy spoke a final time, this time to express his gratitude for their loyalty. "I'm flabbergasted about how supportive you are—even after four months of nearly constant slamming in the press. We will be a better business for going through this, as horrible as it is, because we're thinking about what's really right for the customer going forward."

At that the audience rose almost as one, applauding furiously for ten minutes. Surveying the enormous outpouring of respect and admiration directed at him, Sandy could only stammer, "I love the people in this company," as his eyes welled with tears. "To see that reciprocated at this time is very important to me."

Sandy couldn't tell the two hundred executives and their spouses from all over the world how the biggest upheaval on Wall Street in decades would affect them or their company. Nor could he predict when the scores of lawsuits and investigations would be settled. Nevertheless, he felt their love flowing over him.

Still fighting back tears, Sandy carefully descended the three steps from the bandstand and started walking across the empty dance floor to reach his table. Suddenly, he looked alone, older, more vulnerable. Then someone stood, reached out, and put his arm around him. Others rushed toward him. Sandy quickly disappeared within a swelling throng of Citigroup executives reaching out to shake his hand, pat him on the back, embrace him, or just touch him to show their support. These were his people, the extended family he had always wanted. Sandy felt a renewed determination to fight on.

Back in New York, the Citigroup CEO pushed hard to reach a settlement that would reform Wall Street's research practices and distribution of new stock offerings. With a handful of outside lawyers encamped in the conference room next to his office, Sandy gave the marching orders: Settle this thing even if Citigroup has to take the biggest hit of all the securities firms.

"The whole industry did a lot of things wrong, but we have to show we're willing to do whatever it takes to bring back the confidence of the investor," Sandy told them. But restoring confidence wouldn't be easy. Investors had suffered a mind-boggling $7 trillion in losses since 2000. Even as a mild economic recovery took hold across the country, individual investors, still fearful of tainted research and rigged stock offerings, stayed away from the market in droves.

"I won't like paying the biggest fine, but we make the most money anyway," Sandy said.

Still, certain firms, especially those without huge retail networks, tried to gain a competitive advantage as the negotiations heated up in December 2002. They argued that the regulators shouldn't force them to contribute to a $500 million fund to finance independent stock research. Their position—and the delay it caused—angered Sandy. "They're being shortsighted," he fumed. "To string out this controversy damages all of our reputations and business."

Soon the regulators had enough as well. On Wednesday, December 18, they ordered the top ten Wall Street firms to get behind the sweeping general settlement—or else. Spitzer summoned the firms' lawyers and executives to his drab, cramped office in Lower Manhattan, a few blocks from the

New York Stock Exchange. "Today's the day," he said. "Sign up or we're going into law-enforcement mode." An agreement quickly came to fruition.

By then Sandy was already on his Gulfstream jet en route to Moscow, where Citigroup was poised to be the first U.S. financial institution to open retail banking operations in Russia. Over the air phone, Prince told him a deal was imminent.

"And it looks like you won't face any charges—as it should be," his senior executive said.

"I won't believe it's over till it's over," Sandy replied.

Two days later, on Friday, December 20, 2002, the Citigroup CEO had arrived in Paris for a weekend with Joan before returning home. Prince called again. "Turn on CNBC," he said breathlessly. "It's happening now!"

In his suite at the luxurious Hotel George V, near the Champs Elysées, Sandy watched as Spitzer and the other regulators stood in the boardroom of the Stock Exchange. In a live broadcast presentation, the New York attorney general announced that the ten most important securities firms, which together underwrote the vast majority of all new stocks and bonds sold each year, had agreed to overhaul their research, stock allotment, and investment-banking operations. Without admitting culpability, the firms also would pay a whopping $1 billion fine, with Citigroup incurring the largest penalty, $300 million.

But Sandy wasn't too bothered by the fine's amount—equal to only a week's worth of profits at the huge financial conglomerate. Even better, the penalty was far less than the value that Citigroup stock rose after the settlement was announced, much more important to this Wall Street veteran who watched every blip of his company's stock price like his own heart rate.

It was the beginning of a new era. The changes represented the most significant restructuring of the securities business since 1975, when the Big Board deregulated fixed commissions for stock trading. Now its most visible and seasoned leader, the Citigroup CEO was ready to leave his and his company's missteps behind and lead the business in these history-making changes to win back investors' confidence. But could he?

Just then, a reporter at the press conference asked Spitzer if the Citigroup boss would escape individual responsibility. "We have examined the evidence, and there will not be any charges against Sandy Weill," the attorney general responded.

Sandy breathed a sigh of relief. Feeling drained and exhausted, he called back Prince.

"I guess it's finally over," Sandy said.

"Now you can have your martini," Prince answered.

Sandy stared at the bottle of gin in his Paris hotel room, but didn't pour himself a drink. Since cutting back on food and alcohol, he liked his new physique. He would turn seventy years old in three months. He had no intention of retiring, especially with such monumental changes—and opportunities—before him.

Sandy told Prince, "Let's get back to work."

A NOTE ON SOURCES

This book is based on thousands of hours of interviews with nearly five hundred people who have been associated closely with Sandy Weill or who have been instrumental in the development of Wall Street and the financial industry over the past fifty years. Many sources generously spent hours—and some, dozens of hours—recalling Sandy's role in their lives and careers, for better or worse. Of the people named in this book, only a scant few refused to talk to me at some point over the two-year span of the project. Many of the interviews were done on a not-for-attribution basis, although everyone interviewed understood that the text would reflect their states of mind and quotations they recalled.

Sandy himself played a changing role in this project. His first reaction when I asked for an initial meeting was a question: Can you write a book about me without my approval? Assured that I could, he next asked what controls he could exercise over the finished product in exchange for his cooperation. The answer: none. While he refused at the beginning to participate, he didn't attempt, to my knowledge, to block anyone from talking to me. Nevertheless, the first questions I encountered from any number of people were whether Sandy authorized the book or specifically whether he approved of their speaking with me. In some cases, Sandy's inability to control the book opened doors. In others, it closed them. After all, Sandy Weill is one of the most powerful executives in the world, and his subordinates, friends, and even competitors do not lightly incur his wrath. Only after a year of diligent, thorough reporting, which Sandy clearly learned about from some of those interviewed, did he begin to relax his "neutral" position. Still with absolutely no control over the final results, the Citigroup CEO authorized scores of his colleagues and employees to speak with me. His permission enabled me to spend hours, even days, with his inner circle as they went about the business of running the world's largest financial conglomerate. During the last year of my reporting, Sandy included me at certain Citigroup events and social functions, including gatherings with senior executives and at his home. As a result of this increased access, I witnessed many of the events and conversations in the latter part of the book.

Sandy granted me interviews totaling several hours on different occasions, concluding with a final meeting in November 2002 in his office. At the time, Sandy was under attack from various sources, and Citigroup was the focal point of controversy about Wall Street's stock research and investment-banking practices. Despite all that was going on, Sandy kept his promise to spend the morning with me as I checked facts and sought his explanations for certain critical actions taken over the course of his long career.

To supplement the extensive interviews—and, often, to prepare for interviews—I relied on voluminous documentary material, including corporate records and memoranda, Securities and Exchange Commission filings, annual reports, private correspondence, appointment calendars, records of court proceedings and lawsuits, menus, the archives of the National Climatic Data Center, meeting agendas, diaries, and photographs. News publications and books provided important background and context. *The Wall Street Journal, The New York Times, Fortune, BusinessWeek, American Banker, The Washington Post, The Financial Times, USA Today, The Hartford Courant,* the Baltimore *Sun, Forbes,* and the *New York Post* were valuable reports of unfolding events. Useful books were *The Year They Sold Wall Street* by Tim Carrington, *Greed and Glory on Wall Street* by Ken Auletta, *The New Crowd* by Judith Ramsey Ehrlich and Barry J. Rehfeld, *House of Cards* by Jon Friedman and John Meehan, *The Last Days of the Club* by Chris Welles, *Wall Street: A History* by Charles R. Geisst, *Barbarians at the Gate* by Bryan Burrough and John Helyar, *Liar's Poker* by Michael Lewis, and *Den of Thieves* by James B. Stewart.

For many interview subjects, I constructed a timeline, assembled from the above sources and other interviews, and asked each source to describe his or her actions, conversations, thoughts, and feelings, as well as his or her observations of others present. Where possible, the information was checked against other sources. This methodology made it possible to construct the book as a narrative without specific textual attribution of each fact to a source.

Dialogue has been reconstructed by the same careful reporting methodology. The sources often were the speakers in any dialogue or, in the case of conversations among many participants, at least one or more participants. In a few instances, dialogue was provided by people who did not participate but who were informed about a conversation. The reconstructed dialogue represents the most accurate recollections of the words uttered, as well as the personalities and styles of the individuals involved. In characterizing the inner thoughts of participants, I used in most cases their own recollections of what they were thinking in a given situation. In a few instances, I relied on sources either intimately familiar with a participant's thinking or who had been told by the participant at the time what he or she was thinking.

Many descriptions of places and people are the result of my own observations. In some circumstances they are from published accounts or firsthand accounts told by those who were present. I mercilessly pestered some of the nation's busiest executives about what they were wearing, eating, or doing during their interactions with Sandy. I appreciate their indulgence.

My goal from the outset was to tell the honest, complete, and fascinating story of Sandy Weill's career, which also tells the story of Wall Street and the financial-services industry for a half century. This isn't the book Sandy would write about himself. I told every source that I wanted to write a book that would provide a true portrait of the man they all knew, had worked with or against, loved, feared, admired, or disdained. I hope I have lived up to the pledge I made to the hundreds of sources who generously gave me their time, knowledge, and insights in this quest.

ACKNOWLEDGMENTS

My utmost gratitude goes to *The Wall Street Journal,* which gener-ously gave me the necessary time and support to pursue this pro-ject, and imbued me with the journalistic integrity and professionalism that I so value and appreciate.

I will always be indebted and grateful to Paul E. Steiger, the *Journal*'s brilliant and awe-inspiring managing editor, who has encouraged me in every step of my career, including the decision to write this book. My mentor since I joined the *Journal* straight out of law school in 1983, he whole-heartedly welcomed me back to the newspaper when I ended a midcareer stint practicing law in order to return to my first love, journalism.

Stephen J. Adler, my phenomenal and perceptive editor for several years, both for the newspaper and as the head of Wall Street Journal Books, guided this book from its inception. I appreciate his thoughtful in-put, sound judgment, and adroit stewardship of the project. He also con-tributed the book's title.

I am deeply grateful to Doug Sease, whose enthusiasm, intellect, and superb editing skills helped me immeasurably as we plowed through many late nights and long weekends. As my *Journal* editor on this project, he was truly a godsend whose editorial handiwork graces every page.

I'm fortunate to have benefited from the wisdom and friendship of many other colleagues at *The Wall Street Journal,* especially Daniel Hertzberg, Mike Miller, Alix Freedman, Tom Herman, and Ellen Pollock.

I want to thank the *Journal*'s outstanding librarians, Frances Housten (who did double duty as my indefatigable fact-checker), Lottie Lindberg, and Elizabeth Yeh, for researching thousands of queries. Roe D'Angelo acted as the *Journal* liaison with the publisher, Daniel Nasaw went the ex-tra mile on photo research, and Stuart Karle provided a legal review. I'm grateful to *Journal* associates Cathy Panagoulias, Jim Pensiero, and Jared Sandberg for their help when my notes and research were trapped for months in the World Financial Center following the tragic events of September 11, 2001.

My heartfelt thanks to my able assistants James Kernochan, who transcribed hundreds of hours of interviews, and Ethan Zindler, who supplied critical fact-gathering; both performed flawlessly, often under intense time pressure.

At Simon & Schuster, Frederic Hills, my delightful and astute editor, provided conceptual guidance, sage advice, and enduring patience. A passionate advocate for the book, he munificently educated this first-time author every step of the way. He provided keen insights into every chapter, and then skillfully accommodated revisions as news broke in the final weeks before publication.

Also at the publisher, I am most appreciative of Leslie Ellen for her sharp professional eye for detail and nimble copyediting supervision, Patty Romanowski for her talented copyediting of the manuscript, Kelly Gionti for her efficient and cheerful assistance, and Jennifer Weidman for her incisive observations and wise advocacy. I thank Martha Levin, publisher, and Dominick Anfuso, editor in chief, at The Free Press, for making it possible to publish the book under The Wall Street Journal imprint at Simon & Schuster.

James B. Stewart, the best-selling author, was the first outside reader of the manuscript, and rendered invaluable advice. I will always treasure his exceptional candor and support.

I greatly appreciate the hundreds of men and women I interviewed for the book, some as many as twenty times and for several days. A few sources deserve special mention.

My first exposure to the Citigroup CEO occurred when I wrote a page-one article for *The Wall Street Journal* on Sandy's leadership of Carnegie Hall; Jay Golan, senior director of the famed institution, was particularly helpful. Mary McDermott, an executive in Sandy's companies for three decades, was the one of the first to open up to me when Sandy's initial position on my book was one of neither "encouraging nor discouraging" his colleagues to talk.

Ultimately, I obtained unprecedented access to Sandy and Citigroup. After Sandy received his own accounts of my objective and extensive reporting about his business life, he agreed to occasional interviews in his office. The Citigroup CEO also invited me to several corporate and personal occasions, from the gala of the Alvin Ailey American Dance Theater chaired by his wife, Joan, where he boogied at midnight, to the recent ceremony where he was named CEO of the Year. During the two years I spent on this book, I saw Sandy at least monthly, including at such news events as business meetings, charitable functions, and press conferences.

Members of Sandy's inner circle to whom I am grateful for permitting me to interview them repeatedly include Citigroup president Robert Willumstad, chief executive officer of the global corporate and investment group Charles Prince, chief operating officer of the global consumer group Marge Magner, and longtime Citigroup director and Sandy's close friend Arthur Zankel.

I also thank the two men who worked most closely with Sandy over the years as his deputies for several extensive interviews: Peter Cohen on the first financial empire that became Shearson, and Jamie Dimon on the second empire that became Citigroup.

Many other sources, often extremely busy executives, recalled for me their experiences with Sandy. A great number of these sources provided generously of their knowledge and time, but didn't want to be named. Thank you all.

During this intense and lengthy process, I gained strength and cheer from the love and patience of my friends and family, even as I was frequently preoccupied and unavailable. I wish to thank for their help, in ways large and small, Jennifer Gourary, Jonathan Lampert, Barbara Landreth, Ellen McGrath, Suzanne Meth, Vincent Scotto, and Benjamin Weil (who also proofread the galleys). My apologies to those I'm inadvertently leaving out.

Special thanks go to Faneeza Khan and Margot Golden, the wonderful women who love and care for my four-year-old daughter when "Mommy is working." Also I appreciate the teachers and parents at Langley Grace's preschool, The Episcopal School, for their understanding of my grueling schedule.

I thank my parents for a lifetime of giving and love. My mother, Helen S. Langley, nurtured my love of books with countless hours of reading to me, as well as our weekly visits to the Knoxville, Tennessee, public library during my childhood. A devoted cheerleader, she always believed I would become an author one day. My father, Fred R. Langley, eagerly exposed me, from the time I was knee-high, to his love of finance and entrepreneurship by taking me on frequent business trips and office outings. He and his wife, Faye T. Langley, have been ardent supporters of my career. My sisters, Melissa Langley and Julie Langley Campos, are my best friends whose comfort and conversation were crucial during this process. I also thank other family members, especially Don and Joanne Wallace, James Travis, and Lisa McElvaney.

This book wouldn't have been possible without the unfailing support of my husband, Roger P. Wallace, who bore the brunt of my distractions and absences with understanding and love. I'm indebted to him for his patience and perspective during what was a nearly all-consuming preoccupation, filled with moments of anguish and exhilaration. A fellow journalist, Roger has seen me through it all, from reading my rough drafts at midnight to being the world's best dad with our daughter.

I did my best to keep the book from dominating our home life. Only twice did Langley Grace meet Sandy, when we were guests at the annual apple-picking events at the Weills' mansion. When the Citigroup CEO occasionally appeared on TV news shows, my daughter observed, "There's Mr. Weill, the apple farmer!"

Nevertheless, my four-year-old daughter knew very well that her mother was deeply involved in the solitary process of writing a book filled with "chapters and more chapters." Every evening, she asked if I had finished a chapter as she counted them down until the end. Even though I have worked on this book for half of her young life, Langley Grace Wallace has kept my life in balance and filled it with love and laughter, pride and joy.

PHOTO CREDITS

INDEX

ABOUT THE AUTHOR

MONICA LANGLEY has written for *The Wall Street Journal* for twelve years. Her investigative reports on a wide array of subjects have regularly appeared on the *Journal*'s front page. Formerly a practicing attorney for eight years, she lives with her husband and daughter in New York City.